Blueprint

The policies, principles and personalities
of the New Conservative government

About the author

Lionel Zetter has been involved with the Conservative Party for more than thirty years. During that period he has been chairman of Sussex University Conservative Association and chairman of Enfield Southgate Conservative Association. He has worked for two Tory MPs and he has done a stint in the CCO War Room. In the 2001 general election he was the Tory election agent in Edmonton, and in 2005 he was the Conservative parliamentary candidate in that constituency. He is still Conservative ward chairman for Cockfosters & Hadley Wood and a member of his association executive. He is also a director of the Enterprise Forum, which is the policy interface between the Conservative Party and British business.

Professionally Zetter is the former managing director of Parliamentary Monitoring Services Ltd and Political Wizard Ltd, and the former deputy chairman of Dods Parliamentary Communications Ltd. He is a director of the opinion polling company ComRes and a vice president of PublicAffairsAsia. He is a fellow of the Chartered Institute of Public Relations, a fellow of the Royal Society of Arts and a member of the National Union of Journalists.

Zetter is the former editor of *Vacher's Election Guide*, *The PMS Parliamentary Companion* and *Parliaments and Assemblies of the UK*. He is also the author of *The Political Campaigning Handbook* and of *Lobbying: The Art of Political Persuasion*.

Blueprint

The policies, principles and personalities
of the New Conservative government

Lionel Zetter

totalpolitics

First published in Great Britain in 2009 by
Total Politics, an imprint of
Biteback Publishing Ltd
Heal House
375 Kennington Lane
London
SE11 5QY

ISBN 978-1-907278-00-6

A CIP catalogue record for this book is available from the British Library.

Set in Kepler and Helvetica by SoapBox
Printed and bound in Great Britain by TJ International Ltd, Padstow, Cornwall

Contents

Acknowledgements

Apart from my wife and children, who have had to put up with all of the 4.00 a.m. starts and the resultant tetchiness, I have a considerable number of other people to thank.

Firstly, Iain Dale for having faith in the concept of *Blueprint* and Jonathan Wadman for his excellent editing. In terms of research it was very much a family affair, and credit is due to my niece Stephanie Peate (who was working as an intern in the Commons and is now on her way to Somerville College, Oxford) and my sons Alec (a Politics and Media undergraduate at UEA) and Richard for their research and fact checking.

Many people helped me with their comments and suggestions, but special thanks are due to Craig Hoy, Jonathan French, Mark Fullbrook and Nick Vaughan. The good ideas are all theirs, and the mistakes and inaccurate predictions are, of course, all mine.

Preface

After every general election a plethora of books are published describing in great detail how and why what has already happened actually did happen.

This book is an attempt to provide something altogether more useful: a blueprint for the New Conservative government and a guide for those who will have to deal with it. Of course all good consultants will quite rightly tell their clients that they have to deal with the government of the day – you can, after all, only play what is put in front of you. Equally, those consultants will tell their clients that they have to prepare for change, and that those parties and politicians are more approachable when they are in opposition than when they are in power. This is partly because they have less time when they are in office, partly because they acquire a shield of officials who try to keep the real world at arm's length, and partly because all but the most determinedly modest individuals gradually acquire a veneer of indifference and arrogance which in time ensures that it is they who in their turn are ousted and form the opposition.

So the basic premise of this book is that the Tories are going to win, and that they are going to win with a working majority. What is more, they are probably going to win with a landslide, and there may in fact be a Tory tsunami. This could be 1997 in reverse, and all of those who want or need to inform or influence government should start to try and understand the drivers, the ethos and motivations of David Cameron and his team.

When teaching public affairs I always say that it is about the three Ps – Procedure, People and Policy. I have dealt with procedure in my two earlier books (*The Political Campaigning Handbook* and *Lobbying: The Art of Political Persuasion*) so this book will deal with people and policy. Of the two I have always put people above policy: policies change with circumstances, whilst people rarely change once they have transcended their formative years. If you understand the people, what motivates them and what has shaped their character, then you are considerably more than half way there.

I should make one point very clear. The opinions and views expressed in this book – unless quoted or attributed – are mine and not those of the Conservative Party. David Cameron is determined not to allow any hint of complacency or hubris to creep into his thinking or speaking. His senior colleagues are equally careful not to make any presumptions about the size of any putative majority, or even about whether one will be achieved at all.

Terminology and methodology

Throughout this book I have used the term 'PPC', or 'prospective parliamentary candidate'. There used to be a legal requirement for candidates to use this term, as any other term – such as plain 'parliamentary candidate' – risked triggering the clock on their election expenses. That requirement is now gone, but PPC is still useful shorthand.

I have used the terms 'Tory' and 'Conservative' interchangeably. There is a slight nuance attached to the term 'Tory' which implies traditional Conservatism, but it is a moot distinction. The term 'New Conservative', however, used in the way that Labour used 'New Labour' after Tony Blair became leader, works a lot better than 'New Tory'. CCHQ does not use this term, but it is applicable to the party which David Cameron has fashioned, which is radically different in look, feel, policies and people than the traditional party which Margaret Thatcher led. I have tried to avoid using the term 'Cameroon', because although it is an apt shorthand description for the people and the policies which are in tune with Cameron's agenda, it does sound faintly ridiculous. Perhaps if Cameron stays in power long enough and achieves enough, the term 'Cameronite' might come into widespread usage.

Throughout the book I have referred to current Tory post holders as though they will still be in office come the election. David Cameron resisted holding a reshuffle after Gordon Brown conducted his widespread one in June 2009 – and it is possible that (barring unforeseen circumstances) he will enter the general election with the team in place at the time of writing intact. However, it is equally possible he will have one last reshuffle before the election. It is also possible that, on the advice of the whips and senior colleagues, he will make the painful decision not to take into government some of those who have served him in opposition.

All of the majority and marginality criteria used in this book are drawn from the work produced by Colin Rallings and Michael Thrasher and published in their *Media Guide to the New Parliamentary Constituencies*. This is published by them in association with the University of Plymouth and in collaboration with the BBC, ITN, Sky News and PA News, and is the 'Bible' for pundits and forecasters alike.

Finally, this book is based on the premise that the general election will be held in 2010 – most likely on 6 May. However, that is by no means a given, and if Gordon Brown (or any successor as Labour leader and Prime Minister) calls a general election earlier, I hope that this book will be just as valid and useful.

Lionel Zetter
August 2009

Introduction

I was not only 'up for Portillo' in 1997, I was standing next to him as he waited to ascend the platform to meet his fate, and I comforted his wife as that fate was confirmed. That is because I was chairman of the Enfield Southgate Conservative Association when Portillo – along with a host of other Tory ministers and MPs – was swept away in the Labour landslide of 1 May 1997.

As the long-awaited and long-drawn-out campaign progressed I – and many others – had detected the first signs of the gathering storm. What we maybe did not quite realise was that it would ultimately turn into a perfect storm. Not only was there no enthusiasm for the Tories on the doorstep, there was frequently outright and vehement hostility. Worse even than the anger was the contempt. Voters who had backed Margaret Thatcher over the course of three general elections, and who had stifled their doubts and voted for John Major in 1992, regarded us now with a mixture of indifference and disdain. They had nothing to say to us, and they equally wanted to hear nothing from us.

So as that long night wore on, and Tory scalp after Tory scalp was taken and waved gleefully aloft, we were not shocked, or even surprised. Of course there were regional and local variations, but the trend was the same everywhere. People around the UK were determined to do whatever it took to get the local Tory out – even if that meant voting for a party they did not truly support. In Enfield Southgate the widely disliked Michael Portillo was swept away, but so was the affable, hard-working constituency MP Ian Twinn in neighbouring Edmonton. Almost no matter who you were on that day, Cabinet minister or backbencher, right-winger or centrist, male or female, young or old – if you fought under the Tory banner and you wore a blue rosette you were hunted down and voted out.

In 1997, before his defeat and subsequent Damascene conversion and return via the Kensington & Chelsea by-election, Michael Portillo had been widely regarded as the future of the 'Right' and a future leader of the Conservative Party. He was severely shaken not just by his defeat, but by the widespread delight in his downfall. He was not alone in being dismayed by his fate. For several years after 1997 whenever I was introduced to Margaret Thatcher she would always respond with the same words: 'I know Lionel – he lost Michael his seat.' Fortunately for me she has now either forgotten or forgiven.

There were many explanations for the visceral dislike for the Conservatives in 1997 and for the resultant rout. There was the long-running sleaze saga, where a succession of senior Tories were caught and exposed by the media in a catalogue of sexual misadventures. There was also, after eighteen years, a strong and hard-to-refute feeling that it was simply 'time for a change'.

However, the most obvious and most often quoted reason for the great cull of 1997 was the fallout from the summary ejection of sterling from the ERM on 16 September 1992 – the day which the press dubbed 'Black Wednesday'. On that day interest rates soared, and they would have risen to 15 per cent if the decision to leave the ERM had not been taken. The cost to the Treasury of trying to keep sterling in the ERM was estimated at anything between £3.3 billion (the Treasury's own estimate) and £27 billion (the figure bandied about by some of the more excitable journalists).

The British people never forgave the Major government for the hurt and fear which this episode caused. They also took a long time to forget the misjudgement which had led the country to such ignominy and the economy to the brink of ruin. How much greater is the anger of the British people going to be in 2010? The value of their houses has plummeted, share values have fallen off a cliff and pension pots have been shattered. And the man who had been Chancellor for ten years is now sitting in No. 10, refusing to admit even for a moment that one scintilla of blame for these disastrous events should in any way attach itself to him.

To add to the Labour government's financial woes, the spectre of sleaze has raised its head once again. There has been the MPs' expenses scandal, which has hit all parties – but Labour most of all. There has also been a series of misdemeanours by Labour ministers and advisors. This has created an impression that the party has been in power for so long that it has become careless at best, corrupted by power at worst.

For all of these reasons, the revenge of the British people is likely to be terrible. Whether their verdict is delivered in howling fury or silent contempt, Labour ministers and MPs will suffer the same fate in 2010 as the Tories did in 1997 – an electoral tsunami will sweep them away. It will not matter how clever, competent or hard working they have been: if they wear a red rosette, the electorate will conspire to send them packing.

Scaling the mountain
The electoral challenge for Cameron's Conservatives

On or before 3 June 2010, the United Kingdom will go to the polls to elect a new parliament. The election will mark the first time that any of the three main party leaders – Labour's Gordon Brown, the Conservatives' David Cameron and the Liberal Democrats' Nick Clegg – have led their parties into such a battle with fire.

Against the backdrop of consistently poor opinion poll ratings, factional infighting and humiliating by-election losses in Crewe & Nantwich, Glasgow East and Norwich North, it is easy to forget the relative ease with which Labour despatched the Conservatives at the 2005 general election. The results of that election were a grave disappointment for the Conservatives, despite their protestations to the contrary – and the parliamentary party's largest injection of new blood since 1983.

While minuscule compared to the 179-seat majority the party secured at the 1997 general election, Labour's margin of victory at the 2005 election was without doubt a healthy one. With 9,562,122 votes, Tony Blair's party led Michael Howard's Conservatives by almost 800,000 votes – or 356 seats to 198. Despite polling the lowest share of the vote of any party to ever secure an overall parliamentary majority, Blair's 66-seat majority was larger than that secured by Margaret Thatcher in 1979, treble the size of John Major's 1992 mandate and more than double Ted Heath's majority in 1970. Indeed, of the seventeen general elections held since 1945, only seven have produced governments enjoying majorities larger than the one the Labour Party was handed in 2005.

Labour's precipitous decline from their peak vote share of 43.2 per cent at the 1997 election to 35.3 per cent in 2005 did little help to the Conservatives. Despite modest gains, the Conservative Party's overall vote share increased to 32.3 per cent – only 1.6 points higher than the party had polled at the 1997 general election. Indeed, the only real electoral beneficiaries were the Liberal Democrats, whose support rose by almost a third from 16.8 per cent to 22.1 per cent, in no small part due to their opposition to the Iraq conflict.

While cherished by the Conservatives, the first-past-the-post electoral system only complicates their efforts to achieve an overall majority. Figures compiled by Professor John Curtice of the University of Strathclyde indicate that population movements during the 2001 and 2005 parliaments resulted in the average Labour constituency losing 500 electors while Conservative seats

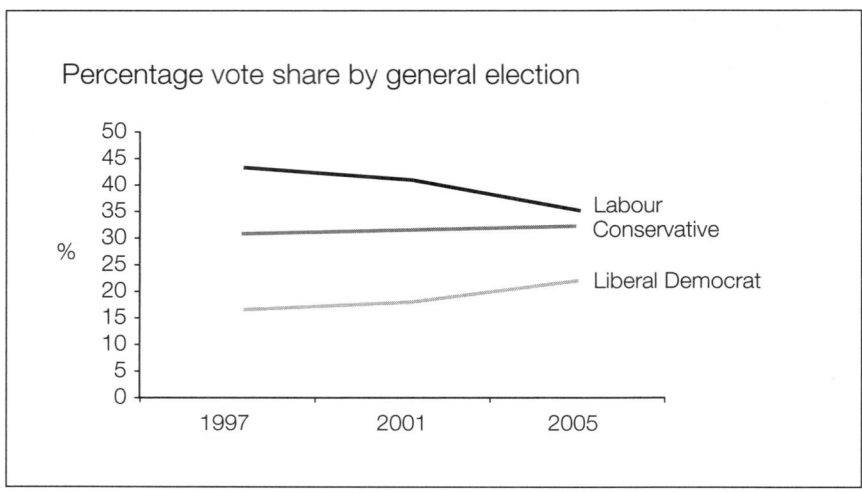

Percentage vote share by general election

gained 1,000. Turnout, Professor Curtice notes, is also higher in Conservative constituencies than Labour seats, by a margin of 65.2 per cent to 58.6 per cent. As such, this disparity in seat size has resulted in a difference of 6,200 voters per seat – or 8,500 votes. A Conservative lead in the popular vote of six percentage points – a greater margin of victory than Labour achieved over the Tories in 2005 – would result in a hung Parliament with Labour as the largest party. Only a nine-point lead would deliver the Conservative Party an overall majority.

When David Cameron and his party chairman Eric Pickles caution Conservative parliamentarian members about electoral complacency, they are correct. To govern effectively, the Conservatives don't just need to lead Labour – they need to win decisively.

The root of Brown's decline
On 24 June 2007, the longest-serving Chancellor of the Exchequer in British history, Gordon Brown, acceded to the leadership of the Labour Party – a job he and his closest confidants had worked tirelessly for him to secure for more than two decades.

Almost as soon as Brown took office, his administration was forced to deal with a foot and mouth disease outbreak and the aftermath of a failed terrorist attack at Glasgow airport. More than three quarters of the general public, reassured by his assertive yet low-key style, felt that he had handled the crisis well. Significantly, the new Prime Minister enjoyed the broad support of a general public who had grown increasingly hostile towards Tony Blair. Some 60 per cent expressed their preference for Brown's premiership over that of his predecessor and twice as many believed the British government would perform more effectively under Brown than Blair.

After a slew of high-profile initiatives which saw previously non-political members of the business community, the medical profession and the armed forces catapulted into high office as members of Brown's 'government of all the talents', his satisfaction level climbed to 67 per cent as he faced his first party conference. Having trailed David Cameron's Conservatives for months, in one opinion poll the Labour government stood thirteen points ahead.

This honeymoon proved short lived. The first sign of the impending economic crisis came on 14 September with Northern Rock's application to the Bank of England for a financial liquidity support facility.

Even with Brown's accession to the premiership, Cameron continued to enjoy modest leads over his opponent in respect of the majority of policy areas, but there was one on which the long-standing former Chancellor appeared unassailable: the economy. In August 2007, opinion polls showed Brown leading Cameron by 67 per cent to 17 per cent on the question of which man would be 'better in a crisis'. Satisfied with Brown's healthy opinion poll lead, his perceived decisiveness in salvaging Northern Rock and putting an end to the near-hysteria which had seen the first run on a bank in more than 100 years, Labour advisors prepared for a general election. Newspapers were abuzz with speculation of possible election dates, advertising hoardings were booked and the Labour Party's spin machine, headed by the now politically exiled Douglas Alexander, went into overdrive. Cameron, in reality fearful of prospect of facing an election against the popular newcomer, taunted Brown with a cry of 'bring it on' in his party conference speech.

The election – which will forever live in political infamy as the 'phantom election' – never came. Brown's credibility was shot and by the end of October 2007, the Conservatives' poll lead reached eight percentage points over Labour.

Within four months of Brown's coronation as Labour leader, three fifths of people disagreed that he had brought about a decisive change in government. Handling the economy had previously been Brown's greatest strength, but 54 per cent of the public now believed that the new Prime Minister had not dealt with the Northern Rock incident well. Despite having enjoyed a massive lead over Cameron on the issue of who would make the best Prime Minister prior to the 'phantom election', Brown now trailed his opponent – and has yet to overtake him to this day.

Hindsight may lead many Labour Members of Parliament and activists to conclude that they ought to have heeded the well-publicised warnings of Blairite former ministers Charles Clarke, Stephen Byers and Alan Milburn,

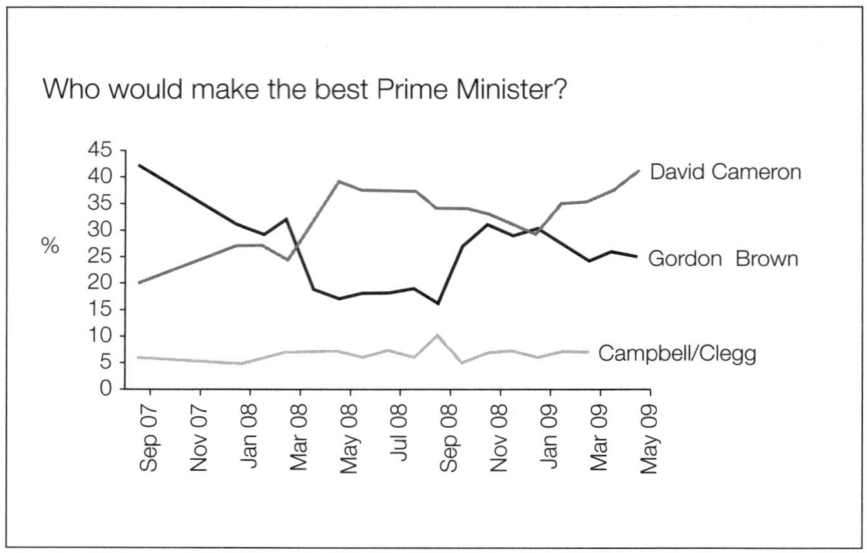

which urged against Brown's coronation as Labour leader, for the signs warning about Brown's leadership were very much apparent:

- In no hypothetical head-to-head match-up conducted after the date of David Cameron's election as Conservative Party leader in 2006 to the day Gordon Brown took office as Prime Minister was the then Chancellor ahead of the opposition leader.
- In January 2007, only 33 per cent of the general public stated their preference for Gordon Brown's election as Labour leader while 55 per cent preferred a 'rising star'.
- In April of the same year, only 25 per cent said the Iron Chancellor would make a 'good Labour leader' while 42 per cent said they believed he would do the job badly.
- The same poll revealed that 71 per cent thought Brown would not represent a 'fresh start' for the country while in May 2007 62 per cent disagreed that his accession to the premiership would make his party more appealing.

The electoral battleground
England
In terms of raw vote share, the Conservative Party 'won' the 2005 general election in England with a margin of more than 70,000 votes over Tony Blair's then party. Despite this lead, Labour captured ninety-two more seats than the Conservatives – largely as a result of hugely advantageous parliamentary boundaries.

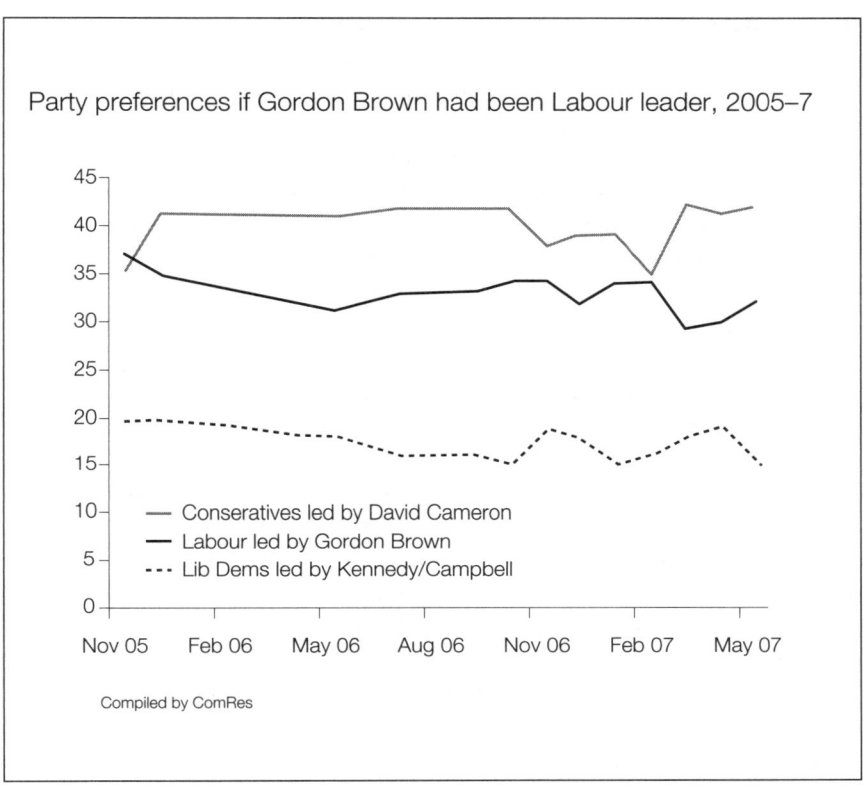

Party preferences if Gordon Brown had been Labour leader, 2005–7

— Conseratives led by David Cameron
— Labour led by Gordon Brown
--- Lib Dems led by Kennedy/Campbell

Compiled by ComRes

Statistically speaking, the 'safest' region for the Conservatives in England at the last election was the South East, where, with 45 per cent of the vote, the party led the Liberal Democrats by a shade under 20 per cent. They were numerically weakest in the North East, where their 19.5 per cent vote share put them in third position behind Labour and the Liberal Democrats.

The electoral success of Tony Blair's New Labour project at the 1997, 2001 and 2005 elections was largely brought about by his party's encroachment into regions in which it had traditionally been weak. While no political observer was surprised to see a long-standing marginal such as Mitcham & Morden or Crawley fall to Labour in 1997, the party's victories in constituencies such as Finchley & Golders Green in north London, Hastings & Rye in East Sussex and Stroud in Gloucestershire were almost entirely unexpected. While these seats have stuck with Labour throughout the last three parliaments, they cannot be expected to do so this time.

Labour Members of Parliament are particularly endangered in the London suburbs, the site of some of their most spectacular gains at the 1997 general election. A modest swing of less than 5 per cent would see the party go down to defeat in Finchley & Golders Green, Croydon Central, Harrow East, Brentford & Isleworth, Eltham and Watford; while a swing to the Conservatives of up to 8 per cent would see further losses in Poplar & Limehouse, Tooting, Hampstead & Kilburn and Hammersmith. Similarly, Labour marginals on the outskirts of other large cities such as Bristol North West, Milton Keynes North, Broxtowe in Nottingham, Birmingham Edgbaston, Bury North, Wolverhampton South West, Wirral South, Leeds North West and Bolton West would fall to the Conservatives on a 5 per cent swing.

Historically speaking, the industrial town of Dartford on the banks of the Thames estuary and Manchester commuter town of Chorley are the most accurate 'bellwether' constituencies, having backed the winner of every general election since 1964. While Dartford is now an ultra-marginal, requiring a swing to the Tories of less than 1 per cent, a more emphatic swing of 8 per cent is needed to hand the Conservatives a symbolic victory in Chorley.

Nobody can forget the sickly sweet grins of Cabinet ministers Malcolm Rifkind in Edinburgh Pentlands, Michael Forsyth in Stirling and, most famously, Michael Portillo in Enfield Southgate on election night 1997 as their electors rejected them in favour of a rapidly advancing Labour Party. If the Conservatives are to advance this time, Labour frontbenchers will not be spared this humiliation. A modest swing of less than 5 per cent will see the end of former Home Secretary Jacqui Smith's and Cabinet minister Jim Knight's parliamentary careers, with government ministers Phil Hope, Michael Jabez Foster, Bill Rammell, Angela Smith, Clare Ward, Tony McNulty, Michael Foster and Ann Keen also going down to defeat.

For the Conservatives, one of the most frustrating aspects of the past three general elections has been the steady advance of the Liberal Democrats into constituencies which had once been considered safe for the party. Of the top thirty marginal seats the Conservatives hope to gain, nine are presently held by the Liberal Democrats. A true test of David Cameron's middle-of-the-road appeal will be whether he is able to lead his party to victory against them in the suburban dormitory constituencies of Romsey & Southampton North, Eastleigh and Carshalton & Wallington and in the well-heeled rural seats of Cheltenham, Chippenham and Taunton Deane.

Scotland

At present, the Conservative Party holds only one seat in Scotland: Dumfriesshire, Clydesdale & Tweeddale. Located on the English border, the seat is held by former MSP and shadow Scottish Secretary David Mundell. Even the most optimistic of Conservatives would concede that the party's prospects for significant gains north of the border – where they failed to win a single seat in 1997 – are severely limited.

Statistically speaking, the party's top two targets in Scotland are Perth & North Perthshire and Angus, yet their prospects for advancement here are checked by these seats presently being held by the Scottish National Party, who can expect to be the main beneficiaries of Labour's slump in vote share. Realistically, the party's best potential for gains is in straight fights with the Labour and the Liberal Democrats. As such, the party will be disappointed not to take Dumfries & Galloway and Edinburgh South.

A Conservative landslide would see the 'decapitation' of Chancellor Alistair Darling in Edinburgh South West and Scottish Secretary Jim Murphy in East Renfrewshire. On the back of incredibly strong local government advances and an unexpected gain at the 2007 Scottish Parliament elections, the party also has an outside chance of defeating former Liberal Democrat foreign affairs spokesman Michael Moore in Berwickshire, Roxburgh & Selkirk.

David Cameron appears likely to find himself in the uncomfortable position of governing – to give his party its full name – as a Conservative and Unionist Party Prime Minister while holding no more than a small handful of Scotland's fifty-nine parliamentary seats. In reality, however, he does not arithmetically require Scottish support in order to secure victory.

Wales
Barren ground for the Conservatives at the 1997 and 2001 general elections, the principality has witnessed the party stage a solid comeback in recent years, gaining the Monmouth, Clwyd West and Preseli Pembrokeshire constituencies at the 2005 general election, increasing its share of Senedd seats in 2007 and topping the poll in the 2009 European elections.

Unlike Scotland, the Conservatives cannot govern without achieving further gains in Wales. At the top of the party's target seats are Aberconwy, Cardiff North, Vale of Glamorgan and Carmarthen West & South Pembrokeshire, all of which would be gained from Labour with swings of less than 3 per cent. A Conservative landslide would deliver the party Gower, Bridgend, Delyn, the Vale of Clwyd and Clwyd South.

On a swing of 5 per cent, the Conservatives will also hope to gain rural Brecon & Radnorshire from the Liberal Democrats. While holding a numerically solid majority, the high-profile Montgomeryshire MP and TV personality Lembit Öpik may well lose to former National Assembly member Glyn Davies, whose locally honed campaign has subtly drawn attention to the incumbent's taste for the metropolitan high life.

Northern Ireland

The 2010 election will be the first electoral test for the Conservative Party's newly formed electoral alliance with the Ulster Unionists, the imaginatively named 'Ulster Conservatives and Unionists – New Force'.

While the UUP's sole sitting MP, Lady Hermon, has refused to sign up to the agreement, the alliance has a realistic chance of victory in the middle-class seats of Belfast South and South Antrim, currently held by the SDLP and DUP respectively.

Boundary changes

It would be an understatement to say that the boundary changes implemented at the 1997 general election were disappointing for the Conservative Party. Labour's then representative to Boundary Commission enquiries, Greg Cook, is broadly perceived as having acted as an exceptional advocate for his party's interests. The boundary changes which will come into force for the 2010 election are significantly more positive for the Conservatives, arguably as a result of the organised and concerted efforts of the Conservative Central Office staffer Roger Pratt.

In total, nine parliamentary constituencies are abolished: six Labour, two Conservative and one Liberal Democrat. Of the thirteen newly created constituencies, ten are notionally Conservative held and three are projected to be Liberal Democrat seats. Furthermore, boundary changes in already ultra-marginal constituencies further strengthen the hand of the Conservatives who notionally 'gain' eleven seats (three of them in the key battleground of Kent alone) while losing only five to Labour.

The key issues

The economy: no time for a novice?

The next general election will be defined by one issue and one issue alone: who the British people trust to steer the country back to economic stability. When asked to state the political issue that concerns them most, 70 per cent of British electors recorded economic concerns – some 49 per cent ahead of immigration, the second highest priority. Never before in British electoral history have voters rated economic concerns so highly.

It is difficult to imagine another politician in recent history whose political destiny has been more influenced by economic attitudes than Gordon Brown, as a former Chancellor of the Exchequer. As such, this issue has the ability to either make or break the Prime Minister.

Brown is clearly comfortable debating the economy: it is an issue he understands and it is one of the few policy areas in which the general public retains a modicum of confidence in his abilities. David Cameron and George Osborne are not yet trusted on the economy; an April 2009 ComRes survey found that by a margin of 49 per cent to 39 per cent the public do not believe the party 'has the right ideas about how to get Britain out of recession'. Similarly, nearly four in five voters (79 per cent) in the same survey agreed that Cameron ought to be clearer about what he would do about the economy if he was to become Prime Minister.

When compared to the scores recorded for the last Conservative government, the Brown–Darling partnership scores relatively favourably. Satisfaction with the current Chancellor stands at minus 16 per cent, while the overall approval rating for the government's economic policies is minus 35 per cent. Conversely, Norman Lamont's rating fell to minus 52 per cent following the 'Black Wednesday' crisis, while Kenneth Clarke's job satisfaction was as low as minus 53 per cent during his spell as Chancellor.

Few can forget the scorn poured upon Baroness Vadera after her suggestion that the British economy was 'beginning to show green roots of recovery'. Among the general public, however, expectations for an improvement in the domestic situation are high with a June 2009 ComRes poll showing 67 per cent of people expect the economy to show 'signs of improvement soon', up from 39 per cent in April. Recent unexpected quarterly figures from France and Germany showing their economies edging back into the realm of positive economic growth will only help fuel expectations for an economic revival in the United Kingdom.

Herein lies Brown's problem – and possible salvation. If the economy fails to improve before the general election, his government's credibility will take another serious hit. On the other hand, all it would take to vindicate Brown's oft-used 'no time for a novice' attack on David Cameron and George Osborne would be solid evidence that Britain is once again moving into positive growth territory. While the Conservatives dithered, Brown could argue, his decisive action in salvaging the British banking sector and reining in the excesses of the City of London resuscitated the country's economy. To this end, the 2009 fourth-quarter economic growth figures are expected to be published at the end of March 2010 – potentially around the time the general election may be called.

'Mr 10% Cuts'
The centrepiece of Labour's attacks on the Conservatives throughout the past decade has been the funding of public services. To condense the Labour attack into one sentence: Labour invests, the Tories cut. From a polling perspective, it is impossible to know yet if the public understands the necessity for

public spending cuts. Labour have, however, already chosen to highlight the Conservative Party's position on this issue, alleging that the party cannot be trusted to make public spending cuts.

Unlike with economic concerns, there is little evidence to suggest that Labour retains any particular residual strength in this area. David Cameron's at times painfully personal defence of the National Health Service and state education provision has done much to neuter any attempts from within the party to paint the Conservatives as a foe of what the public perceive as front-line services. A June 2009 ComRes survey suggests that 31 per cent of voters trust the Conservatives most to decide where public spending cuts should be made, fully ten points ahead of Labour on 21 per cent.

Snouts in the trough

The political profession has never before been viewed in such a negative light, some 80 per cent of the public believing that all of the country's main political parties have let the country down. Fuelled by the *Daily Telegraph*'s lurid allegations about the failure of Labour Cabinet ministers to pay capital gains tax on taxpayer-funded properties, and Alan Duncan's florid description of the way in which comfortably salaried MPs are treated, it would be an understatement to suggest that the public has contempt for the established political classes.

The 2009 European elections proved that the public are at least willing to consider alternatives to the long-standing Conservative, Labour and Liberal Democrat troika. The Conservatives spluttered to victory on 27.7 per cent of the vote – almost three percentage points less than they achieved at their electoral nadir in 1997 – with the Eurosceptic UK Independence Party outpolling the Labour Party by more than 100,000 votes. The British National Party too secured its first two seats in the European Parliament, picking up considerable support in deprived former textile towns in Yorkshire and the north-west of England. The Greens too strengthened their position, taking 8.6 per cent of the vote nationally. The electoral advances secured by UKIP and the BNP in particular did not come so much as a result of an upsurge in support for the two parties – indeed in real terms, their support was lower than at the same poll in 2004 – but rather as a result of supporters of the main political parties boycotting the poll.

Faced with widespread disgust at their actions and the advance of political extremism, the political classes in the United Kingdom are posed a significant challenge as to how to respond to the public's keen appetite for reform. Some 69 per cent of the public now support the introduction of a form of proportional representation, 79 per cent back legislation to fix parliamentary terms at four or five years rather than letting the party in government decide when to call a vote, and 73 per cent favour a 'significant' reduction in the number of MPs sitting in the Commons. But despite Cameron's, Brown's and Clegg's bellicose attacks on abusers of the Westminster expenses system, no one party has yet been able to harness the public's fervent desire for political change.

Conclusion

The next election will be a clear trade-off between the desires of a public, weary after thirteen years of Labour rule, for wholesale political change and their residual – and some could even argue, grudging – respect for Gordon Brown's ability to steer the economy.

Conservative politicians may in public bay for Brown's blood yet in reality, the man is their key electoral asset. The Conservatives are still some way, electorally speaking, from sealing the deal with the British public. Only around half of Conservative voters describe their decision to vote for the party as being an active endorsement of the party's policies while almost as many are simply voting against another party – chiefly Brown's Labour. Similarly, half of the public agree that the Conservative Party 'is not yet ready to govern' (50 per cent) and that the team around David Cameron is 'lightweight'.

A successful challenge to Brown's leadership or a decision by the Prime Minister to stand down at his party conference in October has the potential to be a game-changing moment. Initial figures show that a decision to replace Brown with Home Secretary Alan Johnson would cut the party's deficit to only 10 percentage points – enough to deny the Conservatives an overall majority. It is almost certain that no Labour leadership contender can win the election for their party – but a change of leader could threaten the working majority the Conservatives so desperately want.

Andrew Hawkins
August 2009

The rise and fall of New Labour

Before we venture into Tory territory and look at the people and policies which will shape the new administration it is important to understand how and why the New Labour phenomenon created by Tony Blair, Gordon Brown, Peter Mandelson and Alastair Campbell came to such a disastrous demise.

It is a universal truth, generally acknowledged, that governments lose elections – rather than oppositions winning them. However, in order for a political landslide to be precipitated, the incumbent party has to have run out of energy and ideas, and the opposition party has to have both attractive policies and credible people.

Later in this book we will deal with the Conservatives and measure whether they are up to the task of enthusing the electorate. But for the moment, let us look at the factors which caused New Labour to descend from the euphoria of 1997 to the inevitability of defeat.

Boundary changes

Psephologically the Labour Party has a permanent built-in advantage in the UK. It takes far fewer votes to elect a Labour MP than a Tory MP, and therefore in our 'first past the post' system their votes are more efficiently spread and utilised. This is because inner-city seats (which generally vote Labour) traditionally see many of their voters drift to the suburbs. The boundaries are then never adjusted with sufficient speed to take account of this phenomenon and even up the resulting disparity.

It is technically possible for the Labour Party to achieve a majority in the House of Commons with only 35 per cent of the vote – whilst the Tories need at least 41 per cent to achieve the same result. In the 2005 general election it took an average of just 27,000 votes to elect a Labour MP, 44,000 to elect a Tory MP and a staggering 97,000 votes to elect each Lib Dem MP. This is why the Lib Dems consistently call for some form of proportional representation, and it is perhaps strange that so few Tories join them in that call.

However, the job of the Boundary Commissions (there is one each for England, Scotland, Wales and Northern Ireland) is to work to balance this in-built bias, and periodically there is a big shake-up of seats. Such a shake-up will occur at the next general election. According to the independent UK Polling Report the latest Boundary Commission review will see the Tories gain ten and the Lib Dems three of the thirteen newly created seats. Conversely, of the nine seats abolished, six will be Labour, two Tory and one Lib Dem. The net effect should be that the Tories gain sixteen seats, the Lib Dems and Plaid Cymru one each – and Labour should lose twelve.

More importantly, a great many other seats will be converted from safe Labour seats to marginals by these boundary changes. However, what will ultimately convert these seats for the Tories are not so much the boundary changes as the huge increase in their popularity as consistently chronicled by the opinion polls. Whilst there are always rogue polls, once a party has established a consistent double-digit lead in polls conducted by all of the major polling companies, then this settled public opinion is inevitably reflected in actual election results. Another better indicator of future success is where a party has a consistent lead in the 'iron triangle' of three key questions. They are: which party has the better leader, which party has the best policies for the economy and which party is the most united. Once a party has a consistent lead in all three of these questions – and the Tories do – then it is effectively game over.

Patently all governments make mistakes, and all governments make enemies. Perhaps Labour's biggest mistake was to upset Lord Ashcroft, and he has proved to be their most potent enemy. The Tory deputy chairman has not only poured money into the marginal seats, he has also brought structure and discipline to their offices and their campaigns. It was an adverse poll of the key marginal seats which persuaded Gordon Brown not to call a general election in September 2008 – something which he will undoubtedly regret for the rest of his life. The combination of Ashcroft's money and organisation, boundary changes and a yawning gap in the opinion polls will be strong factors which will ensure that Labour's defeat in 2010 is turned into a rout.

Exhaustion

All governments make mistakes – as we have noted above. That is partly because they are made up of human beings, who are by their nature fallible. It is partly because they have to make decisions every single day, and some of them are bound to be wrong. But it is also because, as time goes by, exhaustion sets into the body of the government and into the bodies and minds of its ministers. In time all governments run out of steam, run out of ideas and run out of road.

When Tony Blair left Downing Street in 2007 he looked dreadful – drawn and overweight at the same time, with deep lines etched in his face. Within months of leaving office he looked slimmer, happier and healthier. The cares of office had been lifted from his shoulders and despite the pressures of his 'portfolio' career, and the increasing grey in his receding hair, he looks ten years younger.

Some ministers have been in government, or even in the Cabinet, since 1997. The pressure of more than a decade in office is bound to take its toll on all ministers – though some are temperamentally better suited to cope with those pressures than others. But after a decade or more in power, many fall off the front bench, because of scandal, illness or simple exhaustion. Sometimes they give way to truly talented rising stars, and as a result they are not missed. In time, however, the whips are forced to scrape the barrel, 'retread' ministers are brought back, and the not quite so able are promoted from within the whips' own ranks or from amongst the 'wannabe' PPSs. The quality of government undoubtedly suffers once this stage has been reached – and in the case of the current Labour government, it undoubtedly has.

Gordon Brown

Nobody in the current Labour government is likely to be more exhausted than Gordon Brown.

After ten years at the Treasury he received a blatant 'hospital pass' from Tony Blair. For non-rugby fans, a hospital pass is where a player, faced with a charging mass of opposition players, unloads a pass to a fellow team member, who then has to take the hit from the onrushing enemy. Such behaviour has been known to result in an exchange of views – and sometimes blows – in the changing room afterwards. By the time Gordon Brown finally assumed the title he had coveted for so many years, he inherited an empty kitty in both intellectual and financial terms, and the reservoir of public goodwill had likewise been exhausted.

Many politicians are labelled 'workaholics' – or label themselves as such. Few of them actually warrant that soubriquet, they merely submit to the tyranny of the civil service with their red boxes, or to the tyranny of constituents who refuse to raise their issue at the appropriate (councillor) level. Gordon Brown, however, is the genuine article. He will routinely rise at 4.00 a.m., pound the treadmill and then hit the phones, before devouring his paperwork as though it were the breakfast which he often neglects to have. That is why he finds it so hard to recruit civil servants who can keep pace with him, and why some ministerial colleagues regard him with a mixture of fear and awe.

Gordon Brown is also, in a literal sense, brilliant. He went to Edinburgh University at just sixteen and graduated with a first. He then became the youngest ever rector of the university. He went on to take an MA in history, before devoting his PhD thesis to the Scottish Labour Party thinker and firebrand James Maxton.

Not only is Brown brilliant, he is also genuinely passionate about alleviating poverty in the UK and in the world at large. Unlike Tony Blair, Brown is steeped in the lore of the Labour Party. The tragedy for this driven man is that for all his intellect and hard work – and his worthy political goals and love of the Labour Party – his party preferred the mercurial Blair when the leadership became vacant in 1994. That is because they knew that Blair – the orator, the charmer, the empathiser – would win elections for them. Sadly for Gordon Brown the same will be true in 2010. The British electorate will prefer the intelligent, ambitious but grounded and rounded Cameron to the driven and workaholic Brown.

Buggins's turn

Just as there is an economic cycle, so there is a political cycle. Just as economies grow and overheat, and then contract, so parties come to power on a wave of enthusiasm, enjoy a brief honeymoon, and then start to decline in popularity as they are forced to make the difficult decisions of government.

In previous eras there were famous double acts that would rotate the premiership between them – such as Gladstone and Disraeli, and Wilson and Heath. In the post-war era (with the Liberals confined to the nation's periphery) the Labour Party and the Tories swapped power on a regular, almost routine, basis.

Then along came Margaret Thatcher, and all of that changed. She spurned the centrist agenda and post-war consensus, and won three straight victories in a row. John Major then replaced her and won by not being Thatcher – and by not being Neil Kinnock either. Next Tony Blair came along with his unprecedented (for Labour) three victories in a row. In theory there is the possibility that Gordon Brown will 'do a Major' and sneak an unexpected victory: in practice Buggins's turn will reassert itself and he will be denied the chance to win his own mandate.

Sleaze

Although John Major's government was primarily derailed by the shock of sterling's enforced ejection from the ERM in September 1992, it was also crippled and ultimately euthanised by the spectre of sleaze.

Politicians, as we have noted, are human. All humans have failings and cravings, but politicians seem to have them in spades. The same drive which propels them into politics also makes them particularly prone to temptation – especially where sex or money is involved. Sometimes the press, no strangers to temptation themselves, are prepared to overlook the fact that an MP (or even a minister) drinks too much, or has sex with a person other than his or her declared partner. However, the one failing neither the press nor the public will forgive is hypocrisy.

When John Major made his disastrous 'back to basics' speech at the Tory Party conference in Blackpool in September 1993, he opened not just a can of worms but also Pandora's box. No sooner had he sat down after his, it must be said, well-received speech than open season was declared on all Tory politicians. The rationale was that if the party leader and Prime Minister was calling for a return to the ethical standards of yesteryear, any of his party colleagues who misbehaved were guilty of hypocrisy by association. The media produced a flood of sleaze stories, and all attempts by the hapless premier and his Cabinet to limp towards the safety of the moral high ground were thwarted.

In the current parliament the issue of MPs' expenses and the additional cost allowance has dwarfed the issue of sleaze under John Major. The drip-drip release of uncensored details of MPs' expenses by the *Daily Telegraph* caused enormous damage to all parties – and to Parliament and the body politic. It also prompted a large number of MPs to stand down – either because they had been brutally exposed by the *Daily Telegraph*'s investigations, or because they did not wish to stay in Parliament and be subjected to this level of scrutiny. However, although the issue hit all parties hard, there is no doubt that it hit the governing party – Labour – the hardest of all.

So politicians are human, sometimes far too human. As parties get used to the trappings of power, and as their politicians grow a carapace of arrogance and indifference, they take dumber and dumber risks. As a party runs out of steam and becomes less popular, civil servants and others are more likely to leak and to 'shop' them to the press. And as the prospect of defeat becomes more apparent, the temptation is to grab anything which is on offer whilst it is still available.

The result is a succession of damaging headlines. These are not usually about breaking any law, but about using, and occasionally abusing, the system. That is why the term 'sleaze' is so damaging – it is not dependent on any actual illegality. But once a government has been labelled as 'sleazy', it is almost impossible to cast off that mantle. That is the stage that the Labour government has arrived at.

Losing touch

To the frequent despair of their own backbenchers, ministers inevitably become insulated to the views of people in the real world and inured to criticism of their policies. They are surrounded by respectful civil servants, they are whisked from one place to another by the Government Car Service, and they regard every media interview as an opportunity to show off their skills at avoiding answering questions. This insulation, combined with the exhaustion mentioned earlier, leads to ministers and government making ever more mistakes. Worse, it also leads to an inability to recognise that mistakes have been made and a refusal to acknowledge the fact even if that realisation does sink in.

In the case of Margaret Thatcher, the poll tax did as much as anything to cut short her ambitions to achieve a historic fourth general election victory. In the case of Gordon Brown, the abolition of the 10p tax band was hugely damaging – something which he actually acknowledged and issued a rare apology for. Since then, however, there have been other completely unnecessary initiatives which have alienated Labour backbenchers, Labour supporters and the electorate at large. The expansion of Heathrow and the proposal to build a third runway was a decision which could easily have been postponed until after the general election. Proposals to partially privatise the Post Office (latterly withdrawn) took Gordon Brown's government into territory where even Thatcher feared to tread.

Health and education

In opposition Tony Blair and Gordon Brown – nervous of the City's reaction to a Labour government – pledged to stick to Tory spending plans for the first two years if they came to power. For the first few years of his Chancellorship Gordon Brown was the very model of prudence, and whilst public spending was gradually increased after those first two years, there was no step change. However, with the confidence of the 1997 landslide behind him, and the huge reservoir of public goodwill seemingly undissipated, the Labour 2001 general election manifesto promised to bring UK spending on health up to the EU average – which stood at about 8 per cent of GDP. This, coupled with Blair's earlier pledge that 'education, education, education' would be his priority, signalled a massive increase in expenditure in these two key areas.

This announcement was very popular and helped to ensure that Labour had another huge majority in 2001, where they won 418 seats to the Tories'

165. People genuinely did feel that greater investment in schools and hospitals was needed, and as long as the economy continued to grow they were happy to pay for it. The problem is that whilst expenditure on health more than doubled between 1997 and 2008 (Alistair Darling, Budget debate, Hansard, 12 March 2008), the difference in standards of frontline healthcare has been discernible – but not significant. Much of this huge increase in spending has been swallowed up in increased salaries and pensions for doctors and nurses – which few people would argue against. However, vast sums have also been spent on NHS managers, who have spent their time ensuring that the same doctors and nurses pursue frequently meaningless targets imposed by Whitehall. It has now got to the point that there are as many people in the NHS wielding pens and clipboards as thermometers and stethoscopes.

In the same Budget statement, Chancellor Alistair Darling boasted that government spending on education had risen by 58 per cent since the Labour government had come to power. And government figures do consistently show an improvement in exam results year on year. However, very few people believe that these improvements are genuine. Study after study has shown that exam standards have been dumbed down, and it is grade inflation, rather than genuine improvements in education standards, which accounts for these improvements.

Driven by Gordon Brown from No. 11 and then No. 10 Downing Street, a positive blizzard of targets has been set for every government department and the agencies they fund in the form of public service agreements. The problem is that it is government which sets the targets, government which seeks to meet them, government which measures the outcomes, and government which announces the results. It has become like Hitler in his bunker trying to deploy long-defunct divisions, or Soviet factories churning out paper tractors to meet five-year plan targets – an exercise in futility. The British public know full well that they have received nothing like value for the doubling of the health budget, or the more than 50 per cent increase in the education budget.

IT projects

Out of all of the waste which has characterised Labour's term of office, IT projects have grabbed many of the headlines. Some projects have over-run in terms of their finances and timescales, whilst others have so exceeded their budget that they have had to be cancelled.

In February 2009 the House of Commons Public Accounts Committee announced that it had ordered the NAO to investigate the cost over-run in government IT contracts. This followed an investigation by *The Times*, which identified government contracts where the amount actually spent was £18 billion in excess of original estimates. An earlier NAO report had concluded that government departments and agencies could save between £160 million and £290 million on the £12 billion which they spent each year on IT service contracts.

The LIBRA project – designed to provide a computer network linking all courts in England and Wales – was seven years late and, at £444 million, £260 million over budget. Despite this delay and huge cost over-run, it was belatedly discovered that the system could not translate documents into Welsh. A last-minute and expensive fix had to be developed.

The NAO highlighted the failure of another project in March 2009. A system designed to track offenders from conviction through prison to parole, the National Offender Management Information System, was projected to cost £234 million in 2004. By July 2007 the cost had soared to £690 million. Ultimately this scheme was scrapped, to be replaced by a simpler system at a cost of £513 million.

Despite these failures the government has persevered with most IT projects. The system designed to link up all NHS facilities and centralise the records of 50 million patients (the National Programme for IT) has cost £12.7 billion to date, is running at least four years behind schedule and still does not function anything like properly. The government is also persevering with its intention to roll out the National Identity Scheme, which will see the issuing of national ID cards with a supporting database, albeit in an increasingly watered-down fashion. This is despite strong libertarian objections to the scheme and the strong possibility that the technical problems which have characterised similar projects will be replicated in this one. Official estimates put the cost of this scheme at £4.8 billion, but external experts predict that this budget will be substantially exceeded.

Welfare reform

All governments and all governments in waiting pledge to reform the welfare system. Tony Blair's government was no exception to that rule, and in 1997 he tasked Frank Field to 'think the unthinkable' and plan for the wholesale reform of the system. Field's efforts were sabotaged by his inability to get on with his nominal boss, Harriet Harman, and by the implacable opposition to his plans of the then Chancellor, Gordon Brown. Field left office within a year, and Harman was also summarily dispatched. After virulent (and sometimes violent) protests by disability groups and representatives of single parents, the Welfare Reform Act of 1999 was a much-diluted piece of legislation.

Safely installed at No. 10, Brown thought that he would try to succeed where Blair had failed. He put rising star James Purnell in charge of the Department for Work & Pensions, and he not only talked tough on welfare reform but also faced off opposition within his own party to the inclusion of private companies in efforts to encourage those on benefits back into work. Not only did he turn to the private sector for solutions, but he also pledged to penalise those on benefits who refuse to actively seek work. His replacement, Yvette Cooper, insists that she will see the reforms through.

The problem is, of course, that it is too late. The system has created hundreds of thousands of households which are entirely dependent on benefits, and has created so many incentives for couples not to live together that the UK has the highest level of single-parent households in the developed world. Meanwhile, many of the vacancies which disincentivised Britons could have filled have instead been taken up by migrant workers from within the EU – or even from outside the EU.

The result of Labour's failure to reform welfare is a whole generation used to being paid for doing nothing, with the jobs which they should be doing instead being carried out by non-UK citizens. Even though Labour said in opposition that welfare payments were 'paying the price of failure', and even though they repeatedly pledged to cut the welfare bill, in 2009/10 the Treasury estimates that the total amount spent on social security payments will be a staggering £186 billion.

Immigration

Since the end of the Cold War there has been a succession of regional conflicts which have led to large-scale population movements. Many of the victims of these conflicts have headed for western Europe, with a substantially disproportionate number aiming to ultimately settle in the UK. A study by the LSE commissioned by London mayor Boris Johnson in March 2009 calculated that as many as 947,000 illegal immigrants were living in the UK. This figure compares with official Home Office estimates published in 2005 which put the figure at 430,000.

The expansion of the EU into eastern Europe has provided opportunities for a large number of migrant workers to work in the UK. The government could have limited the numbers of these migrants, but because the economy was growing and unemployment was low it decided not to do so. Only with the most recent accession of Bulgaria and Romania did the government exercise the option to limit the free flow of labour on a temporary basis. Nevertheless, official government figures show that the quantity of National Insurance numbers issued to eastern European workers in the year to September 2008 was 720,000.

So high is the level of migration into the UK that the UN predicts that by 2050 we will have the largest population in Europe. This is because net migration into the UK – the difference between those entering and those leaving – is predicted to run at 174,000 a year. The UK is already the most crowded country in Europe, according to the ONS, having recently overtaken the Netherlands in this respect. Being much smaller than Germany or France in terms of land area, the UK is going to become a very crowded country indeed.

The Labour government's failure to control both legal and illegal migration has been a source of considerable public anxiety. The Tories have been reluctant to exploit the issue. This is partly because their 2005 general election campaign strongly highlighted immigration but failed to bring the electoral advances which they had hoped for. However, since then public disquiet has sharpened and the BNP have made substantial gains in some areas – at local authority level and European Parliament level – by exploiting the issue of immigration, both legal and illegal.

Figures published by the ONS in June 2009 starkly revealed the failure of Labour's immigration and employment policies. Of the 2.9 million jobs created since 1997, 1.8 million were in the public sector. Of the remaining 1.1 million jobs in the private sector, only 15 per cent were taken up by Britons – the rest were taken up by migrant workers. A study by the OECD the following month suggested that 71 per cent of the new jobs had been taken up by overseas workers.

Devolution

When New Labour swept to power in 1997 it immediately set about honouring the memory of its former leader John Smith by proceeding to roll out devolution throughout the UK.

The Northern Ireland peace process had been ongoing under John Major, and Tony Blair threw his energies and undoubted charm behind giving it new momentum. But away from this troubled province, the incoming government was determined to bring in devolution in Scotland and Wales. The introduction of a Scottish Parliament – with primary legislative and tax-varying powers –

was strongly endorsed by the people of Scotland. However, a Welsh Assembly – without these powers – was only endorsed by a wafer-thin majority, with 50.1 per cent of those who voted doing so in favour of devolution.

Despite the establishment of the Scottish Parliament and the Welsh Assembly, the New Labour government has persisted with the 'Barnett formula', long after its architect has admitted that it is no longer fit for purpose. Under this system, English taxpayers heavily subsidise the people of Scotland and Wales. The largesse of English taxpayers has allowed the Scottish Parliament to freeze council tax whilst it continues to rise strongly in England, and to phase out prescription charges and scrap university top-up fees. Scots also get free personal care for the elderly, and free dental and optical check-ups. The Welsh Assembly scrapped prescription charges back in 2007.

The net effect of devolution and the Barnett formula is that public spending is 30 per cent higher in Northern Ireland than in England – which is perhaps justifiable in view of the Troubles. But it is also 22 per cent higher in Scotland than in England, and 14 per cent higher in Wales than in England.

Regulation

The latest 'Burdens Barometer' estimates the total cumulative cost of all the regulatory burdens on British business since Labour came to power at £76.8 billion. The Burdens Barometer is compiled for the British Chambers of Commerce by the London Business School and the Manchester Business School.

A study by the business lobby group Open Europe puts the cost even higher. This study calculates that the cost to British business of complying with government regulations has escalated to a staggering £28.7 billion a year. This figure was arrived at by studying over 2,000 regulatory impact assessments produced by government departments. The same study also suggests that 72 per cent of these regulations originated in Brussels.

British businesses – not unnaturally – dislike paying tax and will take all reasonable (and legal) measures to avoid doing so. But they do recognise that taxes are needed to pay for public services – including the infrastructure they rely on to function. What they do not regard as inevitable, however, and what they therefore resent strongly, is regulation which appears to have been imposed for its own sake with little thought of the detrimental impact it is likely to have on businesses.

Civil service

Under Tony Blair and Gordon Brown the size and power of the civil service and public sector has increased enormously. The total number of people on the public sector payroll increased by 13 per cent between 1997 and 2006, according to the Institute for Fiscal Studies (IFS), and now stands at 5.8 million, according to the ONS. Whilst the private sector shed 300,000 jobs in the last six months of 2008, the public sector increased its workforce by 50,000.

Again according to the ONS, an extra 600,000 public sector jobs have been created since Labour came to power. Very few people believe that this increase in the number of civil servants has actually added to the sum total of human happiness – or indeed healthiness. What it has done is to underpin a culture of target setting, target checking and target fudging which has created a new – and entirely unproductive – industry.

The problem is not just that these extra civil servants have to be paid a salary. They also have to have offices, desks, chairs and computers. Even more expensively, they have to have gilt-edged, inflation-linked pensions for life. To add insult to injury for private sector workers, civil servants not only have nicer offices, shorter hours, longer holidays, greater job security and better pensions – their wage increases have actually increased ahead of those of workers in the private sector. According to figures provided by the Pensions Policy Institute the average employee in the private sector now earns £25,300, whilst his or her equivalent in the public sector now earns £25,600.

The Conservatives also managed to extract figures from the government in March 2009 showing that claims to be slimming down the size of the civil service are a sham. Whilst £900 million has been spent on redundancy payments for the 15,000 civil servants who have been laid off, an extra 42,020 full-time civil servants have actually been recruited. In theory this might be accounted for by the need to rebalance the civil service and recruit more workers into areas where they are needed – such as in administering benefits and finding work for those who find themselves unemployed as a result of the recession. However, the Department for Work & Pensions has – according to written answers issued by the government – made 8,479 staff redundant at a cost of £401 million.

Now that times are hard and the private sector is contracting, the resentment for this ivory-tower, gold-plated and fireproof existence will undoubtedly build up and will find expression not just in the letters pages of the *Daily Mail* and the *Daily Telegraph*, but also through the ballot box.

Credit crunch

It was Bill Clinton's election guru, the 'raging Cajun' James Carville, who had pinned up on the walls of his campaign war room the phrase 'it's the economy, stupid'. This was to remind supporters and staffers – and himself – that whatever other issues came up in the campaign, George Bush Senior's fatal weakness was his handling of the economy.

When Tony Blair became Prime Minister and Gordon Brown Chancellor in 1997 they inherited a healthy economy and a benign economic outlook. The economy had been growing steadily virtually from the date of the UK's expulsion from the ERM in September 1992. This had given the Tory government the freedom to cut interest rates from the terrifyingly high rate they had been raised to in a futile attempt to maintain sterling's place within the mechanism. After the expulsion of sterling, and the subsequent slashing of interest rates, the UK economy enjoyed a period of unprecedented economic growth. So the Tories took the hit for 'Black Wednesday' – and bequeathed the Labour government a booming economy.

Blair and Brown were determined to show that a Labour government could do a good job of managing the British economy. And to begin with they did. Prudence reigned, Tory spending plans were adhered to, and business was courted and encouraged. However, once Prudence was sent packing, and the civil service expanded enormously, and spending on health and education ballooned, there was only one way to balance the books. That was by borrowing.

For all the talk about the credit crunch being a phenomenon which started in America and then infected the rest of the world, the Blair and Brown governments left the UK highly vulnerable. Not only had the government borrowed, but it actively encouraged business, banks and individuals to do the same. Far from being uniquely well placed to ride out the economic storms sweeping around the world (as Gordon Brown has repeatedly claimed), the UK's economy is one of the worst placed in the west to do so. So says the IMF, and so say the money markets.

The IFS estimates that it will take until 2032 to pay off the debt amassed as a result of the credit crunch and by the government's desperate (but futile) efforts to avert a recession. In his April 2009 Budget the Chancellor, Alistair Darling, had to announce that the government would be borrowing £175 billion. The NAO has announced that tax revenues in 2008/9 were down by £32 billion. London really is 'Reykjavik by the Thames', and there will be a terrible economic and (in Labour's case) electoral price to pay for this decade and more of waste and needless borrowing. The ONS said in July 2009 that the national debt had risen to £799 billion. This represents 56.6 per cent of the UK's GDP, whilst Gordon Brown's 'Golden Rule' stated that it should not rise above 40 per cent.

Of all of the failures of the Blair and Brown administrations, and of all of the reasons why they will suffer an electoral catastrophe in 2010, their mishandling of the economy will be easily the greatest: it's the credit crunch, stupid.

The rise of the New Conservatives

For a change of government to come about, all that needs to happen is for the incumbent to fail. But for a landslide to occur, it is not sufficient for the sitting government to be seen to have failed: the opposition needs to look like a viable government in waiting. Its front bench needs to look attractive and capable, and its policies need to sound credible.

So if there is – as this author maintains – going to be a Tory tsunami in 2010, three criteria need to be met. The government needs to have failed – and to have been seen to fail. This criterion, as discussed above, has certainly been met. The opposition's leaders – and most especially its actual leader – need to look and sound competent and trustworthy. And the opposition party's policies need to ring true.

So, having spent some time cataloguing New Labour's failures, let us spend time examining the alternative. Who are the New Conservatives and what will they try to do when they achieve power?

The people

Political parties are evolutionary beasts. Whilst they generally remain true to the core principles which brought them into being, they have to adapt their policies according to the shifting opinions of the electorate and changes in external conditions and circumstances.

But political parties are made up of people. Hundreds of thousands of people in the case of the Conservative and Labour parties, and tens of thousands of people in the case of the Liberal Democrats. These people change over time as death and unpopularity take their toll – but it is generally a gradual evolutionary process. Perhaps once in a generation, however, the change accelerates and becomes more drastic. This nearly always occurs after a prolonged period in opposition and after multiple defeats.

That is when a new leader comes along and preaches the need for revolution rather than evolution. And generally, after suffering the pain of multiple defeats and after reluctantly enduring years in the wilderness, the mass membership of the party grudgingly accepts the need for real change. That is what Tony Blair accomplished with the Labour Party in 1994 and what David Cameron accomplished with the Conservatives in 2005. Tony Blair – along with a small coterie of trusted advisors – created New Labour. Equally, David Cameron, along with his team, has created the New Conservatives.

That team does not just consist of shadow ministers – or even MPs. It is made up of staffers, thinkers, donors and doers. In this section we will examine the roles and personalities of the individuals who have helped to shape the New Conservative Party to date and who will take it into government.

The inner core

First we will look at the inner core, the closest of the close, the Praetorian Guard, the inner Cabinet in waiting. It is these people that will be appointed to the great offices of state. It is also this close-knit group which will make all the big decisions over all of the major areas of policy.

As with any new government, the team will largely resemble in power the picture it portrayed in opposition. Over time the bonds of friendship and loyalty forged in the wilderness years will be loosened, and the insistent demands of rising stars will have to be satisfied, but for those early halcyon days this is how the inner core of the New Conservative government will look.

David Cameron

Where there is a Praetorian Guard there must be a Caesar, and for the foreseeable future David Cameron will be wearing the laurel crown. The Praetorian Guard will perform its traditional role of keeping Caesar safe from external enemies (and he does have some), until the guards themselves decide that a new leader is required and the daggers come out.

To mix metaphors, Cameron is not in reality a one-man band – but he is the undisputed front man of the Tory band. The Conservatives without him would be like the Doors without Jim Morrison, the Blockheads without Ian Dury, Oasis without Liam Gallagher or the Rolling Stones without Mick Jagger. They would still get gigs, but nobody would be storming the stage. The only foreseeable event which could deprive the Tories of at least a working majority in 2010 would be if something happened to remove Cameron from the stage.

There is a widespread view that everything has fallen easily to the Tory leader, and there is some foundation to this belief. He comes from a happy and comfortable upper-middle-class household based at Peasemore in Berkshire. From there his father Ian commuted into London to earn a very good living as a partner at the stockbrokers Panmure Gordon. On his mother's side the Mount family had sent at least two MPs to Parliament, whilst his father-in-law is Sir Reginald Sheffield – who has large estates in Lincolnshire. Samantha Cameron herself – known as Sam or even 'SamCam' – is the step-daughter of the Tory peer Viscount Astor. She herself has a highly successful career as the creative director of the upmarket stationers Smythson.

Cameron's education was equally top drawer. He was sent to board at Heatherdown Preparatory School near Ascot. The school – now closed – also numbered Princes Andrew and Edward amongst its former pupils. From there it was a short journey – literally – to Eton College, where his elder brother Alex was already ensconced. Initially he did not excel academically, and he had brushes with the school authorities over cannabis and cigarette smoking – both of which (as in most boarding schools then and now) were rife. However, having survived to enter into the sixth form, Cameron started to apply himself academically, especially in politics. In the end he got straight As at A-level in politics and economics, history and history of art – in the days when straight As were very hard to achieve.

As a result of this late surge Cameron was accepted by Brasenose College, Oxford to read the classic PPE – politics, philosophy and economics. He there fell under the spell of the legendary Professor Vernon Bogdanor, who in turn was (and remains) a great admirer of the Tory leader. However, displaying some of the immaturity which had got him into trouble at Eton, Cameron also joined the notorious Bullingdon dining club, along with his Eton contemporary Boris Johnson. Despite this, he graduated with a first, and a career in (or on the fringes of) politics beckoned.

Applying for a job in the Conservative Research Department at CCO (then based at Smith Square) Cameron was interviewed by the then deputy director, the redoubtable Alistair Cooke. The CRD has been a great breeding ground for Tory talent over the years, with Chris Patten and Michael Portillo being two of its politically more successful alumni. It was here that Cameron first met Steve Hilton, who would become one of the architects of the New Conservatives. Despite the strong competition around him Cameron shone, and in 1989 he was appointed director of the Political Section. As such he was part of the team which briefed Margaret Thatcher and then John Major before PMQs – which in those days took place twice a week, on Tuesdays and Thursdays.

During the 1992 general election campaign Cameron was trusted with the key job of briefing John Major every morning ahead of an 8.30 a.m. press conference. To many people's surprise the Tories won the 1992 general election, and this paved the way for the next stage in the advancement of Cameron's career. Partly at John Major's urging, Cameron was installed in the Treasury as special advisor to Chancellor Norman Lamont after the general election victory. Before the end of the year Cameron and Lamont would have to deal with a succession of crises. These culminated in 'Black Wednesday', 16 September 1992, when sterling was unceremoniously bundled out of the ERM. By May 1993 both the Chancellor and his special advisor were out of a job.

Almost by accident Cameron ended up as special advisor to the then Home Secretary, Michael Howard. Ken Clarke had replaced Norman Lamont as Chancellor and wanted to bring his own team to the Treasury. Cameron was temporarily in limbo, but when Howard heard he was available he snapped him up. He knew of Cameron's reputation as an astute observer of the political scene, and he had been briefed by him on occasion ahead of regular TV appearances. Once appointed, Cameron found himself briefing Howard to withstand the onslaught of a rising star within the Labour Party – one Tony Blair. It was Cameron who helped Howard counter Blair's 'tough on crime, tough on the causes of crime' slogan with a simple mantra – 'prison works'.

Cameron and Howard forged a good working and personal relationship which was to benefit them both in the future. However, by 1994 Cameron decided that he needed to get some experience of business if he was to make a successful bid to establish his own political career. Through Samantha's family Cameron had connections with Michael Green – the flamboyant boss of Carlton Communications plc. The company was commercially successful, but under continuous pressure because its programming was widely regarded as being downmarket. Despite this, and the doubts of some of Carlton's executives about employing somebody who made no secret of his political ambitions, Cameron began working in the communications department of the firm whilst applying for a parliamentary seat. Within a short period of time his ability to handle the media – and his difficult boss – earned him the job of director of corporate affairs.

In 1996 Cameron was selected for the supposedly fairly safe Tory seat of Stafford. However, the incumbent Bill Cash had been wise to move to the seat next door, and in the New Labour landslide of 1997 – when many Tory ministers and MPs were swept aside – Cameron lost by 5,032 votes to the unremarkable Labour candidate David Kidney. Cameron returned to Carlton, where his job had been held open for him, and he was to remain there for a further four years. They were not easy years. Carlton's star was fading and Cameron found it ever harder to fend off the aggressive attentions of the financial journalists who loved to prick the sensitive skin of its boss. Cameron's job became less about smoothing and schmoozing and more about blustering and bullying on behalf of his boss.

Salvation came Cameron's way in the shape of the defection of the Witney MP Shaun Woodward to Labour in 1999. The local party was determined to avoid the prospect of any further embarrassment, and the final selection came down to Cameron and the 'retread' Andrew Mitchell. In a prelude of what was to come, Cameron not only spoke without notes at the selection meeting, he spurned the lectern and roamed the stage, addressing the audience without a physical barrier. Cameron won the selection comfortably and in the 2001 general election won the seat with a healthy 7,973 majority.

Despite Cameron's own success in Witney the Tories had been badly beaten in the general election and William Hague immediately tendered his resignation as leader. Cameron backed the modernising Michael Portillo in the first round, but he was squeezed out by the right-wingers supporting Iain Duncan Smith and the Europhiles and traditional 'one nation' Tories backing Ken Clarke. In the end Duncan Smith won, but remorselessly bad poll ratings forced him out in 2003, without having had the chance to contest a general election. The party needed a safe pair of hands and it turned to Cameron's old mentor Michael Howard, who was given a clear run at the leadership.

In the 2005 general election Cameron worked closely with Howard to prepare the simple five-point 'dog whistle' manifesto. Although the Tories again lost, Labour's majority was substantially reduced and the Tories received an infusion of new blood which revitalised the parliamentary party. Many of the 2005 intake have played a leading role in turning the Conservatives into an effective opposition, and they will also play leading roles in the New Conservative government.

Howard regarded his work as being done, and he was determined not to stay on any longer than was necessary. However, he was equally determined to ensure that his protégé would have a good chance of succeeding him. The extended 'beauty contest' he launched to identify his successor was designed to culminate at the Tory conference in Blackpool, when all of the candidates would have the chance to impress the party faithful. As Howard expected, Cameron put on a stellar performance which showed up the comparatively pedestrian speaking style of the clear frontrunner, David Davis. Four years after entering the Commons, having held the comparatively junior posts of shadow local government spokesman and shadow Secretary of State for Education & Skills, Cameron was the Conservative Party leader.

Although Cameron was born and brought up with every possible advantage, he has also suffered setbacks during his career. There was Black Wednesday, when a youthful Cameron was caught just on camera when Norman Lamont was making his *al fresco* announcement that the UK was to leave the ERM. Ken Clarke's refusal to keep him on at the Treasury left him, temporarily at least, unemployed. In 1997 he was to suffer defeat at the hands of the electorate at Stafford, whilst in 2005 those dissatisfied with the Tory's solid but unspectacular gains partly blamed him, as author of the manifesto. In the world of business, at Carlton Communications Cameron found himself trapped between a demanding and occasionally unreasonable boss and a press which was rapidly growing disenchanted with the company and its output.

None of these career setbacks seemed to have much of an effect on the youthful Cameron. What introduced him – and Samantha – to the harsh realities of the world was the birth of their eldest son, Ivan, with cerebral palsy and serious epilepsy. The strain of caring for this severely disabled child – albeit with plenty of professional help – and the heartbreak of losing him at just six years of age finally rubbed the gilt off this gilded youth.

As many of his contemporaries at school have testified, there was – beneath the unfailing courtesy – always a streak of ruthlessness in Cameron. Over the years the steel in him has been honed, and colleagues and opponents alike will testify as to the strength and sharpness of that steel. The death of his son brought about its final tempering.

George Osborne

From the earliest days after entering the Commons in 2001 David Cameron and George Osborne recognised in each other similar talents and an identical ambition to reform the Conservative Party in order to make it electable. The press dubbed them the Blair and Brown of the Conservative Party. Neither Cameron nor Osborne was ever comfortable with that analogy, but it was a hard one to wholly refute.

Osborne's background is every bit as privileged as Cameron's. He is heir to his father, who is the 17th baronet, and also to the family's fortune – generated by the wallpaper firm Osborne & Little. Somehow he escaped the magnetic pull of Eton, but he went to the very upmarket St Paul's School before heading for Magdalen College, Oxford, where he read history. He then followed Cameron's footsteps into the CRD, and like his friend he became head of the Political Section.

This spell at the CRD earned Osborne the dubious reward of being appointed special advisor to the Agriculture Minister, Douglas Hogg, during the BSE crisis. After the defeat of 1997 Osborne worked for William Hague's leadership campaign. When Hague became party leader he rewarded Osborne's loyalty and support by employing him as his political secretary and speechwriter.

Another similarity between Osborne and Cameron is that they both acquired their seats in unusual circumstances. Whilst Cameron had taken over from the defector Shaun Woodward, Osborne was selected for Tatton. In 1997 the white-suited anti-sleaze campaigner Martin Bell had stood as an independent in Tatton and defeated former Tory Trade Minister Neil Hamilton. Perhaps fortunately for Osborne, Bell had pledged to stand for just one parliament, and in 2001 normal service was resumed and Osborne won with a comfortable majority of 8,611 (increased to 11,731 in 2005). At that time he was the youngest Tory MP.

Osborne was barely thirty years old when he was elected, and thereby earned the soubriquet 'Boy George'. He was almost immediately sent to cut his teeth in the Whips' Office. He then joined the front bench as part of the Tory economic team and has stayed there ever since. Within a year of joining the front bench he was appointed shadow Chief Secretary to the Treasury and when Cameron became leader he appointed him shadow Chancellor.

Like Cameron, Osborne supported Michael Portillo in the first round of the 2001 leadership contest. Despite being economically 'dry' and an instinctive Eurosceptic, Osborne is credited with having 'got it' much earlier than Cameron. Whilst Cameron had at least experienced a 'lucky' win in the 1992 general election, Osborne had known nothing but failure during his years of association with the party. This convinced him that, if the party was ever to seriously challenge for power again, the appearance of change would not be enough – it would actually have to embrace real change.

When Michael Howard announced that he was standing down as party leader in 2005, Osborne was just thirty-four years old. Some colleagues and some members of the press expected him to throw his hat in the ring, despite his youth. Osborne was, however, decisive and adamant. He ruled himself out of the contest immediately and threw all his energies into securing the unlikely victory of his friend David Cameron. This doubly unselfish gesture reinforced what was already a strong friendship and alliance, and meant that when he was under pressure over the Deripaska 'yachtgate' incident Cameron never considered moving him. Barring a catastrophic unforeseeable event, George Osborne will be David Cameron's Chancellor of the Exchequer.

William Hague

William Hague, like David Cameron and George Osborne, is something of a phenomenon. He made an electrifying speech to the 1977 Conservative conference at the age of just sixteen – a performance which had led Margaret Thatcher to dub him 'the new William Pitt'. Educated at his local comprehensive school at Wath-on-Dearne he went on to Magdalen College, Oxford (where he got a first in PPE) and was president of the Oxford Union before going on to study at the INSEAD business school near Paris.

After a brief spell working for the world-renowned McKinsey management consultancy firm, Hague was selected and elected for Richmond in the 1989 by-election. This had come about when Leon Brittan resigned the seat in order to take up his consolation post of European commissioner after the 'Westland affair', which had so seriously destabilised Margaret Thatcher's government.

A meteoric political career then ensued. After serving as Norman Lamont's PPS from 1990, he was made a parliamentary under-secretary of state at the Department of Social Security in 1993 and a minister of state in the same department in 1994. From 1995 to 1997 he joined the Cabinet as Secretary of State for Wales, and it was in Cardiff that he met his future wife, Ffion Jenkins. After a short engagement they were married in the House of Commons crypt. Ffion had been Hague's private secretary at the Welsh Office, and she taught him the words to the Welsh national anthem. This was after John Redwood had been captured on camera desperately trying to mumble random words along to the tune.

With the Tories in shock following their catastrophic defeat in 1997, Hague seized what he considered to be his destiny. After an initial hesitation (where he discussed running in tandem with Michael Howard), he ran for the leadership of his party at the age of thirty-six and saw off the vastly more experienced Howard, Ken Clarke and Peter Lilley. However, despite some stunningly good performances at the despatch box, Hague never captured the imagination or the affection of the British public. His accent grated with some sectors of the public, and gaffes such as the baseball cap and the 'fourteen pints' saga ensured that he never really established himself as a Prime Minister in waiting. When the Tories made a net gain of just one seat in 2001 (arguably that one seat being Tatton returning to the fold), Hague resigned with great speed and dignity the very next morning.

After 2001 Hague devoted himself to largely non-political interests. He landed some lucrative consultancies and established himself as an after-dinner speaker of unparalleled wit (and fees), and an excellent performer on television programmes such as *Have I Got News for You*. He also wrote a regular column for the *News of the World* and highly acclaimed books on William Pitt and William Wilberforce, which were lucratively serialised. His outside earnings whilst he was on the back benches ranged between £500,000 and £820,000 a year.

Despite Hague having looked far more relaxed and comfortable away from the front line of politics, when David Cameron asked him to return to the shadow Cabinet as shadow Foreign Secretary he accepted. He has been scrupulously loyal to Cameron and has been rewarded by being anointed the party's *de facto* deputy leader. When Gordon Brown is away and the 'second team' is fielded, it is Hague who takes on Labour's deputy leader, Harriet Harman – and their duels are nearly as eagerly watched as those of Cameron and Brown. Whether Cameron will, in government, appoint Hague deputy Prime Minister is doubtful – but he will certainly be rewarded for his loyalty with the plum post of Foreign Secretary. If anything Hague is more Eurosceptic than his leader, but the years have taught him to temper both his humour and his rhetoric. He will make a very good and a very diplomatic Foreign Secretary.

Kenneth Clarke

In contrast to William Hague, Ken Clarke never made it to the top of the Tory Party's greasy pole – despite running for the leadership three times.

Amongst Westminster watchers there had always been a sense that Clarke was going through the motions when running for the party leadership – that ultimately he did not quite have the fire in his belly, or the patience. However, the prospect of helping a new generation of Tories make the transition from opposition into government – along with the promise of a key ministry for himself – was enough to tempt him back to the front bench.

Despite never having been leader of his party, Clarke has had a highly successful political career, and his return in answer to Cameron's summons in 2009 added a huge amount of literal and figurative weight to the Tory front bench. An MP since 1970 (before George Osborne was born), Ken Clarke had held a raft of senior Cabinet posts under both Margaret Thatcher and John Major. He was Secretary of State for Health from 1989 to 1990, Secretary of State for Education & Science from 1990 to 1992, Home Secretary from 1992 to 1993 and Chancellor of the Exchequer from 1993 to 1997.

It is this last post which is the key to David Cameron's invitation to return to the front bench. For years Gordon Brown – as Chancellor of the Exchequer and Prime Minister – had claimed to be the architect of the UK's extended economic boom. In fact it was Ken Clarke, taking over from Norman Lamont, who had steered the UK economy towards calmer waters following the ejection from the ERM, and who had laid the foundations for that boom. This has equipped Clarke to rebut Gordon Brown's claims – especially in the light of the subsequent dramatic downturn in the economy. Cameron also trusted Clarke to head up his Democracy Taskforce, which amongst other things sought to address the 'West Lothian question' by coming up with a variant of the 'English Votes for English Laws' solution.

There were two other reasons for Ken Clarke's rehabilitation – despite his unapologetic enthusiasm for the EU and the euro, and despite the fact that he had refused to keep David Cameron on as special advisor when he entered the Treasury in 1993. Firstly, Cameron needed to bolster George Osborne in the wake of the Deripaska 'yachtgate' saga – without actually moving him from the shadow Chancellorship. And secondly, Cameron felt that he needed to counter Gordon Brown's masterstroke of luring Peter Mandelson back from Brussels. On his return Mandelson spearheaded the government's communications and headed up the crucial business brief at the Department for Business, Enterprise & Regulatory Reform (BERR) – now the Department for Business, Innovation & Skills (BIS). Whilst Clarke cannot directly face or debate with the ennobled Peter Mandelson, he has effectively countered him in the media.

Ken Clarke is now approaching seventy, but has lost none of his punch or his popular appeal. He would not have been tempted back to the front line during the thankless years of opposition without a firm promise that he would play a key role in the New Conservative government of 2010, and his experience will be invaluable.

Chris Grayling

This tall, balding former BBC journalist, PR consultant and marketing man is largely unknown outside the Westminster village. However, he is rapidly gaining a reputation in the Conservative Party not just as a safe pair of hands, but also as an attack dog capable of dragging down stumbling government ministers. He is given much credit within the party for his onslaught on David Blunkett, bringing about his second (and presumably final) resignation. He also harried hapless Home Secretary Jacqui Smith, both over her numerous housing and expenses mishaps and over the inevitable problems associated with her Home Office brief.

Chris Grayling's seat of Epsom & Ewell was previously held by Tory grandee Sir Archie Hamilton, and he has a rock-solid 16,447 majority. He went to Sidney Sussex College, Cambridge, where he read history. Entering the Commons in 2001, he was appointed a whip in 2002 and shortly afterwards made his way on to the front bench as a health spokesman. In 2003 Michael Howard made him shadow Higher & Further Education Minister, before he returned to Health in 2004. He broke into the shadow Cabinet as shadow Leader of the House of Commons in May 2005, and it was in this role that he gained his reputation as a sleaze buster. He was shadow Secretary of State for Transport from 2005 to 2007 and for Work & Pensions from 2007 to 2009. Finally in 2009 he broke through to the very top ranks of the parliamentary party by being appointed shadow Home Secretary. This followed the quixotic resignation of David Davis to fight a by-election in his own seat in 2008 and Dominic Grieve's brief (but not unsuccessful) sojourn in the post.

Chris Grayling's rise is remarkable because he is by no stretch of the imagination part of David Cameron's 'set'. He is a grammar school boy from High Wycombe, and went to Cambridge instead of Oxford. What is more, he backed Liam Fox in the leadership contest and does not exhibit many of the caring characteristics of the New Conservatives. His job is to use his media skills to attack Labour effectively on the airwaves, and to give first Jacqui Smith and now Alan Johnson a rough ride in the Commons. He is also being groomed to be the kind of straight-talking hard-hitting Home Secretary much loved by the Conservatives of old – along the lines of Michael Howard. This may be a modern, compassionate Conservative Party – but that compassion will not be extended to those who break the law.

Michael Gove

This fiercely intelligent but deeply courteous man is at the heart of the New Conservative project. He was a 'Cameroon' before Cameron.

Born in Edinburgh, but brought up in Aberdeen by adoptive parents, Michael Gove went to a mix of state and private schools before going on to read English at Lady Margaret Hall, Oxford. After a brief spell on the *Aberdeen Press and Journal* he worked for the BBC for four years, including the flagship *Today* and *On the Record* programmes. In 1996 he switched to print and was a columnist and editor for *The Times*. He is married to *Times* leader writer Sarah Vine and they have two children.

Within months of being elected Gove was appointed shadow Housing Minister. Promotion to the shadow Cabinet came in 2007, when he was entrusted with the task of shadowing Ed Balls at the newly created Department for Children, Schools & Families. He has flourished in this role and relishes the regular bouts with one of Labour's brightest ministers.

Initially a right-winger, he wrote a biography of Michael Portillo sub-titled *The Future of the Right*. In foreign affairs he is still tagged a 'neocon', but in reality he has made the same journey as the subject of his biography. He was instrumental, along with Nicholas Boles, Archie Norman and Francis Maude, in establishing David Cameron's favourite think tank, Policy Exchange, in 2003.

As a journalist and as a shadow minister Gove has been highly instrumental in developing the New Conservative philosophy. He is hardline on the EU and hawkish in foreign affairs. Where social affairs are concerned, however, his own innate decency shines through and invariably propels him towards the centre ground. Despite having his reputation damaged by the MP expenses row, Gove will play a central role in putting the nascent New Conservative philosophy into practice in government.

Oliver Letwin

A 1997 'veteran', Oliver Letwin is MP for West Dorset and a highly intelligent and intellectual polymath.

The son of two senior and distinguished academics, Letwin went to Trinity College, Cambridge, before moving on to the London Business School and then becoming a visiting fellow at Princeton. He then returned to Cambridge, where he did a PhD and taught philosophy.

After leaving academia Letwin moved on to advise another Jewish intellectual, the cerebral Thatcher guru Sir Keith Joseph. There then followed a brief spell at the No. 10 Policy Unit, where some credit him with devising the intellectually robust but electorally disastrous 'poll tax'. To balance that, he was also strongly instrumental in devising and implementing the Thatcherite privatisation policies, which have been picked up and replicated worldwide.

A spell at the blue-chip bankers NM Rothschild followed. Letwin worked in the international division which specialised in international privatisation projects, and he became a director and then the managing director of that division. The relationship with Rothschilds survived his election to Parliament and his various spells on the front bench.

As shadow Chief Secretary to the Treasury from 2000 to 2001 Letwin handed the Labour Party a gift by openly speculating about the scope for £20 billion worth of savings in public expenditure. Nevertheless, he survived the resulting furore and went on to be shadow Home Secretary from 2001 to 2003 and shadow Chancellor from 2003 to 2005. He then did a brief spell as shadow Secretary of State for Environment, Food & Rural Affairs, before David Cameron appointed him chairman of the policy review in December 2005.

The similarity with his former mentor Sir Keith Joseph is striking. Letwin is both hugely bright and possessed of a strong social conscience, which makes him very much in tune with the New Conservative agenda. However, like Joseph, he does not always perform at his best under pressure. That said, he could yet be as important to Cameron as Joseph was to Margaret Thatcher.

Francis Maude

One of the longest-surviving members of the Tory front bench, Francis Maude has been MP for Horsham since 1997, having previously been MP for North Warwickshire from 1983 to 1992.

Maude's father, Angus, was a minister under Margaret Thatcher and his mother was an environmentalist. He was educated at Abingdon School before going on to read history at Corpus Christi College, Oxford. He went on to practise law as a criminal barrister, before entering the political world as a Westminster city councillor. He was a minister of state at the FCO (where he reluctantly signed the Maastricht Treaty) and the DTI, before briefly entering the Cabinet as Financial Secretary to the Treasury.

Having lost his marginal seat Maude worked as an advisor on privatisation and globalisation and became a non-executive director at Asda. On his return to the Commons he supported Michael Howard for the leadership, but was nevertheless appointed shadow Secretary of State for Culture, Media & Sport by William Hague. In 1998 he was promoted to shadow Chancellor, but failed to make any headway against the then impregnable Gordon Brown. He was moved to be shadow Foreign Secretary, before becoming chairman of the Conservative Party from 2005 to 2007. He currently occupies the less high-profile – but still influential – position of shadow Minister for the Cabinet Office. He also has the crucial task of heading the Implementation Team, which is planning the steps necessary for when the Tories return to power.

Francis Maude strongly championed Michael Portillo when he returned to Parliament as a chastened moderniser, and he was closely involved in the foundation of two modernising think tanks – Conservatives for Change and Policy Exchange. As party chairman his constant mantra was that the Conservative Party had not changed enough to earn the trust of the electorate, and he has on occasion been brusque in his criticism of those who do not 'get it'. Maude was the first 'tieless Tory' who dared to appear in formal surroundings in an open-necked shirt, and he can lay claim to being the 'midwife' of the New Conservative Party.

Philip Hammond

Philip Hammond has strong business experience, a good grasp of detail and an air of calm competence. This has made him one of the Tories' top choices for fronting the party's economic policies on radio and television.

Having attended Shenfield High School in Brentwood, Essex, he went on to win an open scholarship to University College, Oxford, where he gained a first in PPE. He has worked in the manufacturing, property, construction and energy sectors. His experience in business convinced him that Labour governments were incapable of fostering a positive environment for commerce to thrive.

Having entered the House as MP for Runnymede & Weybridge in 1997, Hammond has only ever spoken from the opposition front bench. He has been a spokesman on health, small business, local government, and trade and industry. He was shadow Secretary of State for Work & Pensions before being appointed shadow Chief Secretary to the Treasury.

Hammond will be a crucial figure in the New Conservative government. It is he who will have to tell the heads of spending departments how much they will have to cut and save. It is he who will then have to explain the reasons for those cuts to the British people. The *Spectator*'s Fraser Nelson, in describing how crucial his role would be, has gone so far as to describe him as the 'Deputy Chancellor'.

Patrick McLoughlin

A veteran who was first elected to West Derbyshire in 1986, Patrick McLoughlin is the only member of the Tory front bench to have done any serious manual labour – unless you count killing people for Queen and country. The son of a miner, McLoughlin was himself both a farm labourer and a miner. Although quietly spoken he has tremendous determination and just enough incipient menace to command respect.

Under Margaret Thatcher (a passionate egalitarian) and under John Major (a man from an almost equally humble background) McLoughlin thrived. He held ministerial posts at the departments of Transport from 1989 to 1992 and Employment from 1992 to 1993. There then followed a brief spell at the DTI which lasted from 1993 to 1994.

However, his performances at the despatch box were not the most fluent, and it was not until he moved to the Whips' Office in 1995 that he discovered his metier. He was an assistant government whip from 1995 to 1996, a government whip from 1996 to 1997, the pairing whip in 1997 and the deputy opposition Chief Whip from 1998 to 2005. Finally, when ill health forced the retirement of David MacLean in December 2005, he became David Cameron's Chief Whip and chief enforcer.

There could be few greater contrasts between David Cameron and Patrick McLoughlin, but they have an excellent relationship which is likely to survive the transition to government. The size of majorities always matters to the whips. Too narrow a majority, and they struggle to deliver consistent victories in parliamentary votes. Too big a victory and backbenchers feel that they can afford the luxury of rebellion, as their actions will not imperil the survival of the government. Either way, McLoughlin will do an excellent job.

Eric Pickles

Like Patrick McLoughlin, a big, bluff northerner. In the case of Eric Pickles it is girth rather than height which is the most striking feature of his frame, but his geniality and self-deprecating humour hide a sharp mind and a natural toughness.

Educated at a grammar school in Leeds and then Leeds Polytechnic, Eric Pickles made his name as the radical and cost-cutting leader of Bradford City Council. He was involved with the local health authority and became active in community relations and anti-racism projects. After a brief career as an employment consultant he was elected MP for Brentwood & Ongar in 1992.

From 1992 to 1994 Pickles was vice chairman of the Conservative Party. In 1998 he moved on to the front bench as shadow social security spokesman, and then in 2001 he moved to Transport. A year later he became shadow Minister for Local Government, but from 2005 to 2007 he filled the role of deputy chairman of the Conservative Party. From 2007 to 2009 he was shadow Secretary of State for Communities & Local Government, before being made party chairman in January 2009.

Very popular within the party, Pickles is also generally a competent media performer (despite his disastrous performance on *Question Time* over the expenses row). He received a great deal of the credit for both the 2008 Crewe & Nantwich and the 2009 Norwich North by-election victories, which were the first that the Conservatives had achieved in decades. It is also undoubtedly the case that in a party somewhat lacking in northern and working-class representation, his bluff Yorkshire presence adds considerable ballast to the shadow Cabinet. All of these factors should see him through to the general election as chairman of the party, and on to a position in government thereafter.

The outer core

These are the Imperial Guard. They are not quite the Praetorian Guard or the inner core, but very close. They are the people who have helped David Cameron in his progress to the leadership of the party, and who have prepared the ground by contributing a lot of the thinking around the New Conservative philosophy and policies.

Some members of this outer core are veterans of many campaigns – and many defeats. Others are fresh to the fray, having only entered the House of Commons in 2001 or even 2005. This combination of grizzled veterans and fresh-faced novices will provide the bulk of the 140 or so ministers and whips who will dictate whether Cameron's New Conservatives are a one-term wonder or destined to keep Labour in opposition for a decade – or even a generation.

Adam Afriyie
Elected Member for Windsor in 2005, Adam Afriyie is the first black Conservative MP. His rapid advance, however, owes nothing to positive discrimination. Afriyie is a self-made millionaire businessman, and he made an immediate and strong impact on the Conservative Party when he decided to move into politics.

A graduate of London University (where he studied agricultural economics) he was also a keen sportsman, being both a long-distance runner and a basketball player. As founder of the IT company Connect Support Services and the information services company DeHavilland, and chairman of the media information company Adfero, he was unsurprisingly a finalist in the Entrepreneur of the Year competition in 2003.

Before being selected to fight Windsor Afriyie had been a Conservative branch chairman in Tonbridge & Malling. He is also a former trustee of the Policy Exchange think tank and a former London chairman of Business for Sterling. He has also been involved as a trustee with the Museum of London and the Docklands Museum. His current post of shadow Minister for Innovation, Universities & Skills suits him well.

Bright and articulate, he is also photogenic and telegenic. This, combined with his impressive record as an entrepreneur, should guarantee him a prominent role in the New Conservative government.

Baroness Anelay of St Johns

A well-liked and highly respected member of the House of Lords, Joyce Anelay has devoted her working life to voluntary causes.

By profession she was a teacher of history and politics. Her voluntary work for the community has included many years of service for the Citizens Advice Bureau and as a UK Trustee for UNICEF. She has also served as a justice of the peace and has sat on Social Security Appeal Tribunals in Surrey, the county where she lives.

Her work as a volunteer for the Conservative Party propelled her to her current position as Chief Whip in the House of Lords. Starting as a local activist, she eventually became chairman of the powerful Conservative National Women's Committee. Before becoming Chief Whip – and a member of the shadow Cabinet – she had spoken for the Tories on social security, home affairs, agriculture, and culture, media and sport.

Gregory Barker

One of the 2001 intake, Greg Barker is strongly associated with environmental issues – to the point where his nickname is 'Green Greg'. However, he is by no means one-dimensional. He is an enthusiastic supporter of his local hunt and a member of the ultra-smart but mission-orientated Honourable Artillery Company.

After a brief spell at the CPS, Barker spent ten years working in the City. He worked for stockbrokers Gerrard Vivian Gray, before moving to the Australian-owned International Pacific Securities. In 1997 he went to work for the world-renowned financial PR firm Brunswick as an associate partner.

Barker initially served on the Environmental Audit Committee, but was appointed to the Whips' Office in 2003. In the 2001 leadership contest he had enthusiastically backed Michael Portillo, and when David Cameron decided to stand for the leadership in 2005 he resigned from the Whips' Office and was one of the 'early adopters' of the New Conservative philosophy.

David Cameron rewarded his support and harnessed his green enthusiasm by appointing him shadow Minister for the Environment. He has succeeded in establishing excellent relations with the 'green lobby', despite his former post as head of international investor relations for a Siberian-based oil company.

His friendship with David Cameron, and his ability and enthusiasm for all things environmental, helped him to survive divorce from his wife and mother of his three children and his belated realisation that he was gay.

Alistair Burt

An inveterate marathon runner and stalwart of the Conservative Party football team, Alistair Burt has also exhibited great stamina in the political stakes. Having lost his Bury North seat in the disastrous Tory defeat of 1997, Burt returned to the Commons in 2001 as MP for North East Bedfordshire.

Burt was educated at Bury Grammar School before going on to St John's College, Oxford – where he was president of the law society. He combined practising law with being a Tory councillor on Haringey Council. In the period when he was out of Parliament he worked as a head-hunter, specialising in the sports and not-for-profit sectors.

When the Tories were last in government Burt served as PPS to Kenneth Baker, before becoming a junior minister in the Department for Social Security. In 1995 he was appointed to the highly controversial role of Minister for Disabled People – at the time when the government was trying to reduce the number of people on incapacity benefit.

In opposition Burt served as PPS to the then leader, Iain Duncan Smith – despite his centrist instincts and pedigree. David Cameron appointed him shadow Minister for Communities & Local Government, but in 2008 he was appointed to the key role of Assistant Chief Whip. He can be expected to play a significant role in the New Conservative government.

Greg Clark

The ultra-brainy Greg Clark was by no means disgusted when he was selected to fight the true-blue seat of Tunbridge Wells for the 2005 general election.

Born in Middlesbrough in 1967, Clark attended the local comprehensive school before studying economics at Magdalene College, Cambridge. He went on to study for his doctorate at the LSE, before spending some time as special advisor to the then president of the Board of Trade, Ian Lang. He also worked for the BBC as controller of commercial policy, before moving to the prestigious Boston Consulting Group. William Hague brought him into CCO as director of policy, and he maintained that position under both Iain Duncan Smith and Michael Howard.

Within a year of entering the Commons Clark was appointed shadow Minister for Charities, Voluntary Bodies & Social Enterprise, before moving briefly to be shadow Minister for the Cabinet Office. In 2008 he was promoted into the shadow Cabinet as shadow Secretary of State for Energy & Climate Change.

As a former member of the SDP Clark is on the centre-left of the party. His intellect, plus an engaging and self-deprecating manner, should ensure his survival and promotion in the New Conservative administration.

David Davis

The man with probably the most interesting back story on the Tory benches, David Davis was brought up on a London council estate by a single mother. He was a member of the territorial SAS before pursuing a career in business and then politics.

Davis's education is equally diverse and impressive. He was educated at Warwick University (BSc in molecular and computer sciences), the London Business School (master's degree in business) and Harvard (Advanced Management Programme). He has also written a range of pamphlets and books, including *Clear the Decks* (on the National Dock Labour Scheme), *How to Turn Round a Company* and *The BBC Viewers' Guide to Parliament*.

In business Davis is best known for having been a former director of – and chief troubleshooter for – Tate & Lyle. However, he is also a former executive member of the Industrial Society and a former member of the CBI Financial Policy Committee.

In politics Davis was a minister in the old Office of Public Service & Science and a minister of state at the FCO. After a distinguished spell as chairman of the Public Accounts Committee, he went on to become chairman of the Conservative Party and then stood for its leadership in 2005. Having failed in his leadership bid, he was then appointed shadow Home Secretary by David Cameron.

Davis stunned the media, the party and his leader by resigning his own seat in 2008 in order to force a by-election on the issue of ID cards and personal liberty. He won back his seat – but not his place on the front bench. It is unlikely, however, that Cameron will be able to ignore this restless talent when he forms his first administration. He must find him a role which will interest him, but which will restrict his opportunities to spring surprises on his colleagues.

Alan Duncan

Witty, debonair and articulate, Alan Duncan's talents are sometimes cancelled out by his willingness – even eagerness – to shock.

An oil trader by profession, Duncan learned his trade with Shell. However, he made his fortune with the controversial oil trading company Marc Rich & Co. Experience with both companies has given him a strong interest in – and wide knowledge of – the energy sector and Middle East politics.

In 1995 he published *Saturn's Children: How the State Devours Liberty, Prosperity and Virtue*. This book attracted controversy because of its libertarian line on drugs. Appearances on radio and TV satirical shows – including *Have I Got News for You* – have made him a well-known figure outside purely political circles. He also gained a great deal of credit for coming out as the first openly gay Tory MP, and he has since entered into a civil partnership.

Duncan was William Hague's campaign manager in 1997, and as a key moderniser was an early and strong supporter of David Cameron's leadership. He has held a wide variety of frontbench posts, including shadow Secretary of State for Transport and then for Business, Enterprise & Regulatory Reform. Having formed an unlikely double act with Harriet Harman when shadow Leader of the House, his indiscretion subsequently caused him to be sidelined to the obscure post of shadow Prisons Minister.

Iain Duncan Smith

Although his brief tenure as leader was not a success for either himself or his party, Iain Duncan Smith has since reinvented himself as a passionate campaigner for social justice.

Educated at Dunchurch College of Management and the Royal Military Academy Sandhurst, IDS was commissioned into the Scots Guards. He saw active service in Rhodesia and Northern Ireland, and also served in Canada and Germany. After leaving the Army he worked for GEC-Marconi, Bellwinch (a property company) and then Jane's Information Group (which publishes military directories).

Under William Hague, IDS served as shadow Secretary of State for Social Services, before becoming shadow Defence Secretary (where his strong links with the United States served the party well). From September 2001 until November 2003 he was leader of the Conservative Party.

David Cameron appointed IDS chairman of the party's Social Justice Policy Group. However, it is through the work of his Centre for Social Justice that IDS is now best known. Although not currently a member of the shadow Cabinet, he can be expected to play a pivotal – and possibly frontline – role in the New Conservative government.

Liam Fox

A Scot and a medical doctor, Liam Fox has long been a favourite of the traditional right of the Conservative Party. He came a creditable third in the leadership contest in 2005.

Born and raised in East Kilbride, Fox attended St Bride's, the local comprehensive school. He did well enough academically to go on to study medicine at the prestigious Glasgow University, where he became president of the Conservative & Unionist Association. Whilst at Glasgow he won national and international prizes for debating.

As well as working as a general practitioner in the NHS, Fox also served as a civilian Army medical officer. This experience gave him a valuable experience into the life of servicemen and women and their families, and instilled in him a strong regard for all those who serve in the armed forces.

Elected MP for Woodspring in 1992, Fox served as PPS to Michael Howard and as an assistant government whip and then a senior government whip. In opposition he has spoken from the front bench on foreign and constitutional affairs, and he was shadow Health Secretary before becoming shadow Defence Secretary.

Fox and Cameron are not natural soul mates, but there is a strong mutual respect. Fox's strong following on the right of the Conservative Party would make it very hard for Cameron to deprive him of the opportunity to serve in his first Cabinet.

Mark Francois

Unassuming but engaging, this 'Essex boy' has risen through the ranks into the shadow Cabinet without making any waves or acquiring any enemies.

Born in Islington, Mark Francois moved to Basildon with his parents in 1971. He attended the local comprehensive school, before reading history at Bristol University and then taking an MA in war studies at King's College, London. He started out working in banking, before switching to the prominent lobbying firm Market Access. In 1995 he set up his own public affairs consultancy, which he wound up on being elected. Throughout this period he maintained a commitment to the TA.

Francois served on Basildon District Council and was instrumental in helping David Amess to hold the constituency in 1992. The announcement that Amess had held the highly marginal Basildon seat was the first sign on the night that Labour might not after all be heading for victory and that Neil Kinnock would never make it to No. 10.

Having won the newly created seat of Rayleigh in 2001, Francois's career has been one of steady promotion. He was a whip from 2002 to 2004, and then shadow Economic Secretary to the Treasury from 2004 to 2005. From 2005 to 2007 he was shadow Paymaster General, and in 2007 shadow Minister for Europe. This became a shadow Cabinet position in 2009.

Ironically this son of an Italian mother with a French name, in charge of the party's European policy, is a firm Eurosceptic. However, this Euroscepticism is expressed calmly, and his demeanour is a long way away from the rabid attitude which has characterised some of his colleagues.

Cheryl Gillan

Although she represents leafy – and ultra-Tory – Chesham & Amersham (which she has served since 1992), Cheryl Gillan's Welsh roots have stood her in good stead.

Born in Llandaff, near Cardiff, Gillan attended local schools before the family moved. She them attended the chic Cheltenham Ladies' College, before going on to study at the College of Law. However, she still has strong family and emotional ties with the principality.

As well as a grounding in the law, Gillan has a strong background in the arts and sports. For ten years she worked for the international sporting consultancy IMG, and she has also worked for Kidsons Impey and Ernst & Young.

In government Gillan served as a PPS and then as parliamentary under-secretary of state at the Department of Education & Employment. In opposition she has been a whip and a frontbench spokesman on trade and industry, foreign affairs, and home, constitutional and legal affairs. She owes her place in the shadow Cabinet partly to her Welsh roots and partly to the fact that the Tories are desperately short of female MPs. However, her experience in business and marketing is also a useful asset.

Damian Green

A Tory wet with a gentle but plausible manner, Damian Green's career was certainly not harmed by the decision of the Metropolitan Police to arrest him and search his office in the Commons for evidence of leaked Home Office material.

Educated at Reading School, he went on to read PPE at Balliol College, Oxford, where he was president of the Oxford Union. He was a financial journalist on *The Times* and then went into broadcasting with the BBC and Channel Four, before joining John Major's Policy Unit.

In 1992 Green contested Brent East, before winning Ashford in 1997. He was frontbench spokesman on education and employment from 1998 to 1999, the environment from 1999 to 2001, education and skills from 2001 to 2003 and transport from 2004 to 2005. In December 2005 he was appointed shadow Minister for Immigration, and it was this appointment which led to the notorious – and ultimately abortive – police raid.

Green is widely liked and admired and has undertaken a variety of roles with equal competence, and his place in the ministerial team is assured.

Justine Greening

Bright, young, attractive and personable, Justine Greening has been one of the stars of the 2005 intake.

Born in Rotherham, South Yorkshire, Greening still retains a northern accent. She attended her local comprehensive school, before reading economics at Southampton University. She has an MBA from the London Business School and is an Associate of the Institute of Chartered Accountants.

Before winning Putney in 2005 Greening had worked as an auditor for Price Waterhouse and then became finance manager for SmithKlineBeecham. She then went on to become marketing finance manager for Centrica.

Shortly after her election David Cameron appointed Greening a vice chairman of the party with responsibility for youth. She has been a shadow minister for the Treasury and for Communities & Local Government, with specific responsibility for London. Although not currently in the shadow Cabinet, she is very much knocking on the door.

Dominic Grieve

When David Davis pulled his surprise resignation in 2008, it was to Dominic Grieve that David Cameron turned in search of a safe pair of hands for the crucial home affairs portfolio.

A barrister (and son of a barrister and MP), Grieve retains an academic and lawyerly manner. However, he has an astute political brain to match his legal skills. This enabled him to inflict a landmark defeat on the Labour government over the issue of ninety days' detention without charge. Educated at Westminster School, he went on to read history at Magdalen College, Oxford – where he was president of the Conservative Association. He then went on to study law at Central London Polytechnic.

Having entered the House as the Tories were swept from power in 1997, Grieve has only known opposition. He has been shadow Minister for Scotland and for Criminal Justice, and shadow Attorney General and Home Secretary. His current role as shadow Secretary of State for Justice suits his manner and his experience.

Nick Herbert

Another über-bright individual, Nick Herbert founded the radical-right think tank Reform before entering Parliament in 2005 as MP for Arundel & South Downs, following the enforced and unfortunate departure of Howard Flight.

After attending the former East India Company's Haileybury College he was offered an open exhibition at Magdalene College, Cambridge, where he read law and land reform. As well as possessing a formidable intellect, Herbert also has a strong record in campaigning, having headed up the Countryside Alliance and Business for Sterling. Before setting up Reform there were spells in the CRD and as a public affairs consultant.

Within months of being elected Herbert was appointed shadow Minister for Police Reform. In 2007 he entered the shadow Cabinet as shadow Secretary of State for Justice, before being appointed shadow Secretary of State for Environment, Food & Rural Affairs in 2009.

His intelligence and campaigning skills will make Herbert hard to ignore in the New Conservative government. However, he supported David Davis in both of his leadership campaigns, and his right-wing leanings and instinctive radicalism may mean that he eventually finds the constraints of collective Cabinet responsibility difficult to bear.

Jeremy Hunt

Another of the 2005 intake, Jeremy Hunt took over from Virginia Bottomley in South West Surrey, where he currently has a 5,711 majority over the Lib Dems. In 2001 the Lib Dems had come within 861 votes of capturing the seat, and he needed a 4.6 per cent swing to achieve that comparatively comfortable majority.

Educated at Charterhouse School, Jeremy Hunt went on to Magdalen College, Oxford, where he read the ubiquitous PPE. He also succeeded in getting elected chairman of Oxford University Conservative Association. After university he travelled and spent time teaching English in Japan, before working briefly for a management consultancy. After that he set up a highly successful company, Hotcourses Ltd, supplying information on education courses.

His early success in business allowed Hunt to give full rein to his strong charitable instincts. He established the Hotcourses Foundation, which provides education opportunities for orphans in Africa. He has also led a campaign to save his local hospital and fire station, and has volunteered in schools, hospitals and care homes.

His relative youth, good looks and energy have marked Jeremy Hunt down as 'one to watch' from his earliest days in the Commons. After a brief spell as shadow Minister for Disabled People he was handed the role of shadow Secretary of State for Culture, Media & Sport in 2007. He is a strong advocate for ensuring that grassroots and local sporting bodies are not neglected, and even with the 2012 Olympics his emphasis is on legacy opportunities for local communities. Popular with the party hierarchy and colleagues alike, he has – perhaps unfortunately from his point of view – already been marked down as a possible future Tory leader.

Andrew Lansley

A slightly grey demeanour and dull delivery marks Andrew Lansley down for what he is – a former civil servant. A veteran compared with many of his shadow Cabinet colleagues, Andrew Lansley has represented South Cambridgeshire since 1997. He was brought up in Essex and studied politics at the University of Essex.

Lansley's father worked for the NHS for almost his entire career, and his two brothers are respectively a policeman and a teacher. He started out life as a career civil servant, before becoming politicised following a spell as private secretary to Norman Lamont. He left the civil service to go and work for the British Chambers of Commerce, before being lured to CCO to head up the CRD by the then party chairman, Kenneth Baker.

Initially a Thatcherite and instinctive right-winger, successive defeats turned Lansley into a moderniser – to the point that he advocated changing the name of the party to the 'Reform Conservatives'. As a result he backed Ken Clarke for the leadership in 2001, having supported Michael Howard in 1997. Under Iain Duncan Smith he spent his time working in select and standing committees. In 2005 he again supported Ken Clarke in the first ballot, but switched to David Cameron in the second.

Most of Andrew Lansley's parliamentary career has been devoted either to formulating policy for general election manifestos, or to spearheading the party's drive to develop and maintain policies towards the NHS which would win the approval of both health professionals and the general public. Since 2003 he has been the Tory's shadow Health Secretary, and he has built up a formidable degree of expertise in the field. He has also succeeded in 'detoxifying' the Conservative brand where health policy is concerned, and his experience and grey hairs add some much-needed substance to the youthful Tory front bench.

Despite his propensity for making gaffes live on air, it is very hard to imagine that he will be denied the chance to put his health experience to good effect in the 2010 government. It is also likely that his extensive policy experience will be put to use in the process of crafting the general election manifesto – although the Conservatives are certainly not short of experienced individuals in the policy-making field.

Theresa May

This former City worker and Merton councillor arrived in the Commons in 1997, just as many of her Conservative colleagues were heading out through the door marked 'real world'. Known for her sharp dressing – especially where shoes are concerned – there is a great deal more to this astute politician than a carefully crafted appearance.

The daughter of an Anglican priest, Theresa May went to the local comprehensive, doing well enough to be offered a place at St Hugh's College, Oxford, where she studied geography. She worked at the Bank of England before moving to take up a number of senior roles at the Association for Payment Clearing Services. She served two terms on Merton Council in south London and fought no-hope seats in North West Durham and Barking.

As one of the few women in the Conservative ranks she was pretty well guaranteed rapid promotion. However, her City background, and her experience as a local councillor, meant that she was a confident performer who adapted well to the predominantly male atmosphere of the Commons. Within a year she was shadow spokeswoman for education and employment, and she entered the shadow Cabinet in 1999 as spokeswoman on women's issues and shadow Secretary of State for Education & Employment. From 2001 to 2002 she was shadow Secretary of State for Transport, Local Government & Regions, and she then did a brief spell as shadow Transport Secretary before being appointed party chairman in 2002. There then followed brief spells covering environment and transport, and then the family and culture, media and sport. May subsequently enjoyed a lengthy spell as shadow Leader of the House of Commons – a post she held from 2004 to 2009 (along with responsibility for women's issues). Then she landed the key role of shadow Secretary of State for Work & Pensions, shadowing the rising star James Purnell, and she now faces another rising star in Yvette Cooper.

An early moderniser, May supported Michael Portillo in the 2001 leadership contest, but this did nothing to halt her rise under Iain Duncan Smith. Her 2002 party conference speech as party chairman shocked and offended some of the delegates, when she told them that many members of the general public regarded them as the 'nasty party'. However, as one of the few women on the Tory front benches, as an early moderniser, as a champion of successive campaigns to make the Tory party more representative, and as a safe performer in the Commons and on the airwaves, her presence in a senior role in the 2010 Tory government is assured.

Andrew Mitchell

Something of a veteran now, and grey haired and bespectacled, Andrew Mitchell has nevertheless never lost his boyish enthusiasm. The son of a Tory MP, Andrew Mitchell lost his Gedling seat in the Tory rout of 1997 – before returning as the Member for Sutton Coldfield in 2001.

Educated at Rugby School, Mitchell went on to study history at Jesus College, Cambridge. He served in the Army, including a brief spell as a UN peacekeeper in Cyprus. He then went on to work for the merchant bankers Lazard Brothers. In the hiatus between 1997 and 2001 he went back to work for Lazards, and was also an advisor to Boots and Accenture.

Having served as a government whip and Minister for Social Security, Mitchell has also spoken from the opposition front bench on economic and home affairs. However, he has been shadow Secretary of State for International Development since 2005, and it is here that he has really made his name. His evangelical espousal of the need to supply aid to the developing world has resulted in his shadow department being only one of two – the other being Health – whose budget is secure when the Tories ultimately win and have to start cutting public spending. He has also organised Project Umubano, which takes Tory volunteers (including MPs and PPCs) out to Rwanda to do development work.

David Mundell

A former MSP, David Mundell in 2005 captured the newly created seat of Dumfriesshire, Clydesdale & Tweeddale – and in the process became the only Tory MP in Scotland.

Born in Dumfries, Mundell went to Lockerbie Academy before going on to read law at Edinburgh University and then business administration at Strathclyde. Having worked as a solicitor he went on to become BT's group legal advisor in Scotland and then its head of national affairs.

Being the only Tory elected to the Westminster Parliament for Scotland, Mundell was a shoo-in to become shadow Secretary of State for Scotland. He is also, however, popular with his constituents and well regarded in Westminster.

Baroness Neville-Jones

A retired spook, Pauline Neville-Jones has something of the air of Judi Dench's 'M' about her.

Educated at Leeds Girls' High School, she went on to study modern history at Lady Margaret Hall, Oxford. She then became a Harkness Fellow of the Commonwealth Fund in the USA.

Having pursued a career in the FCO, Neville-Jones then went to Brussels, where she became chef de cabinet to the UK's commissioner, Christopher Tugendhat. There then followed spells as deputy secretary of the Defence & Overseas Secretariat in the Cabinet Office, before she became chairman of the Joint Intelligence Committee.

Having retired from the civil service Neville-Jones went on to pick up lucrative directorships with NatWest, Hawkpoint Partners and Qinetiq – as well as becoming a BBC governor. In 2006 she was appointed head of the Conservative Party's National & International Security Policy Group, and in 2007 she was appointed shadow Security Minister and national security advisor to David Cameron.

Owen Paterson

Jolly and engaging, Owen Paterson is a right-winger who took over from his mentor, John Biffen, in North Shropshire in 1997. He is a member of the Cornerstone Group and backed Liam Fox for the leadership in 2005.

Having been to school at Radley College, Paterson went on to read history at Corpus Christi College, Cambridge. Before entering politics he was managing director of his family's firm, the British Leather Company. He served for a spell as president of the European Tanners' Confederation.

After a brief stint as an opposition whip – and as Iain Duncan Smith's PPS – he became shadow Minister for Agriculture and then for Transport. His big break came in 2007, when he entered the shadow Cabinet as shadow Secretary of State for Northern Ireland. In that role he has fostered cordial relations with all parties in Northern Ireland – despite being one of the strongest supporters of the setting up of a Tory operation in the province.

Grant Shapps

One of the brightest of the 2005 intake, Grant Shapps's energy and self-belief mark him down as a politician with a promising future.

Educated at Watford Grammar School and with a business qualification from Manchester Polytechnic, Grant Shapps founded a successful printing, design and website company at the age of just twenty-one.

Having failed to gain Welwyn Hatfield by just over a thousand votes in 2001, Shapps used many of the skills he had developed building up his business to achieve an 8 per cent swing to capture the seat in 2005. A combination of Lib Dem-style 'pavement politics' and extensive use of the internet secured him one of the biggest swings of that election. He is now much in demand as a speaker and as a mentor for other Conservative candidates looking to achieve similar swings this time around.

Shortly after entering the Commons Shapps was appointed a vice chairman of the Conservative Party with specific responsibility for campaigning. He held that post until he was appointed shadow Housing Minister in 2007. This is a subject he believes passionately in – and one in which he has developed considerable expertise. He has written several pamphlets on homelessness, and he and David Cameron launched the Conservative Homelessness Foundation together. He has been known to sleep rough to raise money and highlight the plight of the homeless.

A combination of entrepreneurial flair, energetic campaigning and genuine compassion marks Shapps out as a star of the New Conservative Party. The fact that he has a happy marriage with three children, and that he has battled and beaten cancer along the way, identifies a man with a hinterland which transcends his political and business successes.

Baroness Shephard of Northwold

Short, bright, feisty and amusing, Gillian Shephard is popular with all parties in the Upper House.

A former MP for South West Norfolk, Shephard held a string of ministerial posts under John Major, serving in the Cabinet as Employment Secretary and Education Secretary. A confirmed centrist, she supported Ken Clarke in his various leadership bids and was a member of John Major's geographical (and largely non-ideological) 'East Anglian Mafia'.

She is currently chairman of the Association of Conservative Peers – a powerful position which will become even more so once the Conservatives form a government. She also sits on the board of the Conservative Party.

Caroline Spelman

There is something of the head girl about this former party chairman, and a degree of earnestness which did not quite suit the party-facing aspect of the duties of her previous role.

Caroline Spelman was educated at Herts & Essex Grammar School for Girls and London University. A former business consultant, she does not quite fit the usual mould of the New Conservative Party. Her degree was in European studies, and she spent some time as an assistant to a Tory MEP. Her lingering pro-European leanings mark her out as an exception to the Cameroon norm, but the handicap has been overcome by her ability and her patent niceness.

These qualities were much needed when her career was hit by the 'nannygate' scandal, where she was heavily criticised for using her parliamentary allowance partly to pay the wages of the nanny who helped to look after her three children. This led to her losing her post as chairman of the Conservative Party, although she was not banished from the front bench.

First elected in the catastrophic 1997 general election, Spelman was always destined to do well. She was a whip from 1998 to 1999, before becoming the party's spokesperson on health and women's issues from 1999 to 2001. Her breakthrough was her appointment as shadow Environment Secretary, a post she held from 2003 to 2004 – whilst still speaking for the party on women's issues. From 2004 to 2007 she was shadow Secretary of State for Communities & Local Government, before becoming chairman of the Conservative Party. The 'nannygate' controversy saw her return to her previous role as shadow Communities Secretary.

A committed Christian and one of the few women on the Tory benches to really shine, Spelman is assured a prominent role in the next Conservative government. A healthy dose of Euroscepticism might see her propelled into the mainstream of the Cameron Conservative Party and give further impetus to a career which is already promising.

Lord Strathclyde

Tom Strathclyde (as he is almost universally known) is one of the most popular members of the Upper House. A hereditary peer, he was elected to remain in the Lords after Labour's early attempt to expel the hereditaries.

Born in Glasgow, he was educated at the University of East Anglia and the University of Aix-en-Provence. By profession he is a Lloyd's insurance broker, and he continues to ply that trade.

In the Upper House Lord Strathclyde has been a government spokesman on trade and industry, the Treasury and Scotland. He was also a government whip, a minister of state at the DTI and then finally government Chief Whip. He was then appointed opposition Chief Whip, before becoming opposition leader in the Lords in 1998.

If David Cameron is serious about reforming the House of Lords, he will need all of Tom Strathclyde's charm to keep his own hereditary and life peers onside during the dangerous transition period.

Ed Vaizey

Although not in the shadow Cabinet, this barrister-turned-lobbyist has had a considerable influence on Conservative thinking and is close to David Cameron both politically and personally. He is a fully paid-up member of the so-called 'Notting Hill set'.

Educated at St Paul's, Ed Vaizey went on to read modern history at Merton College, Oxford. His father was the eminent Oxford academic Lord Vaizey of Greenwich, who was ennobled by Harold Wilson. After a brief stint with the CRD, he went on to work for Ken Clarke, Iain Duncan Smith and Michael Howard – all of whom valued his abilities to create a narrative. He has also edited a series of essays published as *A Blue Tomorrow*, and is a frequent contributor to the broadsheets.

Although now on the centre-right of the party, Vaizey has been a member of both the left-leaning Tory Reform Group and the Thatcherite Conservative Way Forward. This eclecticism, and his interest in writing books, pamphlets and articles, has perhaps slowed the advance of his political career. His current post as shadow Arts Minister is a lowly one, but his influence on the party – and its leader – should not be under-estimated.

Theresa Villiers

A barrister turned law lecturer, Theresa Villiers was educated at Frances Holland School in Westminster, Bristol University and Jesus College, Oxford (where she read law).

Villiers made her name in Europe. In 1999, when she was just thirty-one years old, she topped the poll in the contest for selection of Tory MEPs for London. She had a glittering career in the European Parliament, successfully defending the interests of British business and the British taxpayer in a succession of campaigns which saw her elevated to the deputy leadership of the Conservative group of MEPs.

When the veteran MP for Chipping Barnet, Sir Sydney Chapman, announced that he was to retire, Villiers beat off a strong field of more than 400 applicants to succeed him in what was then a marginal seat. In 2005 she achieved a strong swing and won with a healthy majority of 5,960. Within months she was in the shadow Cabinet as shadow Chief Secretary to the Treasury, and she was also appointed to the board of the Conservative Party. Her adjustment from Brussels to Westminster was not seamless and she struggled in the highly technical role of shadow Chief Secretary. However, since her appointment as shadow Transport Secretary she has thrived. She has embraced the cause of high-speed rail and has opposed Labour's plans to expand Heathrow with a third runway.

Having got over the breakdown of her marriage and settled into her role in transport, Villiers is now once again exhibiting some of the form which in 1993 saw her gain the runner-up slot in the World Debating Championships and which saw her top the poll in her European elections hustings. The fact that she is one of the few women in the front line of the parliamentary party and that her Euroscepticism in rooted in experience should see her prosper and gain promotion in the forthcoming government.

Baroness Warsi

A highly articulate lawyer, Sayeeda Warsi shot from obscurity to prominence as the first Asian member of the Tory shadow Cabinet under the personal patronage of David Cameron.

Born in Dewsbury, Warsi was educated at Birkdale High School and Dewsbury College. She went on to read law at the University of Leeds and then completed her legal training at the York College of Law. She trained with the Crown Prosecution Service and the Home Office Immigration Department. After qualifying she practised as a solicitor in Dewsbury.

Having been a community relations advisor to Michael Howard, Sayeeda Warsi was appointed a vice chairman of the Conservative Party in 2005. In 2007 she became a working peer and shadow Minister for Community Cohesion. As a woman and an Asian in a party desperately short of both she should make the transition into government, but her outspokenness could ruffle a few feathers amongst colleagues, the press and the public.

David Willetts

Known as 'Two Brains', David Willetts has been at the forefront of Conservative thinking and policy making since the 1980s, when he worked for Margaret Thatcher's Policy Unit and for the CPS.

Educated at King Edward's School, Birmingham, he went on to take a first in PPE at Christ Church, Oxford. After graduating he worked in the Treasury as a civil servant, and he was private secretary to both Nigel Lawson and Nicholas Ridley. After his spells at No. 10 and the CPS he was elected MP for Havant in 1992.

A short spell as PPS to party chairman Norman Fowler was followed by a stint in the Whips' Office. In 1995 he was promoted to Minister for Public Services. In opposition Willetts has spoken from the front bench on education and social security. In the shadow Cabinet he has been shadow Secretary of State for Education & Employment, Trade & Industry and Work & Pensions – and in 2003 he was appointed head of policy co-ordination. When Lord Mandelson absorbed innovation and skills into his mega-department, Willetts was also handed special responsibility for developing family policy for the Tories.

Willetts now shares the education brief with Michael Gove – another shadow Cabinet member respected for his intellectual prowess. The Universities & Skills brief is a crucial but difficult one. It will test both Willetts's intellectual and his pragmatic abilities.

The inner circle

Modern British governments are large and complex organisations – and under Gordon Brown's tenure they have grown even larger and ever more complex.

Although the number of paid ministers and whips is limited by statute, Prime Ministers can appoint as many unpaid ones as they like. The so-called 'payroll vote' actually consists of unpaid parliamentary private secretaries (PPSs), whips and ministers – some of whom are paid, some of whom are not. Governments also need to at least try and get some of their supporters to chair select committees – although technically this is a matter for the House, and not for government or the whips.

So governments do need a large pool of talent which they can draw upon to man the front bench, support the front bench and inhabit the Whips' Office. This section covers the existing sitting MPs – or at least those who, it is reckoned, will be standing again in 2010 – who will provide that cadre. There are relative newcomers from the 2005 and 2001 intake, 'middle-agers' from the 1997 trickle of reinforcements, and even some grizzled veterans from the Thatcher and Major years.

In time, probably very rapidly, these sitting MPs will face competition from the large number of PPCs who will be elected in 2010. For the moment, however, David Cameron and his whips will have to look to sitting MPs when they draw up plans for the next Conservative government.

Peter Ainsworth

A hugely respected environmental campaigner, Peter Ainsworth has held a number of frontbench positions – but is only truly happy when in a position to push the green agenda.

Ainsworth attended Bradfield College before going on to study English at Oxford University, where he fell in love with the Romantic poets. Living in his constituency of East Surrey, he is married to Claire and they have three children. In his spare time he enjoys the arts, particularly music and painting, as well as cricket – he is a member of the MCC.

Before entering Parliament, Ainsworth worked in investment banking. His love of the environment flows from his love of Romantic poetry. His commitment to such causes has earned him much recognition, and he has won three notable environmental awards. He is also vice president of Wildlife & Countryside Link, chairman of the Elgar Foundation, and a board member of Plantlife International.

Before his election to Parliament in 1992, Ainsworth was chairman of the Conservative group on Wandsworth Council. Between 1994 and 1996 he was PPS in the Treasury and the Department of National Heritage before a switch in 1996 to assistant government whip. He was promoted in 1997 to opposition Deputy Chief Whip and held that position for a year. Between 1998 and 2002 he served as shadow Secretary of State for Culture, Media & Sport and then shadow Secretary of State for Environment, Food & Rural Affairs. He returned to the latter position in 2005 and held it until 2009.

Although there are many Tory MPs and PPCs with strong green credentials, Ainsworth has a good chance of putting his beliefs and his experience into practice in office.

James Arbuthnot

A somewhat distracted and aristocratic manner occasionally hides the fact that James Arbuthnot has a first-class mind – and a detailed knowledge of and feel for his party.

The son of an MP and baronet, Arbuthnot is an old Etonian who went on to study law at Trinity College, Cambridge. He was called to the Bar and entered politics as a councillor in the Royal Borough of Kensington & Chelsea – rising to the rank of Chief Whip.

Elected MP for Wanstead & Woodford in 1987, Arbuthnot held a number of government posts. Having served as PPS to Archie Hamilton and Peter Lilley, he spent a spell in the Whips' Office. A short stint as a junior minister in the Department for Social Security was followed by his appointment as Minister of State for Defence Procurement.

In 1997 Arbuthnot shifted to North East Hampshire (his previous seat having been abolished by boundary reviews) and he then spent four years as opposition Chief Whip. In 2001 he stood down as Chief Whip and became a member of the Security & Intelligence Committee. A brief return to the front bench, speaking on trade and industry matters, was followed by his appointment as chairman of the important Defence Select Committee.

Arbuthnot's time as a former Chief Whip, and the experience garnered during his spells as a Defence minister and serving on the Defence Select Committee, could mark him down for another return to the Whips' Office or the front bench in the New Conservative government.

Richard Bacon

A tough inquisitor, Richard Bacon hides a sharp brain behind an amiable manner.

Raised in the West Midlands and educated at King's School, Worcester before going to the LSE (where he took a first in politics and economics), Bacon joined the Conservative Party at the age of just sixteen. Having started out as an investment banker, Bacon moved into financial journalism, and from there it was a logical move into PR. He founded his own company, quirkily named The Word Factory, and had a successful business career before making the transition into politics.

Having cut his political teeth as chairman of Hammersmith & Fulham Conservative Association, Bacon then took on the hopeless task of tackling the popular Kate Hoey in Vauxhall in the Labour landslide of 1997. He was then selected to succeed former Transport Minister John McGregor in South Norfolk, and duly won the seat in 2001. An instinctive right-winger and Eurosceptic, he is reckoned to have backed David Davis and Iain Duncan Smith in the leadership contests.

It is under David Davis's tutelage that Bacon has made his name. In 2001 he was appointed to the Public Accounts Committee, which Davis chaired. Through this powerful committee he has made his name as a forensic inquisitor. His membership of the James Committee (set up before the 2005 general election with a remit to identify waste in government spending) gained him further plaudits. It is his keen eye for savings and keen nose for a story which will ensure that he prospers under the New Conservative government.

John Baron

An ex-soldier who resigned from the front bench over the Iraq War, John Baron is a man of experience and principles.

Having spent his youth on the move following his father (who was in the Army), John Baron attended nine schools before the age of sixteen, ending up in the sixth form at Queen's College in Taunton. He followed his father into the Army, going to Sandhurst in 1984 after getting a degree in law, history and politics at Cambridge.

Baron served in Berlin and Northern Ireland as a platoon commander, and then in Cyprus with the UN. He left the Army in 1988 and became a fund manager, rising to become a director of Hendersons and then of Rothschild Asset Management. Baron is married with two daughters and enjoys tennis, charity fundraising, walking and history in his spare time.

Baron's first experience of politics was in 1997, when he contested the seat of Basildon, though he lost by 13,000 votes. In 2001 he was more successful, elected as Conservative MP for neighbouring Billericay. He served on the Education Select Committee and then as shadow Health Minister from 2002 – though he resigned from that position in 2003 when he voted against the war in Iraq. He was subsequently reappointed to the role, and then in 2007 moved to join the opposition Whips' Office.

Henry Bellingham

A descendant of the only man ever to assassinate a British Prime Minister, Henry Bellingham is a 'retread' who fought back to regain the North West Norfolk seat he lost in 1997.

Having studied law at Magdalene College, Cambridge, Bellingham was called to the Bar at Middle Temple and practised as a barrister for eight years. He then ran a business consultancy specialising in advice on inward investment.

When the Tories were last in government Bellingham never quite made the front benches, but he served as PPS to Malcolm Rifkind when he was both Defence and Foreign Secretary. In opposition he has served as shadow Small Business Minister and as an opposition whip. His legal background then came into play when he was drafted into the shadow justice team. His tenacity and the fact that he is almost universally liked should be enough to see him feature in the ranks of government.

Richard Benyon

The son of an MP and a direct descendant of Lord Salisbury, Richard Benyon has politics in his blood.

Benyon started his career in the Army, where he saw active service. He then qualified as a chartered surveyor, and before being elected to Parliament he ran a business which involved farming, forestry and the management of rural and urban housing. After a couple of years in rural practice he took control of the family farm. He now has five sons, with whom he enjoys sharing his love of the countryside and sport. He is involved with voluntary organisations, having done work for the Citizens Advice Bureau, the Mary Hare School for deaf children and a local rural education charity. He was also president of the Royal County of Berkshire Show in 2002.

In the 1990s Benyon was leader of the Conservatives on Newbury District Council. At both the 1997 and 2001 general elections he was the PPC for Newbury and managed to reduce the Liberal Democrat majority on both occasions. He finally won the seat in 2005 with a majority of 3,400. He is now a member of the Home Affairs Select Committee and is PPS to Lord Strathclyde, the opposition leader in the House of Lords. In 2007 Benyon was selected as an opposition whip, and in January 2009 he became shadow Minister for Environment, Food & Rural Affairs.

Brian Binley

A self-made millionaire with a strongly traditional outlook, Brian Binley was the oldest of the 2005 intake. He is one of the few 'out' freemasons in the Commons.

Binley attended the local comprehensive school in Northampton and left at fifteen. He followed his father into the shoe industry. However, his entrepreneurial flair propelled him out of this environment and into the world of databases and marketing. He started – and sold – a series of companies, including BCC Marketing Services and Beechwood House Publishing. He and his wife and two sons still live in the area.

Binley entered politics early in life. He started out as a Young Conservative and then qualified as an agent, working for several years in CCO. He became a Northamptonshire county councillor in 1997, and served as chairman of the Finance & Resources Scrutiny Committee. In 2005 he was elected to Northampton South with a majority of nearly 4,500. In 2006 he became the chairman of the Conservative Parliamentary Enterprise Group, and he also serves on the Business & Enterprise Select Committee.

Boundary changes give Labour a notional majority of nearly 1,500 in Northampton South, but assuming Binley can hold on he should continue to be a strong voice for business in the Commons.

Crispin Blunt

Perhaps best known for his role in bringing about the defenestration of Iain Duncan Smith, Crispin Blunt inherited his Reigate seat from the ultimate Eurosceptic, Sir George Gardiner.

Blunt's background is military. He was educated at Wellington College and Sandhurst, before going on to study politics at the University of Durham. He was in the Hussars for eleven years, serving in Cyprus and Germany and rising to the rank of captain. Having left the Army he studied for an MBA at Cranfield. Before entering Parliament he was a political consultant and represented the Forum for Private Business. He also acted as special advisor to Sir Malcolm Rifkind when the latter was Defence Secretary and Foreign Secretary.

Having been elected for Reigate in 1997, Blunt became a member of the Commons Defence Select Committee and then the Environment, Transport & Regional Affairs Committee. He has spoken from the front bench on Northern Ireland and trade and industry, and has also been in the Whips' Office.

In January 2009 Blunt was appointed a shadow Home Office minister, with responsibility for security and counter-terrorism. This is where his interest and expertise lie and where he can be expected to serve the New Conservative government.

Peter Bone

Bearing an uncanny physical resemblance to a certain Swedish England football manager, Peter Bone must have been more relieved than most when Sven-Goran Eriksson quit these shores – and disappointed when he returned once again.

Born in 1952 in Billericay, Essex, Peter Bone was educated at Westcliff-on-Sea Grammar School. He lives with wife Jennie and their three children in Rushden, a town in the heart of his Wellingborough constituency. Bone is a keen sportsman, playing cricket and golf. He has run the London Marathon several times, raising thousands of pounds for charity in the process. He is a regular attendee at St Mary's Church, where he is a member of the parochial church council.

By profession Bone is a chartered accountant. During his career he has been in charge of both a public company and a family business. Politically, Bone has been involved at all levels of the Conservative Party. He has been an association chairman, a press secretary, and was a member of the National Union Executive from 1993 to 1996. He first challenged for Parliament in 1992, when he stood against Neil Kinnock, unsurprisingly without success. In 1997 he fought Pudsey and then Wellingborough in 2001, again unsuccessfully on both occasions. He was finally victorious in May 2005, when he was elected as MP for Wellingborough.

Graham Brady

The youngest Tory MP when he swam in against the tide at Altrincham & Sale West in 1997, Graham Brady was a rising star before resigning from the front bench on a matter of principle – something which rarely happens in modern politics.

Born in Salford, Brady was educated at Altrincham Grammar School and Durham University, where he read law. Before becoming an MP he worked in PR and public affairs with Shandwick and then the Waterfront Partnership, and he also did a stint at the CPS.

Brady served as PPS to Michael Ancram when he was chairman of the party and to Michael Howard when he was party leader. He has also served as a whip, and he was opposition Europe Minister from 2004 to 2007. But his main interest has always been education. This led him to resign from the front bench in 2007, when the Conservatives failed to support grammar schools.

Having resigned over a matter of principle, and with the party's attitude to grammar schools now much warmer, Brady can perhaps expect a recall when the Tories return to power.

Julian Brazier

A tall, angular former TA officer who served with the SAS, Julian Brazier is a traditionalist and a practising Roman Catholic.

Born in 1952, Brazier was educated at Wellington College in Berkshire and then Brasenose College, Oxford, where he got an MA. He then went on to the London Business School before beginning work as a project manager with HB Maynard, the management consultants. He now occasionally undertakes some freelance consulting assignments whilst being parliamentary advisor to the British Security Metals Association. He is a strong supporter of Christian Unity, as well as being president of the Conservative Family Campaign and having published two papers on family issues. In his spare time he enjoys philosophy, sciences and cross-country running.

As a student Brazier held the positions of chairman and treasurer of the Oxford University Conservative Association. In 1983 he contested Berwick-upon-Tweed and four years later he was elected as MP for Canterbury. From 1990 to 1993 he served as PPS to Gillian Shephard at the Treasury. Brazier has been a member of the Defence Select Committee, vice chairman and former secretary of the Conservative Backbench Defence Committee, former secretary of the Backbench Treasury Committee, former joint secretary of the Maritime APPG, and a member of the Social Security Support Group. In September 2001 he became an opposition whip. In July 2002 he was appointed shadow Minister for Work & Pensions, before being made shadow Minister for Home Affairs in June 2003. November of that year saw him achieve the role of shadow Minister for International Affairs, and since May 2005 he has been shadow Minister for Transport.

As a hard-working frontbencher with a wealth of experience, Brazier will be hoping to make the cut when the Tories regain power.

James Brokenshire

A survivor, James Brokenshire had to endure several unsuccessful selection contests before landing Old Bexley & Sidcup when the Hornchurch seat he had won from Labour's John Cryer in 2005 was abolished in boundary changes.

Born in Southend-on-Sea, Brokenshire went to Davenant Foundation Grammar School and the Cambridge Centre for Sixth Form Studies before going on to read law at the University of Exeter. He then practised as a lawyer for the international law firm Gouldens, staying with them after they were taken over by Jones Day.

During his brief spell in Parliament Brokenshire has served on the Constitutional Affairs Select Committee and has acted as a shadow Home Affairs minister with responsibility for anti-social behaviour. Now that he has finally secured a safe seat he can be expected to make progress and to enter government in 2010, and he is young enough to have the prospect of a decent ministerial career ahead of him.

Simon Burns

Now something of a veteran but still youthful and enthusiastic, Simon Burns is a survivor who uses his charm and experience to good effect.

In his early years Burns was educated in Ghana, before attending Stamford School and then Worcester College, Oxford, where he read modern history. Before entering Parliament he worked as a journalist and he became a director of *What to Buy for Business* magazine. He also sat on the policy executive of the Institute of Directors.

Having first been elected for Chelmsford in 1987, Burns moved to the new seat of West Chelmsford, where he had a majority of 9,620 in 2005. When the Tories were last in government Burns served as PPS to Tim Eggar and Gillian Shephard, and he also worked in the Whips' Office. He also served briefly as a junior minister in the Department of Health.

In opposition Burns has had lengthy spells on the Commons Health Select Committee, and he has also been an opposition whip and spoken from the front bench on health, social security and the environment. It is his health expertise, and his experience in the Whips' Office, which will probably see him feature in the New Conservative government line-up.

David Burrowes

The 'Twigg-buster', who in 2005 avenged the iconic Labour defeat of Michael Portillo in 1997, David Burrowes was assured of at least a small part in electoral history from that day onwards.

Born and raised in Enfield, Burrowes attended Highgate School before going to Exeter University, where he studied law. Practising as a solicitor in Enfield, he became a councillor at the age of just twenty-five, and was quickly identified as the person with the local qualifications to beat Stephen Twigg. He fought his 'no-hoper' next door in Edmonton, standing against Andy Love in 2001 (when the author was his election agent), before winning Enfield Southgate back for the Tories in 2005.

The fact that Burrowes had beaten Twigg with an impressive 8.6 per cent swing brought him to the attention of the whips. He was put on the influential Public Administration Select Committee, and in 2007 he was appointed shadow Minister for Justice. This portfolio, and his background as a solicitor, has led him to take a close interest in drug and alcohol addiction, and the violent crime which they lead on to.

Whilst at university Burrowes co-founded the Conservative Christian Fellowship, along with ConservativeHome website founder Tim Montgomerie. It is his faith, along with his family (he and his wife Janet have six children), which defines and drives him. He will go far.

Douglas Carswell

Taking on the Labour Party's most electorally successful Prime Minister of all time might not be seen by everybody as a good career move, but that is exactly what Douglas Carswell did in Sedgefield in 2001. And with some success – he achieved a 4.7 per cent swing in favour of the Tories and cut more than 7,000 off Tony Blair's majority.

Having fought Sedgefield as his 'no-hoper' in 2001, Carswell was selected to fight Harwich against the incumbent Labour MP, Ivan Henderson, in 2005. In a highly active and personalised campaign (he drove around the constituency in a Union Jack-emblazoned Mini) he achieved a creditable 3.6 per cent swing – enough to give him a slender majority of 920.

A former investment fund manager and corporate affairs manager, Carswell was educated at the prestigious Charterhouse School, before studying history at the University of East Anglia and then King's College, London. Always interested in policy, he has been involved in Conservatives for Change, and also did a stint at the Conservative Policy Unit.

Carswell is a radical thinker, and his iconoclasm perhaps makes him unsuitable for ministerial office. However, his devotion to 'localism' (since adopted by David Cameron) and his original ideas mark him down as a man to watch. His pamphlet *Direct Democracy* was the first to be published by Conservatives for Change, and his book *The Plan: Twelve Months to Renew Britain* (published with the equally radical Daniel Hannan MEP) shows that he is capable of producing a stream of original policy ideas – at least some of which will end up being implemented by the New Conservative government.

Christopher Chope

A veteran politician and entrenched right-winger and Eurosceptic, Christopher Chope has a strong fan base within the Conservative Party.

Educated at Marlborough College and the University of St Andrews, Chope went on to study at the Inns of Court Law School. He practised at the Bar, and from 1979 until 1983 was leader of Wandsworth Borough Council. He also served on the Inner London Education Authority, the Association of Metropolitan Authorities and the London Boroughs Association.

From 1983 to 1992 Chope was MP for Southampton Itchen. During that time he was a minister of state in the Treasury and Minister for Roads & Traffic. Having lost his seat he acted as a consultant for Ernst & Young. In 1997 he swam back in against the tide as MP for Christchurch. Since returning to Parliament he has spoken from the front bench on Treasury matters and on social security, the environment, local government and regions, and transport.

Chope's experience and versatility, and his long-term leadership of the powerful right-wing pressure group Conservative Way Forward, could see him recalled to government.

James Clappison

A robust lawyer with a combative streak, James Clappison is a much-reshuffled frontbencher with a great deal of experience.

Educated at St Peter's School, York, Clappison went on to read PPE at Queen's College, Oxford – where he was treasurer of the Oxford University Conservative Association. After university he was called to the Bar, and then proceeded to fight a succession of no-hope seats before being elected for Hertsmere in 1992.

In the Major government Clappison acted as PPS to Baroness Blatch whilst she was a minister of state at the Home Office, and then went on to become parliamentary under-secretary of state at the Department of the Environment. In opposition he has spoken from the front bench on education and employment, work and pensions, and Treasury affairs.

Although his career has been more steady than meteoric, Clappison can reasonably expect to survive the transition back into government.

Geoffrey Clifton-Brown

Numbering two previous Speakers amongst his ancestors, Geoffrey Clifton-Brown is steeped in the ethos of the Commons.

An Old Etonian, Clifton-Brown went on to the Royal Agricultural College at Cirencester, before qualifying as a chartered surveyor. He practised as an investment surveyor before entering Parliament. MP for Cirencester & Tewkesbury from 1992 to 1997, he has represented Cotswold since 1997. His strong advocacy of country sports has helped him to build up his majorities in successive general elections.

In opposition, Clifton-Brown has spoken from the front bench on the environment, food and rural affairs and on transport, local government and the regions. He was promoted to become Assistant Chief Whip, before being appointed shadow Minister for International Development in 2007. He is now a member of Ken Clarke's team at Business, Innovation and Skills.

Convivial and popular, Clifton-Brown had a successful innings in the Whips' Office and might expect to return in that capacity after the general election.

Geoffrey Cox

A high-flying lawyer, Geoffrey Cox has carried his libertarian instincts from the court room to the Commons chamber.

Born and bred in the West Country, Geoffrey Cox is the son of a soldier. As his family has for generations, Cox lives in west Devon with his wife and their family of two sons and two daughters. His brother is a local solicitor. He enjoys spending his time walking in the West Country with his dogs, reading, swimming and generally enjoying his surroundings. He is a member of the NFU and the Church of England.

Cox has been a barrister for almost twenty years, having founded his own chambers. Over his career he has appeared in many well-publicised trials – gaining a reputation as a successful advocate. He has also spent many years training young people in the art of public speaking.

Selected as the PPC for Torridge & West Devon in early 2000, Cox spent the next fifteen months campaigning in the largest constituency in England. He managed to cut the Liberal Democrat majority by 40 per cent, many commenting that the UKIP vote ultimately saved the Liberal Democrats from defeat. In 2002 he was selected to fight again, and he finally succeeded in 2005.

Having had such a successful legal career, and having shown such persistence in his efforts to get elected, Cox might well be judged to be worthy of ministerial office.

Stephen Crabb

A compassionate and committed Christian and family man, Stephen Crabb sets aside all trace of that compassion once he sets foot on the rugby field – as the author found out to his cost when playing against the Commons and Lords XV in a charity match.

Raised in Haverfordwest, Crabb went to the local Tasker Milward School before going on to Bristol University – where he gained a first in politics and economics. He also has an MBA from the London Business School. He was parliamentary affairs officer for the National Council for Voluntary Youth Services, and then policy and campaigns manager for the London Chamber of Commerce – before setting up as an independent business consultant.

Having moved to London, Crabb became chairman of North Southwark & Bermondsey Conservative Association. He fought Preseli Pembrokeshire unsuccessfully in 2001, and then in 2005 achieved a 4.6 per cent swing – enough to secure him a majority of just 607. Upon election he became the youngest Conservative MP.

Crabb's politics are influenced by his Christian beliefs and rooted in his Welsh heritage. He supported Liam Fox in the first round of the 2005 leadership elections – as did many Conservative Christian Fellowship members. However, when Fox was knocked out, he publicly backed David Cameron. He was promoted to the Whips' Office in 2009, and the shortage of Tory MPs in Wales should ensure that he secures a berth in the new government.

David Davies

Tough and tough talking, this former TA reservist has ruffled a few feathers in the Welsh Assembly and the Westminster Parliament. In both of these respects he resembles his near namesake David Davis.

Having left the local comprehensive school in Newport, Gwent, David Davies went to work for British Steel. Boredom and wanderlust set in, so he set off to tour Australia and Asia, working at a variety of jobs to pay his way. He then returned to work in the family importing and shipping business. He is also probably the only MP to be sworn in as a special constable.

Davies managed to get elected to the Welsh Assembly twice, in 1999 and 2003, as the only Tory elected by first-past-the-post. The fact that he is a Welsh speaker undoubtedly helped. Having stood down from the assembly he was elected to the Westminster Parliament for Monmouth in 2005. He has been as controversial in Westminster as he was in Cardiff, and he is the champion of the anti-PC brigade.

The Tories are hoping to improve on their three MPs in Wales at the next election, but despite his capacity to shock Davies should still find himself safely ensconced in the Wales Office or the Whips' Office.

Philip Davies

A proud Yorkshireman, in 2005 Philip Davies won Shipley for the Conservatives and saw off Labour's Christopher Leslie, who had himself been the surprise victor over veteran Tory fixer Sir Marcus Fox.

Born in Doncaster in 1972, Davies graduated from the University of Huddersfield with a degree in historical and political studies. It was at university that he met his wife, Debbie. They now live in Baildon with their two young sons. Whilst not busy with politics, Davies enjoys all sports, particularly horse-racing, cricket, football and rugby league. He is also a parish councillor and a school governor.

Before becoming involved with politics, Davies worked for a bookmaker. He then worked on a checkout at Asda, before moving up to become a marketing manager in the retail sector.

Davies was elected to the executive committee of the 1922 Committee in 2006 and is also a member of the Culture, Media & Sport Select Committee. He is a well-known campaigner against political correctness. He has also called for the UK to withdraw from the EU.

A committed backbencher, Davies might be tempted to move into management once the Tories seize power.

Jonathan Djanogly

Scion of a wealthy family, Jonathan Djanogly was impressive enough in his own right to beat a huge field in order to be adopted for John Major's old seat in 2001.

Having been educated at University College School, Oxford Polytechnic and Guildford College of Law, Djanogly qualified as a solicitor with SJ Berwin and became a partner in the firm's corporate finance division. He also ran a small mail order business with his wife.

Djanogly's route into politics was through Westminster City Council, where he chaired the Planning, Environment and Social Services committees. He fought Oxford East in 1997, before winning in Huntingdon in 2001. He served on the Trade & Industry Select Committee and was then appointed shadow Minister for Legal & Constitutional Affairs. He then became shadow Solicitor General in May 2005, and in December of that year moved to become shadow Minister for Corporate Governance.

Able and hard-working, Djanogly should join the ministerial ranks after the general election, although he has been harder hit than most by the MP expenses row.

Stephen Dorrell

In many ways the forgotten man on the Tory benches, Stephen Dorrell is very much alive and well and still considers he has something to contribute.

Having been educated at Uppingham School and Brasenose College, Oxford, Dorrell initially went into the family firm, making protective clothing. Once he left the front bench, Dorrell resumed working for the firm on a part-time basis.

However, his business career was cut short by his being elected MP for Loughborough in 1979 at the age of twenty-seven – at the time the youngest MP in the House. Having served as PPS to Peter Walker from 1983 to 1987, he was then appointed an assistant government whip and then a senior government whip. From 1990 to 1992 he was parliamentary under-secretary of state at the Department of Health, and in 1992 he became Financial Secretary to the Treasury. From 1994 to 1995 he was Secretary of State for National Heritage, and he was Secretary of State for Health from 1995 to 1997. In 1997 he was re-elected in the newly created seat of Charnwood and he returned to the back benches. Since then he has held one brief spell of office in opposition as shadow Secretary of State for Education & Employment.

Although Dorrell – a protégé of Peter Walker – is generally regarded as being too pro-European to have any real influence, he did co-chair the key Public Service Improvement Group, established by David Cameron in 2006. If Cameron's team are looking to make an immediate impact in their first 100 days, drafting back former Cabinet ministers like Dorrell would enable them to avoid some of the pitfalls which will be dug for them by those civil servants who are antipathetic to radical change.

Nadine Dorries

A brash blonde from a Liverpool council estate, Nadine Dorries is an inveterate blogger with trenchant views who is consequently much in demand by the media.

Having initially trained and worked as a nurse, Dorries set up her own business dealing with child healthcare, which she subsequently sold to BUPA. For a while she served on BUPA's board.

In 2001 Dorries stood in Hazel Grove. She fought off a strong field to get selected for Mid Bedfordshire and duly won in 2005. She has worked closely with Francis Maude and sits on the Education & Skills Select Committee.

Although outspoken and sometimes controversial, Dorries has got drive and she is very media savvy. This might eventually earn her a place on the front bench of a party which is notoriously short of women. Even if this does not happen, however, she has – and will retain – influence as a leading light in the blogosphere.

James Duddridge

Energetic, Eurosceptic and entrepreneurial, James Duddridge, MP for Rochford & Southend East, has packed a lot into his business and political lives.

Having gained a degree in government and politics from Essex University, Duddridge went on to work for Barclays. He started out in the City, before moving to Africa – where he ended up running Barclays' operations in Botswana. Upon his return to the UK he helped to found the online polling company YouGov.

Maintaining his interest in Africa, Duddridge is actively involved in the APPGs on Zimbabwe and Africa. He was a member of the International Development Select Committee and the Environment, Food & Rural Affairs Select Committee.

Although he has stayed off the front bench in opposition, the lure of ministerial office might tempt him after the general election.

Philip Dunne

Descended from several MPs from a range of parties, Philip Dunne represents Ludlow. He is a polymath and entrepreneur with a huge range of interests.

Having been to Eton and Keble College, Oxford (where he read PPE) he worked for merchant bankers SG Warburg in London and New York. He then worked for James Gulliver Associates and Phoenix Securities, in London and Hong Kong. He also co-founded the bookshop chain Ottakars and floated it on the Stock Exchange. He still has investment banking and venture capital interests and is still involved in the running of the family farm.

Dunne is actively involved in the Juvenile Diabetes Research Foundation (his daughter suffers from the condition), and he is vice chairman of the Diabetes APPG. He has served on the Work & Pensions, Public Accounts and Treasury select committees, and was appointed as assistant whip in October 2008.

Although Dunne has always insisted on maintaining his outside interests, a job in the Treasury or the new Business monolith should persuade him to put them on ice.

Tobias Ellwood

Young but with wide international experience, Tobias Ellwood is a moderniser who has arrived at the right place at the right time. However, he does have a habit of intervening in disputes on the streets of his constituency – and this has twice led to his being assaulted.

Born in New York (where his parents were posted to the UN), Ellwood was brought up in Austria and Germany. He went to Loughborough University, and then served with the Royal Green Jackets in a variety of overseas postings. He then returned to the UK to gain an MBA from the City University Business School, before working for the London Stock Exchange. Before getting elected he worked as a business development consultant in the financial services sector.

Having worked for Tom King, and on Rudy Giuliani's mayoral campaign in New York, Ellwood fought Worsley in 2001. Soon after being elected he joined the opposition Whips' Office, and he was then appointed shadow Minister for Culture, Media & Sport.

Ellwood's varied career should mean that he gets offered ministerial office in one of the economic ministries, or in the MoD.

Nigel Evans

Popular with parliamentary colleagues and staffers alike, Nigel Evans has a fine singing and speaking voice and is a great raconteur.

Evans went to Dynevor School before studying politics at University College, Swansea. Although he now represents an English seat, Evans still has strong

Welsh connections, having been a West Glamorgan county councillor and having fought Swansea West in the 1987 general election and Pontypridd in a 1989 by-election. He still owns a small retail outlet in Swansea.

Evans fought another by-election in 1991, in Ribble Valley, and won the seat in the general election of 1992. He has served as PPS to Lord Hunt, Tony Baldry and William Hague. He has also served on the Transport Select Committee and the Public Service Select Committee, as well as on a host of APPGs. He has spoken from the front bench on constitutional affairs, and has been a vice chairman of the party. From 2001 to 2003 he was shadow Secretary of State for Wales.

Evans has a wealth of experience and is a confident performer. He may well find his way back on to the front bench.

David Evennett

Nothing if not persistent, David Evennett performed the rare feat of returning after two parliaments in the wilderness.

Having attended Buckhurst Hill County High School, Evennett took a BSc in Economics and an MSc in politics at the LSE. After a spell as a teacher and then a lecturer, he followed in his father's footsteps and became a Lloyd's underwriter.

From 1983 until 1997 Evennett was MP for Erith & Crayford. He fought Bexleyheath & Crayford unsuccessfully in 2001, but had better luck in 2005. Upon his re-election he served in the opposition Whips' Office and in January 2009 became shadow Minister for Innovation, Universities & Skills.

Persistence should be rewarded, and Evennett may finally achieve ministerial rank when the Tories come to power.

Michael Fabricant

A polyglot and a polymath, Michael Fabricant has been there (often on his motorbike), done that, and most probably has pretty well all of the available T-shirts.

A chartered engineer by profession, Fabricant speaks four languages. He has studied at Loughborough University, Sussex University, Oxford University, London University and the University of Southern California. Before getting elected he was briefly a teacher, and was then co-founder of an international broadcasting and management group. He has also worked as a TV and radio broadcaster.

Having been elected MP for Mid Staffordshire in 1992, he switched to Lichfield when the boundaries were changed. He has served on the Home Affairs and Culture, Media & Sport select committees. In 2003 he was appointed shadow Minister for Trade & Industry and since May 2005 he has been an opposition whip.

When the Tories do form their next government, Fabricant may at last be offered the chance to assume ministerial office, or to switch to the government Whips' Office.

Michael Fallon

Despite a deceptively low-key manner, Michael Fallon has a sharp intellect and the credit crunch has given him the chance to prove himself an able inquisitor.

Born in Scotland, Fallon went to Epsom College before reading classics at St Andrews University. Having originally intended following his father into medicine, he ended up in business, founding a chain of nursing homes and nurseries.

Fallon represented Darlington from 1983 to 1992. During that time he was a government whip and parliamentary under-secretary of state for schools. In 1997 he managed to land the safe Conservative seat of Sevenoaks, and he has been an opposition trade and industry and Treasury spokesman. He has most distinguished himself, however, on the Treasury Select Committee, where he has given government ministers and bankers alike a hard time.

Fallon obviously enjoys the freedom which the back benches afford him, but might be tempted by one last stint as a government minister.

Mark Field

Good looking and with an easy-going charm, Mark Field suits the Cities of London & Westminster ('two cities') seat he represents.

Born in Germany to a British Army father and a German mother, Field attended Reading School before going on to read law at St Edmund Hall, Oxford. After graduating he went on to practise with the internationally renowned law firm Freshfields. He then went on to set up his own recruitment and publishing firm in the City.

Having failed to follow Tim Eggar as MP for Enfield North in 1997, Field became MP for the Cities of London & Westminster in 2001. He is involved in APPGs on business services and venture capital, and he has been an opposition whip and shadow Minister for London. He then had brief spells as shadow Financial Secretary to the Treasury and as shadow Minister for Culture & the Arts.

Although he now has a young family, and seems to relish his role as a backbencher, Field might return to the front bench when the Tories return to power.

Edward Garnier

The son of a colonel and the grandson of a Lord, Edward Garnier is very much an establishment figure.

Educated at Wellington College, he went on to read history at Jesus College, Oxford. After the College of Law, London, he was appointed a QC in 1995, a Crown Court recorder in 1998 and a bencher of the Middle Temple in 2001.

Elected MP for Harborough in 1992, he served on the Home Affairs Committee and as PPS to a range of ministers. From 1997 until 1999 he was opposition spokesman for the Lord Chancellor's Department, and from 1999 until 2001 he was shadow Attorney General. In 2005 he was appointed shadow Minister for Home Affairs and since 2007 he has been shadow Minister for Justice.

Probably the most experienced lawyer in the Commons, Garnier's claim to ministerial office will be hard to ignore.

David Gauke

A Eurosceptic with Polish and German ancestry, David Gauke's own roots are East Anglian.

Having attended Northgate High School in Ipswich, Gauke went on to read law at St Edmund Hall, Oxford. After a brief spell as a parliamentary researcher he went to Chester College of Law and then became a solicitor. He worked for the City law firm Macfarlanes, specialising in financial services regulation.

Having fought Brent East in 2001 Gauke was elected MP for South West Hertfordshire in 2005. He served on the Procedure Select Committee, and then in 2007 he was appointed shadow Minister for the Treasury.

Quietly competent, and popular with MPs and staffers alike, Gauke can be confident of advancement in the New Conservative government.

Nick Gibb

Earnest and clever, Nick Gibb was one of the early *Portillistas* who followed his mentor on his journey from right-wing bogeyman to originator of the modernisation agenda.

Gibb was educated at Maidstone Grammar School, Roundhay School, Thornes School and Durham University, where he read law. He went on to work for KPMG as a chartered accountant, specialising in corporate taxation.

Having fought Stoke-on-Trent Central in 1992 and the Rotherham by-election in 1994, Gibb was elected MP for Bognor Regis & Littlehampton in 1997. He spoke from the front bench on Treasury matters the following year, and on trade and industry matters from 1999 until 2001. Since 2005 he has been a shadow Education minister and is currently shadow Minister for Schools.

Although still very 'dry' on anything relating to the economy, Gibb was an early adopter of the modernisation agenda and should be rewarded in power.

Robert Goodwill

A highly Eurosceptic former MEP, Robert Goodwill is a staunch traditionalist in the mould of John Sykes, his predecessor as MP for Scarborough.

Educated at Bootham School and at Newcastle University, Goodwill returned home to run the family farm at Terrington after graduating with a degree in agriculture. He has also run a funeral company offering 'green' burials in woodland areas.

In 1992 Goodwill contested Redcar and in 1997 he fought North West Leicestershire. Between 1999 and 2004 he sat as one of Yorkshire's three Conservative MEPs, and he was briefly deputy leader of the Conservative group. Finally elected MP for Scarborough & Whitby in 2005, Goodwill has served as an opposition whip and is now a shadow Transport minister.

Goodwill is tenacious and has a great deal of experience. He deserves a chance of ministerial office.

John Gummer

A fervent environmentalist and vastly experienced MP and minister, John Gummer is the brother of PR titan Peter Gummer (Lord Chadlington), and they could soon be joined in Parliament by his son, the PPC for Ipswich, Ben Gummer.

Gummer was educated at King's School, Rochester and Selwyn College, Cambridge – where he read history and was president of the Cambridge Union. After a brief spell in publishing he was elected MP for Lewisham West in 1974. Having lost that seat, he transferred to the safer environs of Suffolk Coastal, where he has remained ever since.

Under both the Thatcher and the Major governments Gummer was a fixture on the front benches. However, he made his reputation, and received many plaudits, for his spells as Minister for Agriculture and as Environment Secretary, in which roles he pushed the green agenda and highlighted the dangers of climate change. David Cameron acknowledged his expertise in the area by appointing him (along with Zac Goldsmith) co-chair of his Quality of Life Policy Group.

Whether he chooses to stay on the back benches, or to assume ministerial office in the Commons, or to join his brother in the House of Lords, John Gummer will be extremely influential in the next Tory government.

Stephen Hammond

Amiable but not unambitious, Stephen Hammond has carved himself a niche within the Tory transport portfolio.

Born and educated in Southampton, Hammond graduated in economics from London University's Queen Mary College. He and his wife live with their daughter in Wimbledon. In his youth he was a national league hockey player and is now secretary of the All-Party Hockey Group.

After university Hammond began a career in finance as an investment manager. Before he became an MP he was a director at Commerzbank Securities. He is an associate of the Society of Investment Analysts and also a member of the Bow Group.

Hammond has been actively involved in politics since joining the Conservative Party after university. He was chairman of Stevenage Conservatives for three years in the 1990s and of Wimbledon Conservatives in 2001. After unsuccessful attempts as a parliamentary candidate for North Warwickshire in 1997 and Wimbledon in 2001, Hammond served on Merton Borough Council for four years before being reselected to stand for Wimbledon in 2004.

He was elected to Parliament in May 2005, and later that year he was appointed shadow Minister for Transport, a position which he has since retained. With a particular political interest in financial affairs, he has regularly attacked the complexity of taxation and serves on the Select Committee on Regulatory Reform and is secretary of APPGs on entrepreneurship and financial markets.

The New Conservative government will need ministers like Hammond – unspectacular, but hard-working and knowledgeable.

Greg Hands

Determined and ambitious, Greg Hands typifies a new generation of Tories who have fought Labour toe to toe in London during the wilderness years.

Born in New York, Hands lived in the USA until he was seven years old. He then attended Dr Challoner's Grammar School in Amersham, before going to Cambridge University to study history, gaining a first-class honours degree. Hands, who has lived in Fulham since 1990, is married with two children.

After university Hands embarked on a career in banking, with business involving regular visits to New York and Berlin. He speaks German and French fluently, and learned Czech and Slovak during a gap year in eastern Europe.

Whilst at Cambridge, Hands was chairman of the University Conservative Association and was an elected officer of the Students' Union. He joined Fulham Conservatives in 1991 and was elected to Hammersmith & Fulham Borough Council in 1998, soon becoming the Conservative group leader. He was elected MP for Hammersmith & Fulham in 2005 with a 7.35 per cent swing from Labour and a majority of 5,029 votes. In Parliament he is a member of the Select Committee for Communities & Local Government and the European Scrutiny Committee, and was recently appointed shadow Treasury Minister.

Hands will fight the new Chelsea & Fulham constituency at the next general election, which has a notional Conservative majority of 30.2 per cent. From this power base, Hands should be able to construct a successful ministerial career.

Mark Harper

An instinctive right-winger, Mark Harper nevertheless possesses a strong social conscience.

Harper was brought up in Swindon. His wife, Margaret, is a Forest of Dean district councillor and fought the parliamentary seats of Swansea West and Worcester in 2001 and 2005 respectively. He studied PPE at Brasenose College, Oxford, and then qualified as a chartered accountant. He worked with KPMG until 1995, before working for Intel Corporation in various roles for seven years. In 2002 he set up his own chartered accountancy business in the Forest of Dean.

Born into a non-political family, Harper joined the Conservative Party when he was seventeen and became politically active in his twenties, when he was deputy chairman of South Swindon Conservatives. He fought the Forest of Dean constituency at the 2001 general election, reducing the Labour majority from 6,343 to 2,049, and was elected to Parliament on his second attempt in 2005 with a 4.5 per cent swing. Later that year he was appointed shadow Minister for Defence, and has been a shadow minister on the work and pensions team since 2007. In 2009 he was given the specific brief of shadow Minister for Disabled People on that team. His main political interests are around education, in particular special needs education. Harper's shadow role is a crucial and complex one, and he will almost certainly be asked to cover the same portfolio in government.

John Hayes

A right-winger and a traditionalist, John Hayes is a leading light of the Cornerstone Group of MPs.

Hayes was born in 1958 and was educated at Colfe's Grammar School in Greenwich before attending the University of Nottingham. He left Nottingham with a BA in politics and a PGCE. He married Susan in July 1997 and up until 1999 was a sales director for the IT company The Data Base Ltd.

Hayes started his campaign for Parliament in 1987, when he contested Derbyshire North East, and he contested the same seat again in 1992. In 1997 he won in South Holland & the Deepings and remains its MP today. He had been a councillor in Nottinghamshire since 1985 and from 1988 he was Conservative spokesman on education in the council and chairman of the Conservative group's campaign and politics committees. In the past he has been secretary of the backbench agriculture committee and vice chairman of the backbench education committee.

Until 2000 Hayes was vice chairman of the Conservative Party, after which he became a frontbench spokesman for education and employment. In 2001 he was appointed an opposition whip and then in July 2002 was made shadow Minister for Agriculture. Late 2003 saw Hayes become shadow Minister for

Local & Devolved Government with particular responsibility for housing and planning. In 2005 he was shadow Minister for Transport, and since December 2007 has served as the shadow Minister for Lifelong Learning and Further & Higher Education.

Vastly experienced, Hayes will be hoping for a chance to put some of that experience into practice in government.

Oliver Heald

A veteran on the Conservative benches, Oliver Heald is a great survivor – and he owes that survival to the competence which he brings to every brief he is assigned to.

A law graduate from Pembroke College, Cambridge, Heald was called to the Bar in 1977 and practised as a barrister for over twenty years, specialising in employment law. He is married with three children.

Heald previously contested Southwark & Bermondsey at the 1987 general election but was elected to Parliament in 1992 as the Member for North Hertfordshire. In 1994 he was appointed PPS to William Waldegrave, then Minister for Agriculture, Fisheries & Food. He then became a minister in the Department of Social Security in 1995. After the 1997 general election he spent a period in the opposition Whips' Office and was made a frontbench spokesman for home affairs in February 2000 and then for Health in 2001. A year later Heald was promoted to a shadow ministerial position in the Work & Pensions team and was appointed shadow Leader of the House in November 2003. Between 2004 and 2007 he served as shadow Secretary of State for Constitutional Affairs and as the shadow Chancellor of the Duchy of Lancaster.

More recently Heald has taken a step back from the front bench and is a member of the Work & Pensions Select Committee and of the Committee on Standards in Public Life. He may prefer the life of a backbencher, even when the Tories win, but he has a lot of experience to offer an incoming government.

David Heathcoat-Amory

Dry as dust economically, David Heathcoat-Amory is also one of the most implacable opponents of the EU in the Commons.

Born in 1949, Heathcoat-Amory was educated at Eton College and Oxford University. He left Oxford with an MA in PPE. He won a boxing Blue, and was also president of the Oxford University Conservative Association. In his spare time his hobbies include astronomy, local history, fishing and spending time with his family.

Heathcoat-Amory is a fellow of the Institute of Chartered Accountants. He has been assistant director of finance of the British Technology Group and before that he worked for the British Electric Traction Co. Ltd and Price Waterhouse.

Heathcoat-Amory first stood for Parliament in 1979, when he contested Brent South. He was elected MP for Wells in 1983 and was successfully re-elected in 1987 and 1992. In 1988 he was an assistant government whip and appointed Lord Commissioner of the Treasury in 1989. Since then he has served in a number of positions, including under-secretary of state at the departments of the Environment and Energy, Deputy Chief Whip, minister of state at the FCO and Paymaster General, before resigning from the government in 1996. He was re-elected in May 1997 for the constituency of Wells. Between 1997 and 2000 he served as shadow Chief Secretary to the Treasury and then as shadow Secretary of State for Trade & Industry between 2000 and 2001. March 2002 until July 2003 saw Heathcoat-Amory as the UK Conservative Party parliamentary representative to the Convention on the Future of Europe, and then in late 2003 he was appointed to the European Scrutiny Committee. From May to December 2005 he was shadow Minister for Work & Pensions, and then he was appointed to the Foreign Affairs Select Committee.

There is no shortage of able Eurosceptics on the Tory benches, but Heathcoat-Amory is head and shoulders above most of them in terms of knowledge and experience.

Charles Hendry

Sociable and amiable, Charles Hendry is something of an institution in Westminster.

Born and raised in Sussex, the son of a stockbroker, Hendry was educated at Rugby School and Edinburgh University, where he graduated with a degree in business studies. He spent most of his career in PR working for large international companies, and was special advisor to two successive Secretaries of State for Social Security, John Moore and Tony Newton, in the late 1980s.

After contesting the 1983 and 1987 general elections, Hendry was elected MP for High Peak in 1992. However, he lost his seat to Labour in 1997 and was subsequently appointed chief of staff to William Hague during his leadership of the Conservative Party. Hendry returned to Parliament in 2001, representing the safe seat of Wealden, following the retirement of Geoffrey Johnson Smith. He has held a number of important posts in the party, including shadow Minister for Industry and Postal Affairs, shadow Minister for Young People and deputy chairman of the Conservative Party. He is currently shadow Minister for Energy.

Hendry's wide political interests range from trade and industry to youth policy and rural affairs. He is a patron of the UK Youth Parliament and of the Big Issue Foundation.

Mark Hoban

A Eurosceptic with a quiet and studious manner, Mark Hoban has steadily worked his way up the promotion ladder.

Hoban lives with his wife in Locks Heath, in his Fareham constituency. Outside work he enjoys travelling, reading and cooking. A qualified chartered accountant, he was a senior manager at PricewaterhouseCoopers before embarking on his political career. He grew up in the north-east of England and attended a comprehensive school in Durham. He has a degree in economics from the LSE.

Hoban joined the Conservative Party at sixteen and has worked for it at every level. He first stood as the Conservative PPC for South Shields at the 1997 general election, but was elected MP for Fareham in 2001, increasing his majority in 2005. It was not long before he earned himself a role in the opposition Whips' Office and then on the Conservative front bench as shadow Minister for Education in 2003. He has served as a shadow Minister for the Treasury since December 2005, and it is this key role which should earn him a place in government.

Phillip Hollobone

A former paratrooper, Hollobone brings much of the energy and direct approach of his former regiment to his political life.

Born and raised in Bromley, Kent, Hollobone was educated at Oxford University, where he studied modern history and economics. He spent most of his early career as an investment analyst, specialising in privatisation and public utilities. He also served eight years in the TA, part of that time as a paratrooper. Married with two children, Hollobone lives in his Kettering constituency with his family. In his spare time he enjoys bell ringing and is a member of the band of bell ringers at Kettering parish church.

Hollobone joined the Conservative Party at university. He started his political career as a borough councillor in Bromley in the early 1990s and was later elected a Kettering borough councillor in 2003. He unsuccessfully contested Lewisham East at the 1997 general election and then Kettering in 2001. However, after tirelessly applying himself to local issues, Hollobone was elected as the MP for Kettering in 2005 with a 3,301 majority and a 3.6 per cent swing from Labour. He currently serves as a member of the Transport Select Committee and is chair of the APPG for Victims of Crime.

A tireless campaigner and enthusiastic backbencher, Hollobone may not be able to resist the lure of ministerial office if the call comes.

Adam Holloway

A tough former special forces officer, Adam Holloway has seen service around the world as a soldier and as a reporter.

Holloway was born in Faversham, Kent, and studied theology and then social and political science at Magdalene College, Cambridge. His father, Rev. Roger Holloway, was a priest vicar at St Margaret's, Westminster. He is a former trustee of Christian Aid and is a board member of Map Action.

After spending his gap year amongst the *mujaheddin* guerrillas in Afghanistan, Holloway decided to attend Sandhurst after university, and then served in Germany with the Special Forces Group in the First Gulf War. On leaving the Army in 1992 he took an MBA at Imperial College, London, and worked as an undercover reporter, firstly for the BBC's *Newsnight* and then at ITN.

Having decided to turn to politics later in life, Holloway needed all of his energy and toughness in Gravesham, traditionally a Labour stronghold. He stormed it in 2005, transforming a 4,862 majority to a tight Conservative majority of 645 votes. He is a member of the Defence Select Committee and the Select Committee on Arms Export Controls. His main political interests are defence and crime, and he focused his election campaign on the growing problem of anti-social behaviour and lack of policing in communities. Another committed backbencher, Holloway may be unable to ignore the call to the colours when the Tories form their next government.

John Howell

Elected as Boris Johnson's successor in Henley, John Howell was chosen as the antidote to Boris's shambolic exuberance.

Born into a working-class family, Howell attended Battersea Grammar School before going on to study archaeology at Edinburgh University and gaining a doctorate in prehistoric archaeology from Oxford. Howell has lived in Oxfordshire with his wife and three children for more than twenty years. A keen musician, he is organist and choirmaster at his local parish church.

In the 1990s he was a partner at Ernst & Young, playing a key part in opening up central and eastern Europe to UK businesses following the collapse of communism. He was later an advisor to UK government on overseas trade and aid. For a short time he was also a business presenter for BBC World Service Television. Howell was awarded an OBE in 2000.

Howell was elected an Oxfordshire county councillor in 2004, and was selected to contest the 2008 by-election in Henley from a shortlist of three, all local councillors. He won the seat easily, bumping Labour into fifth place with a Conservative majority of over 10,000 votes. He was appointed to the Select Committee on Work & Pensions in 2009 and is also secretary of the all-party Thames Estuary Airport Group.

Howell's best hopes of ministerial office lie in local government and business experience – but there is no shortage of either on the Tory benches.

Nick Hurd

Nick Hurd is as different from his father Douglas as Bernard Jenkin is from his father Patrick. Both sons followed their father into Parliament, but the younger generation have much stronger views about one of the defining issues of the day – Europe.

The fourth generation of his family to enter Parliament, Nick Hurd was educated at Eton College and Oxford University, where he studied classics. His father was Foreign Secretary. Hurd met his wife at university and together they have four children. He is a trustee of the Greenhouse schools charity, which provides sport for disadvantaged children, and governor of a local junior school.

On graduating from Oxford he followed a career in the financial services and communications industries. For three years he worked in Brazil, representing Flemings Bank, and was more recently advisor to the shadow Trade & Industry team.

Hurd was elected MP for Ruislip-Northwood in 2005 with a majority of nearly 9,000. He was promoted to the opposition Whips' Office in July 2007, and was made shadow Minister for Charities, Social Enterprise & Volunteering later that year. He has since retained both posts and is also a member of the Environmental Audit Select Committee. He also holds various roles in APPGs on Brazil, the Environment, Globe UK, Small Businesses and Penal Affairs. With his background and pedigree, Hurd will hope to emulate his father and achieve ministerial rank.

Stewart Jackson

Cheerful and energetic, Stewart Jackson was a welcome contrast as the MP for Peterborough to his predecessor, Labour's eccentric Helen Clark, who had had a series of run-ins with the press and the voting public.

Jackson gained a degree in economics & public administration from the University of London. He later went on to take a master's degree in human resource management from Thames Valley University. After graduating he worked as a bank manager for Lloyds for nine years. He then advised small companies with human resource issues and was a human resources business advisor with Business Link in London prior to his election to Westminster.

Jackson was elected to represent Peterborough in 2005, having previously contested the seat in 2001. He also contested Brent South in 1997. With eight years' previous experience as a local councillor in the London Borough of Ealing, he was appointed shadow Minister for Communities & Local Government in 2008. He is also a member of the Select Committee on Regulatory Reform and vice chair of the Friends of Islam APPG, secretary of the Philippines APPG and chair of the Pakistan APPG. He is also linked to a number of important charities, working on the board of the Salvation Army's Good Neighbours Scheme and on the 'Light Fantastic' fundraising committee at Sue Ryder Care.

Jackson won Peterborough from Labour with a 2,740 vote majority in 2005, and the boundary changes help him. He is well established locally and has his feet firmly planted on the promotion ladder.

Bernard Jenkin

Good looking and musical, Bernard Jenkin is the son of former Thatcher Cabinet minister Lord Jenkin of Roding (Patrick Jenkin). He is married to the formidable Anne – herself the granddaughter of a viscount and a political operator in her own right.

A former choral exhibitioner at Corpus Christi College, Cambridge, Bernard Jenkin graduated with a degree in English literature. He was also president of the Cambridge Union. He had a career as a venture capital manager at several large private equity firms before moving into politics.

Originally elected as the MP for Colchester North in 1992, Jenkin has represented North Essex since 1997. In his early parliamentary career he was PPS to Michael Forsyth, Secretary of State for Scotland at the time, and served on the Social Security Select Committee from 1993 to 1997. On the opposition front bench he has served as shadow Minister for Transport, shadow Defence Secretary, shadow Secretary of State for Regions and shadow Minister for Trade & Industry. In 2005 he was moved off the front bench to become deputy chairman of the Conservative Party. During this time he was responsible for increasing diversity in the party and launched the Women2Win campaign and the controversial 'A-list'.

Jenkin's constituency is subject to name and boundary changes at the next general election, which mean that he should have a notional majority of about 5,500 in what will be known as Harwich & North Essex. He will undoubtedly hold his seat, and a return to the front benches at some stage is likely.

David Jones

Persistent and ultimately lucky, David Jones became one of only a handful of Tory MPs in Wales when he won Clwyd West by just 133 votes in 2005.

A solicitor by profession, Jones was educated at a grammar school in north Wales and University College, London. Ten years after qualifying as a solicitor he set up his own law firm, David Jones & Company, based in Llandudno. He has specialised in giving legal advice to a number of charities in Wales.

Jones had previously contested four seats before finally succeeding in Clwyd West in 2005. One of three Conservative MPs elected in Wales since 1997, he is a member of the Welsh Affairs Select Committee and deputy to the shadow

Secretary of State for Wales, Cheryl Gillan. Prior to his election, he served on the Welsh Assembly from 2002 to 2003. He is an honorary life fellow of Cancer Research UK, and his outside hobbies include football and travelling. He also speaks French and Welsh.

Although his majority is wafer thin, Jones should hold on next time, and the doors of Gwydyr House may be opened to him.

Daniel Kawczynski

Strikingly tall at 6 feet 8½ inches, Daniel Kawczynski was born in Warsaw and is proud of his Polish roots.

Following a private education at St George's College in Weybridge, Kawczynski graduated with a degree in business studies and French from Stirling University. He speaks five European languages in total, which has helped both his business and political careers. For ten years he worked as a sales account manager in the telecommunications industry, helping British firms to export to Africa and the Middle East.

After failing to win Ealing Southall in 2001, Kawczynski was elected to Parliament as MP for Shrewsbury & Atcham in 2005. He has served on the Agriculture and Justice select committees and is currently a member of the International Development Committee. He is also chairman of the Conservative Friends of Poland and treasurer of the Poland APPG. He also chairs the APPGs on dairy farmers, Libya, Saudi Arabia and first-past-the-post elections.

Having won Shrewsbury & Atcham from Labour with a majority of nearly 2,000, Kawczynski should be safe this time around. So far he has not displayed any lofty ambitions to match his impressive height.

Robert Key

A man of energy and bonhomie, Robert Key is one of the great survivors on the Tory benches.

The son of a former Bishop of Truro, Key grew up in Salisbury and was educated at Salisbury Cathedral School and Sherborne School in Dorset. He then studied economics at Clare College, Cambridge. Before entering Parliament he was a teacher, firstly at Loretto School in Edinburgh and then at Harrow.

Key has been the MP for Salisbury since 1983. One of his earliest appointments was as PPS to Edward Heath. In 1990 he joined Margaret Thatcher's government as parliamentary under-secretary of state at the Department of the Environment. In 1992 he became a minister at the new Department of National Heritage and was responsible for arts, heritage, press, broadcasting, the film industry, sport and tourism. In 1993 he was appointed Minister for Transport, but he soon left the government and instead served on several select committees. He has also served on the front bench in opposition, serving as a spokesman for defence and trade and industry, and as shadow Minister for International Development and for Science.

The Conservative majority in Salisbury has increased steadily over the years, reaching over 11,000 in 2005. If Key decides to fight again he will undoubtedly hold his seat, and one last opportunity to serve as a minister may be offered to him.

Greg Knight

The drummer in the all-MP band MP4, Greg Knight has strong interests in music and charitable works outside Parliament.

The son of a company director and grandson of a miner, Knight grew up in Leicester and attended a local grammar school. A solicitor by profession, he ran his own law firm for ten years and is also the author of four best-selling books on Westminster. During the hiatus when he was out of Parliament he worked as a consultant to showbusiness artistes and companies.

A former Leicester city and county councillor, Knight served as the MP for Derby North from 1983 to 1997. During that time he rose to the position of Deputy Chief Whip and he was made a Privy Counsellor. In 1996 he was appointed Minister for Industry, before losing his seat in 1997. He returned to Parliament in 2001 to represent East Yorkshire. He was soon appointed shadow Deputy Leader of the House. Since 2003 he has served as a shadow minister on the Culture, Media & Sport and Environment & Transport teams, but resigned as shadow Minister for Transport in 2005 in order to become chairman of the Select Committee on Procedure.

Knight has a 6,000-plus majority in East Yorkshire, and when the Tories form their next government he could return to the front bench – or to the Whips' Office.

Eleanor Laing

A proud Scot and a devoted single mother, Eleanor Laing brings a dash of colour (and occasionally plaid) to the Tory benches.

Born in Paisley, the daughter of a builder and Tory councillor, Laing studied law at Edinburgh University and was the first woman to be elected president of the Edinburgh Union. She has practised as a solicitor in Edinburgh, in the City of London and in industry.

After contesting the safe Labour seat of Paisley North at the 1987 election, Laing became a special advisor to John MacGregor in the 1990s when he was Secretary of State for Education, Leader of the House of Commons and Secretary of State for Transport. In 1997 she was elected MP for Epping Forest. She was appointed an opposition whip in 1999, and a year later became a frontbench spokesman on constitutional affairs. In 2005 she was appointed shadow Secretary of State for Scotland, having previously been a shadow Minister for Children and for Women & Equality. Laing has been shadow Minister for Justice since 2007.

Laing's majority in the constituency reached nearly 15,000 in 2005, so she is assured of being returned at the next general election. As one of the most experienced women on the Tory front bench she is also assured of a successful ministerial career.

Jacqui Lait

A cheerful and persistent Scottish PR consultant, Jacqui Lait is another of the great survivors on the Tory benches.

Born near Glasgow, Jacqui Lait attended Paisley Grammar School. She went on to further education at the University of Strathclyde and emerged with a BA in business management. She is married to Peter Jones, who recently retired from work in the City to become the leader of East Sussex County Council.

Lait has been the MP for Beckenham since 1997, having represented Hastings & Rye from 1992 to 1997. In 1974 she joined the Government Information Service in the Scottish Office, the Privy Council Office and the Department of Employment before leaving in 1980 to join the Chemical Industries Association as its parliamentary advisor. From 1984 to 1992 she ran her own parliamentary consultancy.

In 1984 Lait contested the European elections in Strathclyde West before fighting the Tyne Bridge by-election in 1985. Having been selected to fight Hastings & Rye in April 1991, Lait duly won the seat in 1992. She was appointed as the first female member of the Conservative Whips' Office in 1996. Before that she was PPS to William Hague at the Welsh Office and the Department of Social Security. She has served on the Health Select Committee and the European Standing Committee. In 2000 she became a frontbench spokesman for pensions and in 2001 was given the role of shadow Secretary of State for Scotland. In 2003 she was appointed shadow Minister for Home, Constitutional & Legal Affairs and most recently she served as shadow Minister for Communities & Local Government, from May 2005 until January 2009.

Mark Lancaster

A former Gurkha officer and TA veteran, Mark Lancaster has volunteered for active service in Bosnia, Kosovo and Afghanistan.

Raised and educated in Kimbolton, Cambridgeshire, Lancaster went to Kimbolton School, where his father was the chaplain. He served as an officer in the Queen's Gurkha Engineers in Hong Kong for a short time before returning to study for a degree at Buckingham University and for an MBA at Exeter University. He worked for the family's prosperous firework manufacturing company, Kimbolton Fireworks Ltd, before entering Parliament.

Lancaster was elected to Huntingdon District Council in 1995, stepping down four years later to contest Nuneaton, a safe Labour seat, at the 2001 general election. He was elected MP for Milton Keynes North East in 2005, winning back the seat which had been narrowly lost out to Labour in 1997 with a majority of 2,632. He served on the Defence Select Committee until his promotion to the opposition Whips' Office in November 2006. Since July 2007, Lancaster has been shadow Minister for International Development.

With boundary changes at the next general election, Lancaster needs to overcome a notional Labour majority of just under a thousand in the new seat of Milton Keynes North. Assuming he can win this battle, he should have no problem being promoted through the ministerial ranks.

Edward Leigh

A staunch Eurosceptic and arch-traditionalist, Edward Leigh has steadfastly refused to move with the times or to accept his party's modernising agenda.

Born in 1950, Leigh was educated in London at St Philip's School. He moved on to the Oratory School in Berkshire, the French Lycée, London and finally Durham University, where he got a degree in modern history (and where was also president of the Union Society). He is the youngest son of Sir Neville Leigh, former clerk to the Privy Council. He is married with six children, three daughters and three sons.

After university he qualified as a barrister, becoming a member of the Inner Temple. He practised for Goldsmith Chambers in arbitration and criminal law before turning his hand to politics.

Between 1974 and 1981, Leigh was a member of Richmond Borough Council and then the GLC. He worked in Margaret Thatcher's private office between 1976 and 1977 as a private secretary when she was Leader of the Opposition. In the 1974 general election Leigh was chosen to fight the seat of Middlesbrough. Though unsuccessful he was selected to fight again in June 1983, this time for Gainsborough & Horncastle, and on that occasion he won. Leigh was joint secretary of the Conservative Parliamentary Defence Committee and the Parliamentary Agriculture Committee between 1983 and 1985. Between 1990 and 1993 he was parliamentary under-secretary of state at the DTI and then in May 1997 he was elected to the new seat of Gainsborough. From 1995 to 2000 Leigh was a member of the Social Security Select Committee and between 1997 and 2001 he was joint vice chairman of the Conservative Party Parliamentary

Foreign Affairs Committee. Since 2001 he has been the chairman of the extremely influential Public Accounts Committee.

Leigh has made his name as a backbencher, but whether he stays there or moves to the front bench he will undoubtedly have an impact on the next Conservative government.

Ian Liddell-Grainger

A direct descendant of Queen Victoria, Ian Liddell-Grainger was born in Scotland, brought up in the north-east of England, but represents a seat in the south-west. MP for Bridgwater, Liddell-Grainger has always had strong links with Somerset. He was educated at Millfield School and currently lives in the heart of his constituency near Minehead with his wife and their three children.

Liddell-Grainger's background is in business, farming and the Army. He has established a UK-wide building and property management company, maintained a 250-acre arable farm, acted as a consultant to Army Land Command HQ in Salisbury and is still a major on the reserve list. However, upon being elected to Parliament, Liddell-Grainger cut all his professional ties to concentrate on his constituency. He has been MP for Bridgwater since 2001, when he replaced Tom King, who had held the constituency for more than thirty years. He has been a member of three important select committees, looking into public administration, DEFRA and Scottish affairs.

A backbencher by instinct and a select committee aficionado, Liddell-Grainger will nevertheless have an impact on the next Tory government.

David Lidington

Although now a veteran on the Tory benches, David Lidington has never lost his boyish energy and enthusiasm.

A passionate historian, Lidington obtained an MA and a PhD in the subject from Sidney Sussex College, Cambridge. He was captain of the champion team on *University Challenge* in 1979 and on *University Challenge Reunited* in 2002. Prior to entering politics, Lidington worked for BP and Rio Tinto Zinc. He also spent three years as special advisor to the former Home Secretary and Foreign Secretary Douglas Hurd.

In 1987 Lidington stood for the Conservatives in Vauxhall. In 1992 he got himself elected as MP for Aylesbury – a semi-rural, solidly Conservative seat. From 1994 to 1997 he was PPS to the then Home Secretary, Michael Howard, and then he became PPS to William Hague whilst he was the Leader of the Opposition. On the opposition frontbench he has been a shadow home affairs spokesman, shadow Financial Secretary to the Treasury, shadow Minister for Agriculture and shadow Secretary of State for Northern Ireland. Lidington has been William Hague's number two as shadow Minister for Foreign Affairs since July 2007. In that role he has travelled to the USA, China, Saudi Arabia, Egypt, Israel, the Palestinian territories, Qatar and Iran.

Lidington held his seat in Aylesbury with a solid 11,000 majority at the last general election, and he must be reasonably confident that a desk in King Charles Street awaits him when the Tories win next time around.

Peter Lilley

Quiet and on occasion almost shy, Peter Lilley is nevertheless possessed of a fierce intellect and strong political beliefs.

Having studied natural sciences and economics at Clare College, Cambridge, Lilley went on to a career as a financial analyst and economic consultant to several large stockbrokers. He was chairman of the Bow Group in the mid-1970s and he has continued to write pamphlets for it and a number of other centre-right think tanks. His previous Thatcherite and No Turning Back Group tendencies have been replaced by a more centrist approach.

Lilley has been an MP since 1983. Originally elected as the MP for St Albans, he has represented Hitchin & Harpenden since 1997. His first key appointment was in 1984, when he was made PPS to the Chancellor of the Exchequer, Nigel Lawson. After serving as economic and then Financial Secretary to the Treasury between 1987 and 1989, he was appointed Secretary of State for Trade & Industry in 1990 and Secretary of State for Social Security in 1992. In 1990 he was also made a Privy Counsellor. Soon after the 1997 general election, Lilley was appointed shadow Chancellor and subsequently deputy leader of the Conservative Party. In December 2005, David Cameron appointed him chairman of the party's globalisation and global poverty policy group.

Lilley had a very solid 11,393-vote majority in 2005. Assuming he stands again, he will win easily. With his huge experience, and his track record of effectively managing the government departments under his control (including the Department for Social Security), Lilley is strongly tipped for a recall to the Cabinet.

Tim Loughton

Hard-working and unassuming, Tim Loughton has been one of the unsung heroes of the wilderness years.

The son of a clergyman, Loughton was brought up in East Sussex and attended the Priory School, Lewes. He gained a first-class degree in classical civilisation from the University of Warwick, and then went on to study Mesopotamian archaeology at Clare College, Cambridge. After leaving Cambridge he went to work as a fund manager for the blue-blood British merchant bank Flemings, and became a director eight years later.

Loughton joined the Conservative Party when he was sixteen and held various positions with the Young Conservatives in Lewes and the South East region. He stood for Parliament in 1992 as the Conservative candidate for Sheffield Brightside against David Blunkett. He was elected at the following general election as the MP for East Worthing & Shoreham. He has since held a variety of briefs, mostly around health, children and the family. He has been a shadow Minister for Children since 2003. A committed sportsman, he is captain of the Lords and Commons hockey team and a member of the tennis and skiing teams.

Loughton had an 8,184 vote majority at the last general election and will certainly be re-elected next time around. He also has good reason to expect that he will maintain the brief which he has mastered so well in recent years.

Peter Luff

One of the most amiable and able MPs on the Tory benches, former public affairs consultant Peter Luff describes himself as the most lobbied MP in the Commons.

The son of a master printer, Luff was educated at Windsor Grammar School and Corpus Christi College, Cambridge, where he read economics. After working as a researcher in the office of Peter Walker and then in the private office of the late Sir Edward Heath in the early 1980s, Luff pursued a highly successful career in PR and public affairs. Married with two grown-up children (one of whom has followed in his footsteps and works in PR), Luff's outside interests are photography, scuba diving and steam railways. He is vice president of the Severn Valley Railway and chairman of the Worcester Cathedral Council.

Luff has been an MP since 1992. First elected to Peter Walker's old seat of Worcester, he moved to the much safer seat of Mid Worcestershire in 1997, following boundary changes. He had previously contested Holborn & St Pancras in 1987. He was appointed chairman of the Commons Agriculture Committee in 1997, before becoming an opposition whip in 2000. Between 2002 and 2005 he was Assistant Chief Whip. He then went on to chair the highly influential Business and Enterprise Committee.

Mid Worcestershire is subject to minor boundary changes at the next general election, although this will hardly have any effect at all on Luff's rock-solid 13,000 majority. The big question for Luff when the Tories win will be whether to continue his highly successful select committee career – or to accept ministerial office if it is offered.

Anne McIntosh

Not at all an identikit Tory, Anne McIntosh is female (obviously), Scottish (with some Danish blood) and unashamedly pro-European.

McIntosh was born in Edinburgh and educated at Harrogate Ladies' College.

Her father was a doctor but she decided to follow a legal career path and studied at the universities of Edinburgh and Aarhus in Denmark. She practised law in Edinburgh and Brussels before turning to politics.

For the ten years to 1999 McIntosh was MEP for Essex North & Suffolk South, during which she served as an assistant whip and Conservative transport spokesman. She contested Workington at the 1987 general election and was elected to the House of Commons as MP for Vale of York in 1997. She was soon appointed to the Environment, Transport & Regional Affairs Select Committee and the European Scrutiny Select Committee, and has also held a number of shadow ministerial posts. More recently, she has served as shadow Minister for Foreign Affairs, Work & Pensions and Education. She is currently shadow Minister for Environment, Food & Rural Affairs.

McIntosh's seat is to be abolished at the next election and, after several unsuccessful attempts to find a seat elsewhere, she was selected to stand for the safe seat of Thirsk & Malton. This huge rural seat is subject to boundary changes but has a notional Conservative majority of over 14,000. Her Europhilia should be forgiven and a ministerial job should be in prospect, despite her problem with expenses.

Anne Main

Welsh born but now an adopted daughter of Hertfordshire, Anne Main has had to fight every inch of the way in order to get the opportunity to represent ultra-prosperous St Albans.

The daughter of a manual worker from south Cardiff, Main was educated at a local comprehensive school and studied at undergraduate and postgraduate levels at Swansea and Sheffield universities respectively. She then taught English and drama at an inner London comprehensive school. Having lost her first husband to cancer, she then had to bring up three children on her own, before she remarried and had a fourth child.

Main started her political career in 1999, when she was elected to Beaconsfield Town Council. She then became a district councillor in 2001, serving as chairman of planning for South Bucks District Council before entering Parliament in 2005 as the Member for St Albans with an impressive 6.6 per cent swing. With a particular interest in planning and the environment, Main has campaigned to protect the local environment and green belt, opposing housing quotas and planning issues in particular. She currently serves on the Local Government and Works of Art select committees in Parliament, and was recently appointed vice chair of the All-Party Women Parliamentarians Group.

St Albans is subject to minor boundary changes at the next general election and the Conservatives will have a notional majority of around 1,300. Main should hold on, however, and in a party still likely to be short of women – especially with a parliament's worth of experience under their belt – she should make her way onto the front benches, despite her brush with deselection.

John Maples

Tall, grey haired and with an easy manner, this former lawyer and PR man looks every inch the stereotypical Tory MP.

The son of a wine merchant, John Maples was educated at Marlborough College, Cambridge University and Harvard Business School. He qualified as a barrister in 1965 and has had a successful career as a lawyer and businessman. He was chairman and chief executive of Saatchi & Saatchi between 1992 and 1996, and he was also responsible for running the company's lobbying division.

Maples was originally elected to Parliament in 1983 as the Member for Lewisham West, but lost his seat at the 1992 general election. During that period he was PPS to the Chief Secretary of the Treasury and he was Treasury Minister from 1990 to 1992. He returned to Parliament as the MP for Stratford-on-Avon in 1997. He has since held a number of posts in the shadow Cabinet, serving as the shadow Foreign Secretary, Defence Secretary and Health Secretary. He was appointed deputy chairman of the Conservative Party in November 2006 with responsibility for candidate selection and the controversial 'A-list'.

Maples won Stratford-on-Avon with a substantial majority in 1997. Whilst this majority decreased slightly by 2005, the constituency is subject to boundary changes at the next general election giving the Conservatives a notional majority of nearly 11,000. One of the great survivors on the Tory benches, Maples could find himself back on the front line.

Patrick Mercer

A former Army officer, Patrick Mercer combines the straight-talking manner of his former trade with an abundance of energy.

The son of a clergyman, Patrick Mercer grew up in Newark and was educated at Oxford University and the Royal Military Academy Sandhurst. After graduating he joined Nottinghamshire's regiment, the Sherwood Foresters, and served regularly in Northern Ireland, where he was closely involved in the intelligence aspects of the conflict. He has also served in Germany, Canada, Uganda and the Balkans. He was awarded an MBE in 1992 and an OBE in 1996 for service in Bosnia. On leaving the Army, he worked as defence correspondent for the BBC and as a freelance journalist.

Mercer won the seat of Newark in 2001, one of the few Tories to triumph at that election. That year he served on the House of Commons Defence Select Committee before being appointed PPS to the shadow Defence Secretary. He then held the special post of shadow Minister for Homeland Security from 2003 to 2007. He is presently a member of the Home Affairs Select Committee, vice chair of the Transatlantic International Security APPG and chair of the Civil Contingency APPG.

With boundary changes at the next general election, Mercer's majority is set to rise to more than 10,000. Although his plain speaking has landed him in trouble in the past, it is unlikely that the Tories will be able to ignore his unique frontline experience.

Maria Miller

A working mother with a slightly shy and almost diffident manner, Maria Miller is nevertheless widely liked and highly rated.

Born near Wolverhampton, Miller was brought up in south Wales, where she attended a local comprehensive school. She graduated with a degree in economics from the LSE and has worked for both private and public sector organisations in the UK and Europe. Her main area of interest is education, and she has served as a school governor in four different schools over the past twenty years.

Miller was elected to Parliament as the MP for Basingstoke in 2005, having previously contested Wolverhampton North East in 2001. Soon after entering the House of Commons, Miller became shadow Minister for Education. In 2006 she was appointed shadow Minister for Family Welfare, and she has been shadow Minister for Families since 2007.

Miller's constituency is subject to major boundary changes at the next general election, which will effectively halve her majority, but she is still left with a majority of about 2,500. She will survive and she undoubtedly has a bright ministerial career ahead of her.

Anne Milton

Anne Milton is not a Tory MP out of Central Casting – she has spiky hair, a robust sense of humour and an enthusiastic outlook which she applies to her campaigning and her politics.

A former nurse, Milton trained at St Bartholomew's Hospital in London and worked for the NHS for twenty-five years. She has had experience working in hospitals, in research teams, as a district nurse and as a health advisor to local councils and associations.

Before entering Parliament, Milton served as a Reigate borough councillor for five years, two of them as leader of the Conservative group. She was elected to represent Guildford at the 2005 general election, winning the formerly blue seat from the Lib Dems with less than a 1 per cent swing. In 2006 she joined the shadow Culture, Media & Sport team as the shadow Minister for Tourism. She was then appointed shadow Minister for Health in July 2007. She is involved in a huge array of APPGs, being chair of the Health Group, the Primary Care & Public Health Group and the Breast Cancer Group. She is also secretary of the Allergy APPG and vice chair of the APPG on Ageing & Older People.

With boundary changes at the next election, the Conservative result in Guildford will decrease from 0.7 per cent to a notional majority of 0.2 per cent – under 100 votes. However, this hyperactive campaigner should survive and a ministerial job as part of the health team must be in prospect.

Andrew Murrison

Still looking every inch the Royal Navy surgeon commander he once was, Andrew Murrison nevertheless confesses that a place on the green benches was always his primary ambition.

Originally from Harwich, Murrison studied medicine at the universities of Bristol and Cambridge, and spent twenty years as a Royal Navy surgeon. In the 1990s he headed research into neurological decompression illness, which led to the award of the Gilbert Blane Medal in 1994.

Murrison resigned his commission in the Royal Navy in 2000, when he was selected to stand for the relatively safe Conservative seat of Westbury. He was elected in 2001 and got his first frontbench post in November 2003 as shadow Minister for Health. Murrison has a special interest in and first-hand experience of Iraq, having served as a medical officer for six weeks in September 2003, and he is currently a shadow Defence Minister and treasurer of the Iraq APPG.

Boundary changes at the next general election mean he will stand for the seat of South West Wiltshire, which has a notional Conservative majority of around 8,500. Murrison's defence and medical experience should prove invaluable to a future Tory government.

Bob Neill

Genial and astute, there is more than a whiff of Rumpole about this criminal barrister.

The son of a sales executive and a shopkeeper, Bob Neill was brought up in Hornchurch, Essex, where he attended the local grammar school. After studying law at the LSE, he had a successful career as a criminal law barrister.

Despite both his grandfathers being committed socialists, Neill joined the Young Conservatives at sixteen. As a former member of the old GLC, a councillor in the London Borough of Havering and, more recently, a member of the London Assembly, Neill has had extensive experience in local government. Having previously contested Dagenham at the 1983 and 1987 general elections, he was elected MP for Bromley & Chislehurst in June 2006 following the death of

Eric Forth. Neill's experience in local government soon led to his appointment as a shadow Minister for Communities & Local Government in 2007 (with specific responsibility for planning) and a deputy chairman of the Conservative Party in 2008.

Neill's seat is subject to boundary changes and his majority will in theory decrease slightly, but he still has a notional majority of just over 8,000. This will not affect his chances of ministerial office, and Neill should be given the chance to deploy his powers of advocacy from the Treasury bench.

Brooks Newmark

Born in Connecticut and still retaining an American accent, Brooks Newmark has also hung on to the US 'can do' attitude.

Newmark was educated at Bedford School and gained a BA in history and an MBA in business from Harvard. After that he went to Oxford to undertake postgraduate research in politics. Before entering Parliament, Newmark had a successful career in the financial investment sector.

Having narrowly failed to win Braintree in 2001, Newmark succeeded in 2005, overturning a slim 348 majority. His main political interests are in the areas of economic policy, foreign affairs, special needs education and women's issues. He is co-chairman of the Conservative Women2Win campaign (which promotes the selection of female Conservative PPCs), and he has also served on the Treasury Select Committee. He was appointed an opposition whip in July 2007.

Braintree is subject to boundary changes at the next general election, giving the Conservatives a notional majority of around 8,500. Newmark will bring something a little different to the table of the next Tory government.

Stephen O'Brien

Having won Eddisbury at a by-election in 1999 in the teeth of ferocious opposition from the Labour Party, this music-loving supporter of fox hunting has always had at least one eye on retaining his seat.

The son of a businessman and a nurse, Stephen O'Brien was born in Tanzania and attended school in Africa and in the UK. He studied law at Emmanuel College, Cambridge and worked at Freshfields Bruckhaus Deringer for seven years before setting up his own business consultancy specialising in construction and air travel.

Having won the by-election in July 1999 O'Brien has risen steadily within the opposition ranks. In 2000 he was appointed PPS to the then shadow Foreign Secretary, Francis Maude, and later that year to Michael Ancram as chairman of the Conservative Party. He was appointed an opposition whip in 2001 and has since held a number of frontbench posts including shadow Financial Secretary to the Treasury, shadow Industry Secretary and shadow Minister for Education & Skills. He has been shadow Minister for Health since 2005.

The Conservative majority in Eddisbury has increased substantially since O'Brien first won, and with boundary changes he will have a notional majority of around 6,500 going into the next general election. If O'Brien can build up the cushion of a solid majority, then he will be in a position to concentrate on developing his ministerial career.

Richard Ottaway

Quietly spoken and generally self-effacing, Richard Ottaway nevertheless put himself forward to be the Tory candidate for the high-profile role of London Mayor in 2002.

A former Royal Navy officer, Ottaway spent nearly a decade in the Senior Service before leaving to study law at Bristol University. Once he had qualified as a solicitor he specialised in maritime and commercial law with leading City firms.

Originally elected to Parliament as the MP for Nottingham North in 1983, Ottaway lost his seat four years later. He then returned as the MP for Croydon South in 1992. He has served on the front bench as shadow Minister for London and Local Government, shadow Defence Minister, shadow Paymaster General and shadow Secretary of State for the Environment. He also served as a whip during the last two years of the Conservative government. He is currently treasurer of the Singapore and Yacht Club Maritime APPGs and vice chair of the 1922 Committee. He is also a member of the board of the Conservative Party.

Ottaway's Croydon South seat had a majority of around 13,500 at the last general election, and despite boundary changes at the next election, this majority is predicted to stay the same. If the next Conservative government is looking for experienced hands to man the bridge, Ottaway could receive the call – although he may prefer to run for the chairmanship of the 1922 Committee.

James Paice

Born and educated in Suffolk, James Paice attended Writtle Agricultural College and has a career background in farming, but he also had a foray into training management. He still owns 10 acres in Cambridgeshire.

Before being elected to Parliament, Paice was a member of Suffolk Coastal District Council from 1976 to 1987, becoming its chairman in 1983. He contested Caernarvon at the 1979 general election and was elected as the MP for South East Cambridgeshire in 1987. His experience and expertise in agriculture led to him being appointed PPS to two ministers of Agriculture, Fisheries & Food,

Baroness Trumpington and John Gummer. Since 1997 he has served as an opposition spokesman for agriculture, fisheries and food and home affairs and became shadow Minister for Home, Constitutional & Legal Affairs in November 2003. He has served as the shadow Minister for Agriculture since September 2004.

Boundary changes should give Paice and the Conservatives around an 8,000 majority in South East Cambridgeshire. Few people in Parliament have more experience of agriculture than Paice, and some kind of a ministerial role surely beckons.

Mike Penning

A bluff, burly former guardsman and fire-fighter, this arch Eurosceptic was for a time Iain Duncan Smith's pugnacious press spokesman.

Born in north London, Mike Penning attended comprehensive school in Essex and then joined the Army as a boy soldier. He served with the Grenadier Guards in Northern Ireland, Kenya and Germany. He has also been a fireman, a businessman and a political journalist.

Penning entered politics relatively late in his career, first becoming actively involved in 1997, when he ran Sir Teddy Taylor's successful general election campaign in Southend. He contested the safe Labour seat of Thurrock and was finally elected MP for Hemel Hempstead in 2005. Locally he has campaigned to save Hemel Hempstead General Hospital and for a public enquiry into the Buncefield oil refinery disaster. He was appointed shadow Minister for Health in July 2007 and has also served on the Health Select Committee and the Conservative 1922 Committee.

Penning's majority is predicted to decrease to around 150 at the next general election as a result of minor boundary changes. Penning will undoubtedly meet that challenge head on, and a ministerial career should be his reward for success.

John Penrose

A publisher by trade and the son of two teachers, John Penrose is quiet but articulate and able.

After a short spell at the world-famous management consultancy firm McKinsey and then with merchant bankers JP Morgan, Penrose went to work in publishing for Thomsons and then Pearson. He then became chairman of Logotron Ltd, a small company which creates educational software for schools, and was also for a time managing director of the educational publisher Longman.

Penrose was elected as MP for Weston-super-Mare in 2005. He had previously contested the seat in 2001, reducing the sitting Lib Dem MP's majority to just

338 votes, and before that he had contested the safe Labour seat of Ealing Southall in 1997. In January 2009 he was appointed shadow Minister for Business, Enterprise & Regulatory Reform. He is also joint chairman of the Further Education & Lifelong Learning APPG, and has previously served as a member of the Work & Pensions Select Committee and as PPS to Oliver Letwin.

Having won Weston-super-Mare with a majority of 4.2 per cent at the last general election, Penrose should be safe this time around, with minor boundary changes giving him a majority of just over 2,000. Assuming he wins again, he might be presented with the opportunity to use his obvious competence to good effect in ministerial office.

Mark Prisk

A doughty defender of industry and entrepreneurship, Mark Prisk is not averse to engaging in verbal fisticuffs when the need arises.

Born and educated in Cornwall, Prisk went to Truro School before graduating from the University of Reading with a degree in land management. A qualified chartered surveyor, he also worked in the property and economic development markets before starting his own strategic marketing and communication consultancy in 1991.

Prisk stood for Parliament at the 1992 general election in Newham North West and then at the 1997 election in Wansdyke before finally succeeding in Hertford & Stortford in 2001. He is vice chairman of the Small Business APPG and chairman of the East Hertfordshire Business Forum. He was appointed shadow Financial Secretary to the Treasury in November 2002 and became shadow Minister for Economic Affairs a year later. He was made an opposition whip in December 2004, and has been shadow Minister for Business & Enterprise since December 2005. He is also on the executive board of the Enterprise Forum.

With boundary changes at the next election, Hertford & Stortford has a notional Conservative majority of nearly 13,000. Prisk will undoubtedly be fighting British business's corner from the government front bench in the future.

Mark Pritchard

A dog-loving marketeer, Mark Pritchard was helped by many hunt supporters in his campaign to unseat the anti-hunting Peter Bradley.

Pritchard grew up in Herefordshire, which neighbours his parliamentary seat of The Wrekin. By profession he is a marketeer, and he has run two marketing and communications companies.

After unsuccessfully contesting Warley in 2001, he succeeded in The Wrekin in May 2005. He had previously served as a local councillor and was elected to the national board of the Conservative Councillors' Association in 2000. He has served on the Work & Pensions Select Committee, the Welsh Affairs Select Committee and the Environmental Audit Select Committee. He currently serves as joint secretary of the Conservative Foreign Affairs Committee and the Conservative Defence Committee.

Pritchard's seat is subject to minor boundary changes at the next general election, but the Conservative majority remains much the same at just over 1,000 votes. A call-up to the front bench may follow after the general election.

John Randall

One of the few bearded faces on the Tory benches, John Randall is a genial figure much loved by constituents and parliamentary colleagues alike.

Randall spent most of his childhood in Uxbridge, to the west of London, where he attended two local schools before studying for a degree in Serbo-Croat language and literature from the University of London. He also speaks Russian as a supplement to a keen interest in the Balkans and eastern Europe. Four generations of his family have run a furniture shop, Randalls of Uxbridge, and before being elected Randall was a director of the family firm.

Following the death of Sir Michael Shersby, Randall (a former Uxbridge Conservative Association chairman) was selected and then elected as the MP for Uxbridge in July 1997. He was soon appointed to the Deregulation Select Committee and became an opposition whip in 1999. In 2005 he became opposition Assistant Chief Whip.

His constituency is subject to boundary changes and a name change at the next general election. Uxbridge & South Ruislip has a notional Conservative majority of just over 7,000, so the new name and boundaries will not hit Randall's chances. He will be comfortably re-elected and will undoubtedly transfer across the Members' Lobby to the government Whips' Office.

John Redwood

Ultra-bright and unafraid of controversy, the tinder-dry John Redwood has been the Tory's economic conscience for more than a decade.

After graduating from Magdalen College, Oxford at the age of nineteen, Redwood went on to take a DPhil in modern history and he was a lecturer and fellow of All Souls at an age when most students are just graduating. He then moved into banking, becoming a director of Rothschilds investment division. Finally he moved on to become head of Margaret Thatcher's Policy Unit, and is credited with developing the concept of privatisation.

Redwood began his political career as an Oxfordshire county councillor in the 1970s. He joined the front bench as parliamentary under-secretary in the

DTI soon after his election in 1989. After the 1992 general election he served as Minister for Local Government & Inner Cities and then Secretary of State for Wales. He unsuccessfully stood for the leadership of the Conservative Party on two occasions, in 1995 and 1997, and has continued to hold key frontbench posts in opposition since. He has been shadow Secretary of State for Trade & Industry and the Environment, Transport & Regions and spokesman on deregulation. He has been chairman of the party's Economic Competitiveness Policy Group since December 2005.

The Conservatives have a majority of more than 7,000 in Wokingham. Redwood is undoubtedly enjoying life on the back benches, but it is unlikely that he could resist the call of a return to government – especially in an economic role, or a role in a department which needed radical reorganisation.

Andrew Robathan

A super-tough former guardsman and SAS officer, Andrew Robathan had fifteen years of active service behind him when he swapped khaki for the green benches.

Robathan was educated at Merchant Taylors' School in Northwood and Oriel College, Oxford. He then attended the Army Staff College, Camberley, and served in the Coldstream Guards and the SAS before leaving to pursue a career in politics. Prior to his election to Parliament in 1992 he worked for BP, although he briefly returned to the colours in 1991 for the First Gulf War.

Robathan served on Hammersmith & Fulham Council from 1990 until 1992, when he resigned to fight and win at that year's general election. He took over Blaby, a safe Conservative seat, from the former Chancellor of the Exchequer Nigel Lawson. He has served on the opposition front bench as shadow Minister for Trade & Industry, International Development and Defence. He has been deputy opposition Chief Whip since December 2005 and is also vice chairman of the Cycling APPG and the Renewable & Sustainable Energy APPG.

His constituency is subject to boundary changes at the next general election, with a notional Conservative majority of nearly 8,000, and will be rebranded as South Leicestershire. Frontline service of a different variety may be the order of the day when the Tories form their next government, although he does seem to enjoy his behind-the-scenes role in the Whips' Office.

Hugh Robertson

Another former guardsman and Gulf War veteran, Hugh Robertson is a sports fanatic and a playing member of the MCC.

Originally from Canterbury, Robertson attended the King's School before going to the Royal Military Academy Sandhurst. He also gained a degree in land management from Reading University. He served as an Army officer in the Life Guards for thirteen years, seeing service in Northern Ireland, Bosnia, Cyprus and the Gulf. A highlight of his military career occurred in 1993, when he commanded the Household Cavalry at the Queen's Birthday Parade and State Opening of Parliament. Having left the Army in 1995, he worked for Schroders, an investment management company, as head of new business development and as an assistant director.

Robertson was selected to contest Faversham & Mid Kent in March 2000 and won the seat in 2001 with a 20 per cent majority. He was appointed an opposition whip in November 2002. He has been shadow Minister for Sport since 2004, and he is also shadow Olympics Minister, two roles which make the most of his interest in sports. His constituency is subject to boundary changes at the next general election, leaving the Conservatives with a notional majority of nearly 9,000. It seems likely that he will be asked to continue in his current role when the Tories win, since the Olympic Games will be just two years away.

Laurence Robertson

From humble origins Laurence Robertson has made his own way in business and politics. An admirer of Margaret Thatcher, he remains implacably Eurosceptic.

Educated at Farnworth Grammar School and Bolton Institute of Higher Education, Robertson has had a career as a factory owner, charity fundraiser, PR consultant and special events organiser. Over the years he has raised a great deal of money for charity.

Robertson was a candidate in Makerfield in the 1987 general election and Ashfield in 1992. He was successfully voted in as MP for Tewkesbury in May 1997. He had worked hard in politics at a local level before entering national politics, holding numerous roles including local association chairman, a victim support volunteer and chairman of governors at a primary school. He was appointed an opposition whip in September 2001 and has served in a variety of frontbench posts, including shadow Minister for Trade & Industry and for Economic Affairs. He has been shadow Minister for Northern Ireland since 2005.

Robertson held Tewkesbury with a majority of over 20 per cent in 2005. With boundary changes at the next election, the Conservatives have a notional majority of more than 9,000. He will undoubtedly hold his seat and will be hopeful of ministerial office.

Andrew Rosindell

When he first ran for Parliament Andrew Rosindell would take his British bulldog Buster – resplendent in a Union Jack waistcoat – campaigning with him. Although Buster has since passed on, Rosindell still revels in his image as a staunch patriot.

Born and raised in Romford, Andrew Rosindell was educated locally at Rise Park and Marshalls Park schools. Before entering politics he was a freelance journalist and PR consultant. From 1997 to 2001 he was director of the European Foundation think tank.

Rosindell joined the Conservative Party in 1981 and served as a councillor in Romford for eleven years before being elected to Parliament in 2001. During the 1980s and 1990s he was chairman of a number of Conservative youth bodies including Romford, Greater London, national and European Young Conservatives. At the 1992 and 1997 general elections he contested Glasgow Provan and Thurrock respectively. Third time lucky, he was elected as the MP for Romford in 2001, defeating former Labour MP Eileen Gordon with a 9.2 per cent swing and winning more than 50 per cent of the vote. He is currently shadow Minister for Home Affairs and has also served as a vice chairman of the Conservative Party and an opposition whip since being elected.

A working-class Tory seat in north-east London, Romford has traditionally been a marginal seat for both parties. With his firm right-wing views, Rosindell has managed to secure a healthy majority over the last two elections. Subject to boundary changes at the next general election, Romford will have a notional Conservative majority of over 12,000. Now well established and with the rhetoric toned down, Rosindell can expect to feature in the ministerial ranks.

David Ruffley

Fiercely bright and a ferocious interrogator, David Ruffley has unsettled many a minister and civil servant when they appear before any select committee on which he has served.

On leaving grammar school, David Ruffley studied at Queens' College, Cambridge, before practising as a solicitor at Clifford Chance. During the 1990s Ruffley was a special advisor to several senior members of the Cabinet, including Kenneth Clarke in his roles as Secretary of State for Education & Science, Home Secretary and then Chancellor of the Exchequer. He was also a strategic economic consultant to the Conservative Party from 1996 to 1997.

Ruffley was elected to Parliament as MP for Bury St Edmunds in 1997. A specialist in economic and financial affairs, he has served on the Conservative Finance Committee and the Commons Treasury and Public Administration select committees. He is now secretary of the Wholesale Markets & Financial Services APPG and was appointed as shadow Minister for Home Affairs in 2007. He has also served as shadow Minister for Work & Pensions and as an opposition whip.

An active campaigner in the local area, Ruffley is patron of the West Suffolk Voluntary Association for the Blind, the Bury St Edmunds & District Football League, the Bury St Edmunds Town Trust, the Suffolk Deaf Association and the West Suffolk Alzheimer's Society. Despite constituency boundary changes at the next general election, the Conservative majority for this seat remains roughly the same at just over 10,000. Whether Ruffley joins his former mentor Ken Clarke in government, or continues to pursue his career in the ranks of the select committees, remains to be seen.

Lee Scott

Focused and determined, Lee Scott never doubted for one moment that he would make it into Parliament.

Scott has lived in Redbridge, in east London, for most of his life, and was educated at a local school. Before entering politics he had a career as a sales executive and professional fundraiser for several major national and international charities. He has worked with Victim Support, the Barkingside Youth Centre Committee and the Acorns appeals committee at Whipps Cross Hospital. Scott is married and has five children.

Before running his own campaign for Parliament, Scott took part in election campaigns for many well-known political figures, notably President George Bush in 1988. He unsuccessfully contested Waveney at the 2001 general election and was selected as the Conservative candidate for Ilford North in October 2002. He won the seat from Labour at the 2005 general election with a majority of 1,653 votes. Since being elected, Scott has served on the Transport Select Committee and the Health Select Committee. With a special interest in autism, in 2008 he presented a private member's bill dealing with the care of sufferers of the condition.

Ilford North is subject to minor boundary changes at the next general election, leaving the Conservatives with an unaffected majority of just over 1,700. Hopefully after the election Scott will be offered the opportunity to channel his energies into a ministerial role.

Andrew Selous

Tall and thin, Andrew Selous has a somewhat lugubrious air about him which has done nothing to affect his popularity with colleagues – or the electorate.

Before entering Parliament Selous was a TA officer, serving in Germany, Cyprus, the Netherlands, Switzerland and the USA over a period of twelve years. As a qualified chartered insurer, he also previously worked as a reinsurance underwriter for a firm which specialised in helping some of the world's poorest communities recover from natural disasters.

Selous was elected to Parliament as MP for South West Bedfordshire in 2001. In 2003 he was appointed PPS to Michael Ancram, the deputy leader of the Conservative Party and shadow Foreign Secretary. He was made an opposition whip in 2004 and shadow Work & Pensions Minister in 2006. He has also served on the Work & Pensions Select Committee during his time in Parliament and chairs two APPGs – Christians in Parliament and Sustainable Relationships.

Married with three daughters, Selous lives in his constituency, which he holds with a majority of just over 8,000. His experience and quiet competence may secure him the chance of ministerial office.

Mark Simmonds

A very different personality from Sir Richard Body, the arch Eurosceptic and traditionalist from whom he inherited his safe seat, Mark Simmonds is humorous and easy-going. Although he is no enthusiast for the 'project' himself, Simmonds is not fixated on matters European.

The son of two teachers, Mark Simmonds is married and has three children. He attended Worksop College in Nottinghamshire before going on to read urban estate surveying at Trent University. As a qualified chartered surveyor, he worked for Savills in the mid-1980s before moving on to be a partner at Strutt & Parker and then a director at Hillier Parker. In 1999 he set up his own surveying practice, Mortlock Simmonds Brown, of which he is still chairman.

Simmonds served as a Wandsworth borough councillor from 1990 to 1994, during which time he held the position of chairman of the council's Property Committee and Housing Committee. He stood against Geoff Hoon at the 1997 general election, but was elected to Parliament as MP for Boston & Skegness in 2001. He served as PPS to Michael Ancram from January 2002 before being promoted to the front bench as shadow Minister for Public Services, Health & Education in November 2003. He has since been shadow Minister for Foreign Affairs and International Development and is presently shadow Minister for Health. Simmonds is also secretary of the All Party Latin America Group, and he has been a member of the Environmental Audit Committee and the Education & Skills Select Committee.

The Conservatives have a majority of over 6,000 in Boston & Skegness, and Simmonds has a firm foundation on which to build any future ministerial career.

Keith Simpson

With the air of an Oxbridge don, this bespectacled military historian is universally liked on the opposition benches and compiles the annual summer recess reading list for Tory MPs.

Keith Simpson went to the University of Hull, before undertaking postgraduate research in war studies at King's College, London. He has been director of the Security Studies Institute at Cranfield University and a senior lecturer in war studies and international affairs at Sandhurst. He is also the author of five academic books, and he is married with one son.

Before being elected to Parliament, Simpson was an advisor to two Defence Secretaries, George Younger and Tom King, and was the head of the Foreign Affairs & Defence Section at the CRD. Simpson unsuccessfully contested Plymouth Devonport in 1992, but was elected MP for Mid Norfolk in 1997. He was soon appointed to the Conservative Parliamentary Defence Committee and was made a frontbench defence spokesman in 1998. He then served as an opposition whip for two years and was briefly a shadow agriculture spokesman before returning to the shadow Defence team in July 2002. He has been shadow Minister for Foreign Affairs since May 2005.

At the next general election Simpson will stand for the new seat of Broadland, which is mainly formed from the old Mid Norfolk seat. The seat has a notional Conservative majority of over 6,500. It is hard to imagine how he will not be a Defence or FCO minister after the general election.

Chloe Smith

Aged just twenty-seven when elected in Norwich North, Chloe Smith became the youngest member of the current parliament – and the youngest female Tory MP ever.

Smith was typical of the new breed of Tory candidates, with very strong local connections, having lived in Norfolk since the age of three. She was educated at local schools before going to the University of York, where she graduated in 2004 with a BA in English literature.

Since graduating, Smith worked as a business consultant for Deloittes. In her job she advised private businesses, not-for-profit organisations and government departments. For part of that time she was seconded to CCHQ. She also has a strong record of volunteering and charity fundraising.

Smith says that she was inspired to go into politics by Gillian Shephard, who was the MP for her home constituency whilst she was growing up. She has little previous political experience at either local or national level, but she has been fighting campaigns in her constituency, campaigning to keep an NHS walk-in centre open and for a clampdown on speeding drivers.

Very much the right candidate in the right place at the right time, Smith personally benefited from Labour's harsh decision to deselect the respected local MP Dr Ian Gibson. When Gibson decided to retire and force a by-election, the Tories knew they had an excellent chance of winning Norwich North and threw everything at it – turning a Labour majority of 6,769 into a Tory majority of 7,348 on a 16.5 per cent swing. If Smith can hold on to the seat in the general election, she could become one of the stars of the next parliament.

Richard Spring

Perennially youthful, Richard Spring is one of the great survivors on the Tory benches.

Born and raised in Cape Town, Spring is a divorcee with two children. He went to school and university in Cape Town before going on to do a master's degree in economics at Magdalene College, Cambridge. After graduation he moved to London and spent a decade at Merrill Lynch, rising to the position of vice president in 1976. Spring continued to work in financial services until he was elected to Parliament in 1992.

Originally elected as MP for Bury St Edmunds, the constituency title changed to West Suffolk after boundary changes at the 1997 general election. In the 1990s Spring served in the Northern Ireland Office, the DTI and the MoD. On the shadow front bench he has served as an opposition whip and as a spokesman for culture, media and sport and foreign affairs. He was appointed shadow Minister for International Affairs in 2003 and was then shadow Minister for the Treasury until 2005, when he was made vice chairman of the Conservative Party. He is also co-chairman of the Conservative City Circle.

Spring holds West Suffolk with a comfortable majority of nearly 9,000. His City background and contacts will be invaluable to the party in government.

Gary Streeter

A decent and deeply religious man, Gary Streeter's faith informs all of his actions. He is married with two children.

The son of a dairy farmer, Streeter grew up on his family's farm in east Devon and was educated at Tiverton Grammar School. He graduated from King's College, London with a first-class honours degree in law and went on to work for a large City of London solicitors' firm for three years, before joining Foot & Bowden in Plymouth. Four years later he became a partner, specialising in company and employment law.

Streeter started his political career as a councillor on Plymouth City Council in 1986. Originally elected as the MP for Plymouth Sutton in 1992, the constituency was newly formed as South West Devon in 1997. During his first years in Parliament Streeter was PPS to the Solicitor General and then to the Attorney General. In 1995 he was appointed to the Whips' Office before moving to the Lord Chancellor's Department in 1996. In 1997 he was the PPS to the then Leader of the Opposition, John Major. Since 1997 he has served as shadow

Minister for Europe, shadow Secretary of State for International Development and vice chairman of the Conservative Party.

South West Devon has a Conservative majority of nearly 9,500. Streeter may be hoping that his experience will earn him a recall to the front bench.

Graham Stuart

Proudly pugnacious, Graham Stuart is loud and hyperactive, and one of the Tories' most effective hecklers in the Commons.

Stuart was born in Carlisle and was brought up and educated in Scotland. Whilst studying philosophy and law at Selwyn College, Cambridge, he set up a successful publishing business – of which he is still chairman. He is married and has two daughters. He is a school governor and a director of a mental health charity.

Stuart has had an active interest in politics since his student days at Cambridge, where he was chairman of the university's Conservative Association. Before being elected to Parliament as the MP for Beverley & Holderness in 2005, he served as a county councillor in Cambridge and also contested the city's parliamentary seat at the 2001 general election. He is the founder of the Beverley & Holderness Pensioners Action Group, and he also launched the *Holderness Herald* and the *Beverley Bulletin* soon after being elected.

A traditional Conservative seat, Beverley & Holderness was one of their most marginal by 2001. Stuart managed to increase the majority on his election in 2005, and at the next general election he will have a notional majority of over 3,000. He will hope that his tireless efforts in the Commons chamber will earn him a seat on the front benches.

Desmond Swayne

A fitness fanatic, Desmond Swayne cycles and swims to Parliament every day, to the amusement and bemusement of any tourists in the vicinity of the Serpentine in the early morning hours.

Educated at Bedford School and the University of St Andrews, Swayne lives with his wife and three children in the New Forest. He was a schoolmaster for six years in the 1980s before becoming a manager with the Royal Bank of Scotland. He has also served as a TA officer for more than twenty years and served in Iraq for six months in 2003.

After two previous attempts, Swayne was elected at the 1997 general election, as MP for New Forest West. He had contested Pontypridd in 1987 and West Bromwich West in 1992. Swayne has held shadow ministerial posts on the Northern Ireland, Health and Defence teams and has also been a senior opposition whip. He has been PPS to both Michael Howard and David Cameron, famously lending the latter his bicycle on one of the occasions when Cameron's had been stolen.

Swayne has a healthy majority of over 16,000 in New Forest West. He must hope that his years of bag carrying will earn him a red box of his own.

Hugo Swire

Charming and urbane, Hugo Swire is a throwback to how Tory MPs used to look and sound.

Swire attended Eton and St Andrews University. He then trained at Sandhurst and served in the armed forces before entering Parliament. He also has a career background in the arts industry, having been a director of Sotheby's and the head of development at the National Gallery. Married with two daughters, Swire is a fellow of the Royal Society of Arts, and a member of the Countryside Alliance, the NFU and the Royal British Legion. He is also one of the country's leading charity auctioneers.

Having been elected to Parliament as the MP for East Devon in 2001, Swire has served on the Northern Ireland Affairs Select Committee and was chairman of the Speaker's Advisory Committee on Works of Art. In 2003 he was PPS to the then chairman of the Conservative Party, Theresa May, and was made an opposition whip later that year. In 2005 he was appointed shadow Secretary of State for Culture, Media & Sport, a position which he retained until 2007. He has a strong interest in foreign affairs and is secretary of the Conservative Middle East Council and a member of several other related all-party groups.

With boundary changes at the next election, East Devon has a notional Conservative majority of more than 9,000. Swire may be hoping to join either the Defence or Culture ministerial teams after the general election.

Robert Syms

A loyalist and a localist, Robert Syms has been on and off the front bench since he was first elected over a decade ago.

Born in 1956, Syms was educated at Colston's School in Bristol, and after leaving school obtained a Road Haulage Manager's Certificate. He is a former MD of a building and plant hire group and is a fellow of the Chartered Institute of Building. In 2006 he separated from his wife, Fiona, with whom he had two children.

Before being elected to Parliament Syms had a wide involvement with politics. Between 1979 and 1988 he held numerous positions in the North Wiltshire Conservative Association, including chairman and vice president. In 1985 he was elected to Wiltshire County Council and was a whip from 1990 to 1993 as well as being vice chairman of the Finance Committee. He served as a councillor on

North Wiltshire District Council from 1983 to 1987 and was vice chairman of the council and leader of the majority Conservative group from 1984 to 1987. In 1992 he unsuccessfully contested the parliamentary seat of Walsall North.

Elected MP for Poole in 1997, Syms has held a variety of positions since. In late 1999 he was appointed as frontbench spokesman for environment, transport and the regions. In 2001 he became a vice chairman of the Conservative Party and then in 2003 an opposition whip. Between 2003 and 2007 he held the position of shadow Minister for Local Government.

Solid and reliable, Syms must be in the frame for a recall to the front bench at some stage.

Edward Timpson

Somewhat shy but with a pleasant and approachable manner, Edward Timpson shrugged off the 'Tory Toff' image Labour tried to pin on him to win the historic Crewe & Nantwich by-election in May 2008.

Timpson was born and brought up in Cheshire. His family founded the eponymous shoe-repair and key-cutting chain in 1865. His parents fostered children, meaning he and his siblings shared their home with eighty-six other children over the years. Educated at Uppingham School and Durham University, Timpson plied his trade as a lawyer before entering Parliament. He is married with three young children.

Timpson was the first Tory by-election candidate to win a seat from Labour since 1982. His campaign priorities were aimed at cutting crime, increasing police visibility and reducing youth anti-social behaviour. He also led a high-profile campaign against the closure of local post offices, collecting a petition with more than 3,000 signatures. In Parliament he serves on the Joint Human Rights Committee.

Historically, Crewe & Nantwich was a marginal seat but became a secure Labour one after boundary changes in 1997. With more boundary changes at the next election, and based on the 2005 general election results, the seat has a notional Labour majority of just under 7,000, so the Conservatives will need an 8.4 per cent swing to hold it at the next general election. If Timpson can survive that test, a bright ministerial career is in prospect.

Andrew Tyrie

Another policy expert to have made the transition to frontline politics, Andrew Tyrie looks and sounds like what he is – a super-bright economist.

Having been brought up in rural Essex, where his father was a furniture retailer, Tyrie attended Felstead School before going on to study at Trinity College, Oxford. He also did postgraduate studies at the College of Europe in Bruges and

Wolfson College, Cambridge. Before his political career took off, Tyrie was senior economist at the European Bank for Reconstruction and Development.

Tyrie was elected as the MP for Chichester at the 1997 general election. He had already been involved in politics, having worked as a full-time advisor to Nigel Lawson and then John Major when they were Chancellors of the Exchequer. Since being elected, Tyrie has served on the Constitutional Affairs Committee and on the Public Accounts Commission. From 2003 to 2005 he was shadow Minister for Economic Affairs and he has also served on the executive committee of the 1922 Committee. Tyrie is vice chair of the APPG on Parliamentary Reform and chairman of the APPG on Extraordinary Rendition. He has also published a number of pamphlets for the Conservative Party and a number of think tanks, including the CPS.

Chichester is subject to boundary changes and has a notional Conservative majority of nearly 10,500. Tyrie will be hoping for a ministerial position in the Treasury, or as part of the burgeoning business team.

Shailesh Vara

Like the author a martial arts black belt, Shailesh Vara has (also like the author) a wholly reasonable and totally unthreatening demeanour. He attended Aylesbury Grammar School and Brunel University. A qualified solicitor, he has practised in London and in Hong Kong. He is married and has two children.

Vara has been involved with the Conservative Party for nearly thirty years. He has held various posts regionally and nationally within the party. He was vice chairman from 2001 to 2005, during which time he acted as an advisor to Michael Howard and oversaw the youth branch of the party, Conservative Future. He stood as a candidate in the 1997 and 2001 general elections and was elected as MP for North West Cambridgeshire in 2005. He is joint vice chairman of the APPG on Trafficking of Women and Children, treasurer of the BBC APPG and vice chairman of the Executive Committee of Conservative Lawyers. In 2006 he served on the Environment, Food & Rural Affairs Select Committee, which scrutinised the largest bill ever to pass through Parliament. He is now the shadow Deputy Leader of the House.

Vara won his parliamentary seat of North West Cambridgeshire with a majority of nearly 10,000 at the last election, and slight boundary changes are favourable. After his many years of service to the party, Vara will be hoping for a ministerial job.

Charles Walker

Irreverent and iconoclastic, Charles Walker amuses many but offends some vested interests. The author exchanged banter with him when giving evidence to the Public Administration Select Committee (PASC) inquiry on lobbying, an inquiry which Walker, himself a former lobbyist, regarded as being largely a waste of time.

Walker is a graduate of the University of Oregon in the USA. When he finished his degree he returned to the UK, where he pursued a career in marketing and communications, working for both private and listed companies. He is a former director of the recruitment staffing firm Blue Arrow. Married with three children, his hobbies include fishing and cricket.

Walker has been interested and involved in politics from a young age. He started at the age of six, delivering leaflets in his local area at the 1974 general election. He worked actively at a local level before entering Parliament, holding a number of Association posts in Wandsworth and serving as a Wandsworth borough councillor from 2002. He stood as the candidate for Ealing North in 2001 and was elected as the MP for Broxbourne at the 2005 general election. He is a member of the PASC and the Scottish Affairs Committee.

Broxbourne is a rock-solid seat with a Conservative majority of nearly 11,500. Walker certainly has the ability to achieve ministerial rank – but may prefer to continue to play the role of backbench maverick.

Ben Wallace

A military man with a strong Scottish pedigree, Ben Wallace's ambition led him south to Westminster by way of Lancashire.

After leaving school at eighteen, Wallace went on to the Royal Military Academy Sandhurst. Two years later he was commissioned into the Scots Guards, where he served for eight years in many locations including Northern Ireland, Central America and Germany. During his career he served as a platoon commander, company commander, operations officer and intelligence officer. Before his election to Parliament in 2005, Wallace worked as an overseas director for Qinetiq. He lives in Lancashire with his wife and two young children.

In May 1999, Wallace was elected to the Scottish Parliament. He served on the Health Select Committee and was the shadow health spokesman before standing down in 2003 so that he could move to Lancashire and fight the marginal seat of Lancaster & Wyre. He was elected to Parliament in 2005 and was appointed as the shadow Minister for Scotland in July 2007.

At the next general election, Wallace will stand for the new seat of Wyre & Preston North, which has a projected Conservative majority of over 12,000. With the Tories likely to be short of Scottish MPs, a post in the Scotland Office might be on offer.

Robert Walter

A rare creature on the Tory benches, Bob Walter is a pro-European and member of the Conservative Europe Group.

Born in 1948, Walter was educated at Warminster School. He attended Aston University in Birmingham and graduated in 1971. He married his wife Sally in 1970 and they had three children. Sally died in 1995, whereupon he also took responsibility for two step-children. Before his time in politics, Walter was an international banker and farmer. He is a former member of the London Stock Exchange and has been a director of Aubrey G. Lanston & Co. Inc.

Walter's political career began long before his election to Parliament. He was chairman of the Aston University Conservative Association from 1967 to 1969 and chairman of Westbury Constituency Young Conservatives from 1973 to 1976. In 1979 he was PPC for Bedwellty but did not fight another election until 1997, when he was elected MP for North Dorset, the seat he still holds. Walter has been chairman of the Conservative Foreign Affairs Forum and of the Conservative Europe Group, as well as a member of the Conservative Party's National Union Executive Committee. Since 1997 he has been a member of the British–Irish Inter-Parliamentary Body and he is now chairman of its European Affairs Committee. He served on the Treasury Committee from 2003 to 2005. Between 1999 and 2001 he was Conservative frontbench spokesman for constitutional affairs and for Wales. Presently he is chairman of the defence committee of the Western European Union's European Security and Defence Assembly. He is also president of the largest political group in the WEU, the Federated Group of Christian Democrats and European Democrats. In addition, he is one of the UK members of the Parliamentary Assembly of the Council of Europe, where he is chairman of the Media Committee.

Although his Europhilia might count against him, there may be a place on the front benches for a man of Walter's experience and ability.

Angela Watkinson

A big fan of Margaret Thatcher, Angela Watkinson is a right-wing Eurosceptic, reflecting the views of most of her east London constituents.

Watkinson has pursued several career paths, having worked in banking, at a special school for physically handicapped children and also as a local government officer. She was educated at Wanstead County High School and Anglia Higher Education College (now Anglia Ruskin) University. She is a school governor at two secondary schools and also a former governor of two primary schools. She lives with her husband (a retired policeman) and has three children.

Watkinson has served as a councillor in the London Borough of Havering and on Essex County Council. She was elected to Parliament as the MP for

Upminster at the 2001 general election, having previously served as chairman of the Emerson Park branch of the Upminster Conservative Association. She was appointed an opposition whip in July 2002, and has also served on the front bench as shadow Minister for Education and for Local Government Affairs & Local Communities. She was reappointed an opposition whip in 2005.

Her parliamentary seat is subject to boundary changes at the next election, and Watkinson will stand as the candidate for Hornchurch & Upminster. The seat has a notional Conservative majority of over 8,000. Having done spells in the Whips' Office and on the front benches, Watkinson can expect to serve in the next Conservative government.

John Whittingdale

A member of the Tory 'Brains Trust', John Whittingdale has been involved in drafting policy and manifestos for the party for many years.

With a degree in economics from University College London, Whittingdale has always worked in politics, having been an advisor at a senior level within the Conservative Party. In the early 1980s he was head of the Political Section in the CRD, before serving as special advisor to three consecutive Secretaries of State for Trade & Industry. In 1988 he was appointed political secretary to the Prime Minister, and he continued to work for Margaret Thatcher after her resignation until 1992. He was awarded an OBE in her resignation honours list.

Whittingdale was first elected to Parliament as the MP for Colchester South & Maldon in 1992. In his early days he served on the Health Select Committee and was appointed PPS to the Minister for Education & Employment in 1994. He was elected for the new constituency of Maldon & Chelmsford East in 1997 and was appointed an opposition whip that same year. In 1999 he was appointed PPS to the then Leader of the Opposition, William Hague. On the front bench Whittingdale has served as the shadow Secretary of State for Trade & Industry, for Culture, Media & Sport and for Agriculture, Fisheries & Food. He is chairman of the high-profile Culture, Media & Sport Select Committee.

Whittingdale's seat is subject to boundary changes at the next general election, giving him a substantial notional majority of over 13,000. He might conceivably swap the committee corridor for ministerial office should the Tories win power. Alternatively, he could stay on for one more term as chairman of the Culture, Media & Sport committee – or run for the chairmanship of the 1922 Committee when Sir Michael Spicer steps down.

Bill Wiggin

Jovial and hail-fellow-well-met, Bill Wiggin is the son of former Tory MP Jerry Wiggin.

Wiggin's father was a farmer near Upton-upon-Severn before he became an MP and his great-grandfather founded Special Metals Wiggin Ltd. He lives with his wife Milly near Ledbury with their two young children. Outside politics his interests include motorbikes, DIY, diving, shooting, fishing and farming – he keeps chickens and Hereford cows.

Before his election to Parliament, Wiggin worked for Commerzbank, where he was a manager in the foreign exchange department. He has also been a governor of Hammersmith & West London Further Education College, and has served as an officer in the TA with the Royal Welch Fusiliers and the Royal Yeomanry.

Wiggin fought the constituency of Burnley in 1997 and, although unsuccessful, he was selected for Leominster in April 1999 and won the seat in 2001. In 2003 he was given the role of shadow Minister for Environment, Food & Rural Affairs, and he is still a member of the Environment, Food & Rural Affairs Select Committee to this day. From late 2003 to 2005 he was shadow Secretary of State for Wales, before switching to become shadow Minister for Environment, Food & Rural Affairs again – a position he held until early 2009. In January 2009 he was appointed an opposition whip.

After undertaking several frontbench roles Wiggin may at last have found his niche in the Whips' Office. The Lib Dems have announced that they will target Wiggin, following criticism of him over the MP expenses furore, but he has a hefty majority and should survive the transition into government.

Robert Wilson

A serial entrepreneur, Rob Wilson was elected largely because of the bitterness which followed Labour's deselection of their sitting MP, Jane Griffiths.

Born and bred in Oxfordshire, Wilson moved to Reading in 1984 to attend university. He still lives there with his wife and three children. Wilson has successfully built several businesses in his time – mostly in the health and communications sectors – with head offices in central London.

Wilson fought and lost parliamentary elections in 1997 and 2001 before becoming the PPC for Reading East. He has been an advisor to David Davis. In 2004 he was elected as a councillor in the Thames ward of Reading, having previously been one in Caversham. Finally elected to Parliament in 2005, Wilson was appointed shadow Minister for Higher Education in mid-2007, before being selected as opposition whip in early 2009.

Wilson is young enough and fresh enough to have a good career ahead of him, and with his good fortune in getting in in 2005 he will be a few crucial years ahead of the crowd.

Jeremy Wright

Earnest and bespectacled, Jeremy Wright is a lawyer who spent his gap year in the USA and married an American.

As a lawyer Wright specialised in criminal law. Both of his parents were teachers and he attended schools in Taunton and New York City before studying at Exeter University and the Inns of Court School of Law. He was called to the Bar in 1996 and practised in the West Midlands until elected in 2005.

Whilst at university, Wright was national vice chairman of Conservative Students and chairman of Exeter University Conservative Association. Before becoming the MP for Rugby & Kenilworth, he was chairman of Warwick & Leamington Conservative Association, and also served as a constituency vice chairman and ward chairman. At Westminster, Wright is chair of the Dementia APPG and a trustee of the Community Development Foundation, and he has also served on the Constitutional Affairs Select Committee. He has been an opposition whip since July 2007.

At the forthcoming general election, Wright will stand for the new seat of Kenilworth & Southam. This has a notional Conservative majority of nearly 11,000. Although the Commons will not be short of lawyers, Wright's relative youth should see him make his way to the front bench.

Tim Yeo

A Commons veteran and one of the great survivors on the Tory benches, Tim Yeo is much respected.

Yeo was educated at Charterhouse and won an open exhibition to Emmanuel College, Cambridge, where he studied history. Before entering Parliament he had a career in business, and he was also chief executive of Scope, a UK disability charity. He has also served as chairman of the Children's Trust and founded the Charities Tax Reform Group.

Yeo was elected to Parliament in 1983 and has continuously represented his South Suffolk seat since, having won six general elections. He served in the Thatcher and Major governments in the Home Office, FCO, Department of Health and Department of the Environment. He was a member of the shadow Cabinet from 1998 to 2005, holding ministerial posts in the Health, Education, Trade & Industry, Culture, Media & Sport, Agriculture and Environment teams. With special expertise in environmental issues, Yeo has been the chairman of the Commons Environmental Audit Committee since 2005.

Yeo's seat of South Suffolk has a Conservative majority of over 6,500. If the Tories need an expert on charities – or a safe pair of hands – he could get the call.

Sir George Young

Known as the 'bicycling baronet', Sir George Young was for many years the tallest MP – before the arrival of Daniel Kawczynski, who fractionally edged him out of the top position.

Young attended Eton and studied at Christ Church College, Oxford, and the University of Surrey. Before entering Parliament he worked with the National Economic Development Council, and he also worked as an economic advisor to the Post Office Corporation during the 1960s. He is married and has children and grandchildren.

Young started his political career as a councillor in the London Borough of Lambeth and as a GLC member for the London Borough of Ealing in the 1970s. Originally elected as the MP for Ealing Acton in 1974, he now represents North West Hampshire following the abolition of his original constituency in 1997. Having served in the House of Commons for more than thirty-five years, Young has held numerous posts in government and the shadow Cabinet. In particular, he was appointed Financial Secretary to the Treasury in July 1994 and was Transport Secretary from 1995 to 1997. More recently he has served as shadow Leader of the House and shadow Defence Secretary. He was elected chairman of the Select Committee on Standards and Privileges following the 2001 general election.

Young has a majority of over 12,500 for his seat. In June 2009 he once again narrowly missed out on his ambition to become the Speaker of the House of Commons, but ministerial rank might follow and might be an adequate compensation. Alan Duncan's fall from grace has seen him unexpectedly propelled back to centre stage as shadow Leader of the House.

The outer circle

These are the reinforcements which David Cameron and his team will need if the Conservatives are to win the next general election and form a government. They will need to capture at least 130 seats to have even a bare overall majority, and they will be looking to capture 150 in order to give themselves a decent working majority.

In this section of the book we look at the PPCs who are fighting seats where the Tories need to overturn the lowest percentage majorities to win. Some criterion has to be applied to draw up a list of target seats, and the percentage majority – as applied to the seats with their boundaries redrawn – is the most logical one to use.

However, these are not necessarily the seats where it will be easiest for the Tories to win. Other factors apply, such as whether the incumbent MP is standing again or is standing down. Another important factor is whether the seat is held by the Labour Party, or by a Lib Dem or a nationalist. With Labour having been in power for well over a decade, and having slumped in the opinion polls under Gordon Brown, it will be a great deal easier to unseat a Labour MP than to unseat one from another opposition party.

If a Tory PPC is up against an incumbent, then the reputation which that sitting MP has locally for being a good, hard-working MP is also an important factor. Most MPs claim to have a 'personal vote', and this can be worth anything from a few hundred to a few thousand votes. Normally incumbency is a big plus factor – especially when allied with the communications allowance, which has enabled sitting MPs in the 2005 parliament to publicise their work.

However, with few MPs entirely escaping the fallout from the expenses debacle, this normal advantage incumbency may be turned on its head. If the sitting MP is regarded as having abused their allowances, this will undoubtedly be picked up by the local papers and used by their political opponents. Since Labour is the governing party, and has far more MPs than any other party, the fallout from the expenses furore will hit it far harder than any other party.

Apart from the statistics, the author has also applied his own knowledge of the individuals and the seats. This has been built up over the years with his experience as someone who fought a seat – Edmonton – in 2005. This personal knowledge has also been built up at party conferences, at candidates' events, at selection meetings – and during his work as a public affairs consultant.

To be a PPC requires a lot of courage, a lot of resilience and a lot of self-belief. In the case of Conservative candidates it also often requires a lot of money. Apart from the £10,000 or so they will spend on the actual general election campaign, there is all the expense of 'nursing' a seat. This involves travelling to and from the constituency at least once a week, renting or buying a base there, and attending innumerable events – all of which involve a raffle. Gyles Brandreth tells the story about John Major that he always carried around the same blue raffle tickets in his breast pocket, so that when he was approached to buy some at an event he merely had to flourish the ones he had bought several years before.

Whether you buy raffle tickets or not, nursing a parliamentary seat as a Tory candidate is going to cost you about £10,000 a year – on top of the actual general election fighting fund. If you are lucky your Conservative Association might provide some of that money. If you are even luckier you might qualify for a grant from Lord Ashcroft's marginal seats fund. Generally, however, you have to find the bulk of the money yourself.

Which really does beg the question – why do they do it? This question is especially relevant as most Tory candidates will have to take a substantial pay cut if elected. The answer is that they do it for the honour, for the power

– and for the glory. Or at least they do it for the perception of all three, because in modern Parliaments backbenchers have precious little of any of these things.

Looking through the list of PPCs who are likely to win there are some real high flyers – people who have already had successful careers in politics, in the armed forces, in the voluntary sector or in business. There are also a very large number of candidates who have tremendously strong local roots, and many who have been (or still are) local councillors. There are few defining characteristics which mark out this cohort of candidates across the piece. That is not altogether surprising. The only criterion for becoming an MP is to really, really, really want to be one.

Other than the strong local links, there are (as ever) a lot of lawyers. There are quite a few 'professional' politicians as well – PPCs who have worked in public affairs, or for the party, or who have come through the increasingly professionalised councillor route. There are also quite a few soldiers – either full or part time – and a significant number who profess a strong religious faith.

Fortunately for the Tories, there are a good number of female candidates in winnable seats. There are also a reasonable number of candidates from the ethnic minorities and a respectable number of openly gay candidates. David Cameron's ambition – and the initial rationale behind the 'A-list' – was to have a parliamentary party which reflected the society it sought to represent. If the Tories do achieve a substantial swing, he should achieve that ambition.

One final defining characteristic is noticeable. These candidates are overwhelmingly Eurosceptic. With the odd exception, such as Jane Ellison, these PPCs, if elected, will have no truck with any further proposals for EU integration, and indeed they will be pushing very hard for the repatriation of powers. Some, undoubtedly, would happily see the UK leave the EU entirely.

For all of these reasons, whether the Tory majority is large or small, the whips will have problems with this intake. Most of them have strong local roots and local power bases, and many of them have strong professional backgrounds, especially in business and defence. This will make them resistant to unwelcome changes in these areas, and they will certainly be hardline on all policies relating to Europe.

In any event, as the leader and his whips are well aware, this huge new intake cannot be described as Cameron's children. They are, as Tim Montgomerie has pointed out, Thatcher's children. Many of them were inspired to enter politics by her, and they cut their political teeth under her leadership.

Because of their very strong local roots and connections with the armed forces this intake can also be described as the Yeomanry of England. And they are on the march, with a mission to capture Westminster in order to defend the interests of the people they live amongst and who they plan to represent robustly.

Nigel Adams

PPC for Selby & Ainsty

Notional status: Con 2,060

Tory target seat number: N/A

Swing required: N/A

conservatives@selbyandainsty.com

Born in 1966, Nigel Adams was raised in the Selby area and attended Selby High School. He is a governor of Selby High School and also Camblesforth Primary School. He plays cricket and is a Lord's Taverner. He is married and has four children.

Adams is a businessman who specialises in telecoms. He founded his own company at the age of twenty-six and is currently a director of two telecoms companies based in Yorkshire.

Having fought Rossendale & Darwen in 2005, Adams is now contesting Selby & Ainsty. Boundary changes have made this a notionally Conservative seat. The sitting Labour MP, John Grogan, is standing down.

Deirdre Alden

PPC for Birmingham Edgbaston

Notional status: Lab 1,555

Tory target seat number: 39

Swing required: 2.00%

deirdrealden@hotmail.com

Born in Buckinghamshire in 1952, Deirdre Alden was educated at Wycombe High School. She moved to Birmingham to study at the Birmingham School of Speech Training & Dramatic Art and has lived there ever since. She enjoys swimming, playing bridge and collecting curios. Her husband and son are both – like her – Birmingham city councillors. She chairs the council's Health Overview & Scrutiny Committee.

Alden has worked in the theatre and also for the Berlitz School of Languages. Apart from serving on the council Alden is also a freelance writer. She is president of MRSA Support.

Birmingham is an area where the Tories have done well in the past and need to do well this time if they are to form a government. Birmingham Edgbaston should certainly not be beyond their grasp.

Peter Aldous

PPC for Waveney

Notional status: Lab 5,950

Tory target seat number: 116

Swing required: 6.00%

peter.aldous@halesworth.net

Born in Ipswich in 1961, Peter Aldous has lived his whole life in Suffolk and is very much a local boy.

By profession he is a chartered surveyor. He worked for Strutt & Parker before becoming a partner in the family firm. He has been both a Waveney district councillor and a Suffolk county councillor. He was deputy leader of the Conservative group on Suffolk County Council.

Aldous fought Waveney in 2005, and with the Tories riding much higher in the opinion polls he will be hoping to succeed this time around.

Philip Allott

PPC for Halifax

Notional status: Lab 3,481

Tory target seat number: 80

Swing required: 4.38%

allott4halifax@tiscali.co.uk

Philip Allott has been connected with Halifax since his childhood. A Yorkshireman, he spent his younger years helping his father raise thousands of pounds for charity with family-owned racehorses. Having acquired a degree in law, he then went on to set up his own business, a PR and marketing company which specialises in manufacturing, food and education. He is married and has two children – both studying at Oxford University.

In 2006 Allott ran the PR part of a successful campaign to free the Yorkshire-born Mirza Tahir Hussain from death row in Pakistan. In 2007 his book *The Donkeyman* was published, going on to receive critical acclaim both on television and radio. In 2007 he made a speech on law and order at the Conservative Party conference, calling for more police officers. Allott also has a strong track record in local government, having been a former Conservative council group leader and a past mayor in Knaresborough.

In 2005 Allott contested the marginal seat of Bolton West, where he achieved a rare 4.2 per cent Labour to Conservative swing, whilst also reducing the Lib Dem vote by 0.5 per cent. He has a much better chance of succeeding this time around.

Dr Ken Andrew

PPC for Carshalton & Wallington

Notional status: Lib Dem 1,225

Tory target seat number: 26

Swing required: 1.47%

ken@kenandrew.com

Ken Andrew grew up in Tottenham and has spent most of his life in London. Widowed in 2002, he has two sons by his late wife. He now lives with his partner Pamela in Wallington. He is a keen tennis player and enjoys swimming and movies. He has had three books published, one of which made it into the list of top ten non-fiction bestsellers. He has a keen interest in alternative cultures and has travelled throughout the world.

Andrew has always been a businessman and has chaired a public company. He has also been a school governor in Carshalton and has served on the boards of two NHS hospital trusts. He has also served on the board of the British Refugees Housing Committee and as a council member of the IMC Business School.

Politically, Andrew was a candidate in Carshalton & Wallington at the 2005 general election, where he was able to cut the Lib Dem majority to little over 1,000. Despite not succeeding in 2005, Andrew has continued to work with local residents over issues such as schooling, housing, tackling yobbish behaviour and social security and planning applications.

Stuart Andrew

PPC for Pudsey

Notional status: Lab 5,204

Tory target seat number: 111

Swing required: 5.87%

stuart.andrew@leeds.gov.uk

Born in 1971 in Bangor, Stuart Andrew lived for the first few years of his life in the famous village of Llanfairpwllgwyngyllgogerychwyrndrobwllllantysili-ogogogoch on the Isle of Anglesey. After school, he moved into a career in the charity and voluntary sector, where he worked as a fundraiser for the British Heart Foundation. Since the BHF, he has worked at the Hope House children's hospice and the East Lancashire Hospice, and he is now in charge of the fund-raising team at Martin House in Yorkshire, which manages to raise more than £3 million a year.

Andrew served on Leeds City Council after he was successful in winning the Labour-held seat of Aireborough. He now represents the Guiseley & Rawdon ward after boundary changes. He is a member of the Planning Panel and campaigns against excessive development projects. Currently Stuart is the lead member for the Development Department with a responsibility for transport policy in the city. In 1997 he stood for Parliament in Wrexham.

Andrew lives in his ward of Rawdon, where he enjoys walking his dogs on Rawdon Billing, socialising with friends and exercising at the gym.

Tim Archer

PPC for Poplar & Limehouse
Notional status: Lab 3,823
Tory target seat number: 103
Swing required: 5.42%
tim@tarcher.fsbusiness.co.uk

Born in Sutton in 1974, Tim Archer attended schools in south London. His father, born in the East End, moved to Bermondsey after being forced to leave his home due to the war. Archer lives in the Poplar & Limehouse constituency on the Isle of Dogs with his wife Jane.

Archer studied economics and politics at the University of Bath. Since graduating he has worked for a major UK bank and is currently an area director. Archer has also completed a degree in financial services and is an associate of the Institute of Financial Services. On top of this, he is a school governor of a Tower Hamlets primary school and is a trustee of the Isle of Dogs Community Foundation.

Archer is at present the Conservative councillor for the Blackwall & Cubitt Town ward on Tower Hamlets Council, where he is also the deputy leader of the Conservative group. He has stood in local elections in Tower Hamlets for many years. In 2002 he stood in the Blackwall & Cubitt Town by-election, where he was defeated by just ten votes. Archer was also the PPC for Poplar & Canning Town in 2005, where he achieved the largest Labour to Conservative swing anywhere in the country and halved the Labour majority.

Louise Bagshawe

PPC for Corby
Notional status: Lab 1,517
Tory target seat number: 28
Swing required: 1.56%
louise4corby@aol.com

Born in 1971 in London, Louise Bagshawe's family moved to the country when she was seven. She has three children, and in her spare time she enjoys travel and reading.

Having attended local Catholic schools Bagshawe went on to study English at Oxford University. She was secretary of the Oxford Union and she achieved the title of Young Poet of the Year at the age of eighteen. On graduating, she became a writer of popular fiction and has since published a range of bestsellers, after having spent a time working for the PR firm Biss Lancaster.

Bagshawe joined the Young Conservatives at the age of fourteen, but then joined the Labour Party for a few years. She has served as an Association officer and has been a primary school governor. She has also been involved in several charities. Since her selection in Corby & East Northamptonshire in 2006, she has had involvement in both local and national election campaigns. She also helped her mother, Daphne, get elected to East Sussex County Council.

The Tories should definitely capture this seat, and Bagshawe is one to watch – she will presumably campaign in poetry, but govern in prose.

Shaun Bailey

PPC for Hammersmith
Notional status: Lab 3,673
Tory target seat number: 78
Swing required: 4.22%
shaun@shaunbailey.co.uk

Born in 1971 and brought up on the North Kensington estates, Shaun Bailey has made tackling the problems associated with deprivation his life's work. He worked at the Trocadero and as a security guard at Wembley Stadium in order to pay his way through South Bank University.

Bailey set up My Generation, a charity dedicated to combating the problems of young people and their families. He is also a drug rehabilitation worker and chair of the Pepperpot day centre for the elderly.

Hammersmith is a new constituency but eminently winnable for the Tories. Bailey is a powerful speaker, and as one of the Tories' few black candidates will be a very welcome addition to their parliamentary ranks.

Harriett Baldwin

PPC for West Worcestershire
Notional status: Con 3,053
Tory target seat number: N/A
Swing required: N/A
harriett@harriettbaldwin.com

Harriett Baldwin is the daughter of a retired magistrate and a retired headmaster. She grew up in the village of Felsted in Essex. She is married to Jim, who is a businessman and television producer. They have two daughters and a son, the youngest of whom was born in 1995. The family have an interest in country life, animals, canal boats, walking and bicycle rides.

Baldwin was educated at the Friends' School in Saffron Walden and at Marlborough College. She went on to read modern languages at Oxford, where she received a first-class honours degree. After leaving Oxford, Baldwin achieved an MBA from McGill University in Canada.

Since graduating Baldwin has had a twenty-year career in finance and has been on the National Council of Business for Sterling. In 2005 she helped to publish a pamphlet for the Centre for Political Studies entitled *Leviathan Is Still at Large*. Baldwin is also a fundraiser for the CSJ, as well as being involved in several charities such as Make Poverty History and Working Families.

In 2005 Baldwin fought Stockton North for the Conservatives, where she managed a 3.6 per cent swing. This time around she is fighting a seat currently held by the retiring Tory grandee Sir Michael Spicer, and despite the promise of a strong local campaign from the Lib Dems she is virtually assured of success.

Stephen Barclay

PPC for North East Cambridgeshire

Notional status: Con 7,726

Tory target seat number: N/A

Swing required: N/A

necca1@tory.org

Born in 1972, Steve Barclay was raised in the Lancashire town of Lytham St Annes. His life there was dominated by Fylde Rugby Club, where he progressed from the Under-7s up to the 1st XV. Married to Karen, Barclay enjoys rugby, playing the jazz piano and skydiving.

After a local education, Barclay was commissioned as a second lieutenant in the Royal Regiment of Fusiliers. On leaving the Army, he went to study history at Cambridge and subsequently law at the College of Law in Chester. He became a qualified solicitor and then moved into financial services at a range of large organisations.

Barclay made his first parliamentary venture in the safe Labour seat of Manchester Blackley in 1997, followed in 2001 by the marginal seat of Lancaster & Wyre. He managed to win more than 22,000 votes, reducing the Labour majority to a mere 481. In 2005 he became a special advisor to the Conservative Party chairman. In January 2008 Barclay was selected to stand in the Conservative seat of North East Cambridgeshire, in place of the retiring Malcolm Moss.

As a fellow board member of the Enterprise Forum the author can vouch for his intelligence and drive. Equipped with Clooney-esque good looks and a safe seat, Barclay will rise through the ranks very quickly.

Gavin Barwell

PPC for Croydon Central

Notional status: Con 328

Tory target seat number: N/A

Swing required: N/A

gavin@gavin4croydon.com

Born in 1972, Gavin Barwell was brought up in Shirley, Croydon. He was educated at Trinity School and at Cambridge University. He is married with two children, lives in Croydon and is a governor of a local school.

Barwell is a former Conservative Party director of operations. He currently runs his own consultancy, but combines this with being involved with the Tory Party's marginal seats campaign. He has been a Croydon councillor for many years and is currently responsible for the local authority's finances and customer service.

In the run-up to the 2005 general election Barwell was the candidate for Sutton & Cheam, but had to pull out because of a family illness. This time around he is inheriting a seat from the Tory Andrew Pelling, who is standing down. Barwell will not allow this opportunity to pass him by – he will be elected and he will be a great asset to the New Conservative government.

Guto Bebb

PPC for Aberconwy

Notional status: Lab 1,070

Tory target seat number: 37

Swing required: 1.96%

aberconwyconservatives@yahoo.co.uk

Guto Bebb was born in Wrexham in 1968. With strong roots in north Wales, his family has lived in places ranging from Bangor to Blaenau Ffestiniog. After attending three different primary schools, Bebb was educated at Ysgol Syr Hugh Owen and went on to the University of Wales, Aberystwyth. Married to Esyllt, the couple have five children. Bebb is a keen reader and record collector.

Bebb's career has been in development consultancy. Initially working for the Egin Partnership, he has been self-employed since 1993 after establishing his own consultancy, Innovas Wales. He has also been a partner in a public house and in his wife's bookshop.

Bebb was reselected to the new constituency of Aberconwy after a strong performance in the constituency in 2005. He managed to halve the Labour majority with a 5 per cent Labour to Conservative swing. The sitting Labour MP, Betty Williams, is standing down.

Jake Berry

PPC for Rossendale & Darwen

Notional status: Lab 3,696

Tory target seat number: 77

Swing required: 4.18%

jake@jakeberry.org

Jake Berry was born in Liverpool in 1978 and was schooled in the city. He continued his education at Sheffield University, where he studied law, and then Chester College of Law for his Law Society finals. Berry lives with his partner Charlotte. In their spare time they both enjoy walking and water skiing.

After training as a solicitor in London Berry moved back to the north-west to work for a law firm in Manchester, where he specialises in commercial property. He is also a shareholder in Tung Sing Housing Association.

Berry has been a candidate in two local elections in Liverpool and Manchester. He was also the election agent for the Liverpool City Seats Initiative at the 2005 general election.

Tom Biggins

PPC for Telford

Notional Status: Lab 5,651

Tory target seat number: 143

Swing required: 7.50%

toriesintelford@ukonline.co.uk

Born in 1960 and raised in Whitchurch, Tom Biggins now lives in Telford. He went to local schools before going on to Oxford University. His family are local cheese factors and Biggins went into the family business. His hobbies are wildlife and the countryside, and local history.

Biggins has been a Conservative Association chairman, and in the 2001 and 2005 general elections he stood for the Tories in Clwyd South. He is also a Shropshire county councillor. The Tories are resurgent in this area, and with his strong local roots Biggins will be looking to make it third time lucky.

Andrew Bingham

PPC for High Peak

Notional status: Lab 1,750

Tory target seat number: 35

Swing required: 1.90%

hpca@tory.org

Born in Buxton in High Peak in 1962, Andrew Bingham has never left the area. He attended Long Lane School in Chapel-en-le-Frith. He lives in Chapel (at the heart of High Peak) with his wife Jayne. He loves sport, particularly cricket and football and follows Buxton FC. He also enjoys cooking.

After school Bingham pursued a career in business. He set up a company supplying engineering equipment to companies all over the north-west. Bingham was first elected to High Peak Borough Council in 1999. After the council changed control in 2003, he became the chairman of the Social Inclusion & Community Select Committee, and he is also the chairman of the Development Plan Select Committee. He sits on many sub-committees looking at areas such as youth provision and housing.

In 2005 Bingham was the Conservative candidate at the general election, but narrowly lost by 735 votes. This time around Bingham is again fighting High Peak, and despite adverse boundary changes he can expect to win.

Bob Blackman

PPC for Harrow East
Notional status: Lab 2,934
Tory target seat number: 64
Swing required: 3.44%
harroweastconservatives@btopenworld.com

Having been brought up around Wembley, Bob Blackman went to Preston Manor High School, where he became head boy. He went on to Liverpool University, where he was voted president of the Students' Union. Blackman is married to Nicola and they live in Wembley. He takes a keen interest in football and is a Tottenham Hotspur fan. He also enjoys listening to and collecting rock music, reading, bridge and chess.

After graduation Blackman went to work in sales for Burroughs Machines, and then Unisys, before moving on to BT, where he has held several positions in both sales and management. He is now a sales tutor at the BT Training College.

In 2004 Blackman was elected to the London Assembly for Brent & Harrow, and he was Conservative group whip. He has also been councillor for the Preston ward in Brent for twenty years and leader of Brent Conservatives since 1990. Between 1991 and 1996 he was also leader of Brent council. Blackman has run for Parliament on three previous occasions: in 1992 he contested Brent South, in 1997 he tried his luck in Bedford & Kempston, and most recently in 2005 he managed a 7.1 per cent swing to the Conservatives in Brent North. This time around he is standing in Harrow East. A seasoned campaigner, Blackman should win – and, having finally achieved his ambition of being an MP, he will be very hard to dislodge.

Nicola Blackwood

PPC for Oxford West & Abingdon

Notional status: Lib Dem 6,816

Tory target seat number: 130

Swing required: 6.71%

nicola.blackwood@oxfordshireconservatives.com

Born in Johannesburg in 1979, Nicola Blackwood nevertheless has strong connections with Oxford. She spent her early years in Charlbury, where her parents worked for the Oxfordshire NHS. She has been educated in Oxford from GCSE to the DPhil in Music she is currently researching.

A member of the Conservative Party Human Rights Commission, Blackwood spent the 2005 general election as a volunteer with the Political Unit in the CRD and the CCHQ press office – whilst also finding time to help run the Slough Conservative campaign office. In the 2006 Oxford City Council elections she was the candidate for Jericho & Osney. Blackwood has also spent the past year as parliamentary researcher to Andrew Mitchell, shadow Secretary of State for International Development, putting her knowledge of the developing world to good effect.

Fighting Oxford West & Abingdon this time around, Blackwood will need to succeed if the Tories are to gain a substantial majority. The fact that her constituency borders that of David Cameron should help her cause.

Nicholas Boles

PPC for Grantham & Stamford

Notional status: Con 7,308

Tory target seat number: N/A

Swing required: N/A

nick.boles@conservatives.com

Born in 1965, Nicholas Boles was educated at Winchester College. He went on to read PPE at Oxford University.

Boles has had a varied – and mostly successful – career. He founded a decorating supplies company and was central to the formation of David Cameron's favourite think tank, Policy Exchange. He was a Westminster city councillor between 1998 and 2002 and chair of the key Housing Committee. When Boris Johnson stormed in as mayor of London, he appointed Boles as his interim chief of staff. He is now working closely with Francis Maude on the party's Implementation Team, which is mapping out the party's strategy following the general election.

In 2005 Boles narrowly failed to capture Hove for the Tories. This time around he is fighting Grantham & Stamford, the seat of Quentin Davies – who defected from the Tories to Labour. The seat is iconic, as it is Margaret Thatcher's birthplace. This time around Boles will succeed, and the party will undoubtedly make full use of his intellectual powers.

Karen Bradley

PPC for Staffordshire Moorlands
Notional status: Con 1,618
Tory target seat number: N/A
Swing required: N/A
staffsmoorlands@tory.org

Born in Staffordshire Moorlands in 1970, Karen Bradley spent her early years living in Cheddleton before moving to Buxton, where her parents ran a pub. Married to Neil with two sons, Bradley enjoys cooking and reading, and she is also a keen traveller.

Bradley attended local comprehensive Buxton Girls' School before moving to study mathematics at Imperial College, London. Upon graduating, Bradley trained as a chartered accountant and tax advisor, qualifications she has used to help numerous businesses.

Describing herself as a 'couch Conservative' until 2002, it was not until she worked as a technical advisor to the shadow Treasury team that she became fully involved with politics. With new-found enthusiasm and after much campaign work she was rewarded in 2005 when she was given the chance to run as the PPC for Manchester Withington. Prior to 2005 she worked in the Conservative Policy Unit, where she helped to develop economic and fiscal policies.

Standing in Staffordshire Moorlands this time around Bradley should almost certainly succeed – and her financial expertise will be invaluable to the Tory Treasury team.

Angie Bray

PPC for Ealing Central & Acton
Notional status: Lab 839
Tory target seat number: 18
Swing required: 1.08%
help@angiebray.org.uk

Angie Bray was born in Croydon in 1953. She lives in west London (where she returned after graduation from St Andrews University) with her partner Nigel. Outside politics, her interests include cinema, history and playing tennis. Her real passion in life is music, and she plays both the organ and the piano. Before politics, Bray was a radio broadcaster. She worked for British Forces Broadcasting in Gibraltar before moving back to London to work for LBC Radio.

In May 2000 Bray was elected to represent London West Central on the London Assembly. She stayed in the role until 2008, when she stood down. From July 2006 until September 2007 she was also leader of the Conservative group. In 1997 she was the PPC for East Ham. In the past, Bray has also served as chairman of the Conservative Political Forum for the Kensington & Chelsea Conservative Association and she is currently vice president of the Hammersmith & Fulham Conservative Association.

Bray is contesting Ealing Central & Acton, which she should win comfortably. One of the more experienced female candidates standing for a winnable Tory seat, she should be a great asset to the party in the next parliament.

Andrew Bridgen

PPC for North West Leicestershire

Notional status: Lab 4,477

Tory target seat number: 90

Swing required: 4.75%

andrew.bridgen@abproduce.co.uk

Born in 1964 in Burton upon Trent, Andrew Bridgen attended Netherseal Junior School and then the Pingle School at Swadlincote. He went to study genetics and behaviour at Nottingham University. Married to Jacqueline with two young sons, Bridgen is interested in rugby, military history, skiing, fishing and other country activities.

After university, Bridgen trained as an officer in the Royal Marines. At the age of twenty-three he changed paths completely, returning home to help with the family market gardening business. In 1988 he and his brother formed AB Produce, a company which produces pre-prepared potatoes and vegetables and employs more than 230 staff. He has received accolades such as Young Executive of the Year UK and Young Director of the Year (Midlands) for medium-sized businesses.

Bridgen was the East Midlands chairman of the Institute of Directors and also served on the East Midlands Regional Assembly, where he acted as a business representative. As the PPC for North West Leicestershire Bridgen has a fight on his hands, but if the Tories are to have a majority they must win seats such as this. The current Labour MP, David Taylor, is standing down.

Jeremy Brier

PPC for Luton North
Notional status: Lab 6,439
Tory target seat number: 159
Swing Required: 8.18%
jeremyforluton@hotmail.co.uk

Jeremy Brier was born in Watford in 1980 and comes from a family who were not Conservative supporters or voters. Both of his parents worked in the public sector, and he has a disabled sister who requires a great deal of time and care.

At Christ's College, Cambridge, Brier became actively involved in Conservative politics. After graduating, he was called to the Bar and he still practises as a barrister. He has won the World Debating Championships.

Brier is a first-time Parliamentary candidate contesting the slightly more difficult of the two Luton seats – although it was Tory up until 1997.

Steve Brine

PPC for Winchester
Notional status: Lib Dem 6,524
Tory target seat number: 122
Swing required: 6.37%
campaign@stevebrine.com

Born in 1974 in Guildford, Steve Brine lives in Winchester with his wife, a speech and language therapist. He follows football and is a keen golfer.

Brine was educated at Bohunt Comprehensive School. He went on to Highbury College in Portsmouth and then read history at the University of Liverpool. He served a sabbatical year as president of the Students' Union.

After university Brine went into radio, working for a number of local BBC stations, and also had a spell at the CRD. He worked as a freelance journalist, and spent some time in the United States at WGN radio in Chicago. He went on to work for a consultancy specialising in customer care and personnel development. He is now a director of a marketing firm specialising in the golf industry.

Brine has an uphill struggle contesting Winchester for the Tories, but with current Lib Dem MP Mark Oaten stepping down, he might just make it.

Robert Buckland

PPC for South Swindon
Notional status: Lab 1,493
Tory target seat number: 32
Swing required: 1.75%
contact@swindonconservatives.com

Robert Buckland was born in 1968 in Llanelli and educated at St Michael's School in the same town. He then went to Hatfield College, Durham, where he was elected as president of the Durham Union. Married to Sian with twins, Buckland includes music and watching rugby, football and cricket amongst his hobbies.

After university he qualified as a barrister in 1991 and has specialised in criminal law and confiscation of the proceeds of crime. Buckland also helps to organise the Bar Schools Mock Trials Competition, and spends time speaking about careers in law in schools and colleges around the country.

Buckland has been a county councillor and was a governor at his old primary school. Currently he is a governor of Ridgeway School in Wroughton, near Swindon. In the 2005 general election Buckland managed a hefty 6.9 per cent swing towards the Conservatives, finishing slightly behind Labour by 1,353 votes. Again contesting South Swindon this time round, with very little by way of boundary changes, he should easily avoid the disappointment of another second place.

Conor Burns

PPC for Bournemouth West
Notional status: Con 2,766
Tory target seat number: N/A
Swing required: N/A
conor@localconservatives.com

Born in 1972 in Belfast, Conor Burns moved with his family to Hertfordshire in 1980. Burns's interests include biographies, swimming, going to the gym and trekking the countryside. He is also a big fan of snooker.

After being educated in St Albans, Burns moved on to Southampton University, where he obtained a degree in modern history and politics. After university, he moved into the communications and finance sectors, where he has worked for the information provider DeHavilland and the financial services firm Zurich. Voluntary work includes being on the board of the Spitfire Tribute Foundation, and he also works with several other charities.

Having become politically involved at school, Burns was elected as chairman of the Southampton University Conservative Association in 1992. In 1999 he became a member of Southampton City Council and immediately became housing and urban regeneration spokesman. Burns was selected to fight the Eastleigh constituency in 1999. He went on to fight both the 2001 and 2005 general elections, the last time missing out by just 568 votes to the leading Lib Dem Chris Huhne.

Fighting Bournemouth West this time (where he replaces retiring Tory MP Sir John Butterfill), Burns will finally prevail. An astute operator with a strong political pedigree, and a friend of Lady Thatcher's, he will prosper in the new parliament.

Dan Byles

PPC for North Warwickshire
Notional status: Lab 6,684
Tory target seat number: 145
Swing required: 7.62%
mail@danielbyles.com

Born in 1974 in Hastings to a single mother, Dan Byles went to Warwick School under the Assisted Places Scheme. He then became the first member of his family to go to university, obtaining a degree in economics and management studies from the University of Leeds.

After university Byles joined the Army, serving first with the Light Infantry and then with the Royal Army Medical Corps. He saw active service in Kosovo, Bosnia and Iraq. When he left the Army he was the youngest serving major at the age of just twenty-seven. He holds two Guinness world records, for rowing across the Atlantic and for trekking to the North Pole. He married his Indian wife in two ceremonies in the UK and in India.

Byles has proved his ability and his perseverance, but he has an equally tough opponent in Labour's Mike O'Brien.

Alun Cairns

PPC for Vale of Glamorgan
Notional status: Lab 1,574
Tory target seat number: 31
Swing required: 1.68%
alun@aluncairns.com

Born in Swansea in 1970 and brought up in Clydach, Alun Cairns was schooled at Ysgol Gynradd Gymraeg Pontardawe and Ysgol Ddwyieithog Ystalyfera. He is married to Emma and they have one son. In his spare time he enjoys cycling and gardening and regularly takes part in charity cycling events.

Before being elected to the Welsh Assembly, Cairns worked for the Lloyds

Bank Group and gained extensive experience in the business sector. Cairns also has an MBA and specialises in corporate location and inward investment. In 1999 he was elected to the assembly as AM for South Wales West, and he was then re-elected in both 2003 and 2007. He has been the party's spokesman on economic development and transport, shadow Education Minister and shadow Local Government Minister. In 2009 he was appointed shadow Chief Whip and shadow Heritage Minister. On top of this, he is a former spokesman on education and the economy and has also been chair of the Assembly's Finance Committee.

In 1997 Cairns stood for Parliament in Gower. In 2005 he stood for the Vale of Glamorgan seat which he will be fighting again this time. The Tories are resurgent in Wales, having won the popular vote in the 2009 European Parliament elections. Winning seats like this will boost their credibility outside England – and will boost their majority. The sitting Labour MP, John Smith, is standing down.

Darren Caplan

PPC for Hackney North & Stoke Newington

Notional status: Lab 8,002

Tory target seat number: N/A

Swing required: N/A

darren@hackneyconservatives.com

Darren Caplan was born in London in 1973 and has spent much of his life since then living in north London. He helps to run an amateur Sunday morning football club which seeks to recruit players from London's diverse communities. His wife Jo-Anne Nadler has written a series of books on the Tory Party and a biography of William Hague.

Graduating from Birmingham University, Caplan has worked for the Conservative Party before moving to specialise in communications and public affairs. Currently, he is director of public affairs for Brands2Life, a communications agency. He is a member of the Association of Professional Political Consultants management committee and vice chairman of the Public Relations Consultancy Association's public affairs group. Caplan is also a member of the Chartered Institute of Public Relations.

Standing in Hackney North & Stoke Newington, Caplan has got a massive task confronting him – but he is certainly one to watch for the future.

Neil Carmichael

PPC for Stroud

Notional status: Lab 996

Tory target seat number: 15

Swing required: 0.93%

n.l.carmichael@dial.pipex.com

Born in 1961, Neil Carmichael went to St Peter's School in York before going on to study politics at Nottingham University. He is married with three children and lives in Stroud.

Starting out as a livestock farmer, Carmichael moved on to set up his own property management company, specialising in overseas investments. It also provides advice on PFI schemes and planning issues. He has also been a visiting lecturer at the University of Sunderland.

Carmichael contested Leeds East in the 1992 general election and Stroud at both the 2001 and the 2005 general elections. Contesting Stroud again this time around, he must feel that he has finally got the seat within his grasp.

Joanne Cash

PPC for Westminster North

Notional status: Lab 2,120

Tory target seat number: 61

Swing required: 3.30%

joanne@westminsternorthconservatives.com

Born in Portadown, Joanne Cash attended Banbridge Academy. She went on to read English at Lady Margaret Hall, Oxford. She is now a leading barrister in the field of libel and privacy law at One Brick Court. She acts as a consultant to the Policy Exchange think tank.

Cash is a regular commentator on legal issues both on television and radio – having appeared on shows such as *GMTV*, *Newsnight* and *This Morning* and on Radio 4. She has launched STEP UP in Westminster North, with the target of cutting crime and encouraging social mobility, and she is a member of many local charities. She also supports the All Stars boxing gym, as well as Real Action and the Butterfly Reading Group, groups aimed at helping the younger members of her constituency.

Standing in the newly created seat of Westminster North, Cash should get elected and will without doubt be one of the stars of the new intake. She typifies the new breed of Tories who are committed to social action.

Rehman Chishti

PPC for Gillingham & Rainham

Notional status: Lab 15

Tory target seat number: 1

Swing required: 0.02%

raychishti@hotmail.com

Having been born in Pakistan in 1978, Rehman Chishti moved to Kent and has lived there most of his life. He attended Richmond Infant School, Napier Primary School and Fort Luton High School for Boys before going on to Rainham Mark Grammar School and Chatham Grammar School. He did a law degree at the University of Wales, Aberystwyth and on graduation in 2000 was called to the Bar at Lincoln's Inn. He is currently working as a barrister in London.

Chishti is a keen sportsman. He captained Hempstead youth cricket team and went on to represent Medway and Kent Schools at cricket. He is also a keen runner and has completed many half-marathons, raising money for charity.

Chishti was a Labour councillor on Medway Council in 2003. Since 2007 he has also been a Cabinet member for Community Safety & Enforcement for the Conservatives. He worked as special advisor to Francis Maude whilst he was chairman of the Conservative Party, and was for a time special cricket advisor to the late Benazir Bhutto, the former Prime Minister of Pakistan.

In 2005 Chishti contested Horsham for the Labour Party. Having defected to the Tories in 2006, he has been rewarded with the opportunity to contest Gillingham & Rainham – which should be a shoo-in.

Jeffrey Clarke

PPC for Wirral South

Notional status: Lab 3,538

Tory target seat number: 87

Swing required: 4.65%

j.clarke@chester.gov.uk

Jeff Clarke was born in 1962. He lives in Chester with his wife and children. He read law and economics at Keele University.

A practising barrister, Clarke specialises in criminal law, with much of his work in Wirral and Liverpool. Clarke served as a city councillor for five years, but stepped down in March 2009 to concentrate on his campaign for Parliament, having been selected as the candidate for Wirral South in 2007. Clarke has already been involved in many local campaigns, including those for the reinstatement of school patrol crossings and to stop the closure of local post offices.

Having previously been a Liberal Democrat, Clarke was lured over to the Tories by David Cameron. The sitting Labour MP, Ben Chapman, is standing down.

Mark Clarke

PPC for Tooting

Notional status: 5,169

Tory target seat number: 118

Swing required: 6.09%

mark@markclarke.net

Mark Clarke was born in London in 1977. He moved to Tooting at a young age when his mother went to work at St George's Hospital. His family then moved to neighbouring Balham, where Clarke still lives. In his spare time Clarke follows cricket, inspired by his grandfather, who played for the West Indies. He also enjoys skiing.

Clarke read ancient, medieval and modern history at the University of Durham before moving into brand management with Procter & Gamble. He worked there for five years, including spells in Newcastle and Switzerland. He then joined the Boston Consultancy Group as a strategy consultant and now runs his own consultancy business.

Clarke has been involved with the Conservative Party since before university, having spent a gap year working for the party and a think tank. At Durham he ran the University Conservative Association. After graduating he became the chairman of Conservative Future, the youth wing of the Conservative Party.

The Conservatives selected Clarke by means of an open primary election which was open to all Tooting residents. Defeating the Tooting incumbent, Sadiq Khan, will be a tall order. However, Clarke's campaign is being supported by Greg Smith, who orchestrated a 7.35 per cent swing from Labour to the Conservatives in Hammersmith & Fulham, so a Tory gain is possible.

Damian Collins

PPC for Folkestone & Hythe

Notional status: Con 12,446

Tory target seat number: N/A

Swing required: N/A

damian@damiancollins.com

Born in 1974 in Northampton, Damian Collins was educated at St Mary's High School and Belmont Abbey School in Herefordshire. He attended St Benet's Hall, Oxford, where he graduated with a degree in modern history in 1996. Married to Sarah with a daughter, Collins is a keen sports fan. He particularly enjoys football, cricket and rugby union. Outside sport, he enjoys cooking and walking.

In 1995 Collins was the president of the Oxford University Conservative Association and, on graduating, went on to join the CRD. In 1998 he joined the newly created Political Operations Department as media officer for the Foreign Affairs and Agriculture shadow Cabinet teams. An active member of the Bow Group, he was its political officer in 2003 and 2004.

After university, Collins moved into the advertising and communications industry, where he joined the M&C Saatchi advertising agency in London. Currently, he is the MD of Influence Communications Ltd, which he established in 2005. The company specialises in social and political issues campaigns.

In 2005, Collins was the PPC for Northampton North. In 2006 he fought off a huge field to inherit Michael Howard's seat of Folkestone & Hythe. A terrific communicator and campaigner, Collins will do very well in the next parliament.

Oliver Colvile

PPC for Plymouth Sutton & Devonport

Notional status: Lab, 4,472

Tory target seat number: 105

Swing required: 5.56%

oliver.colvile@ukonline.co.uk

Oliver Colvile was born in Guildford in 1959 into a naval family. Both his father and grandfather served in the Royal Navy, whilst his uncle commanded the Royal Marine garrison at Stonehouse.

Colvile is a governor of St Andrew's Primary School and works with Plymouth Cricket Club, where he is a vice president. He is also a member of the Barbican Arts Centre, and he plays at the Stonehouse Lawn Tennis Club. He is also a Plymouth Albion Rugby Club season ticket holder. He is also a senior counsel at Lexington Communications.

Having previously worked as an agent for the Conservative Party, Colvile moved on to set up his own communication business, Oliver Colvile & Associates. This specialises in regeneration and development throughout England. He is also a member of the Federation of Small Businesses and the Institute of Directors.

In 2001 and 2005 Colvile was the Conservative candidate for Plymouth Sutton, where he managed to cut Labour's majority from 9,500 to 4,305. This time around Colvile will be contesting Plymouth Sutton & Devonport. The author sits on the board of the Enterprise Forum with Colvile, where he is an affable and energetic colleague. His strong naval background and his political experience should help him to prevail.

Richard Cook

PPC for East Renfrewshire
Notional status: Lab 6,657
Tory target seat number: 138
Swing required: 7.02%
richard.cook@eastrentories.co.uk

Born in 1973 and raised in the constituency, Richard Cook is married and still lives in the area. He was educated at Carolside Primary School and Williamswood Secondary School. He is keen on sports, particularly golf and tennis.

By profession Cook is a commercial manager for Biffa Waste Services, and takes an active interest in the policy aspects of recycling and waste management. He is also a member of the Institute for Sales and Marketing Management.

Politically Cook has written policy papers for the Conservatives and contributed to *The Blue Book*. He is a vice chairman of the Conservative Party in Scotland, and has stood for Glasgow Cathcart in both Scottish Parliament and Westminster Parliament elections. In 2005 he fought in the more fertile territory of East Renfrewshire, and he is standing there again this time around.

Mark Coote

PPC for Cheltenham
Notional status: Lib Dem 316
Tory target seat number: 6
Swing required: 0.33%
mark@markcoote.co.uk

Born in Hartlepool in 1961, Mark Coote grew up in Cheltenham, and he was educated at Leckhampton Primary School and then Cheltenham Grammar School. He still lives in Cheltenham, and enjoys travelling, walking, gardening and wine collecting. He also has a strong interest in music.

After graduating from Nottingham University, Coote was a teacher of history and politics for twenty years. He was then appointed director of development and marketing at the City of London School for Girls. At present, Coote is the director of community fundraising for Cancer Research UK.

Coote first became involved with politics at the age of fifteen, when he became vice chairman of Cheltenham Young Conservatives. At university he was elected as the president of the Nottingham University Conservative Association. In the general elections of 2001 and 2005 Coote fought the Labour-held seat of Hastings & Rye before being selected to fight Cheltenham in the next general election. He has also been special advisor to a former shadow Home Secretary and a former shadow Secretary of State for Education. Since

1999 he has maintained Ann Widdecombe's website, 'The Widdy Web'. This time around he has the task of unseating the Lib Dem MP Martin Horwood.

Alberto Costa

PPC for Angus

Notional status: SNP 1,601

Tory target seat number: 41

Swing required: 2.10%

alberto.costa@scottishconservatives.com

Alberto Costa was born in 1971 in Carlisle. His parents moved from Italy to the UK in 1967, and he was raised, educated and has worked in Glasgow. He is married and has a young daughter.

Costa attended the University of Glasgow, where he graduated with an MA LLB. At university he was president of the Students' Representative Council from 1995 to 1996. He is now a dual-qualified Scottish and English solicitor, having worked in Glasgow, Edinburgh, the USA and London.

Costa is standing in Angus, where he is up against the SNP MP Mike Weir. A lot will depend on the SNP's standing as the Scottish government – if they suffer mid-term blues Costa could be heading south to Westminster.

Tracey Crouch

PPC for Chatham & Aylesford

Notional status: Lab 3,289

Tory target seat number: 74

Swing required: 4.13%

tracey@traceycrouch.co.uk

Tracey Crouch was born in Kent in 1975 and went to local schools. The daughter of a social worker and insurance broker, she went on to study law at Hull University. In her spare time Crouch enjoys sports, recently having retired from playing football. She now has an FA coaching qualification. Outside sports, Crouch spends her time reading, travelling, listening to music and eating.

On graduation she started work for various MPs, most notably Michael Howard. She also worked as chief of staff to Damian Green as shadow Education Secretary and to David Davis as shadow Home Secretary. Crouch then left Parliament and began to work in public affairs. She went to work for Norwich Union, and is still employed by them under their new name of Aviva.

Crouch is taking on Labour's Jonathan Shaw at Chatham & Aylesford. She is energetic, personable and able, and undoubtedly has a stellar political career ahead of her.

Alan Cullens

PPC for Chorley
Notional status: Lab 7,285
Tory target seat number: 160
Swing required: 8.21%
alan-cullens@btconnect.com

Alan Cullens was born in Rochdale in 1954. He has lived in Chorley for well over twenty years. Married for almost thirty years, Cullens has one daughter. He and his family are heavily involved in the community: his wife is a borough councillor and their daughter is an elected parish councillor. Cullens also finds time to be chairman of a local Scout group and to support Bury Football Club.

For almost two decades Cullens has worked as a learning and development consultant, mainly in the aerospace sector. He has also worked for NatWest and Alliance & Leicester. He is an ex-national president of British Junior Chamber International, as well as a past president of Burnley & Pendle Speakers Club.

Cullens has been involved in local politics for more than fifteen years. In 2004 he was elected to represent the Clayton North ward on Chorley Borough Council and managed to significantly increase his majority in May 2008. He is also vice chairman of Chorley Police Forum and a member of a local residents' group. In 2006 he was appointed to the council's Executive Cabinet in the role of executive member for resources, presiding over finance, a role which has seen him deliver the lowest council tax increase for decades.

Bob Dalrymple

PPC for Stirling
Notional status: Lab 4,767
Tory target seat number: 104
Swing required: 5.46%
rhdalrymple@gmail.com

Born in 1975, Bob Dalrymple is Dumfries born and bred. He studied law at the University of Edinburgh, graduating in 1997. At university he was elected president of the Students' Association. He also won the John Smith Memorial Mace, the British and Irish universities debating competition.

Dalrymple now works in his constituency as a marketing executive for a whisky company. He has previously worked for global brands such as Diageo and Procter & Gamble.

Dalrymple fought the Stirling seat for the Scottish Parliament in 2007, managing to increase the Conservatives' share of the vote. He was selected to fight the Westminster seat at the next general election in December 2007, taking on Labour's Anne McGuire. The seat used to be held by the Tories' former chairman in Scotland, Michael Forsyth.

Byron Davies

PPC for Gower

Notional status: Lab 6,703

Tory target seat number: 165

Swing required: 8.48%

office@gowerconservatives.com

Born in Swansea in 1952, Byron Davies was raised in Gower and attended local schools at both primary and secondary level. Married to Gill, Davies has a son, Warren, who is a barrister. A keen aviator, Davies has a pilot's licence which he has held for over twenty-five years. He is also enthusiastic about rugby and cycling and is involved in rebuilding classic cars.

After acquiring a law degree, Davies followed his father's lead and joined the police force. He spent the majority of his working life in the Metropolitan Police as a detective. He then spent a number of years at the National Crime Squad, before being seconded to the EU as an advisor combating organised crime in eastern Europe. On leaving the force, Davies started up his own consultancy, which advises countries seeking to join the EU. He has written several progress reports on countries in the Balkan region.

Davies got involved with the Tories before joining the police when he joined the Young Conservatives. He sacrificed his political career to join the force, although on retirement he returned to the political fold. In 2007 he was the Welsh Assembly candidate for Gower, achieving a 10.8 per cent swing to the Conservatives.

Suzy Davies

PPC for Brecon & Radnorshire

Notional status: Lib Dem 3,905

Tory target seat number: 96

Swing required: 5.09%

bandrtories@btconnect.com

Born in Swansea in 1963, Suzy Davies went to Aberdare Girls' Grammar School and then Brecon High School. She then went to study law at the universities of Exeter and Glamorgan. She is married to Geraint, a Powys hill farmer, and they have two sons.

Moving into arts marketing and management, Davies then qualified as a solicitor and has worked in practices in Wales ever since. She has now given up her job to concentrate on campaigning, though she occasionally works as a consultant. She has been an Association deputy chairman and deputy chairman of the Welsh Conservatives Mid & West Wales Area Council. Currently she stands as Welsh representative on the national Conservatives' committees for candidates and conferences.

Davies has always been involved in numerous voluntary projects, as well as being a community councillor and school governor. She has been editor of the *Bracton Law Journal* and has had a series of articles published over the years. Davies was one of the founders of the Welsh International Film Festival, and she chairs the Mid Wales Children's Book Festival.

Davies stood as the PPC for Carmarthen East & Dinefwr in 2005. In 2007 she then stood as the Assembly candidate for Brecon & Radnorshire. Standing in Brecon & Radnorshire for Westminster against the Lib Dems' Roger Williams, she will be hoping that the Tories' recent strong showing in Wales continues into the general election.

Kevin Davis

PPC for Yeovil

Notional status: Lib Dem 8,779

Tory target seat number: 169

Swing required: 8.66%

kevin@kevindavis.org.uk

Born in New Malden in 1965, Kevin Davis had until recently lived in and around London for most of his life. However, he has now moved to Somerset with his family.

Until 2002 Davis was the chief executive of an international textiles business. He has now moved into the voluntary sector. He established a social enterprise working in deprived schools throughout the country, and subsequently he resurrected a failing forty-year-old charity working in the disability sector. He has also set up a charity-focused public affairs business.

Davis was a councillor for the Royal Borough of Kingston upon Thames for six years from 1998. During that period he spent time as leader of the council's minority administration. At the 2005 general election he contested the Lib Dem-held seat of Kingston & Surbiton, managing to halve the sitting MP's majority.

Nigel Dawkins

PPC for Birmingham Selly Oak

Notional status: Lab 7,564

Tory target seat number: 166

Swing required: 8.57%

nigeldawkins@consultants2000.co.uk

Nigel Dawkins was born in Birmingham in 1955. He was educated at King Edward VI Camp Hill School, before gaining a physics degree from Imperial College, London. Married with three young children, Dawkins's main interests are karate and British history.

On graduation Dawkins went to work for Rolls-Royce in Derby. He then returned to Birmingham to work for IMI Computing. In 1990 he left and started his own software consultancy company.

A member of the Conservative Party for over twenty-five years, Dawkins has represented Bournville on the city council since 2000. In his time on the council, Dawkins has been Conservative spokesman on regeneration and leisure services and at present sits on the Licensing Committee. He held several positions within the Conservative Association in Selly Oak before being selected as the PPC for the constituency in 2007 at an open public meeting.

Nick de Bois

PPC for Enfield North

Notional status: Con 937

Tory target seat number: N/A

Swing required: N/A

nickdebois@enfieldnorth.org

Born in Ely in 1959, Nick de Bois read business studies at the Cambridge College of Arts. With four children, he spends a lot of time travelling to watch school and university hockey and football matches. When he has the time, he is also a keen traveller and follower of rugby.

After college de Bois went on to join the Advertising Standards Authority, where he worked in the press department. He then joined Rapiergroup, an exhibition design and management company, where he led a management buy-out and went on to become managing director. The company today employs sixty people in the UK and abroad, and de Bois speaks both French and German.

De Bois was motivated to join the Conservative Party by his then local MP, John Major. He served as deputy chairman of Huntingdon Conservative Association. Having stood in Stalybridge & Hyde in 1997, de Bois contested Enfield North in both 2001 and 2005. Over the two elections he has managed to reduce Labour's majority from 7,000 to 2,000. With favourable boundary changes, it has got to be a case of fourth time lucky for this energetic and persistent candidate.

Jackie Doyle-Price

PPC for Thurrock
Notional status: Lab 5,358
Tory target seat number: 125
Swing required: 6.51%
jackie.doyle-price@virgin.net

Born in Sheffield in 1969, Jackie Doyle-Price now lives in Purfleet. When not involved with politics, she enjoys the theatre, pop concerts and watching films and TV soap dramas. She also collects unusual pieces of silver jewellery.

Doyle-Price has worked in public policy and government relations in the City of London. She now works as a consumer advocate, trying to secure fair treatment from financial institutions.

Inspired to join the Tory Party by her parents' battle to buy their council home from a Labour council, she has campaigned for the Conservatives for over twenty years, and she has served in a number of offices at all levels of the party. In the 2005 general election she fought the constituency of Sheffield Hillsborough. This time around she is fighting Thurrock, where she is perhaps fortunate that the sitting Labour MP, the independent-minded Andrew MacKinlay, has announced that he will not be standing again.

Richard Drax

PPC for South Dorset
Notional status: Lab 1,812
Tory target seat number: 33
Swing required: 1.86%
sdorset@online.net

Born in London in 1958 the son of a naval officer, Richard Drax spent his early years in the Far East. At the age of eight, he was sent to Maidwell Hall near Northampton before going to Harrow School. He has four children and is a keen sportsman, enjoying running, sailing, golf, tennis and skiing. He also enjoys reading military history.

Having taken a gap year in Australia, Drax then attended Brigade Squad, a course for those who wish to join the Household Division. From there he went to the Royal Military Academy Sandhurst, after which he was commissioned into the Coldstream Guards in 1978 and posted to Belfast. Before leaving the Army with the rank of captain, Drax served in Kenya, Brunei and Hong Kong.

On leaving the Army, Drax attended an estate management course at the Royal Agricultural College in Cirencester. He moved into journalism, joining the *Yorkshire Evening Press* as a trainee reporter. Two years later he became a fully fledged reporter, having completed the Westminster Press training course. He moved on to work with Tyne Tees TV, the *Express* and the *Daily Telegraph* before finding a job with BBC Radio Solent as their Bournemouth reporter. He remained with BBC South for ten years, where he became a senior reporter.

Drax was selected as the candidate for South Dorset in 2006. He is taking on Labour's Jim Knight, who holds a thin majority.

Flick Drummond

PPC for Portsmouth South

Notional status: Lib Dem 2,955

Tory target seat number: 70

Swing required: 4.00%

flick@flickdrummond.com

Born in Aden (where her father was serving with the Army) in 1962, Flick Drummond went to school at Roedean. She went on to the University of Hull, before doing an MA in politics at the University of Southampton. She is married with four children.

Drummond has worked as an insurance broker in London. In 1994 she trained as a school inspector for Ofsted and has inspected schools all over the country. She has also been an active member of the Winchester & Eastleigh Community Health Council, and she has chaired the local branch of the National Childbirth Trust. She has served as a Winchester city councillor. She has also written a report for the Social Workers Commission, entitled *No More Blame Game: The Future for Children's Social Workers*.

Drummond stood as the candidate for Southampton Itchen in 2005. In 2007 she was selected as the candidate for Portsmouth South, where she takes on the respected Lib Dem MP Mike Hancock.

Peter Duncan

PPC for Dumfries & Galloway

Notional status: Lab 2,922

Tory target seat number: 55

Swing required: 2.87%

peter@peterduncan.org.uk

Born in Ayrshire in 1965, Peter Duncan attended Ardrossan Academy before going on to Birmingham University. He is married with two children. He enjoys sports, especially rugby and cricket.

After graduation, Duncan became a business and communications consultant, before moving on to run his family's textile business. Between 2001 and 2005 Duncan was the MP for Galloway & Upper Nithsdale. Between 2003 and 2005 he acted as shadow Secretary of State for Scotland, and between 2004 and 2007 he was chairman of the Scottish Conservative Party.

Boundary changes lost him his seat in 2005. In May 2007 he was elected to Dumfries & Galloway Council as councillor for Castle Douglas & Glenkens ward. He is now fighting Dumfries & Galloway against Labour's Russell Brown.

Deborah Dunleavy

PPC for Bolton North East
Notional status: Lab 4,527
Tory target seat number: 115
Swing required: 5.99%
deborah4boltonne@aol.com

Born and brought up in Bolton, Deborah Dunleavy was educated at Mount Saint Joseph Grammar School and Abraham Moss College. She lives in Turton, Bolton, with her partner Mark and their three children. She enjoys football and holds an FA coaching certificate. She also spends her time walking in the Lake District, where her sister runs a hotel.

Dunleavy is a director of her family's financial advisory firm and she holds a Certificate from the Personal Finance Society. She specialises in small companies, mainly advising on investments and pensions.

In the 2005 general election Dunleavy stood in Bolton South East. This time around she is contesting Bolton North East against Labour's David Crausby.

Michael Ellis

PPC for Northampton North
Notional status: Lab 3,340
Tory target seat number: 84
Swing required: 4.50%
ellis2win@googlemail.com

Michael Ellis was born in 1967 and raised in Northampton. He went to Wellingborough School and Buckingham University. At university he edited the *Denning Law Journal* and completed a semester in Virginia. After finishing the Bar Vocational Course at the Inns of Court School of Law in London he won the Aylesbury Vale District Council Chairman's Prize for the best performance in public law. In his spare time Ellis goes to the gym and the theatre.

Now practising as a criminal barrister in Northampton, Ellis also works with the Council for Ethnic Minority Communities, where he hosts workshops aimed at educating young people about crime and the criminal justice system.

In 1997 Ellis won the Park ward of Northampton in the Northamptonshire County Council elections. In 2006 he was selected as the PPC for Northampton North in an open primary. He will be taking on Labour's Sally Keeble at the next general election.

Jane Ellison

PPC for Battersea

Notional status: Lab 332

Tory target seat number: 9

Swing required: 0.41%

jane@janeellison.net

Born in Bradford in 1964, Jane Ellison went to St Joseph's College, Bradford before going on to read PPE at St Hilda's College, Oxford.

After graduation she went to work for the John Lewis Partnership. She now works at their head office in Victoria and is responsible for the partnership's in-house magazine.

Ellison has twice been a councillor in the London Borough of Barnet. She has also stood for Parliament on three separate occasions – the Barnsley East by-election in 1996, Barnsley East again in the 1997 general election and the Tottenham by-election of 2000. She is now fighting the eminently winnable Battersea seat. Although she is both experienced and able, her pro-EU stance could affect her promotion prospects.

Charlie Elphicke

PPC for Dover

Notional status: Lab 5,005

Tory target seat number: 99

Swing required: 5.20%

Born in Huntingdon in 1970, Charlie Elphicke was brought up in Kent. He was educated at Felstead School before going on to Nottingham University. He then went on to the Inns of Court School of Law. He is married with two children.

Professionally Elphicke is head of the European tax practice at law firm Hunton & Williams. He is also a research fellow at the CPS. He is a regular blogger and has advised the Conservative Party on tax policies.

Having contested St Albans in the 2001 general election, Elphicke now takes on the pugnacious Gwyn Prosser in Dover. Prosser will be hard to shift, but if Elphicke can achieve that feat then Labour will be staring at a wipe-out in the south-east of England.

Wilfred Emmanuel-Jones

PPC for Chippenham
Notional status: Lib Dem 2,183
Tory target seat number: 43
Swing required: 2.35%
wilfred@theblackfarmer.com

Born in Jamaica in 1957, Wilfred Emmanuel-Jones moved to England and was raised in Birmingham. He is married with three children. He enjoys music, including composing, photography and farming traditional cattle breeds.

As a producer and director for the BBC, Emmanuel-Jones brought many top chefs to the screen, including Gordon Ramsay and Antony Worrall-Thompson. He then founded a food and drink marketing company in London, where he has worked with brands such as Cobra beer and Kettle Chips. He has since purchased a farm in Devon and launched a range of sausages and sauces under the Black Farmer label.

Emmanuel-Jones is fighting Chippenham at the next general election. He should get elected, and if he does his business and broadcasting experience and evocative back story should earn him a chance of ministerial office.

George Eustice

PPC for Camborne & Redruth
Notional status: Lib Dem 2,733
Tory target seat number: 38
Swing required: 1.97%
george.eustice@conservatives.com

George Eustice was born and raised in Cornwall. His family have lived and worked in the Camborne area for more than 400 years. Eustice went to Truro Cathedral School and moved on to Cornwall College. He is a former member of the Cornwall Athletic Club, where he ran for the cross-country team for many years, and he still runs for exercise.

Before politics Eustice worked for nine years in the family business, Trevaskis Fruit Farm – which his parents and brother still run. He first entered politics as campaign director for the anti-euro 'No Campaign'. He was then head of press for Michael Howard in the 2005 general election. From June 2005 until the end of 2008 he was David Cameron's press secretary and was part of Cameron's team during the leadership contest. In March 2009 he joined the PR and PA agency Portland Communications.

With his strong local roots and campaigning experience Eustice should capture Camborne & Redruth at the general election. His experience and close Cameron connections will then make him a shoo-in for ministerial office.

Graham Evans

PPC for Weaver Vale
Notional status: Lab 5,277
Tory target seat number: 137
Swing required: 7.01%
grahamtevans@btinternet.com

Born in Poynton in 1963, Graham Evans is Cheshire born and bred. He still lives in the area with his wife and three children. He was educated at local schools and at Manchester University Business School. He enjoys football, cricket, rugby and fell running and half-marathons, and he has a strong interest in history.

Evans is a sales and marketing professional. He has held senior board positions at a range of blue chip companies within the graphics and manufacturing sectors. He also served for a spell as a special constable.

Having been a Macclesfield councillor since 2000, Evans has also served as chairman of Leisure Services. He fought Worsley at the 2005 general election, and he will have to use all of his marketing skills to capture Weaver Vale this time around.

Jonathan Evans

PPC for Cardiff North
Notional status: Lab 1,146
Tory target seat number: 22
Swing required: 1.26%
jonathan@jonathanevans.co.uk

Born in 1950, Jonathan Evans was raised in Tredegar and went to school at the Lewis School, Pengram. He then went on to the Law Society's College of Law. He lives in Wales with his wife and three children.

Once qualified, Evans joined the well-known and politically connected chambers of Leo Abse & Cohen. He became a partner in 1987 and stayed with the firm until elected as an MP in 1992. Upon losing his seat in 1997 he worked for Eversheds for two years.

In the meantime Evans contested Brecon & Radnor in 1987 without success, but had better luck in 1992. He had a short but successful ministerial career, serving as parliamentary under-secretary for Wales. He then moved to the Lord Chancellor's Department, before becoming Minister for Consumer Affairs at the DTI. He was then elected as an MEP representing Wales. He served on the key Economic and Monetary Affairs Committee and was elected leader of the Conservative group in 2001.

Evans is taking on Labour's Julie Evans in the highly marginal seat of Cardiff North this time around. Another chapter in the career of this versatile politician may be about to be written.

Sian Flynn

PPC for North Cornwall
Notional status: Lib Dem 2,892
Tory target seat number: 63
Swing required: 3.43%
sian@sianflynn.com

Although she was born in Woking in 1952, Sian Flynn's family have strong roots in Cornwall, and she now lives there with her husband and two sons. She studied geography at the University of Exeter. Her hobbies are walking, surfing and gardening.

Before setting up a tourism business in Cornwall with her husband, Flynn worked as a fundraiser for the arts. She has always been involved in voluntary work, and she was chairman of governors of a local school and chairman of her local hospital. From 1991 until 1999 she was a district councillor in Surrey Heath, during which time she chaired the Planning Committee.

The Tories are resurgent in the south-west of England, and Flynn will hope that this tide will help her to sweep away the Lib Dems' Dan Rogerson.

Mark Formosa

PPC for Taunton Deane
Notional status: Lib Dem 1,868
Tory target seat number: 29
Swing required: 1.65%
taunton@tory.org

Mark Formosa was born in Cornwall in 1977. He was educated at Treviglas School and now lives in the Taunton Deane constituency. Having worked in the meat trade for some years, Formosa went on to run his family's catering company. A keen angler, he enjoys country walking and going to the cinema.

Formosa joined the Conservative Party in 2002. In the English local elections of 2003 he was elected to both Newquay Town Council and Restormel Borough Council. In the general election of 2005 he fought the seat of North Cornwall, where he cut the Liberal Democrat majority of 10,000 by almost 7,000. This time around he has one of the top thirty Tory target seats with Taunton Deane, and with the party performing well in the 2009 county council elections he must have high hopes of winning.

Hannah Foster

PPC for Exeter

Notional status: Lab 8,559

Tory target seat number: 167

Swing required: 8.63%

hannah4exeter@mac.com

Born in 1974, Hannah Foster has lived in almost every region of the country. However, she regards Devon as her home as it is where her family have lived for more than four generations. Married to David, a Royal Marine, she now lives in Pinhoe. Foster enjoys films, food and wine, as well as walking, travelling, fly fishing and water skiing.

Schooled in Buckinghamshire, Surrey and Rutland, Foster did a postgraduate at London Guildhall to gain membership of the Chartered Institute of Personnel and Development. She also has a BA (Hons) from Sunderland, which included a year of study in the USA.

Foster now works as a human resources director. She has worked for a number of different businesses, including the *Financial Times* and Penguin Books. Until 2006 she headed up all employment issues for Pearson VUE. She now only works part time so that she has time to work for Exeter.

Until October 2002 Foster was the national chairman of Conservative Future, where she forged a close working relationship with Lord Ashcroft by helping to secure his seat on the national convention as a representative of the organisation. She also won the first Ashcroft Prize for Outstanding Contribution to Conservative Youth Politics. She has written articles for the *House Magazine*, *Heartland* and contributed to the book *There Is Such a Thing as Society*. She was selected as the PPC for Exeter at an open meeting in March 2007.

Kevin Foster

PPC for Coventry South

Notional status: Lab 6,237

Tory target seat number: 144

Swing required: 7.58%

kevin.foster@coventryconservatives.com

Born in 1978, Kevin Foster is Plymouth born, bred and schooled. He is the son of a dockyard worker and a teaching assistant. He studied law at undergraduate and postgraduate level at Warwick University, and was chairman of the university Conservative Association. He was called to the Bar in 2002.

Having worked as a paralegal and company secretary to a computer company, Foster became a researcher for Philip Bradbourn MEP in his Birmingham office. He then gave up work to concentrate on his role as Cabinet member for

City Services on Coventry City Council. He is still a trustee of the Coventry Law Centre and a director of Whitley Community Centre.

Foster has a strong local base with his council position, but he is up against a well-entrenched opponent in Labour's Jim Cunningham.

George Freeman

PPC for Mid Norfolk
Notional status: Con 7,793
Tory target seat number: N/A
Swing required: N/A
george@georgefreeman.co.uk

Born in Cambridge in 1967, George Freeman grew up on a farm near Newmarket, where his family has a long association with horse racing. He moved to Norfolk twenty years ago. When not involved with politics, he enjoys sailing, hill walking and wildfowling.

On leaving Radley College and Cambridge, he spent five years as parliamentary officer of the NFU. In 1996 he left Westminster and started a career in small business, working for a succession of high-tech start-ups. He is now running his own company, 4d Biomedical. He returned to politics in 2003 when he launched the campaign 'Mind the Gap!' – a campaign to promote civic action. In 2005 he stood as Conservative candidate for Stevenage.

Freeman is replacing sitting Tory MP Keith Simpson, who is moving to the new seat of Broadland. Freeman will have no problem holding onto this seat for the Tories.

Mike Freer

PPC for Finchley & Golders Green
Notional status: Con 294
Tory target seat number: N/A
Swing required: N/A
mike@finchleyconservatives.com

Born in Manchester in 1966, Mike Freer was educated at Chadderton Grammar School before going on to Stirling University. He is a keen charity worker, including being treasurer of the Barnet Tsunami Appeal and chairman of Barnet Multi-faith Forum. In his spare time Freer enjoys cycling and keeping fit, as well as travelling and reading. On top of this, he is a member of Friends of Windsor Open Space, Conservative Friends of Cyprus and Conservative Friends of Israel, and he is a friend of British Asian Conservative Link.

Freer is a self-employed financial consultant with previous experience in the banking and finance sectors. He worked for major high street banks (including

Barclays) in a number of divisions before starting his own financial service business. He started out in retail catering and retail gaming.

Freer is currently leader of Barnet Borough Council and is a local councillor for the Finchley Church End ward. He has been involved with the Conservative Party since the early 1980s and was first elected to Barnet Council in 1990. Though he lost his seat in 1994 he regained the Finchley ward by-election in 2001 with a substantial 6 per cent swing. He was selected as PPC for Harrow West in 2005, where he reduced Labour's majority by 66 per cent. In Finchley & Golders Green Labour's incumbent, Rudi Vis, is standing down, and Freer should regain this, Margaret Thatcher's old seat, for the Tories.

Lorraine Fullbrook

PPC for South Ribble
Notional status: Lab 2,528
Tory target seat number: 52
Swing required: 2.71%
lorrainefullbrook@hotmail.co.uk

Lorraine Fullbrook was born in 1959 in Glasgow, where she attended Kilmarnock Academy. She spent over twenty years in business before turning her hand to politics in 2002. In her time before politics she had several different roles including working for several major national and international companies in a PR capacity. Fullbrook has been married to Mark (a well-known political consultant) for eighteen years. She spends her spare time travelling, reading, collecting advertising memorabilia and cooking.

In 2005 Fullbrook was the PPC for South Ribble. She managed to reduce the incumbent Labour MP's majority by half to just over 2,000 and was reselected in October 2005 to contest it next time around. She is a former director of Women2Win. She has also served on South Ribble District Council. Just days after being elected she joined the Cabinet of the council as member for Communications. Later she was selected as Cabinet member for Finance and then as the first female leader of the council. Fullbrook resigned from the council in 2004 to focus on South Ribble. She is also a director of Women2Win.

Fullbrook is a doughty campaigner and with the aid of her husband (who is a former CCO head of campaigns) she should succeed this time around. Assuming she does, a ministerial career is surely in prospect for this experienced campaigner and communicator.

Richard Fuller

PPC for Bedford

Notional status: Lab 3,413

Tory target seat number: 71

Swing required: 4.02%

richard@action4bedford.com

Born in 1951, Richard Fuller is Bedford born and bred, and he has lived there for most of his life. He went to Bedford Modern School, before going on to Oxford and then Harvard (where he was awarded an MBA).

Fuller has worked in management consultancy and in financial services in the UK, the US, Australia and the Far East. He has also been a partner in a venture capital firm.

Having already fought Bedford in the 2005 general election, he will be reasonably confident of succeeding this time around and overturning Labour MP Patrick Hall's fairly slim majority.

Mark Garnier

PPC for Wyre Forest

Notional status: Ind 4,613

Tory target seat number: 91

Swing required: 4.76%

mark@wyreforestconservatives.com

Born in London in 1963, Mark Garnier went to Charterhouse School in Surrey. He is married with two young children. Outside politics, he is a keen photographer and a county standard target rifle shot.

Garnier started his career in the City of London in 1982. He has experience in investment banking, especially with regard to south-east Asia and eastern Europe, and is now a partner in a hedge fund. He is a governor of Kidderminster College as well as a Freeman of the City of London, sitting on the court of the Worshipful Company of Coachmakers.

Only joining the party after the 2001 general election, Garnier was a councillor on Forest of Dean District Council between 2003 and 2007. In 2004 he was selected to fight Wyre Forest and he gained the largest swing in the country in 2005 at 14 per cent. This time around he still has a fairly large majority to overturn, and he is up against the respected independent MP Dr Richard Taylor – assuming he decides to run again.

David Gold

PPC for Eltham

Notional status: Lab 2,904

Tory target seat number: 68

Swing required: 3.80%

office@greenwichconservatives.com

Born in Redhill in 1972, David Gold was educated at Royal Holloway College, University of London. In his spare time Gold is a keen theatre and cinema goer, and he also enjoys travel and gardening. He writes for a variety of magazines and newspapers and also contributed to *A Blue Tomorrow: New Visions from Modern Conservatives* (Politico's Publishing, 2001).

Currently, Gold works as a development director at Brighton College. Previously, he worked in business development in central London and as a business consultant. He has also been a researcher for two different Conservative MPs, and between 1997 and 1999 he was diary secretary to William Hague.

Having been involved in the Conservative Party since university, Gold has stood in local government elections in Ealing and Lewisham as well as having held a variety of positions in local Conservative associations. In 2001 he contested the seat of Brighton Pavilion, where he achieved a 1.6 per cent Labour to Conservative swing. This time around he is contesting Eltham, where Labour's Clive Efford has a slim majority.

Zac Goldsmith

PPC for Richmond Park

Notional status: Lib Dem 3,613

Tory target seat number: 65

Swing required: 3.55%

campaign@zacgoldsmith.com

Born in London in 1975, Zac Goldsmith was brought up in Richmond. He is the son of the famous businessman and founder of the Referendum Party, Sir James Goldsmith. He was educated at Eton College.

Goldsmith is a formidable campaigner on green issues and is editor of *The Ecologist* magazine. He has been involved with the campaigns of Michael Gove and Joanne Cash in the past. In 2005 he was selected as deputy chairman of the Conservative Party's Quality of Life policy group.

Goldsmith has regularly appeared on radio and TV and delivers speeches at colleges, schools and think tanks in the UK. In 2003 he won the Beacon Prize for Young Philanthropist of the Year and then in 2004 the Global Green Award for International Environmental Leadership. He was selected as PPC for Richmond Park in a meeting of almost 400 local residents. He is up against the

Lib Dems' formidable Susan Kramer, but if he can defeat her he is assured of rapid advancement.

John Gough

PPC for Barrow & Furness
Notional status: Lab 4,843
Tory target seat number: 121
Swing required: 6.27%
barrowcon@tory.org

Born in Hartlepool in 1967, John Gough was brought up in Tyneside. He was educated at Ramsey Comprehensive School and at Lancaster University, where he studied economics and politics and was chairman of his university Conservative Association. He is married with one son.

After qualifying as a chartered accountant, Gough worked as a merchant banker in the City of London. He has also worked as a diving instructor and as a civil servant within the Department for Work and Pensions. Having been selected he resigned from the civil service and set up as a consultant in the IT sector.

Having originally been active in Conservative politics in London, Gough switched his attentions to Newcastle and the north-east. This time around he is standing in Barrow & Furness, where Labour's former Defence Secretary, John Hutton, will be standing down next time around.

Richard Graham

PPC for Gloucester
Notional status: Lab 6,063
Tory target seat number: 123
Swing required: 6.47%
richard@richardgraham.org

Born in 1958 and always having been based in Gloucestershire, Richard Graham still lives there with his wife and three children. He went to Oxford University and was awarded Blues in cricket and squash.

Graham's business career has always been international. He has lived and worked in eight countries, always representing British organisations. He was a founder of the British Chamber of Commerce in Shanghai and was on the board of the China–Britain Business Council. He has also served on the board of the charity Care for Children.

Politically Graham has been a Cotswold district councillor and was chairman of the Overview and Scrutiny Committee. He also stood (unsuccessfully) for the European Parliament in 2005. Selected as Tory PPC for Gloucester in December 2006, he has to try and unseat Labour's Parmjit Dhanda.

Helen Grant

PPC for Maidstone & the Weald
Notional status: Con 12,922
Tory target seat number: N/A
Swing required: N/A
helen.grant@grantssolicitors.com

Born in London in 1965, Helen Grant was brought up by a single mother on the Raffles council estate in Carlisle. She went to Trinity Comprehensive School. She gained a law degree from the University of Hull before qualifying as a solicitor in 1988. In 1996 she founded Grants Solicitors, which specialise in the problems of family breakdown. Married with two children, Grant has lived and worked in Kent, Surrey and south London since 1994. She enjoys sport (especially tennis), movies and family life.

Grant is a member of the Conservative Party Family Law Reform Commission and the Conservative Party Social Mobility Taskforce. She was one of the authors of the Social Justice Policy Group Report *State of the Nation: Fractured Families* and the follow-up *Breakthrough Britain*. Grant is deputy chair of the Croydon Central & Croydon South Conservative Federation's diversity group. She is also a member of the Law Society Equality & Diversity Committee and served as non-executive director of the Croydon NHS Primary Care Trust from January 2005 until 2007.

Having only joined the Conservative Party in January 2006, Grant beat off a huge field to win the battle to replace the retiring Ann Widdecombe. As the first black female Conservative MP, she will attract a great deal of attention. Her drive and determination should make her a shoo-in for ministerial office.

Andrew Griffiths

PPC for Burton
Notional status: Lab 2,132
Tory target seat number: 44
Swing required: 2.40%
andrew@andrewgriffiths.org.uk

Born in Staffordshire in 1970, Andrew Griffiths was educated at a local secondary school in Dudley. After leaving college he worked in the family engineering business, manufacturing equipment for the construction industry. He then joined a high street banking and estate agency group, where he rose to become a manager specialising in property and financial services.

In 1999 Griffiths moved into politics when he went to work for the West Midlands MEP team in the European Parliament. He worked on issues such as the economy, industry and transport. He was then appointed advisor on agriculture and worked for the Tory agriculture spokesman Neil Parish MEP and was involved in setting up the foot and mouth inquiry.

Griffiths returned to Westminster in 2004 to work as chief of staff to Theresa May. In 2006 he moved to work for the Culture, Media & Sport team under Hugo Swire. In 2007 Griffiths moved again to work on community cohesion and local government matters as chief of staff to Eric Pickles MP, the shadow Secretary for Communities & Local Government. He stayed with Eric Pickles when he was appointed chairman of the Conservative Party and helped to mastermind the party's stunning by-election successes in Crewe & Nantwich and Norwich North.

In 2001 Griffiths stood as the PPC in Dudley North, managing to reduce Labour's majority. In 2004 he tried again, this time as the Conservative candidate for the West Midlands in the European Parliament elections, but lost out because of the UKIP vote. The sitting Labour MP for Burton, Janet Dean, is standing down, so Griffiths's persistence should finally pay off. He has a great political career ahead of him.

Ben Gummer

PPC for Ipswich
Notional status: Lab 5,235
Tory target seat number: 113
Swing required: 5.91%
ben@bengummer.com

Born in London in 1978, Ben Gummer has lived in Suffolk all of his life. He is the son of former Cabinet minister John Gummer and nephew of PR titan Lord Chadlington.

Gummer read history at Peterhouse College, Cambridge. He runs his own consultancy business in London, specialising in environmental issues. He is also taking time out to write a book. His political interests lie in the areas of education and prison reform, and he has also been actively involved in the campaign to prevent Ipswich Hospital's services from being pared back.

Up against Labour's sitting MP, Chris Mole, Gummer will need all his local contacts and youthful enthusiasm to win at his first attempt.

Robert Halfon

PPC for Harlow

Notional status: Lab 230

Tory target seat number: 5

Swing required: 0.29%

halfon4harlow@roberthalfon.com

Born in London in 1969 and brought up in the north of the capital, Robert Halfon's relatives owned the John Walton clothes shop in Harlow town centre for many years. He was educated at Exeter University, where he got a BA in politics and an MA in Russian and eastern European studies. He is a keen football fan and follows Harlow Town FC and Chelsea. He collects watches and enjoys travelling (including a stint teaching English in Rwanda).

Halfon has worked in public affairs for the now-defunct Market Access and then for APCO. He is political director of Conservative Friends of Israel and has done freelance consultancy work. Additionally, he has been an advisory board member of the CSJ and is a former chief of staff to Oliver Letwin. Halfon has been published in print and online with articles on a wide range of topics. He is a Roydon parish councillor, a trustee for Harlow Employability, a former governor of Passmores School and a former patron of Harlow Homeless Centre.

In the 2005 general election Halfon again failed to unseat Labour's Bill Rammell, that time by a margin of just ninety-seven votes after several recounts. This time around he will ensure that no recounts are needed.

Richard Harrington

PPC for Watford

Notional status: Lab 1,151

Tory target seat number: 38

Swing required: 1.97%

richard@watfordconservatives.co.uk

Born in Leeds in 1957, Richard Harrington was also brought up in Leeds and attended Leeds Grammar School. He went on to read law at Keble College, Oxford. He lives in Watford with his wife and teenage children.

After graduating Harrington worked for Waitrose, before setting up his own company, Harrington Properties. He is also a non-executive director of a financial services company and of a property company. In 2008 David Cameron sought Harrington's advice on how to diversify the party's donor list. He was instrumental in the creation of the Number 10 Club, which has resulted in a substantial boost to the party's coffers.

A former member of the Conservative Party National Union Executive, Harrington was only selected as Tory PPC for Watford at the end of 2008, when his predecessor was charged with harassing political opponents in the constituency. Despite this lack of opportunity to establish himself locally, Harrington will fancy his chances of overturning Labour MP Claire Ward's slim majority.

Rebecca Harris

PPC for Castle Point

Notional status: Con 8,201

Tory target seat number: N/A

Swing required: N/A

rebecca.harris@castlepointconservatives.com

Rebecca Harris's background is in business. She worked at Phillimore & Co., the specialist publishers of British local history. She joined their board in 1997 as marketing director. She lives in Castle Point with her husband and young son.

Harris is a former Chichester district councillor and worked briefly at CCO as a campaign officer. She has also worked at the House of Commons as special advisor to Tim Yeo.

The sitting MP, Bob Spink, was elected as a Conservative but was disowned by his local association. He now sits as an independent in the House of Commons, and Harris should be able to return this seat to the Conservative fold.

Simon Hart

PPC for Carmarthen West & South Pembrokeshire

Notional status: Lab 2,043

Tory target seat number: 51

Swing required: 2.66%

info@simon-hart.com

Born in Wolverhampton in 1963, Simon Hart was educated at Radley College and the Royal Agricultural College, Cirencester. He lives with his wife, Abigail, and their two young children in Llanmill near Narberth. His wife runs a small business selling children's clothes and he is a governor of Tavernspite School, which his children attend. He enjoys playing cricket.

By profession Hart is a chartered surveyor, but he is currently chief executive of the Countryside Alliance, Europe's largest rural affairs lobby group. He also served in the TA for several years.

Hart was selected for the seat in September 2007 by a large majority at an open meeting of more than 250 local people. His campaigning experience and rural credentials should help him to see off Labour's Nick Ainger.

Chris Heaton-Harris

PPC for Daventry

Notional status: Con 11,776

Tory target seat number: N/A

Swing required: N/A

christopher.heaton-harris@europarl.europa.eu

Born in Epsom in 1967, Chris Heaton-Harris lives in Lincoln with his wife and two daughters. He was educated at Tiffin Grammar School and at Wolverhampton Polytechnic.

A qualified Football Association referee, Heaton-Harris used to work in his family fruit and vegetable business in New Covent Garden. However, in 1999 he was elected to the European Parliament for the East Midlands region. Between 2001 and 2004 he was Chief Whip for the Conservative group. He has always wanted to become an MP, and he stood for Leicester South in 1997 and in a by-election in 2004.

Having been selected for the safe Tory seat of Daventry, where the sitting Tory MP, Tim Boswell, is standing down, Heaton-Harris will achieve his ambition. Many former MEPs have carved themselves out successful careers in Westminster and Heaton-Harris is likely to join their ranks.

Gordon Henderson

PPC for Sittingbourne & Sheppey

Notional status: Con 22

Tory target seat number: N/A

Swing required: N/A

sscahalfway@aol.com

Born in the Medway Towns in 1948, Gordon Henderson grew up on a council estate. He attended local state schools but left at sixteen to work for Woolworths as a stockroom assistant in Chatham. By the time he left the company fifteen years later he had risen to the position of senior store manager. He is married with three children, and he likes to write, listen to music and cook.

Since then, Henderson has had a varied career. He ran his own restaurant in South Africa, worked as a senior contracts officer for GEC Marconi and was the director of the Unwins Wine Group. Currently, he is operations manager of the UK's largest alcohol-based gifts manufacturer.

Henderson is a fully qualified political agent and has been the constituency agent for Roger Gale. He has twice been deputy leader of Swale Borough Council, as well as having been a Kent county councillor – sitting on both the Education Committee and the Kent Police Authority.

Henderson was the Conservative candidate in Sittingbourne & Sheppey in the 2005 general election and came within eighty votes of winning. Having been selected to contest the seat again, and with boundary changes fractionally helping the Tories and sitting Labour MP Derek Wyatt standing down, he should certainly succeed this time around.

Damian Hinds

PPC for East Hampshire
Notional status: Con 5,968
Tory target seat number: N/A
Swing required: N/A
damian@easthantsconservatives.com

Born in London in 1969, Damian Hinds grew up in Cheshire, where he attended the local grammar school. He lives in Alton with his wife.

After leaving grammar school Hinds obtained a first-class honours degree in PPE from Trinity College, Oxford. Whilst at university, he was also elected as president of the Oxford Union. On graduating, Hinds moved into strategy, marketing and e-commerce in the hotel and travel business with Greene King and InterContinental Hotels amongst others. He is a former chairman of the policy development group the Bow Group. He is also a Prince's Trust business mentor and works with Trafford United Credit Union.

In 2005 Hinds fought the seat of Stretford & Urmston and achieved a swing of 6.7 per cent from Labour to Conservative, cutting the majority from over 13,000 to 7,850. He is now standing in the rock-solid East Hampshire constituency occupied by the retiring Tory MP Michael Mates.

George Hollingbery

PPC for Meon Valley
Notional status: Con 2,378
Tory target seat number: N/A
Swing required: N/A
ghollingbery@mac.com

George Hollingbery was born in Beverley in 1963. He went to Radley College before going on to study human sciences at Lady Margaret Hall, Oxford. He then went on to study for an MA at the University of Pennsylvania, where he met his wife. He enjoys angling and gardening and is a keen photographer.

After completing his studies Hollingbery spent a short time working as a stockbroker. He then set up in business, discovering and backing small enterprises which showed growth potential but suffered from a lack of capital. In 2002 he sold his company Companion Care to a large chain of pet superstores.

Turning his attentions to politics, Hollingbery was elected to Winchester City Council in 1999 and has been re-elected twice since then, both times with an increased majority. He now serves as a Cabinet member and deputy leader of the council. Since he began his involvement Conservative fortunes in Winchester have improved dramatically, and where they had just nine councillors, they now have twenty-four and an overall majority on the council.

With the sitting Winchester MP, Lib Dem Mark Oaten, standing down and the Tories now running the local council, Hollingbery could well win this new seat.

Kris Hopkins

PPC for Keighley

Notional status: Lab 4,852

Tory target seat number: 100

Swing required: 5.24%

office@kiconservatives.com

Born in Yorkshire in 1963, Kris Hopkins served with the Duke of Wellington's Regiment before getting a degree in communications and cultural studies at Leeds University. After university he became a lecturer in media theory, communications and digital media. He lives in Keighley with his wife and daughter. He enjoys walking and running and is a keen photographer.

Entering politics in 1998, Hopkins was elected to Bradford Council. After getting elected he became portfolio holder for social services and council housing. In 2004 he was re-elected and became deputy leader of the council. In May 2006 he was elected leader of the Conservative group and leader of the council.

In the last two general elections, Hopkins contested the parliamentary seats of Leeds West in 2001 and Halifax in 2005. Ann Cryer, the sitting Labour MP for Keighley, is standing down, which should help make it third time lucky for Hopkins.

Nigel Huddleston

PPC for Luton South

Notional status: Lab 5,698

Tory target seat number: 142

Swing required: 7.34%

nigel.huddleston@gmail.com

Born in Lincoln in 1970 the son of a factory worker and an Asda checkout operator, Nigel Huddleston went to the local comprehensive school before going on to Oxford University. He then gained an MBA from UCLA in Los Angeles. At school he was a keen athlete and rugby player.

After working for Arthur Andersens Business Consulting, Huddleston moved to Deloittes. He is still there, and he is director in the Strategy Practice, specialising in the entertainment and leisure industries.

Huddleston was active in student politics at Oxford (having been a member of the executive of the Oxford University Conservative Association) and he has been involved in the Bow Group and the Tory Reform Group. He also helped the campaign for the Republican governor of California, Arnold Schwarzenegger, in the 2003 recall election.

Initially it looked as if Huddleston would benefit from the MPs' allowances debacle, as the sitting Labour MP, Margaret Moran, was heavily implicated. However, Moran then announced she was to stand down. Despite this, the TV personality Esther Rantzen has announced that she will contest the seat as an independent. This will undoubtedly complicate matters, but could ultimately turn out to be in Huddleston's favour.

Neil Hudson

PPC for Edinburgh South
Notional status: Lab 405
Tory target seat number: 158
Swing required: 8.17%
neil.hudson@scottishconservatives.com

Born in 1971, Neil Hudson lives in Edinburgh with his wife and two children. He and his wife help to run the church Sunday school, and in his spare time he enjoys cricket, music and the theatre.

Hudson went to Cambridge University before going on to study for his PhD at Edinburgh. By profession he is a veterinary surgeon. He has worked both in private practice and in the university academic sector, where he specialises in equine medicine. He has been working with the University of Edinburgh's Veterinary School for the last eleven years.

Hudson has been involved in politics for many years, having campaigned in Edinburgh at all levels. His political interests are health, education, science and rural affairs. If the Tories are to make any impact north of the border, they will need to win seats like this classic three-way marginal.

Maria Hutchings

PPC for Eastleigh
Notional status: Lib Dem 534
Tory target seat number: 12
Swing required: 0.56%
eastleigh@hantsrc.com

Born in 1961 in Romford, Maria Hutchings was brought up in Essex, the daughter of a soldier and a factory worker. She attended Grays Convent School before going on to study first dance and religion, and then switching to social science and public administration, at London University. She still enjoys music and dance as a hobby, along with walking and swimming.

On leaving university Hutchings moved into the communications industry, where she spent twenty-six years working with both small and large businesses. She also worked in Malta, where she was a broadcaster for the first English-speaking radio station. She currently works as a communications consultant in Eastleigh.

Hutchings also spends much time campaigning for special-needs children and carers and hit the headlines when she 'handbagged' Tony Blair over the closing of special schools. Her passion for the issue comes from her son, who was diagnosed with autism, severe learning disabilities and a specific language disorder.

Although Hutchings has only a slim majority to overturn, she is up against the Lib Dems' Chris Huhne, who has proved to be a tough campaigner.

Zahid Iqbal

PPC for Bradford West
Notional status: Lab 3,050
Tory target seat number: 76
Swing required: 4.17%
zahid10@btopenworld.com

Born in Pakistan in 1964, Zahid Iqbal was educated at the local comprehensive school in Leeds, before going on to study at Leeds Polytechnic.

By profession Iqbal is in financial services, specialising in property. He is currently involved in a large-scale project to bring affordable housing to Bradford. In the 2001 general election he contested Bradford North. This time around he is fighting the much more winnable Bradford West, against Labour's incumbent Marsha Singh.

Trevor Ivory

PPC for North Norfolk
Notional status: Lib Dem 8,575
Tory target seat number: 168
Swing required: 8.64%
trevor@trevorivory.net

Born in Crawley in 1978, Trevor Ivory was brought up in the area. He was educated locally, but then moved to Norwich to study law at the University of East Anglia. He has remained in the Norfolk area ever since, having worked as a solicitor for Eversheds in Norwich, specialising in planning law.

Now living in North Walsham, Ivory has a wife, Lisa, and a young son. When not busy with his family he enjoys the theatre, music, wine and travel. He also finds time to be involved with several voluntary organisations including Chatterbox, a Norfolk-based speaking newspaper for the blind and partially sighted.

Before moving to North Walsham, Ivory was chairman of the Norwich South Conservative Association. Whilst at university he held the position of vice president of the university Conservative Association. Boundary changes have considerably improved the Tories' chances in this seat since Iain Dale fought it in 2005.

Margot James

PPC for Stourbridge
Notional status: Lab 1,280
Tory target seat number: 25
Swing required: 1.46%
margot@stourbridgeconservatives.com

Born in Leamington Spa in 1958, Margot James was brought up in Coventry. She was educated at Millfield School in Somerset and then at the LSE, where she gained a BSc in economics and government. She was also chairman of the University Conservative Association. She lives with her partner, a TV presenter, and enjoys collecting wine, walking her dogs, keeping fit, cooking, theatre, opera and travel.

After graduating James co-founded a specialist PR company, Shire Health, which has been voted Consultancy of the Year three times by the British pharmaceutical industry. She sold the company in 1999 and was appointed regional president for the pharmaceuticals division of Ogilvy & Mather in 2005. James has sat on the board of Parkside NHS Trust, chaired its Clinical Governance Committee and its Audit Committee and acted as a mental health manager for the trust. She is also involved in several voluntary projects. For ten years she was a trustee of Abantu, an African women's organisation, and she has worked for the Greater London Forum for Old People as well as the Prince's Trust and Young Enterprise.

In her gap year James worked in the press office at CCO. In 2005 she contested Holborn & St Pancras, where she achieved a swing of 2 per cent. In late 2005 David Cameron appointed James to be vice chairman of the Conservative Party for women's issues, and she formed the Women's Policy Group with Eleanor Laing. In 2006 she was elected as a councillor and has spent some time chairing a review of older people's accommodation in Kensington & Chelsea.

Fighting the eminently winnable seat of Stourbridge against Labour's Lynda Waltho, she should enter Parliament at her first attempt. Progress through the ministerial ranks is then likely to be swift for this serial over-performer.

Ben Jeffreys

PPC for Cheadle

Notional status: Lib Dem 3,672

Tory target seat number: 67

Swing required: 3.70%

ben4cheadle@aol.com

Born in Ilkley in 1975, the son of a teacher and a nurse, Ben Jeffreys was educated at the King's School, Gloucester. He then went on to St Andrews University, where he took an MA in history and international relations, before moving to Cambridge to obtain a Postgraduate Certificate of Education.

He followed his father into teaching and has taught history and drama in Surrey, London and Warwickshire. Currently he is a supply teacher in the constituency of Cheadle, and he is also a consultant to Bellenden Public Affairs. He acts as an advisor to Michael Gove and is a member of the Conservative Education Policy Group and the Conservative History Practitioners Advisory Group.

Jeffreys is up against the Lib Dems' Mark Hunter in Cheadle, but if he succeeds in unseating him he may be given the opportunity to put some of his education policy into practice.

Gareth Johnson

PPC for Dartford

Notional status: Lab 860

Tory target seat number: 16

Swing required: 0.95%

office@dartfordconservatives.com

Born in Dartford in 1969, Gareth Johnson attended Dartford Grammar School. He then went on to the University of the West of England. He lives locally with his wife and two children, and enjoys playing and watching cricket.

Johnson qualified as a solicitor and now practises for a local firm in Dartford. He was formerly an Association chairman and a Bexley borough councillor. He is a governor of the local grammar school and is involved in several local charities.

When he fought Dartford in 2005 Johnson only narrowly missed out. This time around he should succeed, especially as the popular local MP, Dr Howard Stoate, has announced that he will not be standing again.

Andrew Jones

PPC for Harrogate & Knaresborough

Notional status: Lib Dem 7,980

Tory target seat number: 156

Swing required: 8.10%

andrewjoneshk@hotmail.com

Andrew Jones is Yorkshire born and bred. He lives and works in the constituency of Harrogate & Knaresborough. A big cricket fan, Jones has been a member of Yorkshire County Cricket Club for more than twenty years. He has seen many countries in following the English cricket team. He also enjoys squash, walking, going to the theatre and listening to music.

Originally from Ilkley, Jones was educated at Bradford Grammar School and went to study at Leeds University. On leaving university, he started working for Kingfisher's two companies, B&Q and Superdrug, before moving to Going Places and M&C Saatchi. Presently, he works in the sales and marketing department for Bettys and Taylors of Harrogate.

Jones joined the Conservatives in 1987. In 2001 he unsuccessfully contested the seat of Harrogate & Knaresborough. He represents High Harrogate on Harrogate Borough Council and is Cabinet member for resources. Jones is also a member of the Public Services Improvement Group, a group which develops social housing policies for David Cameron's Conservatives. The sitting Lib Dem MP, Phil Willis, is standing down, which should aid Jones's chances.

Debi Jones

PPC for Sefton Central

Notional status: Lab 4,950

Tory target seat number: 117

Swing required: 6.01%

debi@debijones.co.uk

Debi Jones was born in Liverpool in 1955. She lives in Crosby with her husband and daughter. She is a Sefton borough councillor and the Cabinet member responsible for children's services. She is also a governor of a local school.

Originally, Jones wanted to be an opera singer after being offered a place with the D'Oyly Carte Opera Company. However, after a meeting with the head of BBC Radio Merseyside she was offered an afternoon show and built up a substantial audience. Since then she has presented many different programmes, including working for Radio 5 Live, Radio City Gold and Granada Television. She has also done TV work and has produced an award-winning film. Just to add to her versatility, she occasionally does pantomime and after-dinner speaking.

In 2004 Jones was selected as the PPC for Crosby. On that occasion she failed, but she might have better luck this time around in Sefton Central.

Marcus Jones

PPC for Nuneaton
Notional status: Lab 3,894
Tory target seat number: 94
Swing required: 4.87%
marcus@marcus-jones.co.uk

Having lived in Nuneaton all of his life, Marcus Jones attended St Thomas More School and King Edward VI College. He is married and has a young son.

By profession Jones is a conveyancing manager. He has served as a councillor on Nuneaton & Bedworth Borough Council for many years and is now leader of the Council. He was selected to stand as the Conservative PPC for Nuneaton in October 2008, following the resignation of Stephen Rouse. Jones's main campaign priorities include the economy, health, education and law and order.

The seat is currently held by Labour, but the sitting MP, Bill Olner, has announced that he will be stepping down at the next general election.

Simon Jones

PPC for Dagenham & Rainham
Notional status: Lab 6,372
Tory target seat number: 151
Swing required: 7.84%
simon@jonesvision.co.uk

Born in 1974, Simon Jones was born and bred in the London–Essex borders. His family moved to Chadwell Heath in the 1940s and have lived in the area ever since. Outside politics and his career, Jones enjoys sailing, watching football and spending time helping a number of charities.

By profession, Jones is a project manager and has been in the private sector for more than ten years, including working for the telecoms giant Cable & Wireless. He has also been on the executive board of a London technology college, and he has worked as a special advisor to Lord Ashcroft.

Jones has extensive experience in political campaigning. In the 2005 general election he was the Conservative candidate in Pontefract & Castleford and he was on the GLA top-up list in 2004. Jones has been a Waveney district councillor and has been responsible for finance & e-government. In 2005 he became an officer of the International Young Democratic Union, an organisation that brings together centre-right political parties.

Chris Kelly

PPC for Dudley South
Notional status: Lab 3,222
Tory target seat number: 83
Swing required: 4.45%
office@dudleysouthconservatives.com

Born in 1978 in Wolverhampton, Kelly was brought up in the Black Country and is the son of the influential party donor who shares his name. He lives in Pensnett, right in the heart of the Dudley South constituency. His hobbies include sport and fitness – mainly swimming, squash, tennis and skiing.

Kelly attended Wolverhampton Grammar School before going to university at Oxford Brookes. He left with a degree in politics and modern history. He also has an MBA from Imperial College. Kelly joined the family firm, Keltruck Limited, and worked there for three years before going back to studying in order to acquire his MBA. He returned to the family business and in 2006 was appointed marketing director.

A member of the Conservative Party since 1996, Kelly spent some time working for Michael Howard whilst he was leader of the party. He has also been part of the research team at the 'No' campaign against Britain joining the euro. Kelly has a tough battle on his hands to defeat Labour's Ian Pearson, but he has the resources – and the determination – to succeed.

Nick King

PPC for Mid Dorset & North Poole
Notional status: Lib Dem 5,931
Tory target seat number: 128
Swing required: 6.56%
nick@nick4mdnp.com

Born in Cambridge in 1965, Nick King qualified as an agricultural surveyor after leaving school. He has lived around Bournemouth and Poole for more than ten years, and he enjoys walking his dog through the Dorset countryside and along the beaches. Other interests include reading, opera, windsurfing and kayaking – and the Eurovision Song Contest.

King started his own company at the age of twenty-five, dealing in employee relocation. His company achieved top status in the *Sunday Times* Fast Track 100 and went on to win the Virgin Customer Services Award. He now co-owns a chain of cabaret restaurants and has his own property management company. He is also a director of Bournemouth Pride and is treasurer and trustee of the Mayor of Bournemouth's Charity Appeal.

King is a former chairman of Devon Young Conservatives. In 2005 he ran Tobias Ellwood's election campaign in Bournemouth East, and their combined effort gained them the largest swing to the Conservatives in Dorset. He became a Bournemouth councillor after capturing his seat from the Lib Dems in a by-election in 2005. He will be hoping to repeat that feat against the Lib Dems' Annette Brooke at the general election.

Simon Kirby

PPC for Brighton Kemptown

Notional status: Lab 1,853

Tory target seat number: 45

Swing required: 2.42%

brighton@tory.org

Born in Sussex in 1964, Simon Kirby has spent almost all of his life living in and around the area. He lives in Peacehaven with his wife and their six children. He is passionate about football and he has been a lifelong supporter of Brighton & Hove Albion Football Club.

A serial entrepreneur, Kirby was a co-founder of the Brighton radio station now known as Juice 107.2, and he jointly owned a local leisure company, C-Side. He was heavily involved in the campaigning for city status for Brighton & Hove.

Kirby was elected to East Sussex County Council in 1992. In 1995 he was elected to Brighton Borough Council and then in 1996 to Brighton & Hove Council. He is a Cabinet member of East Sussex County Council and is responsible for regeneration across the county. Labour's sitting MP, Des Turner, is standing down at the general election, and Kirby should be able to overturn Labour's slim majority.

Pauline Latham

PPC for Mid Derbyshire

Notional status: Con 5,329

Tory target seat number: N/A

Swing required: N/A

Pauline Latham was educated at Bramcote Hill Technical Grammar and has had a successful career in politics at a local level. She has a special interest in education issues and was a school governor for twelve years, also serving as chair. In 1995 she was awarded an OBE for her services to education. Her husband is a local architect and together they have three grown-up children. The family has lived in Little Eaton for more than twenty years. Outside politics she enjoys horse riding and walking.

A councillor since 1987, Latham served on Derbyshire County Council for six years and Derby City Council for over seventeen years. She was the mayor of Derby in 2007/8, during which time she launched various initiatives to raise awareness of global warming and climate change. She has also helped to raise funds for vital equipment at Derby Hospital's bowel cancer unit. In the past Latham has been a European Parliament candidate and a PPC at Westminster parliamentary elections, contesting the East Midlands region in 1999 and then Broxtowe in 2001.

Latham was one of the earliest candidates to be selected to go onto the 'A-list'. She was selected as the Conservative PPC for the new constituency of Mid Derbyshire in June 2006 and should succeed comfortably.

Bruce Laughton

PPC for Gedling
Notional status: Lab 4,335
Tory target seat number: 92
Swing required: 4.82%
bruce.laughton@btinternet.com

Bruce Laughton was born in Nottingham in 1957. His family has lived in north Nottinghamshire for three generations, and Laughton has always actively promoted the area. He graduated in agricultural science at Nottingham University, has worked in two Nottinghamshire comprehensive schools and presently employs seventy people in his farming and business enterprises across the area. He lives in Rufford with his long-term partner and their two young daughters.

In 1999 Laughton was elected to the Farnsfield seat for Newark & Sherwood District Council and was appointed chairman of the Audit and Accounts Committee on the council in November 2005. He has been county councillor for Caunton ward since 2001, when he won the seat from the Lib Dems with an 11 per cent swing. He has served as the shadow finance and property spokesman and shadow environment spokesman on Nottinghamshire County Council.

In 2005 Laughton stood as the Conservative candidate for Sherwood, significantly reducing the Labour majority. In 2001 he was a member of Patrick Mercer's winning campaign, which achieved a 7 per cent swing. He will need not need anything like such a big swing to succeed for himself at the forthcoming general election.

Andrea Leadsom

PPC for South Northamptonshire

Notional status: Con 11,356

Tory target seat number: N/A

Swing required: N/A

admin@westnorthantsconservatives.com

Andrea Leadsom was born in 1963 in Aylesbury and educated at Tonbridge Grammar School for Girls. She then went on to read political science at Warwick University. Her family is from south Northamptonshire. She is married with three children.

Leadsom has a 25-year career in finance behind her and has worked for Invesco Perpetual, Barclays and De Putron. She has also done extensive charity work for disadvantaged children and was chair of a charity in Oxfordshire which supports families who are struggling to cope with new babies.

Leadsom has been campaigning for the Conservatives for more than twenty-five years. In 2003 she defeated the Liberal Democrat leader of South Oxfordshire District Council by eleven votes in a seat which had been held for sixteen years. Leadsom contested the Westminster seat of Knowsley South, a Labour stronghold, in 2005. She has been the candidate for South Northamptonshire since 2006. This is a new seat, with a strong notional Conservative majority, and Leadsom will soon be able to put her financial expertise at the disposal of the parliamentary party.

Jessica Lee

PPC for Erewash

Notional status: Lab 6,782

Tory target seat number: 150

Swing required: 7.83%

jessica.lee@erewashconservatives.com

Jessica Lee was born in Nottingham in 1976. The only person from her family to go to university, she read history and politics at Royal Holloway, University of London. In her spare time she likes cooking, reading and the theatre.

At university Lee was chairman of the Conservative Association. After reading law at the College of Law in she was called to the Bar in 2000 and she now works as a barrister specialising in family law. She contributed to the CSJ's *Breakdown Britain* report.

Lee has been a member of the Conservative Party since she was a teenager. She has also been held many roles at a local level, from branch officer to Association chairman. In the 2005 general election she contested the Camberwell & Peckham seat, standing against Harriet Harman. She also has a tough fight on her hands this time around, against Labour's Liz Blackman.

Jeremy Lefroy

PPC for Stafford

Notional status: Lab 1,852

Tory target seat number: 40

Swing required: 2.00%

admin@staffordtories.org.uk

Born in London in 1959, Jeremy Lefroy was educated at Highgate School and King's College, Cambridge. He lives in Stoke-on-Trent with his wife and two children. He previously ran a Duke of Edinburgh's Award programme for young people in inner London, and whilst living in Tanzania he helped to develop a successful church-based life skills programme for school leavers.

Lefroy has a background in manufacturing, international trade and agriculture. He is a qualified chartered accountant and started out as a production foreman in a Ford engine plant. In the 1990s he and his family lived in Tanzania, where he worked in the coffee industry and was the foreign director of the Tanzanian Coffee Board. Since returning to the UK in 2000, he has worked for fair trade organisations and assisted smallholder farmers in East Africa to improve the value of their products. He is the co-founder of Equity for Africa, which provides equity funding for growing businesses.

In 2003 Lefroy was elected as a councillor in Newcastle-under-Lyme. He stood as the PPC for Newcastle-under-Lyme in the 2005 general election, and he was also widely commended for his efforts as the Conservative candidate for the West Midlands in the 2004 European Parliament elections – despite being low down on the list. With only a small swing required he should succeed this time around.

Charlotte Leslie

PPC for Bristol North West

Notional status: Lab 2,781

Tory target seat number: 54

Swing required: 2.85%

charlotte@charlotteleslie.com

Born in Liverpool in 1978, Charlotte Leslie went to school at Millfield. She then studied classics at Balliol College, Oxford. Outside politics, she is keen on sports, including boxing, surfing, running and swimming.

Leslie has worked for the BBC, Policy Exchange and the CSJ. She has also worked as a gym instructor and swimming teacher. She is now the editor of the Bow Group magazine *Crossbow*. Her expertise lies in education and she co-authored the report *More Good School Places* for Policy Exchange.

As well as working for major think tanks, Leslie has been an advisor to David

Willetts and currently works for the Conservative Party's public services group. In November 2006 she was selected to contest Bristol North West at the next general election. Boundary changes have made Bristol North West a winnable seat for the Conservatives and the current Labour, MP Doug Naysmith, is standing down.

Brandon Lewis

PPC for Great Yarmouth

Notional status: Lab 3,055

Tory target seat number: 66

Swing required: 3.69%

brandon@brandonlewis.org

Brandon Lewis was born in Essex in 1971. He went to Forest School, Chigwell, before going on to the University of Buckingham and King's College, London, where he studied economics and then law. He grew up in Great Yarmouth and his parents owned a business in the area. Outside politics, he has an interest in theatre and cinema. In 2005 he ran the London Marathon, raising £7,000 for charity.

Lewis is a qualified barrister and a director of two companies – Woodlands Schools Ltd and a corporate communications planning business called i5 Consulting. He is a fellow of the Institute of Leadership & Management and a member of the Institute of Directors.

Lewis was elected to Brentwood Council in 1998 and became leader of the Council in June 2004, standing down in March 2009. He stood for Parliament in 2001 as the PPC for Sherwood and in 2005 he was the campaign manager for Eric Pickles. He has been the candidate for Great Yarmouth since November 2006.

Antony Little

PPC for Norwich South

Notional status: Lab 3,023

Tory target seat number: 157

Swing required: 8.16%

norwich@tory.co.uk

Antony Little was born in Hillingdon in 1979. He lives right in the heart of Norwich with his wife, Louise, and their two daughters. He is an avid follower of Norwich City FC and also enjoys ten pin bowling.

Little went to the University of East Anglia and left with an honours degree and a PGCE. He now works as a teacher at a comprehensive school in the middle of Norwich. He teaches history and is head of Year 10 – a role which sees him responsible for more than 200 pupils. In addition to this, Little is a branch secretary for his teaching union and is actively involved in educational campaigns as well as being a school governor.

In 2005, Little was the PPC for Norwich South, managing to reduce the sitting MP's majority from around 9,000 to 6,000. In May 2006 he was elected to Norwich City Council, winning by just 139 votes in Bowthorpe & Earlham, having overturned a large majority. In 2007 he was the agent and achieved further gains from Labour across Norwich.

Matthew Lobley

PPC for Leeds North East
Notional status: Lab 6,762
Tory target seat number: 148
Swing required: 7.75%
info@matthewlobley.com

Born in 1975, Matthew Lobley now lives in Alwoodley. His family can trace their local roots back to the eighteenth century. He works for BT in Leeds as an IT projects manager, specialising in large scale computer projects.

Lobley's interest in politics was sparked when he started volunteering for Community Actions for Roundhay Elderly, which he now chairs. In 2003 he was elected to Leeds City Council and he has served as lead member for highways. He is also chairman of North East Leeds Development Partnership. In the 2005 general election he stood for Leeds North East, dramatically reducing Labour's majority, and he will be hoping to go one better this time.

Jack Lopresti

PPC for Filton & Bradley Stoke
Notional status: Con 653
Tory target seat number: N/A
Swing required: N/A
jack@jacklopresti.com

Jack Lopresti was born in Bristol in 1969. He went to Bradley Stoke Community School. He lives in Filton with his wife and three children. He has an interest in history and is a member of the International Churchill Society and the General George Patton Historical Society. Every year he takes part in the Bristol half-marathon to raise money for charity.

After school he worked for his family's local ice-cream and catering company for ten years. He then moved on to work as a consultant in the financial services and residential property sectors in the late 1990s. He also serves in the Gloucester Volunteer Artillery as a gunner and has seen active service in Afghanistan.

Lopresti joined the Conservative Party over twenty years ago and represented Stockwood ward on Bristol Council from 1999 until 2007. He stood for Bristol East in the 2001 general election and for the European Parliament South West region in 2004. He has been the candidate for Filton & Bradley Stoke since 2006 and should win this new seat with a notional Tory majority easily.

Karen Lumley

PPC for Redditch

Notional status: Lab 2,163

Tory target seat number: 47

Swing required: 2.60%

karen.lumley@btinternet.com

Born in Barnsley in 1964, Karen Lumley was educated at Rugby High School for Girls and East Warwickshire College. Her father was a head teacher at a local school and her mother was a nurse. She is married and has two grown-up children. Her hobbies are travel, knitting and cooking.

Lumley trained as an accountant at the Ford Motor Company in Brentwood, Essex. She is now company secretary for RKL Geological Services Ltd and chairman of governors at one of the largest schools in Redditch.

Lumley joined the Conservative Party nearly twenty years ago. She has been a district and county councillor in Wrexham and once served as the youngest Tory group leader in Wrexham. In 1997 she was appointed by William Hague to speak for the party in Wales on local government, and she contested the Welsh Assembly elections in 1999. She then moved to Redditch and contested the seat at the 2001 and 2005 general elections. Like quite a few other Tory candidates, she will be hoping it will be a case of third time lucky.

Peter Lyburn

PPC for Perth & North Perthshire

Notional status: SNP 1,521

Tory target seat number: 30

Swing required: 1.66%

pnpconservatives@btconnect.com

Peter Lyburn was born in Dundee and educated at Strathallan School and the Scottish Agriculture College in Edinburgh. He grew up on his family's farm in Coupar Angus and worked for the family business. He is now a manager of a UK-wide recycling firm, but still lives in Perthshire.

In 2007, Lyburn stood for the Scottish Parliament in Dunfermline West. At just twenty-four years old, he was the youngest candidate in history to stand for Holyrood. He was chosen as the Conservative candidate for Perth & North

Perthshire, one of Scotland's most marginal seats, in September 2008. His campaign priorities include crime and safety, support for local business and environmental issues.

Widely regarded as a high flyer, if Lyburn can overturn the slim SNP majority he is up against then a bright future surely beckons, but Pete Wishart is a popular local figure.

Jason McCartney

PPC for Colne Valley
Notional status: Lab 1,267
Tory target seat number: 21
Swing required: 1.26%
jason@jasonmccartney.com

Jason McCartney was born in 1968 in Harrogate and educated at Royal Lancaster Grammar School. He then went on to train at RAF Cranwell. In his spare time, McCartney enjoys running and playing tennis, and he is a keen supporter of the local cricket and football clubs.

Serving as an RAF officer McCartney was responsible for thirty people at just nineteen years of age. He has served at home and abroad in Turkey, Las Vegas and Iraq. He is the vice chairman of a local hospital radio charity and a governor of Sports Aid. He also has a background in journalism, and he has worked as a reporter for BBC local radio in Leeds and Middlesbrough, and more recently as the presenter for *Calendar News and Sport* on ITV Yorkshire.

McCartney reported on the 1997 general election, where Labour celebrated its landslide, at Darlington. In 2001 he covered Northallerton, where the focus was on William Hague. He was chosen to fight Colne Valley in March 2007. The current Labour MP, Kali Mountford, will be standing down at the next election, and this should help McCartney achieve the small swing required.

Karl McCartney

PPC for Lincoln
Notional status: Lab 3,806
Tory target seat number: 89
Swing required: 4.74%
karl@karlmccartney.com

Karl McCartney was born in Birkenhead in 1968. He grew up and attended school in Birkenhead and in the north-west. He went on to study geography at St David's University College in Wales. Aside from politics, McCartney is an accomplished sportsman. He played football to a high standard whilst at university and now enjoys cricket, croquet, golf and rugby. The author played alongside him for the Lobbyists RUFC for many years and can personally vouch for his physicality – and verbosity – on the rugby field.

In the 1990s McCartney worked in the City before becoming the director of a consultancy owned by one of his brothers. After achieving an MBA from Kingston University Business School in 1999, he worked as a corporate strategy and communications consultant. He has also been a councillor, as well as a school governor and local magistrate. He worked for the Conservative Party in the mid-1990s and has held a number of key voluntary positions.

After leading a strong campaign as the PPC for Lincoln at the 2005 general election, McCartney was reselected to contest the seat at the next general election. With his combination of communication and strategic skills, he should prevail this time around.

Gareth McKeever

PPC for Westmorland & Lonsdale

Notional status: Lib Dem 806

Tory target seat number: 13

Swing required: 0.85%

westmorlandtories@btinternet.com

Gareth McKeever was born in 1977 in Portstewart in Northern Ireland. He was educated at Coleraine Academical Institution and has a degree in PPE from Oxford. In his spare time McKeever enjoys running, cycling and playing bridge. He also serves as a board member and volunteer for Honeypot, a charity which supports young carers.

Now living in London, over the last decade McKeever has worked in finance. He worked for UBS and then more recently as a senior executive for the international bank Morgan Stanley.

McKeever was selected to contest Westmorland & Lonsdale following the resignation of Tory candidate Richard Bell in July 2008. Despite not being a local man, McKeever has run a strong local campaign, focusing on issues such as the NHS and challenges faced by rural communities.

Mary Macleod

PPC for Brentford & Isleworth

Notional status: Lab 3,633

Tory target seat number: 75

Swing required: 4.14%

mary@marymacleod.com

Born in London in 1969, Mary Macleod was raised in Scotland. She went to

Dingwall Academy and Glasgow University. Outside politics she has a wide range of interests, including music, art, sport and reading.

Since graduating from Glasgow University, Macleod has built up a career as a management consultant, specialising in the banking and financial sectors. After working for Andersen Consulting for many years, she now runs her own consulting firm in the City. Macleod has also worked as a policy advisor in the Queen's private office at Buckingham Palace. She was also an ambassador for ActionAid, a charity working with global poverty, for many years. She is a school governor and runs conferences in schools and universities across the country to promote learning about business to students.

In politics Macleod has worked for some of the key members of the shadow Cabinet, including Liam Fox, David Willetts, Theresa May, Caroline Spelman and Lord Strathclyde. She is the chairman of the Conservative Candidates' Association and stood as a Conservative candidate in the 1997 general election against Charles Kennedy. This time around she has an eminently winnable seat and a bright political career ahead of her.

Stephen McPartland

PPC for Stevenage
Notional status: Lab 3,288
Tory target seat number: 72
Swing required: 4.03%
stephen@stephenmcpartland.co.uk

Born in Liverpool in 1971, Stephen McPartland was educated at St Joseph's School, Widnes. McPartland is married to Emma, a primary school teacher. He has worked for several local and national charities, and is a trustee of the Living Room, a local charity which offers addiction treatment, and a volunteer for Asthma UK. He is also a fan of Stevenage and Liverpool football clubs.

McPartland worked for a while as a Conservative Party agent. He has business experience at every level, having worked for small local businesses and large global organisations. He is now a director of the leading transatlantic business organisation British American Business.

When McPartland moved to Hertfordshire in 2001 he was selected to contest Stevenage. He has campaigned against the closure of the A&E department at Lister Hospital, for better cancer services in the area and for more community policing. He is up against Labour's Barbara Follett, who has been damaged by the MP expenses row.

Esther McVey

PPC for Wirral West

Notional status: Con 569

Tory target seat number: N/A

Swing required: N/A

esther@winningwomen.co.uk

Born in Liverpool in 1967, Esther McVey was educated at Belvedere School. She went on to study law at Queen Mary & Westfield College, University of London. She also has a postgraduate diploma in journalism from City University and an MSc in corporate governance from Liverpool John Moores University.

Having started working for the family construction firm, McVey went on to have a successful career as a presenter and producer in the media. She is currently the managing director of her own PR company and is the founder of Winning Women, an organisation which promotes women in business. She also does extensive charity work, and is patron of Wirral Holistic Therapeutic Cancer Care and of the disabled children's charity Full Life. She is an ambassador for Action Medical Research and Wirral Women and Children's Aid. Having known Kate McCann for over twenty years, McVey helped set up the Madeleine McCann Fund and remained on the board for eight months.

McVey contested Wirral West in 2005. Until 1997 the area was safe Conservative territory, but it has been held by Labour MP Stephen Hesford since then – although boundary changes are favourable for the Tories and give them a notional majority. Energetic and articulate, McVey will be one of the stars of the new intake.

Simon Marcus

PPC for Barking

Notional status: Lab 12,183

Tory target seat number: N/A

Swing required: N/A

simonmarcus2003@yahoo.co.uk

Born and brought up in north London, Simon Marcus has an MA from King's College, London. Apart from boxing, he enjoys cricket, rugby, yoga and military history.

Marcus has had a spectacularly varied career. He has been involved in publishing, small business management and financial services. He has also worked for the British Chambers of Commerce in Brussels.

Outside business, Marcus's passion is charitable work and community service. He now runs the hugely successful London Boxing Academy in Tottenham. The academy has a strong track record of turning troublesome youths into model citizens. He is also involved with the CSJ, the YMCA and Policy Exchange.

Marcus has been selected to fight Barking at the general election. He will need all his fighting spirit to take on not just the Labour incumbent Margaret Hodge but also the BNP – who have the seat as one of their top targets. Likely defeat in this round will not deter this pugnacious pugilist.

Paul Maynard

PPC for Blackpool North & Cleveleys

Notional status: Lab 3,241

Tory target seat number: 79

Swing required: 4.24%

paul@bncconservatives.com

Born in Crewe in 1975, Paul Maynard was educated at St Ambrose College, Trafford. He then went on to study modern history at University College, Oxford. Outside politics, Maynard enjoys the arts and theatre.

After graduating, Maynard worked as a legal management consultant. He spent some time as a special advisor to Dr Liam Fox and also had a spell at the Reform think tank.

Maynard is well established locally, having been a governor at his local Catholic primary school and a lay reader at his local church. He contested Twickenham in 2005 and was chosen as the candidate for Blackpool North & Cleveleys in December 2006.

Mark Menzies

PPC for Fylde

Notional status: Con 11,117

Tory target seat number: N/A

Swing required: N/A

mark.menzies@virgin.net

Born in Ayrshire, near Glasgow, in 1971, Mark Menzies has lived in Leeds since 1997. He graduated from Glasgow University with a degree in economic history and has had a career in marketing, working for some of the largest supermarket chains in the country. He got his first job with Asda when he was fifteen years old, he has worked for Marks & Spencer and he now works for Morrisons.

Menzies has been actively involved in politics for twenty years. He stood as a Conservative PPC in the last two general elections. He fought the Glasgow Govan seat in 2001 and Selby in 2005, which he came very close to winning from Labour. He was selected as the Conservative PPC for Fylde in November 2008.

Fylde is a safe Tory seat, having been represented by the Conservatives for more than sixty years. The current much-respected Conservative MP, Michael Jack, will be retiring at the next election after twenty-one years' service in the House of Commons, leaving behind a majority of 12,459. Menzies will soon be swapping the supermarket aisles for the corridors of power.

Stephen Metcalfe

PPC for South Basildon & East Thurrock

Notional status: Lab 905

Tory target seat number: 17

Swing required: 1.07%

stephen@vote4metcalfe.com

Steve Metcalfe was born in Essex in 1966. He is married with two teenage children. Outside politics he enjoys, amongst other things, amateur dramatics, watching rugby and helping out at his local church.

Metcalfe runs a family printing business with his wife. The business is based in Romford and employs around forty people. He has also been a governor of a large secondary school, where he led budgeting and management changes which saw the school improve its rating from 'poor' to 'good'.

Metcalfe has extensive political experience, having campaigned at every level for over twenty years from parish council to European Parliament. He is a former Epping Forest district councillor and stood as the Conservative PPC in Ilford North in the 2005 general election. This time around Metcalfe is fighting a wafer-thin Labour majority and should return the iconic Basildon & Billericay seat to the Tories.

Gerald Michaluk

PPC for Ochil & South Perthshire

Notional status: Lab 688

Tory target seat number: 163

Swing required: 8.42%

perth@scottishtories.com

After leaving Lendrick Muir School in Rumbling Bridge, Gerald Michaluk went on to study chemistry and then management at Heriot Watt University. Outside politics, Michaluk likes to spend his time playing field sports, flying and writing. He is the author of two professional books on marketing. He has also worked as a volunteer with the British Red Cross for over twenty-five years, and is a civilian gliding instructor with the Air Cadets, the RAF youth movement.

After graduating Michaluk held a post at Strathclyde University and was an elected member of the university's senate for many years. He then moved on to run his own business as a marketing consultant, and is now a member of the Market

Research Society, a fellow of the Chartered Institute of Marketing and a chartered marketer. He owns several businesses, with his head office based in central Glasgow.

Michaluk contested Glasgow Pollok in the 2007 Scottish Parliament elections. As well as being selected as the Conservative PPC for Ochil & South Perthshire, he also stood as a candidate for Scotland in the June 2009 European Parliament elections. This is a three-way marginal, and if the Tories are to re-establish themselves north of the border this is the kind of seat they need to win.

Nigel Mills

PPC for Amber Valley
Notional status: Lab 5,512
Tory target seat number: 120
Swing required: 6.27%
nigel@ambervalleyconservatives.com

Having been born in Jacksdale in 1975, Nigel Mills has lived in the Amber valley area all of his life. He went to local schools before studying classics at the University of Newcastle upon Tyne. He is a season ticket holder for both Notts County and Nottinghamshire Cricket Club.

By profession Mills is an accountant. He works for PricewaterhouseCoopers as a tax advisor, specialising in advising UK businesses on international tax issues. He has also advised international companies on how to invest in the UK.

Mills has served on Amber Valley Borough Council since 2004. At the general election he will hope to leverage his local connections and unseat Labour's Judy Mallaber.

Philip Milton

PPC for North Devon
Notional status: Lib Dem 5,276
Tory target seat number: 102
Swing required: 5.35%
pjmilton@miltonpj.net

Born in Barnstaple in 1962, Philip Milton's can trace his north Devon roots back to the seventeenth century. His father worked for BT and his mother ran a bed and breakfast hotel and fostered children. He is married with four children. He is actively involved in Christian life in the area and enjoys taking part in numerous local clubs, societies and charities.

Milton left school at sixteen and went straight into work at Lloyds Bank, before setting up his own business at the age of twenty-three. He has run his prosperous finance business for over twenty years and also owns a local restaurant, bookshop and art gallery.

Milton's business experience and links with the local community will help him in the contest for this Lib Dem seat, but it is held by the tenacious Nick Harvey.

Stephen Mold

PPC for Derby North
Notional status: Lab 5,691
Tory target seat number: 154
Swing required: 8.07%
stephen@stephenmold.com

Born in Banbury in 1968, Stephen Mold does not have a typical Conservative background. Both his parents were Labour voters and he was brought up on a council estate. Married with one child, Mold's interests outside work and politics include Formula 1 racing, motor cruising and flying small aircraft.

Mold attended the local comprehensive school but had to give up his plans to go into higher education, as his father injured himself, forcing Mold to go straight to work in order to help pay the bills. He worked in a variety of manual jobs and then set up his own flooring business. However, having always been interested in computers, he has since worked his way up to being the European sales and marketing director for an international software company.

Mold fought his first council election thirteen years ago in Daventry. He then moved to Bicester and managed to win a council seat and hold it until he moved from the area. Recently, he has been elected as a governor of Northampton General Hospital Trust.

Penny Mordaunt

PPC for Portsmouth North
Notional status: Lab 315
Tory target seat number: 8
Swing required: 0.38%
portsmouthnorth@tory.org

Born in Torbay in 1973, Penny Mordaunt was educated at Oaklands Comprehensive School. Her mother, father and step-mother were all teachers, and she has a strong interest in education. She read philosophy at Reading University, where she was president of the Students' Union. When not working, she enjoys painting, astronomy and fundraising for local and national charities. She also runs the League of Friends visiting team at the Queen Alexandra Hospital.

Mordaunt's career has not always been conventional. Whilst studying at college she worked as a magician's assistant, and she spent her gap year working in orphanages and hospitals in post-revolutionary Romania. Since graduating, she has had a successful career in communications. She has worked for the National Lottery, the Freight Transport Association, Diabetes UK and Hanover Communications.

Mordaunt has been involved in politics at a voluntary and professional level for many years. She has been deputy chairman political of several associations, and was the Conservative Party's head of youth under John Major and head of broadcasting for two years under William Hague. In 2000 she was head of foreign press to George W. Bush during his first presidential election campaign.

She first contested Portsmouth North in 2005, achieving a 5.5 per cent swing to the Conservatives. This is one of the Tories' top target seats and Mordaunt seems sure to get in – and she is certainly one to watch.

Nicky Morgan

PPC for Loughborough
Notional status: Lab 1,816
Tory target seat number: 36
Swing required: 1.94%
nicky@loughboroughconservatives.com

Born in Kingston upon Thames in 1972, Nicky Morgan went to Surbiton High School. She then studied law at St Hugh's College, Oxford. She is married and has a baby son. She regularly attends her local church, and enjoys running and cooking in her spare time.

Morgan has a strong legal background. She qualified as a solicitor in 1994 and has worked as a corporate lawyer specialising in mergers and acquisitions. She now acts as an in-house counsel advising on corporate law matters. She was also a school governor for eight years.

Morgan joined the Conservative Party in 1989 and has been a Conservative candidate in two previous general elections. She was the candidate for Islington South in 2001 and fought Loughborough at the 2005 general election, achieving a 5 per cent swing. When she was first selected as the candidate for Loughborough in 2004, Morgan launched the 'Listening to Loughborough' campaign to enhance the voices of the local residents. As Loughborough University forms a significant part of the constituency, Morgan has tried to build up a strong connection between its students and Loughborough Conservatives.

Only a small swing is required in order for her to win at the next election, placing Loughborough within the top Conservative target seats. Another one to watch.

Anne-Marie Morris

PPC for Newton Abbot

Notional status: Lib Dem 4,830

Tory target seat number: 101

Swing required: 5.25%

annemarie@annemariemorris.co.uk

Born in London in 1957, Anne-Marie Morris is the daughter of a maritime trader. She grew up in Brixham, where her family has lived for over two centuries. She studied law at Hertford College, Oxford. She lives in Newton Abbott with her family and enjoys walking her two dogs in the Devonshire countryside.

After university, Morris pursued a successful career in law and international marketing. She now runs a successful local marketing and executive coaching consultancy, and is a member of the Devon and Cornwall board of the Institute of Directors and of the Federation of Small Businesses.

Morris is also a school governor at Rydon School in Kingsteignton and at Newton Abbott College. She was elected a county councillor in 2005 and became chairman of the county's Health Scrutiny Committee. As the Conservative PPC for Newton Abbott, Morris has campaigned vigorously on local healthcare, education, investment for new jobs and affordable housing.

David Morris

PPC for Morecambe & Lunesdale

Notional status: Lab 4,849

Tory target seat number: 110

Swing required: 5.87%

morecambeandlunesdale@tory.org

With a father who worked in port administration, David Morris was brought up in Hong Kong and the Bahamas. However, the family has strong Lancastrian connections. No longer married, Morris has two sons with his former wife.

By profession Morris is a company director. His firm specialises in the property service and retail sectors. Once the youngest Conservative Association chairman in the country, Morris has frequently spoken for the party on youth affairs.

Having fought Blackpool South in 2001 and Carmarthen West & South Pembrokeshire in 2005, Morris is contesting Morecambe & Lunesdale this time around, against Labour's Geraldine Smith.

James Morris

PPC for Halesowen & Rowley Regis
Notional status: Lab 4,010
Tory target seat number: 93
Swing required: 4.83%
james@halesowenandrowleyregis.com

James Morris was born in Nottingham in 1966 and educated at Nottingham High School and Birmingham University, where he studied English literature. He then undertook postgraduate research at Oxford. He also has an MBA from Cranfield School of Management. He is married and has two young children, and in his spare time he enjoys playing cricket.

Morris has had a successful career as a businessman specialising in software companies. He is presently chief executive of Localis, a local government think tank. In 2003 he launched Mind the Gap, an independent campaign which aimed to encourage more local involvement in politics, and in 2004 wrote a pamphlet called *Change Starts Small*, which carried forward the ideas of Mind the Gap.

Unusually for the current crop of Tory PPCs, Morris has no previous experience as a candidate or councillor. He was selected as the candidate for Halesowen & Rowley Regis in July 2008.

Wendy Morton

PPC for Tynemouth
Notional status: Lab 5,490
Tory target seat number: 109
Swing required: 5.83%
wendy.morton5@btinternet.com

Having been born in Northallerton in 1967, Wendy Morton has spent most of her life in Yorkshire and the north-east. She went to Wensleydale Comprehensive School, and later in life studied for her MBA at the Open University. She enjoys running and cooking.

After a spell in the Diplomatic Service, Morton moved into the private sector to work in sales and marketing. When her husband left the Royal Navy they set up their own electronics and manufacturing business.

Having been a district councillor since 2001, Morton fought Newcastle Central in the general election of 2005. This time around she is taking on Labour's Alan Campbell at Tynemouth.

Stephen Mosley

PPC for City of Chester
Notional status: Lab 973
Tory target seat number: 19
Swing required: 1.10%
stephen@stephen-mosley.co.uk

Born in Solihull, Stephen Mosley graduated from Nottingham University with a BSc in chemistry. He is married and has two young children, and his big hobby is cycling.

Mosley worked for IBM for four years before setting up his own IT consultancy in 1997. His business has since developed into property management and has expanded into north Wales. He also has family and business relationships in Malawi.

Mosley was elected to Chester City Council in 2000 and was re-elected in 2004 with the largest number of votes ever obtained in his ward. He has been the deputy leader of the council since May 2007, following the defeat of its twenty-year Labour and Lib Dem coalition. He was selected as the Conservative PPC for City of Chester in 2007 and must be hopeful of overturning Labour MP Christine Russell's slim majority.

David Mowat

PPC for Warrington South
Notional status: Lab 4,337
Tory target seat number: 85
Swing required: 4.58%
davidmowat@btinternet.com

David Mowat was born in 1957 and grew up in Rugby, where he attended the local grammar school. He is married and has four children. The family has lived in Cheshire for more than twenty years. Outside work, his main interests lie in sport, including golf, rugby and football. He is the director of Warrington Town Football Club.

After grammar school Mowat went on to study civil engineering at Imperial College, London, before qualifying as a chartered accountant. He then worked for Accenture for twenty-four years as a global managing partner. He left Accenture in 2005 and is now chairman of Fairbridge, a Salford-based charity which is dedicated to rebuilding opportunities for young people from deprived backgrounds. He is also governor of his local primary school.

Mowat joined the Conservative Party whilst at university. He is a borough councillor and is presently treasurer of the Tatton constituency. He was selected to be the Conservative PPC for Warrington South in March 2007.

Julia Mulligan

PPC for Leeds North West

Notional status: Lib Dem 2,064

Tory target seat number: 95

Swing required: 5.08%

julia.mulligan@leedsconservatives.com

Julia Mulligan was born in Bradford in 1968 and has lived in the area for most of her life. She is married and has two young daughters. Outside politics she has done extensive charity work. She has spent time volunteering in Rwanda, supporting a movement against modern-day slavery. She has also raised money for Great Ormond Street Hospital and several local hospices and animal refuges.

Mulligan has a degree in European politics and economics from the University of Buckingham, and she has built up a successful career in marketing. She started out in sales and marketing at a car dealership in Leeds and has since worked for several major international communications agencies. She now runs her own marketing agency in Leeds.

Mulligan is a local councillor for Upper Wharfedale on Craven District Council and is a member of the Policy Committee. She has been the candidate for Leeds North West since November 2006.

Gary Mulvaney

PPC for Argyll & Bute

Notional status: Lib Dem 5,636

Tory target seat number: 126

Swing required: 6.52%

gary.mulvaney@scottishconservatives.com

Born in Kirkcaldy in 1968, Gary Mulvaney lives in Helensburgh with his fiancée and her daughter. He volunteers for the Young Enterprise Scheme.

Mulvaney has a degree in accounting from the University of Abertay in Dundee. By profession he is a chartered certified accountant and finance director, and he has worked in a local authority finance department. He currently works for a Toyota dealership.

Mulvaney has been a local Argyll & Bute councillor since 2003 and formerly chaired the Audit Committee. He will be contesting Argyll & Bute this time around against the Lib Dem Alan Reid.

Sheryll Murray

PPC for South East Cornwall

Notional status: Lib Dem 5,485

Tory target seat number: 112

Swing required: 5.89%

smurrayuk@gmail.com

Born in Millbrook in 1956, Sheryll Murray was educated at Torpoint Comprehensive School. She still lives locally and can trace her roots back many generations. She is married to a local trawler owner and they have two grown-up children.

By profession Murray works in primary healthcare. She also worked for a time as a representative of the fishing industry. She is a former Cornwall county councillor and is still a Caradon district councillor and leader of the Conservative group.

Murray will be hoping that her strong local roots and vigorous support for the local fishing industry will help her to win this seat. The Lib Dems' sitting MP, Colin Breed, is standing down.

Simon Nayyar

PPC for Hackney South & Shoreditch

Notional status: Lab 9,629

Tory target seat number: N/A

Swing required: N/A

simon@hackneyconservatives.com

After graduating with a degree in history from York University, Simon Nayyar has been working for over twenty years in the public affairs industry, advising large organisations in the public and voluntary sectors. He was brought up in London and has lived in the capital for most of his life. He is a school governor for a local nursery school and the trustee of a central London Citizens Advice Bureau.

Before his career in public affairs, Nayyar was a parliamentary researcher for a Conservative MP. He has been a member of the party for over twenty years, working as an activist across the country and in Westminster. Recently he was involved in the Conservative Party's Umubano mission project in Rwanda.

Nayyar was selected as the Conservative candidate for Hackney South & Shoreditch in March 2009, a seat which has been held by Labour in every election since its creation in 1974. On paper at least Hackney South & Shoreditch is a safe Labour seat. Nayyar, however, has a combination of sophisticated charm and political nous – and should achieve a substantial swing to the Tories.

Sarah Newton

PPC for Truro & Falmouth

Notional status: Lib Dem 3,931

Tory target seat number: 86

Swing required: 4.63%

sarahnewton1@aol.com

Married with three children, Sarah Newton was educated at Clare Terrace, Falmouth School and King's College, London. Her hobbies are sailing, skiing and beekeeping.

Newton has had a varied career. She has worked in financial services for Citibank and American Express, but she has also worked in the voluntary sector. She has been a director of Age Concern and the International Longevity Centre, and has also volunteered for a range of charities and educational establishments.

Newton is standing for the new seat of Truro & Falmouth and will hope that the Tory revival in the south-west will help her to win. The sitting Lib Dem MP for Truro & St Austell, Matthew Taylor, is standing down.

Caroline Nokes

PPC for Romsey & Southampton North

Notional status: Lib Dem 204

Tory target seat number: 4

Swing required: 0.23%

caroline@romseyconservatives.co.uk

Born in 1972 in Lyndhurst, Caroline Nokes went to La Sagesse Convent before going on to the University of Sussex, where she gained a BA in politics. The daughter of an MEP, she has been actively involved in the world of politics from a young age.

Nokes worked for her father, Roy Perry MEP, for ten years, gaining experience in the conduct and handling of a busy constituency office. She is married and has one daughter. Since 2008 she has been the CEO of the National Pony Society.

Nokes was elected to Test Valley Borough Council in 1999, becoming the youngest member on the council. She was re-elected in 2003 and has continued to represent the Romsey Extra ward on the borough council ever since. In 2001 she was elected to the council's ruling executive and is responsible for leisure and culture. In 2005 the council's facility for young people, the Depot, was opened and several Healthy Living Centres have been established under her remit.

When she fought Romsey in 2005 Nokes achieved a 2.3 per cent swing from the Liberal Democrats – making it the most marginal Lib Dem seat in the country. One more heave and she should do it.

Jesse Norman

PPC for Hereford & South Herefordshire
Notional status: Lib Dem 1,089
Tory target seat number: 20
Swing required: 1.19%
jesse4hereford@gmail.com

Born in London in 1962, Jesse Norman has a wide range of business, public and third-sector experience. He was educated at Oxford University and has an MA and a PhD from University College, London. He was a director of Barclays for several years, but left the City in 1997 to teach and research at UCL.

Norman has published several books and written extensively for the national press. His book *Compassionate Conservatism* was hailed as the 'handbook to Cameronism' by the *Sunday Times*, and the follow-up, *Compassionate Economics*, was described as the 'best analysis of the credit crunch' by Dan Hannan MEP. He has also made regular appearances on national radio and TV. He is married and has three children.

Norman joined the Conservative Party whilst at university in the 1980s and has taken part in campaigning for over twenty years. He worked with Oliver Letwin during the 2005 general election and has been a policy advisor to George Osborne, the shadow Work & Pensions team and Boris Johnson during his mayor of London campaign. He has led numerous local campaigns, including Save Our Post Offices in Herefordshire, and he set up Herefordshire Schools First to help fight against school closures.

Norman was selected to be the candidate for Hereford & South Herefordshire in December 2006. With the sitting MP, Lib Dem Paul Keetch, retiring, he should win the seat. Recently described by Boris Johnson as the 'Clark Kent of British politics', he is widely tipped for high office.

David Nuttall

PPC for Bury North
Notional status: Lab 2,059
Tory target seat number: 46
Swing required: 2.52%
nuttall4burynorth@aol.com

Born in Sheffield in 1962, David Nuttall went to Aston Comprehensive School in Rotherham. He then went straight into work, joining a local solicitor's firm in Sheffield. He has since stayed with the same firm and, after years of part-time study to obtain a law degree and qualifying as a fellow of the Institution of Legal Executives, was admitted as a solicitor in 1990. He became senior partner in 1998, employing more than forty staff. He was admitted as a notary public in the same year. He is married, a regular church attender who enjoys walking and bird watching.

Nuttall has been a member of the Conservative Party since 1980. He was a Rotherham borough councillor for six years and contested Sheffield Hillsborough at the 1997 general election. He also contested Morecambe & Lunesdale in 2001 and Bury North in 2005. Bury North is subject to boundary changes at the next general election and he should succeed this time around, especially with the sitting MP, David Chaytor, standing down.

Matthew Offord

PPC for Hendon
Notional status: Lab 3,231
Tory target seat number: 73
Swing required: 4.03%
fingold@btinternet.com

Matthew Offord was born in Alton in 1969 and educated at Amery Hill School and Nottingham Trent University. He lives in Hendon and currently works at BBC Television Centre in London. He enjoys travelling with the Royal Geographical Society. In 2005 he undertook a 2,000 kilometre exploration of the Libyan desert and he has visited many countries, including Cyprus, India and Israel.

Offord became involved with the Conservative Party when he was a student. After capturing the only Tory council seat in Doncaster, he went on to become a councillor in Hendon in 2002. He is now the deputy leader of Barnet Council and the Cabinet member for environment and transport. In 2004 he became chairman of the Hendon Conservative Association. In the past he has also worked as an agent for the party in numerous campaigns and seats, and acted as the Conservative election agent in Hendon at the 2005 general election, where the Labour majority was reduced from 7,417 to 3,005.

Offord was selected to contest Hendon in July 2007 and needs only a small swing to win the seat at the next election. Given his campaigning experience – and his knowledge of the area – he may soon have to restrict his expeditions to the parliamentary recesses.

Eric Ollerenshaw

PPC for Lancaster & Fleetwood

Notional status: Lab 3,428

Tory target seat number: 81

Swing required: 4.41%

lancasterwyre@tory.org

Eric Ollerenshaw was born and educated in Lancashire. He taught history at a number of comprehensive schools for many years before launching his political career.

Ollerenshaw was a councillor on Hackney Borough Council in the 1990s and was elected to the London Assembly in 2000. In 1990 he was awarded an OBE for public and political service. Ollerenshaw currently leads the Cities and Diversity Section of the Conservative Party at CCHQ. In addition to his political commitments, he has been a governor of a number of primary and secondary schools and a board member of several charities, including Great Ormond Street Hospital.

He was selected as the candidate for Lancaster & Fleetwood at an open primary in March 2007, and has since led a number of major local campaigns including the Conservative petition against the closure of four Lancaster post offices and the launch of Lancaster's 'Stop Cantaxx Again!' campaign. A canny operator with a wealth of experience of political street fighting, Ollerenshaw should get elected.

Guy Opperman

PPC for Hexham

Notional status: Con 4,957

Tory target seat number: N/A

Swing required: N/A

hexham@tory.org

Born in Marlborough in 1967, Guy Opperman was brought up in Wiltshire, son of a mother who worked for MI6. He went to Harrow School and the universities of Buckingham and Lille. He is a marathon runner and amateur steeplechase jockey. His partner is a journalist.

By profession Opperman is a lawyer, and he is a practising barrister specialising in public law and human rights. He is also a published author, and was a councillor in Wiltshire for four years. He also acted as an advisor to Michael Ancram when he was shadow Foreign Secretary.

Opperman served as a one-term councillor in Wiltshire. He then fought Swindon North in 1997 and Caernarfon in 2005. This time around he is inheriting Peter Atkinson's safe Hexham seat – so it will be third time lucky.

Adrian Owens

PPC for West Lancashire

Notional status: Lab 6,084

Tory target seat number: 139

Swing required: 7.05%

adrian@adrianowens.com

Born in the Wirral in 1965, Adrian Owens lives in Newburgh with his wife and three young children. He is a science graduate from Trinity College, Cambridge. His hobbies are cricket, walking and camping.

Owens runs his own consultancy business advising companies on health, safety and environmental regulations. He is also an external grant assessor for the Community Foundation for Merseyside and a Prince's Trust business mentor.

Having been a councillor in Ormskirk since 1999, he has held the finance portfolio on West Lancashire District Council since 2002. He contested South Ribble in the 2001 general election. He is fighting West Lancashire this time around, taking on Labour's Rosie Cooper.

Neil Parish

PPC for Tiverton & Honiton

Notional status: Con 9,007

Tory target seat number: N/A

Swing required: N/A

nparishmep@bridgwest.demon.co.uk

Neil Parish was born in Bridgwater in Somerset. He comes from a background in farming, having managed his family's arable farm in Somerset for many years. He is married and has two children.

Parish served as a parish, district and county councillor in Somerset before standing for the Westminster Parliament in 1997 and winning a seat in the European Parliament for the South West region in 1999. He has served as Conservative spokesman on agriculture and animal welfare. He was also chairman of the Agriculture and Rural Development Committee and sits on the Fisheries Committee. He played a leading role in the establishment of the European Parliament's public inquiries into the foot and mouth outbreak and the collapse of Equitable Life.

Parish was selected as the Conservative PPC for Tiverton & Honiton in February 2007. He replaces the Conservative MP Angela Browning, who has decided to step down.

Priti Patel

PPC for Witham

Notional status: Con 7,241

Tory target seat number: N/A

Swing required: N/A

priti@working4witham.com

Priti Patel was born in London in 1972. She went to Watford High School before going on to study economics at Keele University and the University of Essex. She is married and has a young son. Outside politics she enjoys cricket, travelling and watching horse racing.

Her parents ran a number of small businesses in the south-east and east of England. However, Patel has followed a career in public affairs and communications, working at various stages for Weber Shandwick and Diageo. In the 1990s, Patel worked in the CRD and became deputy press secretary to the then Leader of the Opposition, William Hague, in 1998. She also had a brief spell working for the Referendum Party.

Patel was the Conservative candidate for Nottingham North at the 2005 general election and was selected to represent the new constituency seat of Witham in November 2006. The seat has a notional Conservative majority. She will get elected, and after that there is no doubt that she will rise rapidly through the ranks of the parliamentary party.

Mark Pawsey

PPC for Rugby

Notional status: Lab 2,397

Tory target seat number: 48

Swing required: 2.60%

mark@rugbyconservatives.com

Born in Meriden in 1957, Mark Pawsey comes from a large family, with four younger brothers. He grew up in Rugby, attended Lawrence Sheriff School and then went on to study estate management at Reading University. He is married and has four children, and as a former rugby player still enjoys watching the game.

Moving to London, Pawsey worked as a trainee chartered surveyor. He then worked as an account manager for several years, and in 1982 set up his own catering supply company in Rugby with one of his brothers.

In 2002, Pawsey was elected to Rugby Borough Council and has served on the Cabinet as spokesman for housing and affordable homes. He was also a founding member of the Anti Rugby Airport Committee, which successfully opposed government plans to build a large airport in the area. Pawsey has a special interest in planning issues and the local environment. In 2005 he fought Nuneaton, reducing Labour's majority from around 7,500 to 2,200. He will fancy his chances of beating Labour's Andy King at the next general election.

Stuart Penketh

PPC for Ellesmere Port & Neston

Notional status: Lab 6,713

Tory target seat number: 153

Swing required: 7.99%

penkethstuart@hotmail.com

Born in Bury in 1981, Stuart Penketh has lived in the north-west all his life. He likes to spend his spare time hill walking, sailing and going to the theatre.

Having gone to the University of Manchester, Penketh graduated in 2003 with an honours degree in geology. At university he was in the Royal Naval Reserve, and before leaving in 2004 managed to become a sub-lieutenant. He now works as a geological consultant at an engineering company.

Penketh's first involvement with the Conservative Party came at university, when he was a member of Conservative Future. Between 2005 and 2007 he was chairman of Greater Manchester East Conservative Future before standing down when he became an elected councillor. He first contested a council seat in 2003, whilst still at university. Since then he has stood for his home ward of Radcliffe North. He finally won his seat on Bury Council in 2007.

Andrew Percy

PPC for Brigg & Goole

Notional status: Lab 3,217

Tory target seat number: 69

Swing required: 3.92%

brigg.goole@gmail.com

Andrew Percy was born in Hull in 1984. He went to William Gee School before studying at York University and then taking a postgraduate law degree at Leeds University. He is a teacher by profession and has taught history at a number of the toughest secondary schools across the Humber region. He now teaches part time and also works as a researcher for David Davis, the former shadow Home Secretary. He is a governor at two local schools.

Percy started to become involved with the Conservative Party as a teenager. He has served as a councillor in the region for the past seven years and he has led successful campaigns against anti-social behaviour, protection of the local environment and the closure of a popular local primary school. He is a member of the NASUWT and is a supporter of a number of pressure groups, including

Countryside Alliance and the Campaign Against Political Correctness. He contested Normanton at the 2005 general election and was selected to represent the Conservatives for Brigg & Goole in November 2006. He will be taking on Labour's Ian Cawsey.

Christopher Pincher

PPC for Tamworth
Notional status: Lab 2,569
Tory target seat number: 56
Swing required: 2.94%
christopher.pincher@tamworthconservatives.co.uk

Christopher Pincher was born in Walsall in 1969 and grew up near Wolverhampton. He graduated from the LSE with a degree in government and history, and went on to work for Accenture, a major consultancy firm.

As well as his political commitments, Pincher is a governor of North Westminster Community School and a member of Tamworth's Hodge Lane nature reserve. In his spare time he enjoys playing golf and is a keen supporter of horse racing. He joined the Conservative Party in 1987 and has since campaigned on various local issues. Most notably, he is leading a high-profile 'clean up' campaign across the streets of Tamworth and the local villages.

Pincher contested Tamworth in 2005 and was narrowly defeated. The Conservatives won Tamworth Borough Council in June 2004 after seventeen years of Labour control, and Pincher needs a small swing in order to win at the next general election. A veteran of the CCO General Election Voluntary Agency (GENEVA), Pincher has the skills and experience to succeed.

Brenda Porter

PPC for Southport
Notional status: Lib Dem 3,838
Tory target seat number: 88
Swing required: 4.66%
brenda.porter@talktalk.net

The daughter of an army officer, Brenda Porter was born in Liverpool but spent most of her childhood living in Hong Kong with her family. She now lives in Southport, where she has been settled for more than thirty years. She originally trained as a cook, but has worked in management for several charitable and religious organisations.

Porter is married and has three children and six grandchildren. She is a strong supporter of the local community and is a founding member of the Ainsdale Civic Society and a member of the Ainsdale Horticultural Society. She was elected as an Ainsdale ward councillor in 2000 and has held a number of key posts, including chair of licensing and spokesperson on health. In 2005 she became the Conservative Chief Whip and was made deputy leader in 2007. She was selected to contest Southport in October 2007, and she will be taking on the Lib Dem MP John Pugh.

Will Quince

PPC for Colchester
Notional Status: Lib Dem 6,388
Tory target seat number: 149
Swing required: 7.79%
willquinceforcolchester@live.co.uk

Born in Ascot in 1982, Will Quince was educated at the University of Wales, Aberystwyth. He works for the Britvic soft drinks company.

Quince worked his way up through the party by way of Conservative Future (CF). He has sat on CF's national committee and he has been deputy chairman of Hertford and Stortford Conservative Association. He has also been an East Herts district councillor. He will have his work cut out to unseat the Lib Dems' Bob Russell, who is well entrenched in the seat, but he is certainly one to watch for the future.

Mark Reckless

PPC for Rochester & Strood
Notional status: Con 503
Tory target seat number: N/A
Swing required: N/A
markreckless@hotmail.com

Born in London in 1970, Mark Reckless studied PPE at Oxford University, and he also has an MBA from Columbia Business School. A former economist and banker, he recently trained as a barrister and was called to the Bar in 2007.

In the past, Reckless worked for the Conservative Party's Policy Unit, developing policies for tackling youth crime and police governance. He is a Medway councillor for Rochester West ward and previously stood as the Conservative candidate for Medway in two general elections. In 2005, he missed out by just 213 votes.

Reckless was selected to be the candidate for Rochester & Strood, a new seat, in July 2008. The seat has a notional Conservative majority, and the sitting Labour MP for Medway, Bob Marshall-Andrews, is standing down.

Annunziata Rees-Mogg

PPC for Somerton & Frome

Notional status: Lib Dem 595

Tory target seat number: 11

Swing required: 0.56%

areesmogg@sfca.org.uk

Annunziata Rees-Mogg was born in Bath in 1979. She was brought up in Somerset and London. She has been a journalist for over ten years and worked as the deputy editor of *MoneyWeek* and editor of the *European Journal* before her present position as a leader writer for the *Daily Telegraph*.

Rees-Mogg has been a member of the Conservative Party for more than twenty years, during which she has set up a number of high-profile campaigns – particularly relating to Europe. In 2003 she set up Trust the People, a campaign for a referendum on the European constitution. She continued to fight for the same cause in 2008, lending her support to the independent group 'I Want a Referendum' in Somerton & Frome. Rees-Mogg was the candidate for Aberavon in south Wales at the last general election, increasing the Conservative vote by 34 per cent.

She has been the Conservative PPC for Somerton & Frome since October 2006. This is a new seat, with a narrow notional Lib Dem majority. Part of a journalistic and political dynasty, she is the daughter of Lord Rees-Mogg and sister of Tory PPC Jacob (see below).

Jacob Rees-Mogg

PPC for North East Somerset

Notional status: Con 212

Tory target seat number: N/A

Swing required: N/A

jacob@northeastsomersetconservatives.co.uk

Jacob Rees-Mogg was born in 1969 and grew up in Somerset. He was educated at Eton and studied history at Trinity College, Oxford. He is married with two children. His hobbies include politics and history – and he is a staunch supporter of Somerset Cricket Club.

Rees-Mogg's career has focused on pension fund management. He worked for Rothschilds and spent three years working in Hong Kong in the mid-1990s. He now runs his own company, Somerset Capital Management, which specialises in pension fund management for charitable organisations. He is also a trustee to several non-profit-making and charitable organisations.

He has been a Wansdyke councillor for many years. He previously stood as a Tory candidate in Fife Central in 1997 and The Wrekin in 2001. He is known for his strongly Eurosceptic views. Rees-Mogg has been the candidate for the new constituency of North East Somerset since 2007. The Conservatives have a notional majority, and Jacob should join his sister Annunziata in the Commons – with father William just along the corridor in the Lords.

Simon Reevell

PPC for Dewsbury
Notional status: Lab 3,999
Tory target seat number: 82
Swing required: 4.44%
simon@wattonabbey.co.uk

Born in Doncaster in 1966 and brought up in Yorkshire, Simon Reevell is married to Louise, a barrister. They have two dogs and support the RNLI, Help for Heroes and the Dogs' Trust. Simon also enjoys playing tennis.

Reevell obtained a degree in economics from Manchester Polytechnic and then intended to pursue a career in the military. His career was, however, cut short by injury. He therefore went to Lincoln's Inn and qualified as a barrister. He practises in Leeds, specialising in defending members of the armed forces.

Politically Reevell has been an association chairman and regional deputy chairman. He is standing in Dewsbury against Labour's Shahid Malik, who was badly hit by the MP expenses scandal.

Fabian Richter

PPC for Bath
Notional status: Lib Dem 5,624
Tory target seat number: 134
Swing required: 6.78%
fabianforbath@hotmail.co.uk

Born in Munich in 1972, Fabian Richter was brought up in Germany. He went to state schools before going on to Oxford University. He enjoys cooking, cinema, concerts and playing squash.

Professionally Richter is a management consultant in financial services. He also spent a year working for a charity which helps aged and disabled people. He currently works part time as chief of staff to David Willetts.

Politically Richter was Association chairman and then election agent for North Southwark & Bermondsey. He is standing in Bath this time around. He is up against the sitting Lib Dem MP Don Foster, and it might take a small earthquake to shift him.

Caroline Righton

PPC for St Austell & Newquay
Notional status: Lib Dem 5,723
Tory target seat number: 119
Swing required: 6.22%
caroline@carolinerighton.com

Caroline Righton was born in London in 1958 and attended La Retraite High School and Cardiff College. She has lived in Cornwall since she was nineteen years old, where she initially trained as a journalist on local newspapers. She is married with two grown-up sons, and her hobbies include cooking and voluntary work.

Righton has worked in the media for most of her career and has experience as a journalist, television presenter, producer and author. She has worked for the main national newspapers and national television channels, including the BBC, Channel Four and Sky. She is a member of the Media Society and the Society of Authors. She also has extensive experience in business. She previously set up her own independent production business, which was bought out by a large corporate media company, and in 2003 she set up her own management consultancy. The same year she created *The Life Audit*, an international best-selling self-help plan.

Righton was selected as the candidate for St Austell & Newquay at an open primary in December 2006. This is a new seat with a substantial notional Lib Dem majority.

Douglas Ross

PPC for Moray
Notional status: SNP 5,676
Tory target seat number: 141
Swing required: 7.32%
office@morayconservatives.com

Born in Aberdeen in 1984, Douglas Ross has lived in Moray all his life. He went to Alves Primary School and Forres Academy, before going on to study agriculture at the Scottish Agricultural College. He is still involved with the Young Farmers, and he enjoys refereeing football games.

Ross worked in farming with cattle until he was elected to Moray Council in 2007. He now sits on various panels and sub-committees, and he also works for MSP Mary Scanlon. Despite his strong local credentials, Ross will struggle to unseat the SNP's Westminster leader, Angus Robertson. If the Tories are to re-establish themselves north of the border, it will be candidates such as Ross who will have to take on the task.

Amber Rudd

PPC for Hastings & Rye

Notional status: Lab 1,156

Tory target seat number: 23

Swing required: 1.27%

harcon@freeuk.com

Amber Rudd was born in London in 1963. Having been brought up in London, she studied at Edinburgh University and also spent a year studying at the University of Pennsylvania. She lives in Hastings with her husband and two teenage children.

After a career in banking, Rudd gained experience as a financial journalist before setting up her own head-hunting firm. She also writes for local and national magazines, specialising in finance and recruitment.

Rudd is an active Conservative campaigner and has campaigned locally in Hastings & Rye on education, health and business enterprise. Recently she has been involved with a programme to encourage a link between local businesses and schools to highlight the opportunities are available for young students. She is also governor of a local primary school and sits on its finance committee. She was selected to represent the Conservatives in Hastings & Rye in December 2006 and needs only a minimal swing to defeat Labour's Michael J. Foster.

Jason Rust

PPC for Edinburgh South West

Notional status: Lab 7,242

Tory target seat number: 161

Swing required: 8.24%

jason@jasonrust.co.uk

Born in 1978, Jason Rust was educated at the University of Strathclyde and Glasgow School of Law.

A practicing solicitor, Jason Rust is also a convener of Pentlands Neighbourhood Partnership and a member of Lothians and Borders Fire and Rescue Board. He is director of Edinburgh International Jazz and Blues Festival and of Edinburgh International Science Festival Limited.

Rust was elected to City of Edinburgh Council in 2004 to represent Colinton ward – at the time he was the youngest councillor in the city. He now represents the larger ward of Colinton/Fairmilehead, a position he was elected to in 2007. He is the economic development spokesman for the Conservative group.

Laura Sandys

PPC for South Thanet

Notional status: Con 810

Tory target seat number: N/A

Swing required: N/A

laura@sandys.org.uk

Laura Sandys was born in London in 1964. She started working at seventeen, and by the time she was nineteen had set up her own business. She has since set up and sold two further companies, both of which specialised in campaigning, communications and marketing. She lives in Ramsgate with her husband.

Sandys is deputy chairman of the Civic Trust, a trustee of the Open University and chairman of OpenDemocracy. As the daughter of the former Conservative MP and Cabinet minister Duncan Sandys, she has been a Conservative campaigner all her life. She has done extensive work on human rights and campaigned strongly against Saddam Hussein's abuses of them. Sandys also worked for the MoD during the Iraq War and has been an advisor to the shadow Defence team on energy security. She is now a member of David Cameron's Democracy Taskforce and Quality of Life Taskforce. She is also a founding member of the Conservative Women's Group and was formerly a director of the Enterprise Forum.

South Thanet is a new constituency seat with a notional Conservative majority. With her political pedigree and business experience Sandys can be expected not just to be elected, but to quickly achieve ministerial rank.

Alok Sharma

PPC for Reading West

Notional status: Lab 4,931

Tory target seat number: 108

Swing required: 5.74%

office@readingwestconservatives.com

Born in Reading in 1968, Alok Sharma attended local schools and has lived in the town all his life. He is married with two young daughters.

By profession Sharma is a chartered accountant working for a Swedish bank in London. He is a fellow of the Royal Society for the Arts and was previously chairman of the Bow Group's economic affairs committee. He also works as a volunteer for a UK charity which supports health and social projects in the developing world.

Sharma is standing in Reading West, where the sitting Labour MP, Martin Salter, is standing down.

Alec Shelbrooke

PPC for Elmet & Rothwell

Notional status: Lab 6,078

Tory target seat number: 107

Swing required: 5.71%

elmetconservatives@tory.org

Born in Bromley in 1976, Alec Shelbrooke was educated at the local comprehensive school. He then went on study at Brunel University. His hobbies are football, motor racing, cricket and music.

After a brief spell as an officer cadet at Dartmouth, Shelbrooke moved into a career in project management within engineering through the University of Leeds. He is a mechanical engineer and now acts as a consultant and troubleshooter for UK and international projects.

Politically Shelbrooke was elected to Leeds City Council in 2004 and still sits as a councillor. He stood in Wakefield in the 2005 general election. This time around he is standing for the newly created seat of Elmet & Rothwell. The sitting Labour MP for Elmet, Colin Burgon, is standing down.

Chris Skidmore

PPC for Kingswood

Notional status: Lab 6,145

Tory target seat number: 135

Swing required: 6.88%

chris@chrisskidmore.com

Born in 1981 in Bristol, Chris Skidmore attended Bristol Grammar School before going on to study modern history at Christ Church, Oxford.

Starting out as a journalist for the *Western Daily Press*, Skidmore went on to help Robert Lacey by researching his series *Great Tales of English History*. He is now an author in his own right (his first book on Edward VI was the *Guardian*'s Book of the Week) and advises David Willetts on a part-time basis. He is chairman of the Bow Group and has published several reports for the group.

Taking on Labour's Roger Berry in Kingswood is a tall order, but even if he does not get in this time around Skidmore is definitely one to watch for the future.

Janice Small

PPC for Batley & Spen
Notional status: Lab 6,060
Tory target seat number: 133
Swing required: 6.77%
janice4batley@aol.com

Born in London in 1966, Janice Small grew up in south London. She attended Blackheath and Bluecoat Grammar School, and is married with two sons. She describes herself as a 'rugby mum'.

Having previously been a Conservative Party regional press officer, and having worked with Tim Yeo, Nick Hurd and Adam Holloway, Small now runs her own marketing and communications company. The firm specialises in the pharmaceutical, automotive, financial services and politics sectors.

Standing in Batley & Spen at the general election, Small will need all of her marketing skills and media experience to unseat the Labour incumbent, Mike Wood.

Henry Smith

PPC for Crawley
Notional status: Lab 37
Tory target seat number: 2
Swing required: 0.04%
henry4crawley@aol.com

Henry Smith was born in Surrey in 1969 and attended Frensham Heights School. He then read philosophy at University College, London. In the past he has been governor to three local schools. He lives in Crawley with his wife (who is a local councillor) and their two young children.

Owner of a property investment company, Smith was first elected as a county councillor in Crawley in 1997, and he has also been a borough councillor. At thirty-four years old he became the youngest county council leader in the country when he was selected for that position in West Sussex in 2003, a post which he has since retained. Under his leadership the county council has invested around £80 million in new schools for Crawley, and he has overseen many other developments in local amenities for young people. Locally, he has campaigned extensively on health issues. He is chairman of the South-East County Leaders group and in 2005 he co-authored *Direct Democracy*, an agenda which argues for greater devolution and power to locally elected bodies.

Smith stood as the Conservative PPC for Crawley at the last general election, reducing Labour's majority from 6,770 to 37. Crawley is a super-marginal seat, and a move from council chamber to Commons chamber seems inevitable.

Anna Soubry

PPC for Broxtowe

Notional status: Lab 2,139

Tory target seat number: 42

Swing required: 2.22%

annasoubry@broxtoweconservatives.com

Anna Soubry was born in Lincoln in 1956. She was raised in Nottinghamshire, where her mother was a radiographer and her father ran a garage. She was educated at Hartland Comprehensive School in Worksop and Birmingham University. She is a single mother of two teenage daughters.

Originally trained as a barrister, Soubry then worked as a presenter and reporter for many years on local and national television. She returned to the Bar around twelve years ago and now works as a criminal barrister in Nottingham.

Soubry has not always been Conservative. Whilst both of her parents were lifelong supporters of the party, she supported the Liberals as a teenager. Soubry first joined the Conservative Party over thirty years ago as a student, left in the 1980s and returned in 2002. At university she was elected as the first woman Tory to the National Union of Students Executive. In 2003 she stood for Nottingham City Council and was the PPC for Gedling at the 2005 general election, where she reduced Labour's majority by more than 2,000 votes. She was selected to stand as the candidate for Broxtowe in July 2006.

Mark Spencer

PPC for Sherwood

Notional status: Lab 6,869

Tory target seat number: 152

Swing required: 7.95%

sherwood@tory.org

Born in Sherwood in 1970, Mark Spencer's family has lived in the area for four generations. He attended Lambley Primary School and Colonel Frank Seely School, Calverton, before moving on to Shuttleworth Agricultural College in Bedfordshire.

After college Spencer joined the family farm business and garden centre, which now employs fifty people. He still lives in Sherwood, along with his wife and two children, and he has served as a school governor and trustee of the local adult education centre.

In 2001 Spencer contested the Hucknall seat on Nottinghamshire County Council. In 2003 he won the Ravenshead seat on Gedling Borough Council and then in 2005 the Calverton seat on Nottinghamshire County Council. In 2006 he was appointed shadow spokesman for community safety and partnerships for the county council. At present he represents four parish councils – Ravenshead, Calverton, Woodborough and Lambley.

Andrew Stephenson

PPC for Pendle
Notional status: Lab 2,180
Tory target seat number: 49
Swing required: 2.65%
pendle@tory.org

Andrew Stephenson was born in Manchester in 1981 and educated at Poynton High School. He then went on to study business management at the Royal Holloway College, University of London. With the exception of his years studying, Stephenson has lived in the north-west all of his life. He currently runs the family's small insurance consultancy business in Greater Manchester and lives in Colne.

Stephenson first became involved with the Conservative Party in 1997. From 2001 to 2002 he was the national deputy chairman of Conservative Future, the party's youth group wing, and was a councillor in the north-west from 2003 to 2007. During that time he played a leading role in the development of housing policy, fighting to protect the green belt and environment, and he has held a variety of important positions in the local Conservative Association including chairman and area officer.

Stephenson was selected as the Conservative PPC for Pendle in September 2007 and has since led a number of high-profile campaigns in the area. He organised a successful petition against the reduction of rail services which attracted thousands of signatures, and also fought against the closure of local post offices.

John Stevenson

PPC for Carlisle
Notional status: Lab 5,085
Tory target seat number: 132
Swing required: 6.73%
woodvilla@btinternet.com

Born in Aberdeen in 1963, John Stevenson was educated at the local state school before going on to study history and politics at Dundee University, followed by law at Chester College. He is a keen sports fan, playing tennis and running marathons.

After eighteen months of travelling around the world, Stevenson joined the firm of Bendles Solicitors in Carlisle and was then made a partner. His father had had a successful career as a university lecturer before becoming a minister in the Church of Scotland and a local councillor.

Stevenson has been chairman of Carlisle Conservative Association and the Penrith & the Border Association. He has sat on Carlisle City Council for ten years and is also chairman of the North Cumbria Conservative Federation. He was selected to contest Carlisle as the Conservative PPC in December 2006. The sitting Labour MP, Eric Martlew, is standing down.

Iain Stewart

PPC for Milton Keynes South
Notional status: Lab 1,497
Tory target seat number: 27
Swing required: 1.52%
iainastewart@hotmail.com

Iain Stewart was born in Glasgow in 1972 and grew up in central Scotland, where his father worked as a computer systems analyst. He was educated at Hutchesons' Grammar School in Glasgow and the University of Exeter, graduating with a degree in politics. He has lived in Milton Keynes for more than fifteen years. Outside politics Stewart is a committed runner and has run for charity on many occasions, including at the London marathon and Milton Keynes half-marathon.

For some years Stewart ran the Parliamentary Resources Unit, supplying research to Tory MPs. He also had a spell as head of research for the Scottish Conservative and Unionist Party. Initially he had trained as an accountant, but he now works for executive search firm Odgers, Ray & Brendston.

Stewart first became involved in politics whilst at university. He is a member of his local parish council, Shenley Brook End & Tattenhoe. In 1999 he stood at the Scottish Parliament elections as the candidate for Glasgow Rutherglen, and stood again as a candidate in Milton Keynes in 2005, reducing Labour's majority from 10,000 to 4,000. He was selected by the local Conservatives to contest the new seat of Milton Keynes South soon after the last general election.

Mel Stride

PPC for Central Devon
Notional status: Con 2,338
Tory target seat number: N/A
Swing required: N/A
melstride@centraldevonconservatives.com

Mel Stride was born in 1961 in Perivale. He was educated at Portsmouth Grammar School and went on to study PPE at St Edmund Hall, Oxford. He is married and has three daughters.

Stride has a strong interest in history and culture and is a qualified tourist guide. He was awarded the Tourist Board Guide of the Year Award in 2005 and enjoys giving talks to local groups as an extension of his hobby. He is the owner and chairman of the Venture Marketing Group.

Whilst at Oxford he became involved in debating and was president of the Oxford Union and of the Oxford University Conservative Association. Stride has a social entrepreneurial background and is committed to social justice. He has served on the Commission for Social Justice and he runs his own community action team, which provides voluntary support to local communities in central Devon.

As the candidate for Central Devon, Stride has campaigned vigorously to support local post offices, protect hospitals and improve schooling. He is co-chairman of the Crediton Hospital Campaign Group and a governor at a local school. He has also campaigned on green issues by launching the 'One Tonne Green Challenge'. Central Devon is a new seat with a notional Conservative majority, and Stride can be expected to take the seat and apply his energy and flair to the Commons.

Philippa Stroud

PPC for Sutton & Cheam
Notional status: Lib Dem 2,689
Tory target seat number: 59
Swing required: 3.11%
phillippa.stroud@centreforsocialjustice.org.uk

Philippa Stroud was born in Devon in 1965, but she was raised in Surrey. She studied French at the University of Birmingham. She is married and is the mother of three children, including a set of twins. She plays the flute and is also a keen sportswoman, having played lacrosse at university.

After university, Stroud spent a year abroad leading a centre for heroin addicts in Hong Kong, an experience which led her to train and establish dedicated staff teams in five residential support units across the UK. During this project she has worked alongside local councils, health authorities and the police in an effort to find lasting solutions to combat drug addiction.

Stroud is now executive director of the CSJ, a centre-right think tank which works closely with the Conservative Party in developing policy proposals. She oversaw the production of two key reports, *Breakdown Britain* and *Breakthrough Britain*, which have been central to the formation of Conservative social policy.

In 2001 Stroud was the Conservative PPC against Clare Short in Birmingham Ladywood. She was selected to represent the seat of Sutton & Cheam in January 2007. Should she succeed in capturing the seat, Stroud will have a great political career ahead of her.

Julian Sturdy

PPC for York Outer
Notional status: Lib Dem 203
Tory target seat number: 3
Swing required: 0.22%
julian.sturdy@btconnect.com

Julian Sturdy was born in Harrogate in 1971. He has spent all of his life in Yorkshire. After studying agriculture at Harper Adams University, he set up a successful farming business which he still runs today. Within his local community Sturdy is a governor of a local school educational foundation, a director of Harrogate District Community Transport and senior steward for the Great Yorkshire Show. He is married and has two young children.

Sturdy has been involved with the Conservative Party since leaving school and has been campaigning for the local party in Yorkshire since 1992. He was elected as a councillor for Marston Moor ward on Harrogate Borough Council in 2002. In 2003 he became the council's spokesman for transport and was the Cabinet member for planning and transport until 2007, when he decided to stand down from the council in order to focus on his campaign as PPC for York Outer.

Sturdy previously fought the safe Labour seat of Scunthorpe at the 2005 general election. York Outer is a new seat with a slim notional Liberal Democrat majority.

Jason Sugarman

PPC for Lewes

Notional status: Lib Dem 7,889

Tory target seat number: 164

Swing required: 8.43%

jason@jasonsugarman.co.uk

Born in 1969 in Brighton, Jason Sugarman was educated at Brighton College and then Durham University, where he read history. On graduation he went on to get a law diploma from the University of Westminster. In 1995 he was called to the Bar and he is now a member of the chambers of Lord Carlile QC.

Sugarman is married to Kate, a journalist, and they have two young daughters. He has a special interest in criminal justice as well as history. He enjoys diving and riding on the Sussex Downs, having lived in Sussex all his life.

From 1995 until 2003 Sugarman was a councillor on Lewes District Council. In his time as councillor he successfully campaigned to prevent a development of more than 300 houses on green fields in the area which he represented. In the 2001 general election he contested Dudley South, managing to halve Labour's majority from 14,000 to 7,000. Standing against the well-entrenched Norman Baker, Sugarman certainly has a battle on his hands.

Maggie Throup

PPC for Solihull

Notional status: Con 124

Tory target seat number: N/A

Swing required: N/A

maggie@maggiethroup.com

Born in Shipley in 1957, Maggie Throup was educated at Bradford Grammar School. She went on to the University of Manchester, where she gained a degree in biology. She is divorced and lives in Solihull.

Throup started her career as a laboratory scientist before moving on to medical diagnostics for Nycomed, and then into sales and marketing. Since 1996 she has run a marketing and PR consultancy, offering her expertise to businesses of all sizes.

She has appeared regularly on TV and radio and has also featured in the press. She has spoken out strongly to protect the green belt and the environment around Solihull. She was the Conservative candidate for Colne Valley at the 2005 general election, significantly reducing the Labour majority from 10 per cent to 3 per cent. Minor boundary changes make Solihull a new seat with a notional marginal Tory majority.

Justin Tomlinson

PPC for North Swindon

Notional status: Lab 2,675

Tory target seat number: 60

Swing required: 3.12%

justin@swindonconservatives.com

Born in Kidderminster in 1976, Justin Tomlinson was educated at Harry Cheshire High School. He went on to gain a degree in business and marketing from Oxford Brookes University. He is recently married and lives with his wife in Swindon. Outside politics he is a football fanatic, and he was a committee member of Bracknell Town Football Club from 2003 to 2005.

Tomlinson has a career background in marketing. After graduating he went on to work as a sales and marketing manager for First Leisure, and then as a marketing executive at Point to Point. He has been a director of TB Marketing Solutions Ltd, a printing and website design service in Swindon, since 2000. His clients include a number of fellow PPCs.

During his time at university, Tomlinson was chair of the Conservative Students' Association. He was elected to Swindon Borough Council in 2000 and served as the deputy chair of the North Swindon Conservative Association from 2000 to 2004. He has been the council's Cabinet member for leisure, culture and recreation since 2003. He was also the national chair of Conservative Future from 2002 until 2003. Tomlinson previously contested North Swindon at the 2005 general election, slashing the Labour majority to just over 2,000 votes, and he should succeed this time around.

Paul Uppal

PPC for Wolverhampton South West

Notional status: 2,114

Tory target seat number: 50

Swing required: 2.66%

office@wolverhamptonconservatives.com

Born in Birmingham in 1967 into a Sikh family of east African descent, Paul Uppal considers himself a model modern Conservative, representing all social, ethnic and cultural backgrounds. A football fanatic, he is a season ticket holder for Wolverhampton Wanderers. He is married and has three children.

His father was a magistrate, and Uppal has worked in a variety of careers. He currently runs his own business and in the past has worked as a builder, secretary, accountant, lawyer and cleaner. He is also a trustee for a large Sikh temple in Wolverhampton.

Uppal was the Conservative PPC for Birmingham Yardley in 2005, and he was selected as the candidate for Wolverhampton South West in February 2007 in an open primary. He has since appeared on national TV on several occasions and has also been interviewed on Radio 4 for *The World Tonight*. Labour holds the seat with a hefty majority, so this jack of all trades will need to focus his energies on the general election campaign in order to succeed.

Martin Vickers

PPC for Cleethorpes

Notional status: Lab 2,640

Tory target seat number: 58

Swing required: 3.03%

vickers4cleethorpes@msn.com

Born and educated in Cleethorpes, Martin Vickers has lived and worked in the area his whole life. He went to Havelock School in Grimsby and recently graduated from Lincoln University with an honours degree in politics after six years of part-time study. He is married and has one daughter. He enjoys football and cricket, reading and music. He also has a special interest in railways.

For many years Vickers was in the printing industry and retail trade. He acted as the constituency agent to Edward Leigh MP in 1994. With twenty-four years' experience as a councillor under his belt, including six years as a Cabinet member on North East Lincolnshire Unitary Council, Vickers is well established locally. As well as his service as a councillor, he has also been a local churchwarden.

Vickers fought the Cleethorpes seat at the 2005 general election, significantly reducing the Labour majority to just 2,642. He was reselected to contest Cleethorpes in November 2006 and has a very good chance of success this time around.

Chris Walker

PPC for Berwickshire, Roxburgh & Selkirk

Notional status: Lib Dem 5,901

Tory target seat number: 124

Swing required: 6.50%

chris.walker@scottishconservatives.com

Born in Keighley in 1966, Chris Walker has lived in the south of Scotland for the last twenty years. He is married with one daughter.

Walker went to school in Sedbergh before going on to gain an HND in hotel management at Blackpool College. He then went to work for Trust House Forte as a management trainee. He is still involved in the hospitality trade, but is now self-employed. He sits on the local community council, is a member of the chamber of trade, chairman of his local tourism committee and a board member of Visit Scotland.

At the general election Walker will be taking on the incumbent Lib Dem, Michael Moore, for the Berwickshire, Roxburgh & Selkirk seat. If the Tories win here they will be looking at a landslide.

Robin Walker

PPC for Worcester
Notional status: Lab 3,144
Tory target seat number: 62
Swing required: 3.39%
ask@worcesterconservatives.com

Following in his father's footsteps, Robin Walker has been interested and involved in politics from a very young age. His father, Peter Walker, was the MP for Worcestershire for thirty-one years, so Robin grew up with his family in the area. He later won a scholarship to Oxford to read ancient and modern history. In his spare time he enjoys listening to music and supporting the local rugby, football and cricket clubs.

After university Walker set up his own internet business and later built up a successful career offering communications advice to some of the leading industrial companies in the country. In the 2005 general election he worked for Oliver Letwin, the then shadow Chancellor, as his press officer.

Walker described himself as 'the happiest man in Worcester' when he was selected to be the Conservative PPC in 2006. Engaging with the local needs of the constituency, he has based his election campaign on defending local services. Walker needs to achieve a sizeable swing at the next election in order to gain the seat from Labour, so he needs both Worcester man and Worcester woman to vote for him on the day.

Michael Weatherley

PPC for Hove
Notional status: Lab 448
Tory target seat number: 10
Swing required: 0.50%
mike@mikeweatherley.org.uk

Born in Clevedon in 1957 and educated at Kent College and South Bank University, Mike Weatherley has lived in the Brighton and Hove area for over thirty years. Outside work and politics, Weatherley is passionate about live rock music. He is a former qualified football referee and skiing instructor. He has also travelled around Europe and South America, and recently made a trip to Israel with the Conservative Friends of Israel.

Weatherley has had a colourful career in the music industry, working as a finance director and independent advisor to a number of large international businesses. Until 2000 he was co-owner of South Coast manufacturing company Cash Bases, a business which won a number of prestigious awards including Sussex Company of the Year and two Queen's Awards. He is currently vice president for a worldwide film licensing company.

Weatherley has considerable political experience. In 2005 he stood as the PPC for Brighton Pavilion, achieving an impressive 6 per cent swing. He was a borough councillor on Crawley Council from 2006 until 2007, when he decided to step down and focus on his parliamentary campaign as the candidate for Hove. The seat is within the top ten of Conservative target seats at the next election, and Weatherley needs to achieve a fractional swing from Labour in order to win at the next general election. Hove should return to being Conservative – actually.

James Wharton

PPC for Stockton South
Notional status: Lab 5,834
Tory target seat number: 131
Swing required: 6.72%
james@jameswharton.co.uk

Born in Stockton-on-Tees in 1984, James Wharton attended Yarm School before going on to study law at Durham University.

Wharton completed his legal practice course at the College of Law in York and now practises as a solicitor in Stockton and Darlington. He has also practised in Newcastle and Durham. He specialises in business and company law.

In the 2005 general election Wharton worked with James Gaddas, the Tory candidate for Stockton South. This time around he is the candidate himself and must take on the well-entrenched Labour MP Dari Taylor.

Heather Wheeler

PPC for South Derbyshire
Notional status: Lab 2,436
Tory target seat number: 53
Swing required: 2.73%
heather@heatherwheeler.co.uk

Born in 1959, Heather Wheeler has lived in the Midlands since her marriage in 1986. She is married and has one daughter. In her spare time she enjoys DIY and watching sport.

Wheeler is qualified as an associate of the Chartered Insurance Institute and worked in the City for ten years as an insurance broker at Lloyd's of London before fully devoting her time to politics. She served on Wandsworth Council from 1982 and was elected to Derbyshire District Council in 1995. She has been the leader of the Conservative group since 2002 and she led the Conservatives to victory in 2007 for the first time in the council's 33-year history.

She contested Coventry South in 2001 and 2005, and was selected to contest South Derbyshire at an open primary in 2006. The current Labour MP for South Derbyshire, Mark Todd, will step down at the next election, which should help her cause and see her win.

Chris White

PPC for Warwick & Leamington

Notional status: Lab 4,393

Tory target seat number: 98

Swing required: 5.17%

chris.white@wlca.org.uk

Chris White was born in Sydney, Australia, in 1967. He was educated at Manchester University and now lives in Warwick.

Having previously worked for Rover at Longbridge, White now works locally in PR. He is a governor of a local school, and a trustee of Victim Support and the Warwickshire Association of Youth Clubs.

In 2002 White stood for Birmingham Hall Green, and in 2005 he missed out on capturing Warwick & Leamington by just 266 votes. He was elected a Warwick district councillor in 2008. With the Tories now much higher in the opinion polls, he has a good chance this time around.

Christopher Whiteside

PPC for Copeland

Notional status: Lab 5,157

Tory target seat number: 129

Swing required: 6.62%

chris4copeland@btinternet.com

Born in St Albans in 1961, Chris Whiteside was educated at St Albans School and the University of Bristol (where he got a BSc in economics) and the University of East Anglia (where he received an MA in the same subject). He lives in Copeland with wife and young family.

Working in the telecommunications industry, Whiteside is currently employed by BT Global Services. He has been a councillor for sixteen years and has been a member of a health authority. He has also been a school governor for many years and has served in various capacities on the court of Bristol University.

Whiteside was a St Albans councillor from 1987 to 1995 and from 1999 to 2007, and he served as Conservative group leader and deputy leader of the council. He is currently a Copeland borough councillor. Having already contested Copeland in 2005, he will be hoping that the Tories' improved poll rating will help him to see off Labour's Jamie Reed this time around.

Craig Whittaker

PPC for Calder Valley
Notional status: Lab 1,303
Tory target seat number: 24
Swing required: 1.37%
craig@craig40.wanadoo.co.uk

Born in Bury in 1962, Craig Whittaker was taken to Australia by his parents at the age of five. He attended Belmont State High School and returned to the UK in 1984. He is divorced and has two daughters and a son.

By trade Whittaker is a general manager working in the retail sector, starting out with Wilkinson Home and Garden Stores and moving on to PC World. Having previously been a parish councillor Whittaker now sits on Calderdale Metropolitan Borough Council and is the Cabinet member responsible for children and young people.

Calder Valley is one of the Tories' top target seats, and Whittaker should succeed. The sitting Labour MP, Christine McCafferty, is standing down.

Matthew Williams

PPC for Newport West
Notional status: Lab 5,458
Tory target seat number: 146
Swing required: 7.63%
nwca@tory.org

Born in 1973, Matthew Williams grew up in the Forest of Dean and the Wye valley. He went to Monmouth School before going on to the University of Surrey, where he studied business economics and computing. His hobbies are walking, tennis, cycling, football and rugby.

Since graduating Williams has worked for David Tredinnick MP. He is also manager of the Integrated & Complementary Healthcare APPG. Despite the Conservative' resurgence in Wales he may struggle to unseat Labour's veteran MP Paul Flynn.

Susan Williams

PPC for Bolton West

Notional status: Lab 5,041

Tory target seat number: 114

Swing required: 5.98%

boltonwestppc@hotmail.co.uk

Susan Williams was born in Cork in 1967, but she was brought up and educated in the north-east of England. She is a qualified nutritionist and spent ten years working for a charity specialising in support for multiple sclerosis sufferers. She is married and has three children. Outside politics, she enjoys squash, gardening and hill walking in Scotland. She and her family live in Hale, Cheshire.

Williams's involvement in politics began in 1997 when she led a successful campaign in Trafford to protect grammar school education. She was elected to Trafford Council in 1998 and is now its leader. She was the first female leader of Trafford Conservative group and led the Conservatives to a landslide victory in 2004. She was the Conservative candidate for Wythenshawe & Sale East at the 2001 general election and was selected to contest Bolton West in December 2006. Williams is especially interested in education and health, which is where her experience and expertise lie.

Bolton West is currently represented by Labour MP Ruth Kelly, who is not standing at the next general election, and this should help Williams's cause.

Sarah Wollaston

PPC for Totnes

Notional status: Con 2,693

Tory target seat number: N/A

Swing required: N/A

The 47-year-old GP and lecturer Sarah Wollaston made history in August 2009 when, in the UK's first truly open primary, she became the first parliamentary candidate to be selected by a postal ballot of all those entitled to vote in a constituency.

Wollaston is married with three children, She has pledged to wind down her medical duties between now and the general election, and to give up practising medicine entirely if elected.

The vacancy came about because of the much-criticised expenses claims of the sitting Tory MP, Anthony Steen. After some pressure, he announced that he would not be standing at the next general election. Offered a shortlist of three local candidates, the electorate backed Wollaston with 47.6 per cent of the 16,639 votes cast. Although she only joined the Conservative Party three years ago, Wollaston beat two experienced politicians in the form of Sara Randall

Johnson, the chairman of East Devon District Council, and Nick Bye, the mayor of Torbay.

Marcus Wood

PPC for Torbay

Notional status: Lib Dem 2,727

Tory target seat number: 57

Swing required: 3.01%

mw@banfu.com

Marcus Wood was born in Maidenhead in 1959. He was educated at Maidenhead Grammar School and Slough College and has an OND in hotel management from Thames Valley University. He lives in central Torquay with his wife and two daughters. In his spare time he is keen amateur artist and enjoys DIY, skiing and motorcycling.

Wood began his business career at twenty-one, setting up his own frozen food business in 1981. The business soon expanded into a high-class delicatessen and catering company, and he later opened a restaurant near Windsor Castle. In the 1990s Wood turned his expertise to management consultancy and today he runs Fleming Banfu International, an executive search firm.

Wood joined the party in 1997 and was the Conservative candidate for Torbay in the 2005 general election, where the 4.9 per cent swing was amongst the highest Lib–Con swings anywhere in the country. If he achieves the same swing next time around he will unseat the Lib Dem incumbent, Adrian Sanders.

Matt Wright

PPC for Vale of Clwyd

Notional status: Lab 4,629

Tory target seat number: 140

Swing required: 7.09%

matt@valeofclwyd.orangehome.co.uk

Born in 1962 in Stockton-on-Tees, Matt Wright lives in Nannerch, Flintshire, with his wife. They are both members of the Friends of Theatr Clwyd Cymru and the Friends of the Scala Cinema.

Wright has a very strong background in manufacturing, business management and consultancy. He has been a director of Enterprise Business Solutions and a consultant to the North West Development Agency, and has worked for Tube Investments and Qinetiq. He now works as a freelance management consultant.

Politically, Wright also has a long track record. He is a former chairman of North Wales Conservatives, and he is deputy leader of the Conservative group on Flintshire County Council. He stood for the Welsh Assembly in both 2003 and 2007, although this is his first effort to capture a Westminster seat.

Tory staffers

These are the individuals who work either at CCHQ or in the Palace of Westminster. Some work in the mainstream departments (CRD, press office etc.), whilst others work directly for individual frontbenchers – either as chiefs of staff or as special advisors. Most are young and low profile, but some are higher profile and veterans of previous campaigns.

Many of these individuals have been targeted by headhunters, instructed by public affairs consultancies and others to find them anyone who has worked closely with the Tories. Of particular value is any person who has worked with David Cameron or George Osborne and who can therefore give an insight into their views and likely policies and actions. Of those approached, some have been tempted and some have succumbed. Most, however, are hanging on for the chance to work within government, possibly even in Downing Street itself.

When the general election is called many others will volunteer or be drafted into work at CCHQ at Millbank Tower, in the War Room or out in the regions or key marginals. The people below, however, are at the time of writing the team which will be tasked with securing the Tories a decent working majority.

Gavin Barwell

A former CCO director of operations, Gavin Barwell is still closely involved with the Ashcroft marginal seats campaign at its Cowley Street headquarters, despite being the PPC for Croydon Central. *See 'The outer circle' for full biography.*

Gabrielle Bertin

Having been David Cameron's press officer since his election as leader in 2005, Gabby Bertin is one of the constants in his inner circle. She is also married to his former campaigns director George Bridges. A confident and competent operator, she has won the respect of the press. She worked on the 2005 leadership campaign and will follow Cameron into Downing Street.

Olivia Bloomfield

A former banker with Bank of America and ex-headhunter with Russell Reynolds, Olivia Bloomfield is now chief of staff to party treasurer Michael Spencer. She is the CCHQ contact point for local and regional Tory party treasurers and fundraisers.

Peter Campbell
A former CRD staffer of a decade's standing, Peter Campbell is David Cameron's private secretary. He undertakes and oversees research for the leader and co-ordinates the team which prepares him for PMQs.

Simon Cawte
A former researcher in the European Parliament, Simon Cawte is now chief of staff to the shadow Secretary of State for Communities & Local Government (and former party chairman), Caroline Spelman.

Ramesh Chabra
A former CCHQ staffer who manned the local government desk, Ramesh Chabra is now George Osborne's press secretary. He formerly worked for David Davis and Dominic Grieve.

Tim Chatwin
Head of planning, Tim Chatwin reports direct to Steve Hilton. He is in charge of the crucial 'grid', a device originally invented by Peter Mandelson and Alastair Campbell. The 'grid' ensures that major party policy announcements do not clash with key internal or external events.

Elana Cheah
Previously a financial analyst for a City merchant bank, Elana Cheah has worked with William Hague for more than five years. She is his research assistant specialising in the developing world and the Commonwealth.

Samuel Coates
Still in his early twenties, this rising star is former deputy editor of ConservativeHome. He was one of David Cameron's speechwriters, reporting to Ameetpal Gill, but has now joined Rishi Saha's New Media Unit. Not to be confused with *The Times*'s Sam Coates.

Alistair Cooke
Veteran author of the Conservative Campaign Guides, Alistair Cooke has been a fixture at the CRD for more years than many of its staffers have been alive. A former deputy director of the CRD, Cooke is still on the scene.

Andy Coulson
The former editor of the *News of the World* has transformed the Tories' relations with the media. His timing was right, because the Tories were on the way up in

any event, but Andy Coulson is widely admired and credited with at least some of the Tories' strong opinion poll standing. Very much a member of the core team.

Seth Cumming
Formerly with Accenture and the think tank Reform, Seth Cumming is now an economic advisor to George Osborne.

Dominic Cummings
A former Business for Sterling and 'North East Says No' referendum campaigner, Dominic Cummings is now chief of staff to Michael Gove, shadow Secretary of State for Children, Schools & Families.

Chloe Dalton
A Middle East specialist, Chloe Dalton is a special advisor to shadow Foreign Secretary William Hague.

Denzil Davidson
William Hague's chief foreign affairs advisor, Denzil Davidson is also head of the International Affairs Section at the CRD.

John Deans
A veteran former *Daily Mail* political correspondent and former secretary of the Parliamentary Press Gallery, John Deans is now the news manager at CCHQ, responsible for producing the morning press briefing.

Oliver Dowden
A former PR man with Hill & Knowlton, Oliver Dowden was drafted into CCHQ to be director of operations in late 2008. Dowden had previously been deputy campaigns director before being lured away by H&K. His return is a sure sign that he – and CCHQ – expect to win in 2010.

Christina Dykes
Previously a CCHQ director of candidates, Christina Dykes is now special advisor to shadow Justice Secretary Dominic Grieve.

Catherine Fall
Kate Fall is David Cameron's deputy chief of staff, working under Edward Llewellyn. She is the leader's principal gatekeeper and a key member of the team, having worked for him since the days of his leadership campaign.

Andrew Feldman

An old Oxford University friend of David Cameron's who is now one of his closest aides and confidants. A lawyer by training, Andrew Feldman went to work for the family clothing business before being approached to raise the funds for Cameron's leadership bid. As well as being chief executive of the Conservative Party, he is chairman of the Leader's Group, whose members get to socialise with the Tory top brass for an annual membership fee of £50,000.

Clare Foges

Having previously worked for Boris Johnson, Clare Foges is now a speechwriter to David Cameron, reporting to Ameetpal Gill.

Gareth Fox

Low key but diplomatic and highly competent, Gareth Fox has presided over the candidates list at CCHQ since 2006. During that time he has had to defuse the row over the priority list (or 'A-list' as it has become known) and handle the fall-out over the positive discrimination in favour of women candidates. He has also had to handle the huge surge in new applications following David Cameron's reopening of the list following the furore over MPs' expenses.

Peter Franklin

A former CRD staffer, Peter Franklin is now chief of staff to Greg Clark, the shadow Secretary of State for Energy & Climate Change.

Blair Gibbs

A former think-tanker with Reform and the Taxpayer's Alliance, Blair Gibbs is now chief of staff to shadow Environment Secretary Nick Herbert.

Stephen Gilbert

Head of field campaigning – including polling – Stephen Gilbert is a former Tory agent. He is now Lord Ashcroft's right-hand man in his campaign to target marginal seats. Although Eric Pickles was closely involved in the crucial Crewe & Nantwich by-election victory in May 2008 and the Norwich North victory in July 2009, much of the credit belongs to Gilbert.

Ameetpal Gill

A former researcher for the author and historian Niall Ferguson, Ameetpal Gill is lead speechwriter to David Cameron.

Andrew Griffiths

Secretary to the board of the Conservative Party and chief of staff to party chairman Eric Pickles, Andrew Griffiths is also Tory PPC for Burton. *See 'The outer circle' for full biography.*

Matthew Hancock

Formerly at the Bank of England, Matt Hancock has been chief of staff to George Osborne since 2005. He advises the shadow Chancellor on economic policy.

Rupert Harrison

With the title of chief economic advisor to George Osborne, Rupert Harrison advises the shadow Chancellor on taxation issues and macro-economic policy.

David Hass

As chief of staff to the famously casual Ken Clarke, one of David Hass's tasks is making sure that his boss gets to the right place at the right time. Hass is bright and able, and will be a great asset to his boss in government.

Arminka Helic

A former venture capitalist and defence policy specialist, Arminka Helic is now William Hague's chief of staff.

Nicholas Hillman

A policy expert formerly with the Policy Exchange think tank, Nicholas Hillman is now chief of staff to David Willetts, shadow Secretary of State for Universities & Skills.

Steve Hilton

Shaven headed and casually dressed, Steve Hilton is one of David Cameron's oldest and most trusted friends and advisors – often cited as his 'Svengali'. Hilton studied PPE at Oxford and worked with Cameron during his time at the CRD. A marketing specialist, Hilton is widely credited with the successful strategy to 'decontaminate' the Conservative brand. He is married to Rachel Whetstone (*see below*).

Sian Jones

A former CRD staffer, Sian Jones is now chief advisor to the shadow Chief Secretary to the Treasury, Philip Hammond. As Hammond's role as the guardian of the public purse gains in importance, so will Jones's.

Edward Llewellyn

A friend of David Cameron's from Eton and Oxford days, Ed Llewellyn runs the leader's private office. He is a former CRD staffer and has worked as an advisor to Chris Patten in Hong Kong and Paddy Ashdown in Kosovo. Not only is he one of Cameron's closest confidants, he is one of his principal advisors on foreign affairs.

Ian McIsaac

As finance director and registered treasurer of the Conservative Party, Ian McIsaac has the statutory duty to vet, approve and register all donations and loans. He is a former partner at Deloittes.

Henry Macrory

Veteran CCHQ head of media, Henry Macrory is the Tories' link to lobby correspondents, who respect him enormously. He reports to and works closely with Andy Coulson.

Poppy Mitchell-Rose

After a spell at the BBC and then Reuters, Poppy Mitchell-Rose joined George Osborne's private office in 2006. She has the title of deputy chief of staff, and organises the shadow Chancellor's tours, visits and events.

James O'Shaughnessy

Lured from Policy Exchange to become director of the CRD when George Bridges departed, O'Shaughnessy is much more than a policy wonk. He is credited with reviving the flagging fortunes of the CRD and ensuring that it worked in tandem with Andy Coulson and his revamped Communications Department.

Jenny Parsons

A former television journalist, Jenny Parsons is now chief of staff to shadow Health Secretary Andrew Lansley.

Claire Perry

Having worked for Credit Suisse, McKinsey and Bank of America, Claire Perry now advises George Osborne on economic and business policy.

Stephen Phillips

A Tory election agent of long standing who has held numerous CCHQ posts, Stephen Phillips now reports to Stephen Gilbert at CCHQ Field Campaigning.

Caroline Preston

Having worked in the press office at CCHQ since 2005, Caroline Preston has been David Cameron's press officer since 2008.

Dominic Raab

A former diplomat and lawyer, Dominic Raab is chief of staff to shadow Justice Secretary Dominic Grieve. He is the author of *The Assault on Liberty*.

Annabel Roycroft

A former City worker and CCHQ staffer, Annabel (Bee) Roycroft is now chief of staff to Theresa May, taking over from Nick Timothy when he moved to CCHQ.

Rishi Saha

A former charity worker, Rishi Saha is the head of the six-strong New Media Unit. He is the man behind 'WebCameron' and the party's new interactive website, and he is credited with revolutionising the party's e-communication strategy.

Sir James Sassoon

The author of the Sassoon report, which set up the tripartite system of financial regulation, Sir James Sassoon is now economic advisor to George Osborne on all matters relating to financial regulation.

Eleanor Shawcross

Having formerly worked with Boris Johnson, Eleanor Shawcross now advises George Osborne on financial services policy.

Rohan Silva

Previously a Treasury civil servant, Rohan Silva is now an economic advisor to George Osborne.

Douglas Smith

A former speechwriter for David Cameron, Douglas Smith is now head of the Political Section at CCHQ. He is in charge of opposition research.

Campbell Storey

A former businessman and a PPC for Wansbeck, Campbell Storey is chief of staff to shadow Home Secretary Chris Grayling.

Liz Sugg
Head of operations and events at CCHQ, Liz Sugg previously worked for Sky and the Conservative Press Office in the European Parliament. In this key role she oversees all of the leader's visits, including the crucial party conference programme.

Nick Timothy
Former chief of staff to Theresa May, Nick Timothy was poached by the CRD to beef up the team headed by James O'Shaughnessy.

Sheridan Westlake
Still young but already a veteran of the CRD, Sheridan Westlake makes up the top triumvirate with James O'Shaughnessy and Nick Timothy. Westlake is a Tory councillor and specialises in local government issues – and in taking on the Lib Dems.

Sean Worth
A former CRD staffer who has also worked at the Association of British Insurers, Sean Worth is head of the CCHQ Policy Unit.

Tory doers

This somewhat diverse group of individuals are influential either because they have the ear of David Cameron, or because they are already putting Conservative thinking into operation. The Tories are already in 'government' in London and many town halls, and much can be learned from the way they have gone about running their administrations.

Also detailed below are the backgrounds of some of the external experts who may be drafted in for the general election campaign and to aid the transition into government. Their task will be to try and ensure that any Tory majority is big enough to provide a mandate for some of the tough decisions which will have to be taken in government, and that those decisions are efficiently put into practical effect.

Lord Ashcroft
Should the Tories romp home in 2010, *The Sun* could (but no doubt won't) carry the headline 'It Was Ashcroft Wot Won It'. When Gordon Brown pulled out of the 'general election that never was' in the autumn of 2007, it was because a Labour Party internal poll showed him that he was behind in the key marginal

seats. Michael Ashcroft, who sits on the Conservative Party board, has not just provided the party with money – although he has certainly done that. He has also provided it with ideas (he published the pamphlet *Smell the Coffee* after the 2005 defeat), organisation and focus. It is he who has been chiefly responsible for making sure that the Tories concentrate ruthlessly on the key marginal seats.

Viscount Astor

An elected hereditary peer, Viscount Astor is not only Tory frontbench spokesman on culture, media and sport in the House of Lords, but also a big wheel in business and in the City. He is also, of course, Samantha Cameron's stepfather, and the family socialise and holiday together. During the leadership campaign the Astor connection did much to reassure traditional Tories that David Cameron could be trusted.

Richard Barnes

London mayor Boris Johnson's only statutory deputy, Richard Barnes is a consolidator and a consensus builder. A former leader of the London Borough of Hillingdon, Barnes speaks a wide range of languages and has a genuine interest in equality issues. His low-key approach complements Johnson's ebullient style.

Samantha Cameron

The daughter of Baronet Sir Reggie Sheffield and the step-daughter of Viscount Astor, Samantha Cameron (or 'SamCam' as the tabloids refer to her) is impeccably connected. She is a mother and a career woman (she is creative director of the stationers Smythson of Bond Street) who still finds time to support her husband's political ambitions – even though she has little interest in politics herself. Her appearance – visibly pregnant – on the stage at Blackpool after David Cameron's leadership speech in December 2005 did a great deal to reinforce his triumph on the day.

Merrick Cockell

Tory councillor Merrick Cockell has been leader of the Royal Borough of Kensington & Chelsea since April 2000. It is one of only five local authorities in England to receive the maximum four-star ratings for its comprehensive performance assessment. He is also a member of the board of the Conservative Party and he is chairman of London Councils.

Lynton Crosby

This tough-talking Australian is not technically a Conservative – he is a gun for hire. However, he prefers working with right-of-centre parties and is credited with helping former Australian Liberal Party Prime Minister John Howard to his 1998 and 2001 general election victories. He asked the author how to win London, and when told to concentrate on the suburbs he went on to devise the 'doughnut strategy' and deliver an unlikely victory for Boris Johnson in the 2008 mayoral elections. If the Tories do not draft Lynton Crosby in to help them win the 2010 general election they will be missing a trick.

Margaret Eaton

Following on from the late Lord Bruce-Lockhart and Sir Simon Milton (now at City Hall), Margaret Eaton is the chairman of the powerful local authority pressure group the Local Government Association. She is the former leader of Bradford Metropolitan District Council – the first woman to hold that position – and former leader of the Conservative Councillors' Association.

Mark Fullbrook

A former CCO head of campaigns, Mark Fullbrook runs Parliamentary Liaison Services Ltd. This company provides support and advice for Conservative and Unionist MPs and candidates – building websites and drafting newsletters and communications material. Fullbrook is married to Lorraine Fullbrook, the Conservative PPC for South Ribble.

Annabel Goldie

In a way, as leader of the Scottish Tories, Annabel Goldie has nothing to lose – expectations are low. However, she has impressed north of the border, deploying logic and humour in equal measure to ensure that the Tory voice is not lost in the battle between the governing SNP and the formerly dominant Scottish Labour Party.

Guto Harri

A former BBC journalist, Guto Harri was lured away to work for international PR firm Fleishman Hillard. They in turn lost him to London mayor Boris Johnson, who appointed him as his spokesman and director of external affairs.

Lady Hodgson of Astley Abbotts

Recently elected to the party board, Fiona Hodgson is credited with rejuvenating the Conservative Women's Organisation. She is one of four members of the voluntary party on the board, and she has the ear of David Cameron. She takes much of the credit for the boost in the number of women on the approved candidates list.

Boris Johnson
His victory in May 2008 surprised many – but not the author, who bestowed his CIPR President's Medal on Boris Johnson when he was still an outside bet. Johnson is super-bright and hyper-ambitious. Now that he has a strong team around him, Johnson will start to deliver for London and will be looking for a second term. In the long run, his ambitions could be even loftier.

Kit Malthouse
A former investment banker and a Westminster city councillor from 1998 until 2006, Kit Malthouse was elected to the London Assembly in 2008. Boris Johnson appointed him his deputy mayor with specific responsibility for the Metropolitan Police. In that role he was instrumental in securing the retirement of Sir Ian Blair as Metropolitan Police commissioner, and his robust attitude towards law enforcement makes him a key player at City Hall. His success or failure in curbing crime in London will have an impact on the incoming Conservative government.

Sir Simon Milton
Shy and unassuming, Sir Simon Milton is nevertheless a key player in London politics. He made his name as leader of the flagship Westminster City Council. He then went on to become chairman of the Local Government Association, before being lured to City Hall by Mayor Johnson as one of his deputy mayors. Milton plays a crucial role behind the scenes. He has brought order to the mayor's office, following the confusion of the early months. His knowledge of London planning – and London politics – will be crucial to securing Johnson a second term and ensuring that relations with a Conservative government at Westminster remain cordial.

Shireen Ritchie
Mother of Madonna's ex-husband Guy Ritchie, Shireen Ritchie is the doyenne of the large, active and powerful Kensington & Chelsea Conservative Association. She is also one of the principal gatekeepers who controls access to the approved candidates list, and she has used her position and influence to try and ensure that the gender imbalance within the parliamentary party is addressed.

Lord Turnbull

Formerly Cabinet Secretary and Head of the Home Civil Service under Tony Blair, Andrew Turnbull is now advising the CCHQ Implementation Team on making the transition to government.

Tory fixers

This section is composed mainly of former CCO and CCHQ staffers who have moved into the private sector. The Tories rely to some extent on these people to ensure that British business buys into Tory policies. They also rely on them to help to make the party conference a commercial success, and to secure funding and venues for events and launches.

After the general election some of these individuals will make the transition into government as special advisors. Neil O'Brien of Policy Exchange says that the next Conservative government will be a government of policy wonks. There certainly will not be a lack of intellectual firepower on the Tory benches. However, it is not possible to govern solely with a bunch of wonkers. Where the fixers come into their own is that they can see every side of an argument, and they are therefore well equipped to work out how to counter it. More importantly, they get things done.

Alex Aiken

Straight talking and occasionally acerbic, Alex Aiken is the former head of the Campaigns Unit and Head of News at CCO. Now head of communications at Westminster City Council, Aiken has been called in to firefight at a number of other local authorities.

Iain Anderson

This quietly spoken Scots-born lobbyist heads chief corporate counsel of the public policy consultancy Cicero. Iain Anderson specialises in the field of financial services and has good links with the Conservative Party.

David Beamer

A former CCO staffer, David Beamer is a director and co-founder of Politics Direct. Having advised a range of secretaries of state when the Tories were last in office, Beamer has kept his contacts with the party fresh.

Kevin Bell
A veteran lobbyist with strong Conservative connections, Kevin Bell is currently regional president, UK and Africa, for the global PR agency Fleishman-Hillard. A former advisor to Margaret Thatcher, Bell is well connected and well liked.

Lord Bell
One of the lobbying industry's great names and great survivors, Tim Bell successfully navigated the sea change of 1997. A range of political and commercial giants have turned to Bell for advice in times of crisis, and his company, Chime Communications, has thrived under both Tory and Labour governments.

Peter Bingle
Energetic and ebullient, Peter Bingle is a lobbying legend. He is now chairman of Lord Bell's Bell Pottinger Public Affairs, but remains very much a hands-on PA man. Probably the only living lobbyist who could out-lunch the author.

George Bridges
A former chairman of the CRD and campaign director, George Bridges knows the Conservative Party inside out. Bridges has done spells at Quiller Consultants and has also written for the *Daily Telegraph* and *Sunday Telegraph*. He is very much in tune with the party's thinking.

Jonathan Caine
A former assistant director of the CRD, Jonathan Caine remains an expert on the intricacies of Northern Ireland politics. Caine worked closely with William Hague when he was party leader. After a short spell at the Communication Group, Caine is now happily ensconced at Bell Pottinger Public Affairs.

Darren Caplan
Director of public affairs at Brands2Life, Darren Caplan has also been selected as the Tory PPC for Hackney North & Stoke Newington. *See 'The outer circle' for full biography.*

Lord Chadlington
Brother of Tory MP and former Environment Secretary John Gummer, and uncle of Tory PPC Ben Gummer, Peter Gummer is the former boss of the PR company Shandwick, who founded his own empire with the mighty Huntsworth.

Alex Challoner

A former BBC journalist who went into public affairs, Alex Challoner has his own vehicle with Cavendish Place Communications. He worked (as did the author) on both of Steve Norris's mayoral campaigns and is still closely associated with Norris – and the Conservative Party.

Andrew Cumpsty

A lobbyist with Fleishman Hillard, Andrew Cumpsty is the leader of the Tory group on Reading Borough Council. He is also the co-founder of the Enterprise Forum, which facilitates the exchange of policy ideas between the Tory Party and British business.

Simon Elliott

At a towering 6 feet 6 inches, Simon Elliott was one of the mainstays of the Lobbyists RUFC. He stood as a parliamentary candidate for the Tories, before concentrating on building a highly successful career in PR and PA. He heads up the communications consultancy FD's public affairs division.

George Eustice

A former press secretary to Michael Howard and David Cameron, George Eustice is now at Portland Communications. He is standing for the Tories in Camborne & Redruth at the next general election. *See 'The outer circle' for full biography.*

Malcolm Gooderham

Following his time as Michael Portillo's press secretary, Malcolm Gooderham went on to work for Weber Shandwick and as a producer for LWT, before setting up his own agency, the Ledbury Group (or TLG).

Geoff Lawler

Previously Tory MP for Bradford North, Geoff Lawler now runs the Public Affairs Company, a lobby shop based in Leeds.

Charles Lewington

A former political editor of the *Sunday Express* and John Major's former director of communications, Charles Lewington set up his own PR and PA company, originally called Media Strategy – now renamed Hanover.

Chris Lewis
CEO of the eponymous PR company, Chris Lewis has been closely involved with the Tories in the years of opposition, offering support and training, particularly on the media side.

Simon Nayyar
A top lobbyist now running Citigate Dewe Rogerson's public policy division, Simon Nayyar is a Tory PPC for Hackney South & Shoreditch. He is known to be close to Francis Maude. *See 'The outer circle' for full biography.*

Steven Norris
Although he has taken a step back from frontline politics in recent years, Steve Norris is still a top Tory fixer and the man with the best address book in London.

Adrian Pepper
As well as having his own agency in Pepper Media, Adrian Pepper works closely with Lynton Crosby, a man the Tories could still turn to to run their general election campaign.

Katie Perrior
A former CCO staffer, Katie Perrior is now one half of the top team at In-House PR. She and Jo Tanner (*see below*) kept Boris Johnson on an unwavering course through selection to election as London mayor.

Stephan Shakespeare
One of the founders of pollsters YouGov and involved in 18 Doughty Street, Stephan Shakespeare is well connected with senior figures in the Tory Party and worked closely with Jeffrey Archer on his abortive mayoral campaign.

Jo Tanner
Another former CCO staffer, Jo Tanner is the other half of In-House PR, and along with Katie Perrior steered Boris Johnson towards victory in the London mayoral elections.

Nick Vaughan
The former national chairman of Conservative Future, Nick Vaughan has since set up his own boutique communications agency, Quay Public Affairs. Not as yet tempted by the green benches, he maintains close links with all levels of the voluntary and professional party.

Tory funders

These are the people who are either top funders of the Conservative Party themselves (in terms of either donations or loans) or who organise and control fundraising on behalf of the party.

The Tories will go into the next general election with a big advantage in financial terms. Since David Cameron became leader and the party started to look electable once again, the funds have flowed in. CCHQ has been well resourced, and the Tories will have no problem in finding the £25 million they need to fight the next general election.

This is in contrast with the Labour Party. Since the departure of Tony Blair, the funds have dried up and Labour may struggle to put together a decent war chest. Ultimately the trade unions will, as ever, step in and supply the necessary cash. They might, however, make the Labour Party sweat, and this brinkmanship could have a negative effect on their general election campaign.

Lord Ashcroft

An extremely generous donor, Michael Ashcroft has not only given (and loaned) the party millions of pounds in good times and bad, he has also provided expertise. He has led the CCHQ unit which has focused on the key marginal seats.

Bamfords

J. C. Bamford Excavators Ltd and Joseph and Anthony Bamford as individuals have donated more than £1.5 million to the Tories over the last seven years. They have made donations to CCHQ and to individual constituency associations – including David Cameron's Witney Association.

Maurice Bennett

This wealthy retail magnate has donated well over £1 million to the Tories during the last five years. Maurice Bennett is also a substantial donor to charity, and he is a treasurer of the Conservative Party.

Sir Tom Cowie

The business tycoon Sir Tom Cowie has donated more than £660,000 to the Tories over a period of five years. He is a serial entrepreneur and life president of the Arriva transport group. His donations included a crucial £500,000 in the run-up to the 2005 general election. When David Cameron was first elected leader he ceased all donations, but these have now resumed – albeit on a more modest scale.

Robert Edmiston

The entrepreneur and owner of the IM Group has donated £280,000 to the Conservatives over the last five years and has also loaned them £2 million. Robert Edmiston is also closely involved with the Midlands Industrial Council, which raises large sums for the Tories. Edmiston is a committed Christian and also donates to charities and schools, including city academies.

Michael Farmer

A serial donor to the Tories, Michael Farmer has given more than £1.5 million to the party in England and Scotland over the last decade. Farmer is a commodities broker and owner of the hedge fund Red Kite Metals.

Stanley Fink

This wealthy businessman has donated nearly £1.5 million to the Tories over a period of six years. Stanley Fink is a lawyer and accountant by background, and he is the former chairman of the mighty hedge fund the MAN Group. He is now the Conservative Party treasurer charged with procuring substantial donations and loans from his former City colleagues.

Roger Gabb

A wealthy wine entrepreneur, Roger Gabb has donated more than £600,000 to the Conservative Party over the last five years.

Lord Harris of Peckham

The carpet and retail tycoon Philip Harris has donated millions of pounds to the Conservatives over the years, either as an individual or though his companies. He is also a substantial donor to charity and supports the City Academies programme.

Michael Hintze

The owner of CQS Management has donated nearly £1 million to the Conservatives over the last decade. Michael Hintze, who is Australian born, has also loaned the Tories large sums over the years, and he is a generous donor to a wide range of charities.

Lord Laidlaw

Irvine Laidlaw, a wealthy Scottish entrepreneur, has donated more than £3 million to the Tories in the last six years, as well as making loans to the party. He was ennobled in 2007 for services to charity – he has pledged to give £20 million a year to charitable causes for the rest of his life.

George Magan

Over the last decade George Magan has donated nearly £1.5 million to the Conservative Party. He is a well-known figure in the City (where he specialised in mergers and acquisitions) and he is a former treasurer of the Conservative Party. He is a trustee of the Conservative Party Foundation.

Jonathan Marland

Another former Conservative Party treasurer, the wealthy Jonathan Marland has donated around £250,000 to the Tories in recent years. He made his money in the City and is a former Tory PPC.

Malcolm Scott

Malcolm Scott is treasurer of the Conservative Party in Scotland. He has donated over half a million pounds to the Tories north and south of the border.

Tom Scott

The son of one of the wealthiest men in the Channel Islands, Tom Scott Senior, Tom Scott Junior lives and works on the mainland. He is a wealthy accountant and businessman in his own right and has donated more than half a million pounds to the Tories in recent years.

Michael Spencer

The Conservative Party treasurer is charged with obtaining loans and donations from the City, where he is a well-known figure as the former chairman of ICAP and owner of the City Index spread betting company. Michael Spencer is also a regular and substantial donor to the party.

Lord Steinberg

Since 2001 Leonard Steinberg has donated nearly £1.4 million to the Tories. A Merseyside-based entrepreneur, he founded Stanley Leisure and is a former deputy treasurer of the Conservative Party.

Diana Van Nievelt Price

The wife of a wealthy Midlands businessman, Diana Van Nievelt Price has donated well over half a million pounds to the Tories. A strong admirer of Lady Thatcher, she paid £440,000 for a portrait of the former Prime Minister in an auction at a Tory fundraising ball. She has since given nearly another £100,000.

David Whelan

This wealthy businessman has donated a round figure of £1 million to the party in the last two years in four payments of £250,000. David Whelan is a sports shop tycoon and chairman of Wigan Athletic Football Club.

Tory thinkers

These are a combination of CCHQ policy staffers, think tank personnel and Tory-inclined journalists and bloggers. They are the key opinion formers who are so loved by PRs on both sides of the Atlantic – because they are able to get to the key decision makers.

Politicians rely on their staffers to develop and research viable policies. All political parties also rely on think tanks to undertake blue-sky thinking and fly the proverbial policy kites. Additionally, virtually all politicians are media obsessed. Whether in opposition or in power, they devour the newspapers and always have one ear on the radio and one eye on the television. Neither backbenchers nor ministers operate in a vacuum, and nor do their advisors, and the media plays a key role in shaping their opinions. Different political parties also give more weight to the opinions of different newspapers, leader writers and columnists.

Below are some of the people whose opinions are likely to have the most impact on Tory thinking as they prepare for, and enter, government.

Sir David Arculus

Sir David Arculus is the former head of the Better Regulation Task Force. He was appointed to that post by Tony Blair, but is now advising the Tories. He is heading an independent review on regulation, and will work closely with Ken Clarke to devise methods of easing the regulatory burden on British business.

Donal Blaney

A no-nonsense blogger who was appointed by William Hague as national chairman of Conservative Future, Donal Blaney is now chief executive of the Young Britons' Foundation, which promotes conservatism in universities. Although independent of the party, the foundation has trained more than 2,500 activists, councillors and aspiring MPs.

John Blundell

The long-serving director general of the right-wing think tank the IEA is an unashamed Thatcherite. John Blundell is carrying on the work of the

IEA's founder, Lord Harris of High Cross, who had a strong influence on the Thatcherite agenda. Although he is handing over the helm of the IEA, he will still be involved.

Vernon Bogdanor
Professor of government at Oxford, a fellow of Brasenose College and one of the UK's leading constitutional experts. Vernon Bogdanor taught David Cameron, and there is a strong mutual respect between the pair.

Nicholas Boles
One of the founders of the highly influential Policy Exchange think tank, Nicholas Boles works closely with Francis Maude in overseeing the work of the Implementation Team. He is also the Tory PPC for Grantham & Stamford. *See 'The outer circle' for full biography.*

Christopher Booker
A *Daily Telegraph* columnist, Christopher Booker delights in identifying and highlighting some of the EU's greater idiocies. He is highly sceptical of the Tory line on Europe, believing that the party in power would do little to halt the advance of federalism.

Benedict Brogan
Having been political editor of the *Daily Mail*, Benedict Brogan is now an assistant editor and chief political commentator for the *Daily Telegraph*. He is also a habitual blogger.

Michael Brown
A former Tory MP and now a political correspondent for *The Independent*, Michael Brown makes frequent appearances on radio and TV talking about the policies and personalities of the party.

Anthony Browne
A former *Observer*, *Times* and BBC journalist and former director of Policy Exchange, Anthony Browne was headhunted by Boris Johnson to be director of policy. He is not afraid to be radical, and his proposal to offer an amnesty to illegal asylum seekers in London caused apoplexy amongst some of the more conservative media pundits – and considerable disquiet at CCHQ.

Sir Alan Budd

Sir Alan Budd is a former economic advisor to Tory Chancellors Norman Lamont and Ken Clarke, and he is advising the current Tories on the setting up of the proposed Office for Budget Responsibility.

Dr Eamonn Butler

A former academic and radical conservative thinker with experience on both sides of the Atlantic, Eamonn Butler is co-founder of the ASI.

Iain Dale

A serial entrepreneur, former Tory PPC and inveterate blogger and Twitterer, Iain Dale is at the heart of the Conservative Party. He is the managing director of Biteback Media and the publisher of *Total Politics*. When the media want a commentator who understands the Tories, they turn to Dale.

Janet Daley

American born and a former liberal, Janet Daley is now a trenchant right-wing commentator and columnist for the *Daily Telegraph*. Now verging on the libertarian, she is as yet unconvinced by the Cameroons.

Matthew d'Ancona

This former *Times* and *Telegraph* journalist was until recently editor of the influential *Spectator* magazine. As part of the political establishment, Matthew d'Ancona is well regarded by politicians of all hues, but his instincts are primarily conservative.

Matthew Elliott

The chief executive of the Taxpayers' Alliance (TPA), Matthew Elliott has led the charge against the Labour government's debt and its spending plans. He has often been far more direct in his criticism of the Labour government than Tory frontbenchers. A cross between a think tank and a pressure group, the TPA is likely to be a thorn in the side of governments of all hues for many years to come.

Danny Finkelstein

This former CRD staffer and advisor to John Major and William Hague is one of the most perceptive pundits currently pontificating on the field of politics – and football. Danny Finkelstein is a *Times* columnist and leader writer and an avid blogger. He makes frequent TV appearances, where he largely interprets Tory thinking.

Lord Freud

A former journalist and City operator, David Freud has carved out a new niche for himself as a leading expert on welfare reform. He has previously advised the Labour government, but is now advising the Tories on measures which will be needed to curb the size and cost of the welfare state when they gain power. He should become a Tory minister in the Lords.

John Glen

A former director of the CRD and former Conservative PPC, John Glen set up the secretariat for the Conservative Party's policy review groups. Currently working for the Accenture Institute for High Performance, he is a major contributor to policy thinking around the sustainability agenda, and is still closely involved with the party.

Stephen Glover

A *Daily Mail* and *Spectator* columnist, Stephen Glover is a keen observer of the political scene and his opinions are more inclined towards the Tories than any other party. A staunch critic of Gordon Brown, he is nevertheless not a paid-up member of the David Cameron fan club.

Andrew Haldenby

A former head of the political section of the CRD, Andrew Haldenby went on to work for the CPS and Business for Sterling, before becoming co-founder (along with Nick Herbert) of the Reform think tank.

Sir Max Hastings

The former editor of the *Daily Telegraph* and London *Evening Standard* has strongly held traditional Tory views. Max Hastings excoriates the current Labour government for ruining the economy, but doubts if the New Conservatives have the steel to take the necessary tough decisions.

Simon Heffer

An acerbic traditional right-winger, Simon Heffer is a columnist for the *Daily Telegraph*. Whilst strongly critical of the Labour government, he saves most of his venom for the New Conservatives.

Dieter Helm

Professor of energy policy at Oxford University and a fellow of New College, Dieter Helm is a leading expert in energy and climate change issues. He has worked closely with both the Blair and Brown Labour governments, but he has also influenced Tory thinking in this area and will undoubtedly inform it in government.

Jonathan Isaby

A former BBC and *Daily Telegraph* journalist, Jonathan Isaby is now co-editor of the highly influential ConservativeHome website. Isaby is also a blogger and has co-written a book on how Boris Johnson beat Ken Livingstone to become mayor of London.

Rachel Johnson

The journalist sister of London mayor Boris Johnson has written for the *Financial Times*, the *Daily Telegraph*, the *Spectator* and the *Evening Standard*. Rachel Johnson is now a columnist for the *Sunday Times*.

Jill Kirby

Jill Kirby is director of the CPS, the think tank set up by Sir Keith Joseph and Sir Alf Sherman which (along with the IEA and the ASI) dreamed up privatisation and other Thatcherite policies. She is an expert on all matters relating to family policy, and on the relationships between individuals and the state. She has been closely involved in developing policy for the New Conservatives and served on George Osborne's Tax Reform Commission.

Ruth Lea

A staunch monetarist economist, Ruth Lea was a civil servant for many years. She then became a director of the CPS and then head of the Policy Unit at the Institute of Directors. Now economic advisor to the Arbuthnot Banking Group, she is director of the Global Vision think tank and is a frequent media pundit on all matters relating to the economy.

Quentin Letts

The *Daily Mail*'s highly rated parliamentary sketch writer, Quentin Letts does not hesitate to get personal in his attacks on politicians. Letts launched a long-running campaign against Speaker Michael Martin (who he dubbed 'Gorbals Mick') and is no great fan of his successor, John Bercow (who he has dubbed the 'Squeaker').

Richard Littlejohn

The *Daily Mail*'s licensed attack dog, Richard Littlejohn uses his column to lambast politicians of all parties. He refers to David Cameron as 'call me Dave', but currently directs most of his fury at the Labour government and the politically correct culture which he accuses them of fostering.

Tim Montgomerie

The joint founder (along with David Burrowes) of the Conservative Christian Fellowship, Tim Montgomerie was Iain Duncan Smith's private secretary during his brief period as leader. He then went on to set up ConservativeHome, providing a forum for all schools of thought within the party. Not a huge fan of David Cameron, Montgomerie will nevertheless be keen to see the back of the Labour government and ensure that IDS's social justice agenda is fully implemented by the Cameron administration.

Charles Moore

The author once introduced Charles Moore at a Tory fundraising lunch as 'the high priest of high Toryism'. He did not demur. The former editor of the *Daily* and *Sunday Telegraph*, Moore went on to edit *The Spectator* – which he still writes a column for. An ardent Thatcherite, he will regard the incoming Tory administration as being on probation.

Ferdinand Mount

A veteran author and columnist for the *Sunday Times* and other newspapers, Ferdinand Mount was head of Margaret Thatcher's No. 10 Policy Unit in the early 1980s and a director of the CPS in the late 1980s and early 1990s.

Fraser Nelson

One of the rising stars in the firmament of political journalism, Scots-born Fraser Nelson is the Tory-inclined editor of *The Spectator* and a columnist for the *News of the World*. He is also a director of the CPS. Not uncritical of Cameron, he is in great demand as a TV pundit – partly because of his informed views and partly for his youthful good looks.

Lord Norton of Louth

Philip Norton is professor of government at the highly rated Department of Politics at the University of Hull. An acknowledged constitutional expert, he is frequently consulted by Tory leaders on plans to reform the House of Lords.

Peter Oborne

A former *Spectator* political correspondent who now writes a column for the *Daily Mail*, Peter Oborne is a scathing critic of the whole political class. However, he reserves his most virulent outpourings for New Labour, and he has a much larger following on the right than on the left.

Neil O'Brien

Former head of the Open Europe think tank, Neil O'Brien now heads up the hugely influential Policy Exchange. It is widely regarded as being David Cameron's favourite think tank, although it is far from being the creature of the New Conservative leadership.

Matthew Parris

A former CRD staffer, MP and correspondence secretary to Margaret Thatcher, Matthew Parris is steeped in Tory lore. After standing down as an MP he began a brief career as a broadcaster, before picking up his pen and becoming a widely admired parliamentary sketch writer. He now writes a regular comment column for *The Times*, and his offerings to that and other publications on the political scene and (most especially) on the Tory Party are always worth reading.

Melanie Phillips

A *Daily Mail* columnist, Melanie Phillips is a keen observer of the political and social scenes. She regularly appears on radio and TV shows, and always views issues through a right-of-centre prism. She is married to the BBC's legal correspondent Joshua Rozenberg.

Madsen Pirie

A radical free market academic with transatlantic connections and experience, Dr Madsen Pirie is co-founder (along with Dr Eamonn Butler) of the ASI.

Amanda Platell

Born in Perth, Western Australia, Amanda Platell shot to fame when she was appointed William Hague's press secretary in March 1999. She joined CCO after having been controversially removed from her post as editor of the *Sunday Express*. She is now a columnist for the *Daily Mail*.

Stuart Polak

Head of the powerful Conservative Friends of Israel, Stuart Polak is a highly effective lobbyist for the Israeli cause. He regularly takes delegations of Tory MPs, peers and PPCs on fact-finding trips to Israel.

Michael Portillo

Now reinvented as a media pundit, Michael Portillo came close to becoming Tory leader on at least one occasion. He was ahead of his time, but the modernising agenda which he espoused was taken up by Francis Maude and others, and eventually it was put into effect by David Cameron.

Lord Rees-Mogg

Veteran former *Times* editor and columnist, and a former PPC himself, William Rees-Mogg is the father of current PPCs Annunziata and Jacob.

Andrew Roberts

Andrew Roberts is a respected historian, biographer and chronicler of right-wing causes and champions. His books are read with interest on both sides of the Atlantic. A personal friend of David Cameron's, they regularly holiday together.

Roger Scruton

A polymath, Roger Scruton has been a lecturer and professor and writes on food, wine, the arts and philosophy. He is also, however, an expert on conservative and liberal politics and he often conjoins the two in his writings. Although not in tune with the modernised New Conservative Party, Scruton is still influential.

Paul Staines

A prolific and influential blogger, Paul Staines plies his trade under the *nom de plume* Guido Fawkes. In this guise he has exposed a number of political scandals, and he has excoriated the political classes for their greed and duplicity. More a libertarian than a conservative, Staines does, however, dip his keyboard in a particularly potent vat of poison when writing about Gordon Brown and his colleagues.

Irwin Stelzer

Reckoned to have the ear of Rupert Murdoch, Irwin Stelzer writes for the *Sunday Times* and *The Spectator* and is respected on both sides of the pond. He is also director of economic policy at the Hudson Institute. Initially impressed with Gordon Brown as Chancellor and in the early days of his premiership, he is now appalled at the level of debt which the government has taken on.

Philippa Stroud

A charity worker who is now executive director of the influential CSJ and director of the Conservative Party's Social Justice Policy Group, Philippa Stroud is also the Tory PPC for Sutton and Cheam. *See 'The outer circle' for full biography.*

Baroness Thatcher

The prosperity of the late 1980s and the 1990s, and the halt in the UK's post-war decline, were down to Margaret Thatcher's clear vision and iron determination. The likes of Keith Joseph, Alf Sherman and Ralph Harris supplied the policies, but it was her will which saw them put into effect. A hate figure for many on the left, the true extent of her achievements will probably only be acknowledged after her death.

Elizabeth Truss

A Tory councillor and former Tory PPC, Liz Truss is deputy director of the Reform think tank. She has previously worked in the private sector for Shell and Cable & Wireless.

Rachel Whetstone

Michael Howard's former chief of staff, Rachel Whetstone left politics to start a career in PR and lobbying. After a spell at Carlton Communications and Portland PR she is now vice president, communications and public affairs, for Google. She is married to Steve Hilton (*see above*).

Think tanks

There are around 100 think tanks in the UK, some dealing with specific policy areas such as transport or the environment, some dealing with the whole spectrum of policy issues.

Since think tanks are registered charities they are not allowed to be officially allied to a particular party. Many do, however, have strong links with one of the main political parties or another. For the sake of form they are described as 'right leaning' (i.e. associated with the Tories), 'left leaning' (i.e. associated with Labour) or 'centrist' (i.e. associated with the Lib Dems).

These are the think tanks which are traditionally most closely associated with the Tories (or even specifically to David Cameron), or which are having and will have the most influence on the thinking of the New Conservatives.

Adam Smith Institute

Named after the author of *The Wealth of Nations*, the ASI is a free market think tank which the great man would have been proud of. It states its aims as being to inject competition into public services, extend personal freedom, prune regulation and cut government waste.

Centre for Policy Studies

A venerable think tank set up by Sir Keith Joseph and Alf Sherman in the 1970s to 'convert the Tory Party to economic liberalism'. The CPS came up with many of the policies which underpinned the Thatcher administration and is still influential in the development of Tory policy.

Centre for Social Justice
Having lost the Tory leadership, Iain Duncan Smith set out to analyse the root causes of the UK's social ills and to come up with radical but practical solutions. The result was the CSJ, a think tank which has a profound influence on David Cameron and the New Conservative project.

Institute for Economic Affairs
Describing itself as the UK's original free market think tank, the IEA is in direct competition with the ASI. But then free marketeers believe that competition is healthy, and these two long-established right-of-centre think tanks have certainly kept each other sharp. Not as influential as in the days of Thatcher.

Institute for Fiscal Studies
The IFS is the UK's most respected and authoritative economic think tank. Politicians of all parties look to it to corroborate their figures and economic policies – or to undermine those of their opponents.

Policy Exchange
Probably the leading Cameroon think tank, Policy Exchange has originated much of the New Conservative agenda and produced many of its brightest staffers and candidates.

Reform
The clue is in the title – this think tank looks at existing public bodies and structures and recommends radical policies for their reform. When David Cameron launched his plans to curtail the power of the quango state, he chose Reform as the platform from which to do so.

Taxpayers' Alliance
Officially nothing to do with the Tory Party, the TPA wittingly or unwittingly often acts as its outrider, savaging government spending plans and pushing policies which the Conservatives may like to adopt but cannot. The TPA will be a constructive critic of the next Tory government.

The policies

David Cameron was the joint author of the highly focused Tory general election manifesto of 2005. Michael Howard had wanted to replicate Labour's success with their 'pledge cards', whilst the general election campaign supremo, Lynton Crosby, wanted to reprise the triumph of some of his 'dog whistle' campaigns in Australia.

So the Tory manifesto – a fairly slim document in itself – was boiled down to five key pledges in ten words. These pledges were based on widespread opinion polling and the extensive use of focus groups. These had been used to identify the five key concerns of the British public, which were then translated into the five key pledges designed to address those concerns. They were:

- Cleaner hospitals
- School discipline
- Controlled immigration
- More police
- Lower taxes

Although the Tories fell a very long way short of winning the 2005 general election, they did gain an extra thirty-one seats – and a vital infusion of new blood. Counting those new MPs who had replaced retiring MPs, there were nearly fifty reinforcements who came in with the class of 2005 – younger, fresher and untainted by the traumatic defeat of 1997.

When Cameron won the Tory leadership in December 2005 he immediately set in motion a total overhaul of Conservative policy. He set up six different groups – each headed by senior Tory politicians – to look at key policy areas and to make radical suggestions. The policy reviews covered:

- *Social Justice* – headed by Iain Duncan Smith
- *National and International Security* – headed by Dame Pauline Neville-Jones
- *Globalisation and Global Poverty* – headed by Peter Lilley
- *Economic Competitiveness* – headed by John Redwood
- *Public Service Improvement* – headed by Stephen Dorrell and Lady Perry
- *Quality of Life* – headed by John Gummer and Zac Goldsmith

From the outset Cameron had made it clear that the reviews would produce recommendations, which would not necessarily translate into official party policy – never mind make it into the manifesto. In reality, the credit crunch intervened and made many of the recommendations unaffordable or irrelevant. Since the initial policy reviews were set up, other more tightly focused reviews have been put in train – but their findings have not been published.

The policy review process served several useful purposes. It bound senior Tory figures into Cameron's leadership. It also came up with some useful policy ideas – some of which will ultimately make it into the manifesto. More important, however, was the fact that four of the reviews (Social Justice, Globalisation and Global Poverty, Public Service Improvement and Quality of Life) were concerned with areas which were not traditional Tory priorities. This sent out the clear message that this was a new, modern, compassionate Conservative Party. The policy review process was a vital part of the programme of decontaminating the Tory brand.

After the formal policy reviews had reported the frontbench teams concerned with particular policy areas began to digest their findings and to report back to the shadow Cabinet. In the meantime, however, an unofficial inner Cabinet had been formed which started to plan the way forward in policy terms. This was made up of David Cameron himself, George Osborne (perhaps more of a policy person even than Cameron), William Hague (the unofficial shadow Deputy Prime Minister), Francis Maude (the midwife of the New Conservative Party), Oliver Letwin (technically in charge of policy formulation) and Philip Hammond (the man who will have to wield the knife to re-establish the public finances). Also closely involved were Steve Hilton (part of the time from California) and Andy Coulson (once he had joined the team). Their job was – and is – to put together a set of policies which are practical and popular (or at least not wildly unpopular) and which conform to a consistent narrative.

The key themes which have emerged from the policy reviews and their aftermath are reform of education and of the welfare system, and support for the family. The buzz-words which reverberate around the walls of Millbank Tower are decentralisation, localism – and moving into the post-bureaucratic age. What this will mean in practice is that the state will be made much smaller, much less expensive and much less intrusive.

But the New Conservatives will not allow themselves to make the perceived mistakes of their predecessors – they will not permit a vacuum to develop which will suck in the disadvantaged. The role of the central state will be greatly diminished, but it will be replaced by an enhanced role for families, local government and the third sector – in effect, by people who are closer to the problems and therefore better able to provide the appropriate solutions.

The challenge for any opposition party entering a general election with an opinion poll lead is to demonstrate that the country's faith is justified by unveiling a policy platform which can be translated into an agenda for change within weeks of polling day. A government in waiting should have a well-drafted Queen's Speech. This should outline legislation in the areas which were the dividing lines in the general election campaign, and it should address the centre-ground issues in which every citizen has a real stake. It should not have more than a handful of measures which deal with the issues which are close to the hearts of the mainstream Whitehall departments.

Realpolitik dictates that opposition parties have to keep things simple and straightforward. It also dictates that they must be sure not to announce too much too soon. This is because of the danger of the incumbent government seizing upon the policies and making them their own – possibly even introducing them and putting them into effect ahead of a general election. Of even greater concern is that existing governments – with the full resources of the civil service behind them – will have time to unpick and ridicule opposition policies before they have had a chance to even try to put them into effect. Both of these factors provide strong disincentives against revealing too much, too early. The development and revelation of policies should be a slow strip-tease, with the 'full monty' reserved for the actual general election manifesto launch.

In 1997 Labour was elected on a manifesto which was opaque in many fundamental respects – and which left out many of the most crucial of its policies. The independence of the Bank of England did not feature anywhere in the party's manifesto. Labour's view then was that as governments supposedly lose elections, rather than oppositions winning them, it would only complicate matters to dot every 'i' and cross every 't' prior to taking office. Indeed one of Labour's few firm policy commitments in 1997 was to stick rigidly to the Tory's two-year public spending freeze. Ken Clarke, then Chancellor of the Exchequer and now shadow Secretary for Business, subsequently conceded that he would have found it very hard to stick to his own spending plans had the Tories won. Going back as far as 1979, Margaret Thatcher's manifesto was thin to the point of anorexia. It said nothing about privatisation – one of the policies which defined her premiership.

So for Cameron and his team the challenge is to develop a far-reaching, coherent and modern Conservative policy agenda: and then to reveal just enough to suggest that they have solutions for the tough challenges which inevitably lie ahead. In no area is the challenge greater than the economy and public finances. This is the issue which, despite his own planned cuts in public spending, Gordon Brown will attempt to turn into the great dividing line of the forthcoming general election.

This conflation of the importance of the economy and of society is summed up in a passage from a speech which Cameron delivered at Davos in January 2009:

A lot of people are angry with capitalism. Instead of representing hope for a better future, they think capitalism threatens it. This matters because in the future, social, economic and environmental progress will only come from the drive, energy and enterprise of individuals. So if we want capitalism to be a success again, we need to make capitalism popular again.

When the Tory Party marches into Downing Street it will not be short of brainpower. Apart from veteran thinkers such as Oliver Letwin and David Willetts, they will have in their MP ranks relative newcomers such as Greg Clark, Nick Herbert and Nicholas Boles. They will also have a raft of former think tank personnel there as advisors, to the point where at a conference in July 2009 organised by *Total Politics* and ComRes, Policy Exchange director Neil O'Brien went so far as to say that they would be a 'government of policy wonks'. For the sake of the Conservatives, and for the sake of the country, it is to be hoped that those policy wonks will be overseen by seasoned, pragmatic politicians. It is also to be hoped that the civil service will be sufficiently fed up with the outgoing government to enthusiastically embrace the New Conservative agenda.

The economy, taxation and business

This policy section is being put first – and out of sequence – because all of the proposals and aspirations which follow will be entirely dependent on how business performs, whether the economy recovers quickly and strongly, and therefore whether there are any funds available to pay for the policies which the spending departments will wish to put into operation.

David Davis, freed from the shackles of frontbench responsibility, has been very honest about what the priorities for the incoming Tory government would be. Whereas Tony Blair came to power espousing 'education, education, education' as his mantra, for the Tories it will be very simply, and in the immortal lyrics of Abba, 'money, money, money'. If a policy proposal does not generate money or save money, it will almost certainly get strangled at birth.

George Osborne set the scene when in a speech to the Birmingham Chamber of Commerce on 6 March 2009 he promised to 'tell it how it is'. He said that 'the age of irresponsibility is over'. He then went on to say that 'the unsustainable debts in our banks are a reflection of unsustainable debts in our households, our companies and our government ... The truth is that Britain is going to have to work hard and save hard to get out of this hole.'

In a later speech to the Association of British Insurers in June 2009 Osborne clearly set out the economic priorities of an incoming Tory government. They would be:

- to restore the UK's international economic credibility and preserve its 'Triple A' credit rating
- to bring about a transformation of an economy based on debt to an economy based on savings and investment
- to refocus the economy and investments on long-term gains, rather than short-term gains.

The following month Osborne announced proposals which would dramatically change the way in which the financial sector would be governed. The Bank of England would be given sweeping new powers to oversee the banks, the building societies and the insurance sector. The Financial Services Authority – blamed by the Tories for failing to spot that the banks were over-lending and over-borrowing – would be stripped of much of its powers, or even abolished completely. In its place, a powerful new Consumer Protection Agency would be set up.

Before the 2005 general election the Tories set up the James Commission (headed by Lord James of Blackheath) to look for efficiency savings across Whitehall. The commission found efficiency savings worth £34 billion. The report and its findings were howled down in that more affluent age, when the public had no appetite for cuts in public spending. This time around such 'salami slicing' exercises are not going to be anything like enough. What will be needed this time around are wholesale 'Canadian model' reductions in public spending.

This model was created and put into effect in the mid-1990s, when the Canadian economy had stalled and the Canadian currency had been badly battered. This was because of the unsustainably large size of the budget deficit, which at 9.2 per cent of GDP was causing serious concern and major problems. Between 1984 and 1992 successive governments had implemented no fewer than twenty-two rounds of spending cuts – but they had not achieved the desired results. Drastic measures were called for.

With the very real prospect of the IMF having to be called in, Jocelyne Bourgon (a senior civil servant) and Marcel Massé (a senior civil servant turned politician) devised a strategy which resulted in savings from the budget of $29 billion. There was a cut of 20 per cent in the size of the state, and this resulted in the loss of 47,000 civil service jobs. In the process of reducing the budget deficit, spending cuts outweighed tax rises by a ratio of seven to one. Responsibility for devising the drastic cut programmes were devolved down to the people actually running the departments. Once the headline reduction rates had been agreed, the decisions as to how the cuts should be implemented were devolved to the ministers concerned. Crucially, these were the people who would be running those departments after the reforms – so they had every incentive to cut fat, not muscle.

This process, known as *La Relève*, was as much about improving the delivery of public services as saving money – and it worked on both levels. This drastic medicine quickly had the desired effect – the size of the budget deficit was slashed by two thirds to a manageable 3 per cent of GDP and the Canadian economy has prospered ever since. The Tories have been studying this project to see if there are any lessons which can be translated and used to address the UK's current similar twin problems of an enormous budget deficit and a failure to deliver improvements in frontline public services to match the huge increases in spending over the last decade.

It is not just the Tories who are interested in the Canadian model for bringing the deficit back under control. In an interview for *The Times* Blair's former advisor David Halpern called for the model to be followed. He said that public spending cuts of around £130 billion would have to be found in order to cope with the projected £175 billion budget deficit. Efficiency gains, as espoused by both the Labour government and Tory opposition, would simply not be enough, he maintained.

Despite Labour's assault on 'the Tory cuts agenda' there is strong evidence to suggest that whoever forms the new government will have to make some bold decisions and tough choices. A study of the 2009 Budget and Red Book by the independent – and highly respected – Institute for Fiscal Studies (IFS) concluded that after the general election whoever formed the government would have to cut spending across the board by 7 per cent, and that that figure for cuts would rise to at least 10 per cent if spending on the NHS were ring fenced.

The Tories were prematurely prompted into admitting that there would have to be comprehensive cuts in spending by the unscripted remarks of shadow Health secretary Andrew Lansley during a live interview on the *Today* programme. However, he may have done them a favour. The slip was seized on by Gordon Brown, who proceeded to try and label David Cameron as 'Mr 10 Per Cent'. What emerged from this row, however, was the fact that the public were not only expecting heavy cuts in public services no matter who won the general election, but a substantial proportion of them were actually quite relaxed about the prospect. What has prompted this change of mood by the general public is the impact of the recession – and the knowledge that the burden of coping with its ill effects were being borne almost exclusively by the private sector.

The former minister David Davis, also a former chairman of the Public Accounts Committee, has described what he refers to as the 'bleeding stump' solution which civil servants put forward when asked to find areas to cut. Their solution, he says, is along the lines of 'Yes, Minister, of course you can lose 10 per cent of your body weight – we will simply cut off your arm'. In other words, they will try to portray cuts as being so painful – and so debilitating – as to be impracticable. Fortunately, the Tories are being advised by former senior civil servants on ways to circumvent all the obstacles which Whitehall traditionally puts in the way of new ministers and new governments.

Two sets of figures reinforced and underlined the feeling amongst the general public that the public sector was not bearing its fair share of the pain. One set of figures from the IFS showed that average public sector pay had now outstripped that of the private sector – despite the fact that public sector employees had greater job security, worked shorter hours, had longer holidays and retired earlier. The other set of figures came from the Pensions Policy Institute and showed that private sector workers were having to put more money into public sector pension pots than they did into their own. These two figures starkly demonstrated how distorted the economy had become under the Labour government.

The Tories' promise to ring-fence spending on health (as well as international development) would undoubtedly cause huge problems in other departments. A joint study by the IFS and the King's Fund estimated that if the Department of Health were protected against cuts other departments would face a 16 per cent cut over six years. Alternatively, every family in the UK would have to pay an extra £340 in tax every year, or there would have to be a 1.6 per cent rise in VAT, in order to maintain spending in those two departments.

Although no senior Tory or Labour politician has as yet admitted as much, the scale of the UK's debt is so vast that neither public spending cuts nor tax rises will be enough to tackle it. Borrowing in the fiscal year 2009/10 is projected by the Treasury to be £175 billion, and the ONS estimates that this will bring the national debt up to £799 billion. This represents 56.6 per cent of the UK's GDP, as against the 40 per cent maximum figure which Brown had stipulated when he was Chancellor of the Exchequer and still espousing his 'golden rules'.

Whoever wins the next general election will have to both cut public spending and raise taxes in order to effectively deal with the unsustainable level of national debt. The CEBR, in a study published in July 2009, estimated that an incoming Conservative government would have to cut public spending by £80 billion, and also raise taxation by £20 billion, in order to address the problem seriously. However, when you consider that public spending has risen from £396 billion in 1997 to £720 billion today, cuts of that magnitude look more manageable and less painful.

George Osborne, quizzed about his preference for tax rises over budget cuts, was clear. He said: 'I have not ruled out tax rises, but I do think that after a decade of over-spending, people should not be over-taxed because of that mistake. The bulk of the strain in dealing with this debt crisis has to be cutting public spending.'

Some of the tax and spending policies which the policy and manifesto teams on all sides will be looking at in order to mitigate this massive debt burden include:

- a new 'Beveridge report' on the role of the state
- scrapping the unaffordably generous public sector pension scheme
- the freezing or even cutting of public sector pay
- a freeze on public sector recruitment
- the abolition of middle-class benefits such as child tax credit, free bus passes for the over-sixties and the winter fuel allowance
- the reining in of expensive programmes such as education maintenance allowance and Sure Start
- raising the standard VAT rate to 20 per cent
- substantial increases in alcohol duty on strong beer, cider and alcopops
- the introduction of new 'green taxes' both to raise revenue and to encourage environmentally responsible behaviour
- scrapping the favourable tax treatment of corporate debt in order to discourage unsustainable borrowing
- the sell-off of national assets such as the QEII Conference Centre, the Royal Mint, the Met Office, Ordnance Survey and British Waterways
- the cancellation of 'big ticket' items. Tempting targets include Building Schools for the Future, ID cards, Trident replacement, the two new CVF aircraft carriers, the Joint Strike Fighter and Crossrail.

That is not to suggest that the Tories will do all of these things if they get elected, but they will certainly have to do some of them. In the case of projects like ID cards they will scrap the programme even if the savings are minimal – because they have pledged to do so, and because they are ideologically opposed to the programme in any event. In the case of the sell-offs, there is no downside for them – they need to raise money, and they do not believe that the state should be performing many of the functions which it currently performs.

The Tories have pledged to look at the role – and the budgets – of quangos, and some will undoubtedly be abolished or downsized. Two quangos they have pledged to create, however, are an Office of Budgetary Responsibility and an Office of Tax Simplification. The hope is that these bodies will not only keep the Tory government honest, but will also bind their successors with the bonds of fiscal prudence.

The Tories are acutely aware that government is not the engine of wealth creation. They will, therefore, not just be looking to downsize the size and role of the state for the sake of it, they will do so because they realise that this is the only way of allowing business the room it needs to function and grow. The Tories have signalled their determination to re-energise business as the economy returns to growth. They say that they want to make Britain the easiest and best place in the world to set up and grow a business. 'Under Labour, business has become increasingly burdened by corporate taxes, red tape and the lack of enterprise leadership in government. As a result, we are falling down the global scale of economic competitiveness,' the party's policy business blueprint states.

The party will bring forward detailed measures to help businesses, which it claims have been pushed close to breaking point by increased red tape. The Tories say that a partnership between business and government is essential to end a system of 'micro-managing from the top down'. According to the official party website, business-side measures which will be implemented include:

- establishing a temporary National Loans Guarantee Scheme with £50 billion to get credit flowing again and help protect jobs – an idea since adopted by the Labour government
- allowing struggling firms to defer their VAT bills for up to six months – another measure which the Labour government has adopted
- cutting small firms' payroll taxes by halting the planned increase in national insurance contributions
- refocusing the efforts of RDAs on attracting inward investment
- helping companies with the costs of hiring new staff by giving tax breaks for new jobs with a package worth £2.6 billion
- changing the pattern of government procurement to develop greater engagement with small and medium enterprises
- cutting the main rate of corporation tax to 25 per cent and the small business rate to 20 per cent.

At the macro level George Osborne and Ken Clarke, the shadow Business, Innovation and Skills (BIS) Secretary, will also seek to remove some of the disincentives to business development. They plan to reduce the burden of regulation to give businesses more freedom and greater flexibility. Employment law will also be simplified to remove the red tape which can be a barrier to the creation of new jobs, and the Tories are pledged to try and secure the UK's withdrawal from the Social Chapter. The Tories also want to improve the system of skills and apprenticeship training to plug the remaining skills gaps in growth areas.

Clarke agrees with this line of thought. He has said: 'BIS should build a new regulatory framework which supports and promotes entrepreneurship.' He went on to say that 'the tax code should be simplified so that corporation tax can be cut'. All opposition parties pledge to cut bureaucracy and red tape when they get into power. The difference is that the Tories really do mean it. They realise that the only way to seriously tackle the huge debt burden they will inherit is to get the economy back to working at full throttle.

The Tories realise that in the medium term the UK (along with other western economies) faces a huge challenge from China, India and the rest of Asia – which is why they have pledged to strengthen UK Trade & Investment. People in the Far East now study harder, work harder and save harder than their western competitors. They also have the huge advantage of not having to cope with the restrictions which western companies have imposed on them by their own governments and – in the case of the UK – by the EU. If the west – and the UK – is to compete, then it will have to work harder and smarter and come to terms with the fact that regulation simply cannot safeguard every worker from every conceivable hazard at all times.

The former head of the Better Regulation Taskforce, Sir David Arculus, has been advising the Tories on how to cut red tape. Speaking at a 'Listening to British Business' event in July 2009 he said that:

- there were 150 regulators – far too many
- all proposed regulations should be costed before they were introduced
- there should be a 'one in, one out' policy for regulations
- 'sunset clauses' should be introduced, meaning that new regulations would automatically be rescinded unless renewed by Parliament
- new employment laws should only be brought in once a year – in order to give them a higher profile and in order to give business a chance to absorb them.

The Tories have been very circumspect and have made few firm pledges over taxation. They have stuck to their pledge to raise the threshold of inheritance tax to £1 million – but then this was the pledge which helped to give them the bounce in the polls which was one of the factors which dissuaded Gordon Brown from going to the country in 2007. Even with IHT, however, the implication is that the threshold will be raised in the first parliament – not the first Budget.

They have also stuck firmly to their promise to 'prioritise' reversing Labour's planned increase in the rate of national insurance contributions – but then whilst this benefits everybody, it benefits those on lower wages most of all, and it can be regarded as a 'tax on employment'. They have also promised to scrap stamp duty for first time buyers (up to £250,000), and they have promised to recognise marriage in the tax system.

The Tories will not necessarily implement even these few pledges in their first Budget, although all should be honoured in their first parliament. The public finances are in such a dreadful state that even the firmest of pledges may have to wait until the signs of economic recovery are unmistakable. This is also partly the reason why the Tories have avoided falling into Alistair Darling's and Gordon Brown's elephant trap of promising to reverse the 50 per cent top rate of tax – although that is certainly something else they would like to do in their first parliament. David Cameron is on record as saying that 'the wealthy will have to pay their fair share'.

The Tories know it is going to be tough – tough on British business, tough on the British people, and therefore tough on them as a government and a party. If, however, they can gain power without making too many hard-to-keep promises, and if they can take the really tough decisions early on in the next parliament with a swiftly announced early emergency Budget, then they can look forward to an extended period in power. During the course of that period in power they will see the beneficial effects of the hard choices which they will have had to make early on. At that point they will be able to resume their mantra about 'sharing the proceeds of growth'.

Agriculture, food and rural affairs

Although this policy area was subsumed into DEFRA years ago, it is sufficiently vital to the Conservatives that it may be reinstated as a separate department at some stage. The Tories have not made many policy announcements in this area – mindful that much agricultural and regional policy is decided in Brussels. Instead they have tried to woo the countryside with mood music, convincing rural communities that they have their interests at heart. They say that it is their ambition 'to rebuild the broken bond of trust between rural communities and the government'.

The Tories have always dominated the countryside in electoral terms – although in bad times they have had to share rural seats with the Lib Dems and the nationalists. Even when the electoral map was drenched in red in 1997, geographically large areas remained blue because of the rural seats which the Tories still held. They will be looking to consolidate – and extend – the natural hold they have over the countryside in 2010.

Whilst the Tory Party was effectively banished from many metropolitan areas during the Blair years, it was still propped up in a rump of rural seats by a core and committed vote. The most notable exceptions to this, however, were in rural south-west England, where the Lib Dems used local government power bases to mount successful bids to turn once true blue seats yellow. The results of the May 2009 county council and unitary elections, however, indicate that even this process is now in decline and about to be reversed.

David Cameron is well aware of the need to harvest the rural vote. Addressing the CPRE's 2009 annual conference, he said:

> My constituency . . . is a permanent reminder of the connections between agriculture and landscape, the past and the present, economic activity and often breathtaking beauty. And the whole area, which is not some vast museum, has a buzzing 21st-century economy. This combination of farming, history and landscape is considerably enriched by local traditions and culture that links people with their place and the past.

In policy terms the Conservative believe that the countryside and the many rural communities which populate it are struggling with a poor transport infrastructure, a lack of affordable housing and hidden poverty. They are aware that many rural communities are lacking the provision of even the most basic public services. Schools, post offices and healthcare facilities have all come under threat in recent years.

The Tories want to challenge some of the central notions which have become embedded in rural policy over recent years. David Cameron used another speech to the CPRE in May 2008 to lambast Labour's focus on economic rather than social values in rural areas, saying:

> The attitude that the only thing that matters when it comes to policy and administration is economic value – that social value doesn't matter – has done great damage. The real world effect has been post office closures, library closures, police station closures, the closure of small shops, small schools and now GP surgeries under threat.

The Conservatives want to develop a holistic strategy which, for example, sees agriculture and tourism as aspects of a wider rural policy. They say that they would decentralise decision making, improve access to public services, reduce regulation on local business, increase affordable housing and integrate the transport system.

The party will aim to revitalise the countryside with a series of measures, including:

- shifting decision-making away from central government and the RDAs to local communities
- Maintaining and even increasing access to public services, by encouraging small rural schools and protecting family GP services
- Addressing the issue of rural poverty by creating opportunity, with less regulation on rural businesses, more power to local people to tackle the shortage of affordable homes and a more integrated transport system
- Allowing local authorities to use their revenues to support vital local amenities – such as village shops, post offices – and even pubs.

The Tories strongly maintain that rural communities need 'a thriving farming industry'. They are placing farming and food production at the heart of their rural strategy, and have pledged to overhaul farming regulations to lift the burden of unnecessary paperwork and inspections. Their strongly sceptical attitude towards the EU will undoubtedly lead them to try and seek the 'repatriation' of many of the powers which the EU has over farming and regional issues.

The party is also committed to making it easier to buy British by improving food labelling. shadow Environment, Food & Rural Affairs Secretary Nick Herbert launched an 'Honest Food' campaign at the NFU annual conference with a call for clearer food labelling. Under current rules, meat imported from abroad and processed into products like bacon, sausages and pies in Britain can be labelled as 'British'. Instead the party wants a system of compulsory 'country of origin' labelling introduced, so that meat products that are labelled 'British' can only come from animals born and bred in the UK.

In his speech Herbert said that 'Honest Food' is not about protectionism – consumers should be free to choose food from any country. Clear labelling, he maintained, would empower consumers, not restrict their options, adding that 'other EU countries fight for the interests of their consumers and their farming industry within the trading rules. It's time for the British government to show the same spine.' The Conservatives will also use public procurement to strengthen the link between food grown on British farms and the meals served in the country's schools and hospitals.

Finally, David Cameron has promised that if elected he will allow a free vote on whether or not the ban on hunting with hounds should be overturned. This is an iconic issue. Many rural inhabitants feel that the hunting ban was brought in to 'punish' rural voters for voting Conservative. If the Tories win the next election, there should be enough pro-hunting votes in Parliament to reverse the ban – and what was widely perceived as a 'wrong' in rural communities will be righted.

Constitution and devolution

One of Labour's most significant legacies will be in the area of constitutional reform. If Tony Blair can point to nothing else which he achieved in his ten years of power, he can at least say that he brought devolution to Scotland, Wales and London. He also saw through the peace process in Northern Ireland – and he oversaw the partial reform of the House of Lords with the removal of most hereditary peers.

However, the Conservative Party (the clue is in the title) will come to office warning that not all reform is good reform, and that not all change is progress. They will argue that the government has put in place a series of conflicting structures and systems which are undermining confidence in Parliament and resulting in increased tensions between the component parts of the United Kingdom.

To correct the situation David Cameron has spoken of a 'radical redistribution of power' – saying that the political crisis surrounding MPs' expenses has illustrated the need for 'sweeping reform'. Speaking in May 2009 he said that 'a bit of technocratic tinkering here, a bit of constitutional consultation there' would not be sufficient to address the feeling that people are 'increasingly powerless' and 'at the mercy of powerful elites that preside over them'. He pledged to devolve power 'from the state to citizens; from the government to Parliament; from Whitehall to communities. From Brussels to Britain; from judges to the people; from bureaucracy to democracy'. He also promised to 'replace bureaucratic accountability with democratic accountability' with local control over schools, housing and policing and more elected mayors.

Central to the Conservatives' policy plan will be measures to tackle the 'unbalanced devolution settlement', which critics say gives Scotland an unfair advantage – both economically and in terms of representation. In order to address the 'West Lothian question' first posed by the anti-devolution Labour MP Tam Dalyell during home rule debates thirty years ago, the Conservatives will reform Westminster to create a system of 'English votes for English laws'. Under these plans Scottish MPs and members from Wales and Northern Ireland would no longer be permitted to vote on measures which do not apply to their own constituencies.

Under a scaled-back version of this plan, it has been suggested by the Tories that non-English MPs (by which they mean MPs who do not represent English seats) would be able to participate at second and third reading debates and votes, but would be barred from the standing committees which examine bills in detail. The Conservatives hope these proposals will address the resentment felt by many English voters that they are the only part of the UK without their own unique parliament or assembly.

The Tories are also expected to reiterate their unwavering support for the United Kingdom. They will continue working on a vote-by-vote basis with Alex Salmond's SNP in the Holyrood Parliament. The recent announcement that the Conservative Party will now be collaborating with the Ulster Unionist Party in Northern Ireland is also seen as being a reaffirmation of the Tories' belief in the integrity of the Union.

A Conservative government would also seek to restore confidence in public life by expanding public engagement in the decision-making processes at local and national level. The party is describing this approach as being an exercise in 'direct democracy'. The Conservative Party website states: 'We want to see decisions taken at the lowest possible level, and where possible, by those directly affected. So we will encourage greater use of direct democracy, with measures including the introduction of directly elected police commissioners [and] enabling local residents to veto excessive council tax rises.'

One policy commitment already on the table is a system of individual voter registration. This follows a report from the Electoral Commission which called on the government to replace the current system of household registration with individual voter registration. The commission said such a move would 'make the electoral register – the foundation of the electoral process – safer and more accurate'.

At Westminster the Conservatives will support moves towards a substantially elected House of Lords – although this is certainly not a priority and has been described as a 'third term' issue. They also plan to introduce further direct controls by developing a system of petition which will force the legislature to consider any measure which has the support of one million signatories. This measure could be used by faith groups or pressure groups to force Parliament to debate issues such as banning abortion or the reintroduction of the death penalty.

Any reform in the House of Lords may be mirrored by reforms of the House of Commons. The Boundary Commissions may be instructed to draw up proposals to make sure that all constituencies are of uniform size – thus scrapping once and for all Labour's in-built electoral advantage. At the same time, the size of the House of Commons may be reduced, possibly by 100 – or even 150 – seats.

The Tories have also let it be known that they would be willing to give detailed consideration to a system of fixed-term parliaments – likely to be for a period of four years. There are elements within the Conservative Party who have advocated some form of proportional representation – but they are still very much in the minority. Any moves towards a system of PR received a possibly fatal blow with the election of two BNP Members to the European Parliament.

The Conservatives have also issued a clear commitment to replace the controversial Human Rights Act, which they say 'has undermined the government's ability to deal with crime and terrorism'. They plan to replace it with a British Bill of Rights and Responsibilities, thus reversing another one of Tony Blair's key constitutional reforms.

In opposition the Tories have also been hinting that they will oversee a crackdown on the role of lobbyists. Conservative candidates for the European Parliament had to sign a pledge that they would publish details of all formal meetings with lobbyists and declare all gifts or entertainment with a value in excess of £50. They are also keeping a close eye on President Obama's campaign to rein in the power of lobbyists on Capitol Hill. Ultimately, under either government, some form of statutory regulation of the industry in Westminster is likely, and a natural body to oversee it would be the new Independent Parliamentary Standards Authority.

The Conservatives genuinely believe that the Labour government, for a variety of political reasons, has presided over a period of 'constitutional vandalism' which may take many years to correct. Following the MPs' expenses scandal, trust in Parliament as an institution is at a historic low. The Tories are determined to ensure that they are in a position to correct the imbalances which a system of patchy devolution has created. They are also determined to enhance the role which the public has in the decision-making processes at both the local and the national level. The Conservative policy agenda is all about decentralisation and direct democracy, and devolving decision making down to the lowest practical level.

Culture, media and sport

A New Conservative government would come into office pledging reform in key areas within the Department for Culture, Media & Sport's (DCMS) portfolio, although suggestions that the Tories might scrap the department are probably wide of the mark. The Tories invented the precursor of the DCMS, the Department for National Heritage. They will not be looking to strangle their own offspring.

Whilst the most pressing issues, such as housing, welfare reform and economic recovery, are likely to be given top billing in the first Queen's Speech of a New Conservative administration, the party will also seek to focus on some of the softer issues which it has been accused of neglecting in the past. They are mindful of the role which tourism and the creative industries play in the UK economy. Tourism is the UK's fifth largest industry, and the creative industries together account for nearly 7.5 per cent of GDP. The Conservative Party website says that the party is 'committed to fostering an environment in which sport, the arts, and the creative industries can flourish, and in which people can take control of the most enjoyable aspects of their lives'.

One of the priorities of a New Conservative government will be a push to deliver a broadband-enabled digital Britain. The Tories have given a clear signal that they will act quickly to push ahead with the roll-out of high-speed broadband across the country. In June 2009 shadow DCMS Secretary Jeremy Hunt accused the government of 'digital dithering' following the publication of their *Digital Britain* report. He said that the report, which announced twelve new consultations, did not contain a single action and 'reads more like a top-down attempt to protect and prop up old business models using yet more public cash'. The Tories, like the other main parties, realise that fast broadband is not only a requirement for recreation, it is also nowadays essential for education and for business.

The party is still to offer a radical policy on broadcasting, although an attempted vote-winning move in the form of a £3 reduction in the BBC licence fee was criticised by some media commentators. To back up its policy in March 2009 the Conservatives detailed a raft of examples of BBC 'waste', including £13.8 million on taxis and £170,000 on parties to promote one BBC drama series.

Writing in *The Times*, Adam Sherwin, a former lobby correspondent turned media analyst, said:

> Since the proposal was not presented as part of a strategic Conservative plan to preserve the BBC's future whilst ensuring it does not obliterate struggling commercial rivals, many will see it as merely a populist gesture. As much as Mr Cameron would like it, the £68 million that the Conservatives hope to lop off the licence fee will not come out of the generous pay packets enjoyed by the corporation's top brass.

The Tories are ambivalent about the BBC. Like all politicians they wake up to the *Today* programme, and nod off with *Newsnight* or *Question Time* on in the background. They also realise that the BBC does a tremendous job of promoting the UK overseas. And yet, despite all this, they cannot help thinking that it is monopolistic – and that most of its journalists are anti-Tory. As an indication of the Tories' thinking, their media and arts spokesman, Ed Vaizey, has mooted the idea of privatising the BBC's Radio 1.

Whilst there may not be a lot of votes connected to a party's media, culture and sport policy, given the importance of all three issues on the day-to-day lives of the public, the Conservatives will be determined to bring forward some distinct policies. Whilst some within the arts and heritage world have criticised the Conservatives' general approach to the culture agenda in the past, others point to significant policies such as the creation of Channel 4 as a sign of creativity in the party's arts policy.

The party will seek to expand areas such as tourism, which are a key part of the British economy. With the Olympic Games looming sport and tourism will be important drivers of future growth and should deliver a lasting legacy for London and the country as a whole. The Conservatives believe that despite the economic pressures the country faces, the Olympic Games offer an opportunity to showcase British sport, talent and tourism. In its policy paper the Conservatives state: 'We must make sure that the Olympics leave us with a lasting legacy focused on inspiring young people to take part in sport.'

More is also being pledged in the areas of the arts and the creative industries. When he was in office John Major established the National Lottery and directed the proceeds towards good causes in the communities – often arts, sport or heritage-related projects. In opposition the Conservatives have repeatedly criticised the way much of the proceeds of the National Lottery have been siphoned off and spent on areas which would normally be funded from mainstream tax revenues. The incoming administration will pledge reforms which would put an end to any further government interference and 'ensure a greater share of Lottery funding goes to the arts, sport and heritage'.

The finer details of the Conservatives' DCMS policy are still under development by Jeremy Hunt's team, who are also known to be consulting the influential CMS Select Committee chairman, John Whittingdale. Some indication of their thinking can be gleaned from their response to the Arts Taskforce, headed by former Barbican Centre managing director John Tusa. His report called for responsibility for funding England's national performing arts companies to be taken away from Arts Council England and given to central government – mirroring the situation in Scotland. The report called for responsibility for the National Theatre, Royal Shakespeare Company and the Royal Opera House to be taken away from the Arts Council.

The Tory front bench made it clear that not all of Tusa's suggestions would be adopted – with Hunt ruling out a recommendation that sport be taken out of the DCMS to create a de facto Department of Culture. Hunt said:

> John Tusa and the Arts Taskforce have put together a comprehensive and ambitious document and have brought a wealth of expertise and fresh thinking to arts policy. We're very grateful for all their work putting this report together. In it there are many proposals that would reform the arts; some we support, some are aspirational, and some, such as the plans to move sport out of the DCMS, are not something we would support.

This is not going to be a top priority area for the New Conservative government. Having said that, it does offer an opportunity to demonstrate radical thinking and to introduce policies which have a direct effect on the everyday lives of citizens – without involving substantial expenditure from the Treasury's much-diminished coffers.

Defence

The Conservatives have traditionally always been the party of strong defence. A quick scan of the PPC section of this book will show that a large number of future Tory MPs have served either with the regular armed forces or with the TA. Notwithstanding these two factors, given the dire state of the country's finances, the Tories will have to look to see if there are savings to be made in the MoD's equipment budget.

In his conference speech of 2007 David Cameron issued a direct pledge on defence. He said: 'I think the key principle that we must apply to these great challenges in our dangerous and insecure world is keeping our defences strong.' Yet despite the clarity in commitment to maintaining a robust defence capability, the Tories are somewhat vague about on some of the key issues confronting the armed forces. The simple reason for this is that nobody around the shadow Cabinet table is entirely sure that a Tory government will be able to afford to maintain every one of the defence equipment programmes which the MoD is currently pursuing.

In office the Conservatives have also said they will oppose the defence provisions in the Lisbon Treaty and ensure that NATO and not the EU 'remains the cornerstone of the UK's defence strategy'. This fits in with their core foreign affairs policies of keeping close to the USA – whilst striving to keep the EU at arm's length without actually precipitating a situation where the UK is asked to leave.

The Conservatives view defence as relatively strong territory in election terms. However, the party's central concern appears to be related to the mounting problems around funding and equipping modern forces in the increasingly sophisticated defence arena. One commitment which the party may allow to slide into the long grass is the pledge to restore the three infantry battalions abolished by Labour – which, according to defence analysts, could prove logistically and operationally difficult to achieve. Instead the Conservatives may focus their efforts on increasing troop numbers and improving the lives of the servicemen and women engaged at home and abroad.

The Tory defence team in opposition does not look entirely comfortable in its role. Former medical doctor Liam Fox is not a defence specialist, whilst

Gerald Howarth and Julian Lewis are both veterans – of politics if not defence. At least Andrew Murrison served in the Royal Navy for twenty years – albeit as a surgeon. It is likely that in government this team will be refreshed with some of the younger MPs with a more recent defence background. Defence might also be fruitful ground for the rehabilitation of Patrick Mercer – and possibly even David Davis. He would relish the role of Secretary of State for Defence – and it is a role which would keep him firmly out of mischief.

Defence equipment

A large part of the defence budget is allocated to acquiring and maintaining the equipment which the Army, the Royal Navy and the Royal Air Force require. Every new requirement is put out to tender, and negotiations over contracts can drag on for years – with UK, US and European defence manufacturers lobbying, bidding and then counter-bidding.

One iconic programme is that to update the ageing UK nuclear deterrent. shadow Chancellor George Osborne is said to have led calls for a rethink of the full £21 billion Trident modernisation proposed by Labour, and which was backed by the Conservatives in the division lobbies. An about turn on Trident is said to be supported by senior Conservatives, including former Defence Minister Nicholas Soames and James Arbuthnot, chairman of the Commons Defence Select Committee.

Whilst David Cameron has spoken of his support for the government's Trident plans, the party does appear to be having senior-level second thoughts on the wisdom of the revamp. William Hague and Liam Fox are reported to believe that the party should match Labour's commitment, whilst some suggest Cameron is leaving the door open for a future change in policy, telling a press conference in early 2009:

> We are in a very similar position to the government. We support things that are
> in the forward defence programme because we think there is good justification
> for all of them. But that doesn't mean in these difficult circumstances that you
> don't have to look – just as you're looking across government – at all these things.
> But when you are reviewing spending you have to review all spending.

However, although there has been serious discussion around the issue, it is hard to see a Tory government cancelling the Trident upgrade unless a serious viable alternative nuclear deterrent can be found.

Aware that the room for any major spending commitments is highly restricted, David Cameron is hoping to delay any wholesale decisions by pledging a major strategic defence review upon taking office. Along with the first defence review a new Tory government will pledge a US-style system of quadrennial defence reviews. The party has said it is 'completely unacceptable' that the last strategic defence review was conducted over a decade ago under the stewardship of former Defence Secretary George, now Lord, Robertson. The current Labour government has also now pledged to hold a strategic defence review.

The Tories believe that a succession of blows to the MoD's budget could leave a litany of problems for an incoming administration. Senior Conservatives have admitted that the country's defence budget is in a desperate state, and they concede that their room to spend any further money will be severely restricted by cross-Whitehall financial pressures. In office, the party's review will assess the threats posed to UK national security – assessing whether more should be done to equip mobile armed forces and to determine whether the two extremely expensive new CVF aircraft carriers are still essential.

The Tories say that future defence procurement projects will be determined according to five criteria: capability, interoperability, adaptability, affordability and exportability. Writing for the website ConservativeHome, Shadow Defence Secretary Liam Fox said:

> A Strategic Defence Review under a Conservative government would follow a logical sequence:
> - First, it would determine what the national interests of Britain are and where they exist in a truly global economy. These need to go wider than the traditional definitions and include threats in areas such as energy and cyber-security.
> - Second, we need to make an assessment of how we perceive threats developing in the foreseeable future, which is never an easy task.
> - Third, we must determine the defence capabilities we require to protect our interests from these threats.
> - Only then, fourth, will we be able to decide the specific resources needed to make a reality of these capabilities.
> - Finally, we need to take account of the financial constraints that will ultimately decide what we can and cannot afford to do.

Where defence equipment is concerned, the Tories have promised to 'ensure the speedy delivery of equipment' and to 'match resources with commitments'. Fox has said he fears that a succession of 'unpleasant, unpaid bills' could enlarge a black hole in the MoD's budget – already conservatively thought to be at least £1 billion.

As far as defence exports are concerned the Conservatives have promised to restore the Defence Export Service Organisation, with the implication being that the UK will set off on a worldwide arms sales drive. Deals such as the Al Yamamah contract with Saudi Arabia have maintained the UK defence industry over the last two decades but have been frowned upon by New Labour. The Tories, however, are intent on ensuring that defence sales become a key component in reviving the manufacturing and export base.

In opposition the Conservative Party has focused its attention on what it perceives as the chronic neglect of the armed forces under Labour, leaving them 'overstretched, undermanned and in possession of outworn equipment'. It has also made major pledges on the future handling of procurement and the welfare of service personnel and their families. Whilst the party has repeatedly advocated an expansion of the Army, believing that it is currently too small for recent operations in both Iraq and Afghanistan, any increase in headcount will add to the MoD's financial pressures.

The Conservatives have supported the Future Rapid Effect System (FRES), the programme to deliver a fleet of more than 3,000 armoured vehicles for the British Army. This new generation of armoured fighting vehicles will be rapidly deployable, network-enabled and capable of operating across a range of terrains and climates. The total FRES fleet is expected to comprise five families of vehicle: Utility, Reconnaissance, Medium Armour, Manoeuvre Support and a family of simpler variants known as the Basic Capability Utility. The FRES programme has continually been under review and under pressure, but the Conservatives seem committed to maintaining it.

Although recent Conservative announcements contain no pledge to insulate defence spending against any future cuts, it is unlikely that they will look for many savings in this area. What will undoubtedly happen, however, is that the defence reviews will recommend that the focus of investment should switch away from hugely expensive projects designed to equip the armed forces to take on Warsaw Pact-type enemies, and instead refocus manning levels and equipment programmes so that they will be better able to take on Iraq-type and Afghanistan-type operations.

Service personnel

Looking after service personnel is certain to feature high up the list of discussion points between the Tory Defence Secretary and his generals. The Conservatives' Military Covenant Commission has recommended ways of taking better care of service members and their families. The commission provides the basis for the armed forces manifesto, which they claim will establish a strong relationship between the armed forces and the next Conservative government.

Amongst the recommendations contained in the Military Covenant Commission's report are preferential NHS treatment for forces personnel –

including military wards for injured personnel returning from combat – and the extension of free parcel deliveries outside the Christmas period. The Tory leadership has also spoken about reviewing leave regulations to replicate the US system, whereby leave period only begins when the personnel set foot on home soil, rather than the clock starting when they leave their bases. Measures to improve housing and schooling for service families will also be under active review.

The Conservatives realise that defence capability is as much about the training and morale of the armed forces as it is about equipment. They are determined to be seen as – and to act as – the friend of the armed forces, and to that end their website contains a firm pledge:

> A Conservative Government will repair the broken Military Covenant, respect our Armed Forces, and ensure that Forces' families and veterans are taken care of.

Education

Education is certain to become a key election battleground issue. Two of the brightest politicians in the Labour and Conservative parties, Ed Balls and Michael Gove respectively, go head to head on schools policy. David Willetts, another extremely intellectually able individual, heads up Tory thinking in the area of higher education and skills.

Education is a continual learning experience for all political parties. The three main parties are committed to what amounts to a permanent revolution in schools, despite complaints from the teaching profession that constant change is undermining their attempts to get on with the job in hand. The Tories have pledged to trust the professionals – whether they be healthcare professionals, teachers or the police – to go about their work relatively unhindered by the attentions of the 'man in Whitehall'. It remains to be seen, however, whether they will be capable of sticking to this self-denying ordinance.

Labour, which tried to make education its core issue following Tony Blair's 'education, education, education' pledge, has sought to retain moral ownership of this central plank of social policy. As recently as July 2009 Gordon Brown unveiled new thinking in the form of the latest education white paper, which heralded the end of key Blairite reforms such as centrally controlled national strategies, including those on literacy and numeracy in primary schools. However, Brown's record on loosening control over key policy areas is not good, and there may not be time before the general election to see whether he is serious about relinquishing control in this area.

The Tories are set to propose what they claim will be a 'commonsense' approach to schools, FE colleges and universities. In a policy foreword written in November 2007, David Cameron expressed confidence in his education team's ability to develop a bold strategy which he said contrasted with 'the top-down centralisation and endless short-term tricks that characterise Labour's efforts and explain their failure'. He went on to say: 'After all the promises Labour have made and all the money they've spent, Britain today is a country where it is harder, not easier, for children to achieve their potential.'

The party's policy blueprint *Schools: Raising the Bar, Closing the Gap* was designed to show a commitment to raise standards, create more good school places and make opportunity more equal. In the skills and FE arena, an often overlooked sector, the Tories stated in their Policy Green Paper Number 1 that they 'will remove the bureaucracy that is suffocating our colleges, put students and employers in the driving seat so training matches the needs of the market, and introduce real apprenticeships with true, on-the-job-training'.

Following on Labour's decision to dismantle the two-year-old DIUS – a move which they criticised – the Tories are unlikely to want to create any further structural instability in relation to education and may leave responsibility for schools and universities and skills with separate Whitehall fiefdoms.

David Willetts, the shadow Minister for Universities & Families, admitted in June 2009 that the latest Labour restructuring, which saw Lord Mandelson take responsibility for higher education, had left his party without a clear plan in relation to departmental organisation. 'We have not decided what would happen to Whitehall if we won the election at this stage. There will always be a business department. What we are wary about is putting these big education roles – colleges and universities – in with it,' he said. 'We would keep universities and colleges separate from the super-ministry. To be honest, this is a muddle caused by Gordon Brown creating DIUS in a rushed way and destroying it in a rushed way.'

Schools

The Conservatives are determined to try to wrest schools education, as a core aspect of public policy, from Labour as they set out their agenda for government. According to Tory policy plans, the party says it believes that education is the most powerful means by which individuals can be given the freedom to shape their future – and they have placed their schools reform plan at the heart of their drive to increase opportunity.

Central to the Tories' policy, as in other key areas, will be moves to shift the balance of power away from Whitehall and towards service users, in this case the parents. The current obstacles which prevent local demand for new schools leading to their creation are to be removed. Grammar schools will be retained – although the party is still pledged to prevent the creation of any further grammar schools, despite their popularity amongst many Tory voters. They have also promised to provide state funding for Montessori and Steiner schools – provided that there is demand for them from parents.

The Conservative Party will present plans to develop a more diverse schools system, taking failing schools out of local authority control and developing a greater supply stream through a wider range of providers. Sixth forms will be expanded, and more academies and trusts will be created as the party seeks to provide more choice.

The Tories are also considering radical plans for the creation of up to 3,000 new schools within the state system – following the so-called 'Swedish model' for the provision of as diverse a range of schools as possible. This model allows parents' groups, charities and companies to set up schools – provided that they are free. Initially the Tories were only considering allowing new schools to be created and run by voluntary and third-sector groups. In a radical rethink, however, they are now considering allowing such schools to be run by the private sector. However, they would have to be free to parents, the fees paid by the state would be capped (probably at £6,000 per pupil per year) and dividend payments would be controlled.

The Tories say they want a greater concentration on reading skills and appear opposed to any moves to increase the learning leaving age. Reflecting the need for a diversity of supply, they are unlikely to adopt the line that schools are the sole solution. Instead they are likely to opt for a mixed system of academic and vocation routes though a system of school, further education and higher education.

As the party seeks to drive resources to the front line the Conservatives are also likely to push for smaller schools which more closely reflect the communities they seek to serve. At the same time they will be taking what the Tory high command has said will be 'a number of immediate steps to improve standards in all our schools'.

Just as the Conservative Party wants to see pupil and parent empowerment, it also believes that empowering teachers to take control of discipline is essential if the respect culture is to be engendered across society from an early age. They point to the fact that there were roughly 140,000 pupils suspended from secondary schools for violence or persistent disruption in 2005/6, and have noted that there are over a quarter of a million persistent truants per year. They also highlight the fact that 100,000 custodial sentences are being passed for 10–17-year-olds every year, and they have pledged to offer further support to teachers who have faced false allegations from pupils.

The Tories have also signalled a determination to restore standards and reduce the red tape which results in teachers spending time filling forms rather than marking homework or addressing classroom concerns. On the crucial issue of testing, the Tories commissioned a review by Sir Richard Sykes. In June 2009 the party announced that it would abolish SATS for eleven-year-olds if elected. They will be replaced by a test which pupils will take in their first year in secondary school. Speaking on *The Andrew Marr Show* in June 2009, Michael Gove said: 'Our principal aim is to ensure we have a system of testing which allows us to measure how well individual children are actually doing and also to accurately measure how well schools are doing and what we are doing as a country.'

The Conservative Party has signalled that GCSEs and A-levels will stay in the early years and that there will be a greater emphasis on British history and culture throughout the education system. 'Our children are either taught to put Britain in the dock or they remain in ignorance of our island story. That is morally wrong, culturally self-defeating and we would put it right,' the *Daily Mail* quotes Gove as saying.

The Tories' determination to push responsibility down to the lowest practical level will see a big reduction in the powers of local education authorities – or even their complete abolition. This will not be a case of 'let a thousand flowers bloom', but more a case of 'let a thousand schools bloom'.

Higher education

Despite what some have seen as a not necessarily desirable year-on-year increase in the numbers of students pursuing undergraduate degrees, the Conservatives will fight the next election on a commitment to making higher education places available to all those who seek them.

The party will offer universities a greater freedom from detailed bureaucratic instructions and seek to develop a system which offers more support for the increasing numbers of part-time and mature students. They also say that they are committed to creating a clearer pathway from vocational routes into further and higher education.

In a concession to Labour government policies, the Tories acknowledge that tuition fees have brought benefits to universities. However, they stress that all academic bodies need to ensure that they are providing a better student experience in return.

Having committed this U-turn on student finance, the Tories are now committed to the expansion in student numbers, but they will seek to inject a sense of reality into the overarching mission to achieve a better-educated population. The party wants to ensure that students get value for money and that student numbers rise in line with realistic expectations. Its website says:

> We believe that every person who could benefit from a university education should have the opportunity to do so if they wish. But the proportion of young people going to university has scarcely changed in eight years. At the current rate, it would take Labour over a century to meet their 50 per cent target.

The Tories have said that they will try and ensure that there is closer collaboration between universities and British business. In an article written in *The House* magazine in July 2009 Ken Clarke said: 'Universities should develop stronger links with the business community, translating innovative research into marketable products.'

As they edge closer to government the Tories will be anxious not to alienate students – or their parents. Perhaps that explains the comparative dearth of concrete policy proposals in this area.

The skills agenda

The Conservative Party has consistently claimed that Labour has failed on the skills agenda – pointing to the record number of young people not in education, employment or training (NEETs). They say that the numbers of real apprenticeships, FE enrolments and adult learners have dropped, and in order to address this problem they will pledge a series of significant reforms in relation to training and skills.

The Tories will fight the general election pledging a 'massive expansion' in the provision of real apprenticeships. As many as 100,000 additional apprenticeships will be created every year through a system which makes it easier for companies to establish entry-level training systems.

The Tories are also pledging greater community-level learning via a new NEETs Fund. This will be aimed at young people who have failed to secure a place in any formal education, training or employment. A new Community Learning Fund is also likely under a New Conservative government, as it seeks to push funding to the front line. This process would see the creation of a streamlined funding model through which government support for training 'follows the learner'.

A wider careers advisory service, which covers people of all ages and at all stages of their careers or working life, would also be established by an incoming Conservative administration. Currently such advice is largely restricted to pupils of school age, and private schools are able to offer much more career advice than their state-funded counterparts.

Energy

The Conservative Party, when it returns to government, will seek in its energy policy to extend the mixed economy in provision, whilst also striving for an overall reduction in fuel consumption. They are also determined to ensure security of supply, both by boosting domestic energy generation and by securing energy supplies from politically stable regions.

In government the Tories are also committed to measures to achieve a low-carbon economy – and will use nuclear provision where the economics stack up. In a speech to the Local Government Association in July 2006 David Cameron said: 'The future is decentralised energy.' He went on to say that nuclear power is 'a last resort' in policy terms.

The party's website states that the UK is 'uniquely placed to be the world's first low-carbon economy, with the natural resources to generate wind and wave power, a skilled workforce trained in the energy industry, a high-tech manufacturing sector and a green financial centre in the City of London'.

Green campaigners predict that by 2010 renewable energy could be the engine of green growth, and to this end the Tories have pledged a series of renewable and low-carbon energy policies, which will involve:

- transforming electricity networks with 'smart grid' and 'smart meter' technology, which will automatically match supply and demand, thereby allowing for a huge increase in renewable power
- providing up to £6,500 worth of home insulation improvements, enabling households to reduce their gas and electricity bills
- creating a decentralised energy revolution by introducing a system of feed-in tariffs to encourage micro-generation of electricity
- expanding offshore wind and marine power and providing government backing for a network of large-scale marine energy parks
- supporting the vast expansion of offshore wind power with incentives to build the necessary undersea grid network
- fast-tracking planning for the offshore marine energy parks.

Alternative energy lobbying groups have welcomed the Tories' focus on renewable energy sources. Commenting on the plans, the British Wind Energy Association chairman, Adam Bruce, said in early 2009: 'The Conservative plans recognise that moving to a green economy will create jobs, secure our energy supplies and tackle climate change. Britain needs a green energy revolution that delivers security of supply and better management of demand.'

The Tories, however, insist that they will ensure that the UK has 'adequate, safe and reliable access to conventional fuels'. They will permit coal-fired power stations to be built, but only where clean carbon capture and storage technology is in place. The criterion applied will be that new coal-fired power stations must be able to restrict carbon emissions to the level achieved by modern gas power plants.

The Conservatives concede that nuclear power can form part of the energy strategy, but only where it is economically viable. The party believes that new nuclear power stations should not leave taxpayers with liabilities for their running, decommissioning or waste. 'Nuclear is not an alternative to developing and expanding renewable forms of energy', party policy states. The party line on nuclear power has, however, softened recently. The Tories now recognise that nuclear power has a role to play both in security of supply and in countering climate change.

The Conservatives have also announced measures to tackle the rising cost of energy, which they believe is pushing more and more families into fuel poverty. Amongst the measures they are likely to introduce in government is legislation to make it illegal for energy companies to charge unfair price premiums on prepayment meters – a move which it is estimated will cut bills for 5.8 million households. A future Conservative administration would also force energy companies to offer low rates for electricity and gas to vulnerable households, and force them to state how much less a customer would pay if they moved to the cheapest tariff.

Shadow Energy Secretary Greg Clark has also criticised Labour over its 'frustratingly slow' progress towards the installation of smart meters. Despite previously promising to install smart meters in every home by 2017, the government has now announced that full roll-out will not take place until 2020. 'In other countries around the world, smart meters are already being rolled out now, resulting in savings of up to 15 per cent on energy bills and reduced CO_2 emissions', Clark has said.

David Cameron has also highlighted the potential of deep geothermal technology and promised to provide 'generous incentives' to kick-start the industry in Britain. That pledge, delivered in May 2009, followed a report by the Geothermal Research Programme which estimated that deep geothermal energy could generate almost 10 per cent of the UK's electricity needs.

The priorities for the Conservatives in government will be simple. They will want to boost the supply of green energy, they will accelerate the home insulation programme – and they will look for security and diversity of energy supply. This agenda will be paid for by a mixture of government, consumers – and the energy companies.

Environment and climate change

During the campaign for the Conservative leadership David Cameron led the charge on the environment. He spoke of the need to take the politics out of climate change, and he called for the creation of a new independent body with powers to require future governments to stick to agreed year-by-year reductions in carbon emissions.

In office the Conservatives say that they will seek to tackle the UK's domestic environmental issues, whilst pressing for further international co-operation to tackle global climate change. Whilst Cameron has insisted he does not want Britons to 'live like monks', early in his leadership he signalled a determination to tackle global warming when he instructed environmentalist Zac Goldsmith and former Environment Secretary John Gummer to consider radical measures to create a system of 'green growth'.

Cameron's visit to a Norwegian glacier was widely seen as a PR stunt, although green groups said they hoped he would follow through with a series of radical measures domestically and internationally. In April 2006 Cameron used an article in *The Independent* to set out his environmental concerns: 'I want to see for myself the effects of climate change, not just to see a retreating glacier but to meet leading scientific and research experts,' he said. 'Climate change is one of the biggest threats facing the world and we must have a much greater sense of urgency about tackling it.' The party's website makes clear: 'Quality of life and environmental issues must be at the heart of politics – which is why we have pledged to improve Britain's environment by reversing the decline in our biodiversity, improving urban green spaces, providing incentives to recycle and working towards zero waste.'

The Tories concede that Britain has yet to find a coherent strategy to cope with growing mountains of waste. To achieve a new approach they want to develop a new mindset about packaging and waste. They say that ending landfill through increased recycling targets and finding better ways of coping with waste through discarded products will not be enough. Instead they will call on manufacturers to consider the waste implications of their products at the design phase.

A future Conservative government would introduce a Responsibility Deal on waste – which the party says will come in the form of voluntary arrangements amongst producers to cut back on the production of waste and improve its disposal. The party would also encourage councils to adopt a scheme which gives incentives to households who recycle.

The Conservatives also consider that much more should be done to improve the protection of the marine environment. The party warns that fish stocks have been over-exploited and has called for legislation to conserve the UK's marine habitats. In opposition the Tories pressed to ensure the Marine and Coastal Access Bill was strengthened. At a European level the Conservatives will call for further reform of the Common Fisheries Policy to deliver a 'fair deal for our fishermen' and, through the development of a pilot scheme, will aim to bring to an end the practice of fish discarding.

The Conservatives have also outlined the need for greater flood prevention measures as part of a mitigation package to deal with the effects of climate change. Although urban flooding is an increasing phenomenon as drainage systems are overwhelmed by flash floods, many of the areas affected are in the Tories' rural heartland.

On the question of forestry, the Tories have insisted that timber dealers and furniture makers using illegally logged wood could face criminal charges under plans which they have put forward to help save rainforests from destruction. In a speech in June 2007 David Cameron pledged to press for an EU-wide definition of sustainable timber, and to push for an EU-wide ban on products which did not meet these criteria, which would phased in to allow countries time to reach the required standard.

There are a number of committed environmental campaigners within the Conservative Party. Apart from Cameron himself, there are Greg Clark (the current shadow Energy & Climate Change Secretary), Greg Barker, Peter Ainsworth, former Environment Secretary John Gummer and Zac Goldsmith – who was an environmentalist before he was a Conservative. Although the exigencies of government will inevitably have an impact and soften the 'green line' to some degree, this is not an agenda which the Tories will discard in government. They will simply try and shift the emphasis away from forcing people to turn green, to incentivising them to do so.

Equality

David Cameron has said that by the end of the first parliament one third of his ministers will be women. This pledge is his way of underlining his commitment to the equality agenda.

Women have always formed the backbone of the Conservative Party's activists, and they have also always been the party's core vote. However, the Tories now realise that they need to reach out beyond their traditional middle-aged and elderly workers and supporters, and engage with a younger generation of mothers and single female workers if they want to secure their electoral position.

A series of initiatives have secured 'Cameron woos women' headlines for a party leader keen to stress his modern male, metrosexual credentials. The Conservatives policy on women revolves around five key areas:

- women in the workplace
- vulnerable women
- women in the community
- women and ethnicity
- the role of women in international development.

Through its 'fair play on women's pay' initiative the party has noted that men still get paid 17.2 per cent more than women, and the average woman will lose or forgo £300,000 over her lifetime because of the gender pay gap. The party's website states: 'This is an issue that affects every woman, not just those doing part-time or lower-paid roles. Full-time women earn less than men in every occupation – and last year the gender pay gap amongst managers in Britain actually increased.'

The Conservatives are committed to measures to tackle the gender pay gap. These include stronger legislation to prevent employers discriminating against the female workforce, and also the provision of better careers guidance for young women. To effect change on gender-related pay, Theresa May, the shadow Minister for Women, has teamed up with the TV presenter June Sarpong to launch the 'fair pay' campaign. May will also introduce an Equal Pay and Flexible Working Bill in Parliament – and with cross-party support seek effective legislation to help narrow the pay gap.

The Tories are also pledged to introduce a new system of flexible parental leave, which will give parents a year of shared leave after they have a baby. They have also promised to support the extension of the right to request flexible working to all parents with children under the age of eighteen.

The party supports a new strategy to tackle violence against women. This includes a greater focus on preventative work in schools, better training for police and frontline professionals and new rape crisis centres.

The female vote is vital to any political party – it is not possible to get elected without it. The Tories understand, through polling and focus groups, that female voters are quicker to pick up changes in policies and the electoral cycle – and that they are more prepared to admit that they may have been wrong in the past and to therefore switch their votes. It was women voters who were primarily responsible for Gordon Brown's 'bounce' in the opinion polls after he became Prime Minister, and it is women voters who have largely deserted him since.

If the Tories do well enough to form a government after the next general election they should have more than fifty women on their benches, and, as has been noted, David Cameron has promised to have a third of his ministerial team made up of women by the end of the next parliament. Nobody – including the Tories – pretends that these figures are anywhere near enough. But compared with Tory parliamentary parties of the past, the new intake will look radically different, and this should dramatically extend the party's appeal in future elections.

Family

Developing policies which support families is a top priority of Conservative strategists ahead of the next general election. Responsibility for the development of family policy will run through all domestic departments of a New Conservative administration. David Cameron has identified the issue as a distinct focus for the Tories. This underlines one of the central philosophical beliefs of an incoming Conservative government: that many of the country's problems can be attributed to the failure of the traditional family unit. At the macro level the Tories have pledged to end the 'couple penalty' in the benefits system and to recognise marriage in the tax and benefits system. But deeper in the Tory thinking is the development of policies designed to support families when times get tough and relationships run into difficulties.

Delivering the annual Relate Lecture, the Conservative leader set out his belief that family breakdown was at the heart of problems such as crime, deprivation and educational failure. Cameron believes that strong relationships create strong families, which in turn can create a strong society. In the lecture he said:

> Britain has one of the highest rates of family breakdown in Europe. And we also have some of the worst social problems. That is why I say it is time for change to make this country more family friendly so we can turn around the social breakdown, turn around the crime and anti-social behaviour, turn around this unacceptable situation where our cost of living is going up and the quality of life is going down.

To tackle problems before they develop into family breakdown the party has promised to do more to help people stay together and deal with relationship stresses, including compulsory teaching about relationships as well as sex education in schools.

Practical measures likely to feature in the Tories' family policy include the creation of an extra 4,200 home health visitors and a possible expansion in the number of maternity nurses. The party is also developing policies proposed by Iain Duncan Smith's Centre for Social Justice which would see the creation of a national network of family relationship centres which would provide support and advice to couples whose marriage was in difficulty. The party is also considering a proposal for the introduction of a compulsory three-month 'cooling-off period' before divorces could become final. This would provide time for mediators to try and effect a reconciliation.

The Conservative front bench, several of whom have young families, also want to work with business leaders to create a more family-friendly environment. The party has plans to extend parental leave to twelve months. This extended period could be shared by the mother and father as they choose, in order to create a work–life balance. The Tories would also extend the right to request flexible working to all parents with children under the age of eighteen and ensure the public sector becomes 'a world leader in providing flexible working opportunities'.

Through its education portfolio, led by Michael Gove, the party has also detailed measures to support a diverse childcare system, with parents' needs being met by a variety of providers, including childminders and private, voluntary and independent nurseries.

Tory thinking in this area has been heavily influenced by Iain Duncan Smith's Centre for Social Justice. It has also been driven by the ongoing need to change the electorate's perception of the party – and to attract a younger and more diverse electoral base.

Foreign affairs

The Conservative Party's foreign affairs priorities next time around will be much the same as they have been over the last thirty-five years: to make sure that the UK maintains its position as the most important ally of the USA, and to maintain membership of the EU without being dragged further along the path of European integration.

William Hague, however, has sent strong signals that he wants to look beyond the EU – and the USA – and to strengthen the UK's relations with the Commonwealth. He emphasised the importance of taking a global view in a speech which he gave at the International Institute for Strategic Studies shortly before the Commons summer recess in July 2009, and in the same speech he seemed to suggest a return to *Realpolitik*, saying:

> Foreign policy is above all about the protection and promotion of our national
> interest, and even narrowly defined, the British national interest requires our

continued fully active engagement in world affairs. Idealism must always be tempered with realism – even those countries like many of the Gulf states, which are making democratic reforms, will do so at varying paces and sometimes over an extended period.

If Hague becomes Foreign Secretary many believe the UK will have one of its most strategic political thinkers in recent memory in that role. The notion that Hague could effectively become Deputy Prime Minister appears to have been challenged by the ongoing partnership between David Cameron and George Osborne. Therefore Hague may apply his shrewd political skills and mastery of policy detail to the development of a far-reaching foreign policy. Aside from the specific overriding focus on relations with the USA and the EU, this policy will involve a focus on three issues: hard-headed liberalism, deeper engagement and a greater focus on human rights.

A Conservative government will develop an 'intense and energetic' foreign policy, Hague said in a speech in spring 2008. The Tories will also press for greater Cabinet-level decision making on foreign policy matters. Hague will wrest responsibility for foreign affairs away from 10 Downing Street, where it largely resided in the Blair years.

Hague has made clear that Afghanistan, which in an intractable problem confronting those engaged on its soil, is his number one specific priority. In a speech to the 2008 Conservative Party conference he said: 'We regard progress in Afghanistan, and in the closely related problems of Pakistan, as the single most urgent focus in foreign affairs for our work as a new government. Failure there would leave the world, ourselves included, much more open to terrorist attack.'

Hague has also warned that a firmer foreign policy will be required to prevent more potential rogue states emerging and causing damage to the geo-political framework. In an interview with the *Daily Telegraph* in 2008 he said that European nations needed to 'carry a bigger stick' when dealing with countries such as Iran. He went on to say that 'this is a very serious issue affecting the future peace of the world. If the Iranians develop a nuclear device then you have a nuclear arms race in the Middle East, you have a much greater likelihood that Israel will take matters into its own hands.'

The Conservatives have also said that the issue of human rights will be at the heart of its foreign policy agenda. Their desire for greater engagement in problematic states was also underlined when the Conservatives strongly criticised what they say is the Labour government's failure to act over the humanitarian situation in Darfur. The involvement of many Tory MPs – frontbenchers and backbenchers – in the humanitarian Project Umubano in Rwanda demonstrates the level of their commitment.

The European Union

Closer to home the Conservatives will propose some significant reworking of European policy. Ahead of the European elections the Conservatives insisted it was not too late to modify the Lisbon Treaty. If a Conservative government takes office whilst the Lisbon Treaty remains on the table but unratified by any one nation of the EU, the Conservatives will offer the country a referendum.

If the treaty is in force the Tories have admitted they will then be forced to confront a different situation. 'In our view, then, political integration would have gone too far, the treaty would lack democratic legitimacy in this country and we would not let matters rest there,' states the party's policy blueprint. 'A Conservative government would also amend the 1972 European Communities Act so that any future EU treaty that transfers powers from the United Kingdom to the EU would be subject to a referendum of the British people. The British people must be in charge of their future in Europe.'

As an indication of how serious the Tories are about resisting the move towards an 'ever closer union', they have made good their promise to leave the openly federalist European People's Party – even though it is the largest group in the European Parliament. They have now formed the European Conservatives and Reformists, which with fifty-four members is the fifth largest group. Although dominated by the British Conservatives, it is led by a Pole, Michał Kamiński.

Hague has spoken of an EU closer to its people. He told his party's 2009 spring conference that he would demonstrate 'cool-headed engagement of a country that will protect its national interest and seek common cause with its neighbours on issues that concern them all'. The Tories are pledging to champion the enlargement of the EU, and to anchor in Europe the war-torn nations of the western Balkans. The party also supports building a bridge to the east through Turkish accession.

Just as he did when serving as the Leader of the Opposition, Hague repeats his party's commitment to retain the pound. The rhetoric is, however, less intense and shrill than it was when the Conservatives fought the 2001 election with a pledge to 'save the pound' as one of their key policies.

The Conservative Party will also commit to measures seeking the return of social and employment legislation to national control – although it has repeated its commitment to 'a completed single market, the lowering of trade barriers, and collective action on climate change'. They also want to see reform to the European Emissions Trading scheme and an overhaul of the EU's aid policy. On global trade and the environment the Conservatives will also seek a greater EU-level effort to find a successful conclusion to the Doha trade round and a renewed focus on global policies to combat climate change.

Hague may now never achieve his ambition to become Prime Minister. But if he becomes Foreign Secretary, and is given the freedom to act to develop a far-reaching international policy, he may find himself able to shape world events from an office which is considerably grander than that of his boss.

International development

This is one of the few areas where the Tories have unambiguously pledged to maintain spending – international aid will be insulated against the threat of any future spending cuts. As stated earlier, Tory politicians have also demonstrated their concern for issues affecting the developing world by actively participating in Project Umubano in Rwanda.

The Conservatives have pledged to honour the UK's commitment to the UN to provide 0.7 per cent of its GDP as aid to the developing world by 2013. However, if the UK economy continues to shrink, that gross contribution figure will as a result become smaller. Not all Tories are convinced by this commitment in any event. Some regard aid as being a mechanism whereby poor people in rich countries give money to rich people in poor countries. Those Tories who are opposed to the aid pledge are especially exercised by the fact that the UK provides aid to China – which has one of the fastest-growing economies in the world.

However, Tory policy on international development is firmly set, and it will exhibit a radical departure from that of the current government. Whilst the level of aid will be maintained, it will be more closely tied to results – recipient countries will have to demonstrate that the money is being well spent. As in other areas of policy, the Tories will also try to disentangle UK aid from the clutches of the EU – the focus will be on bilateral aid, rather than multilateral.

Finally, William Hague will ensure that the situation where the Department for International Development gets a higher priority than the FCO is reversed. The FCO has always been the lead department in all aspects of relations with the rest of the world, but under Tony Blair and Gordon Brown this situation has been turned on its head. William Hague, one of the 'big beasts' in the incoming Tory government, will ensure that normal service is resumed.

Health

The first challenge any Tory leader faces in relation to the NHS is to prove that it will be safe in their hands. David Cameron, whose late son Ivan's cerebral palsy and epilepsy resulted in frequent late-night hospital visits, has spoken with genuine passion about his faith in the NHS.

Although he is committed to the NHS as an institution, David Cameron is highly critical of what he refers to as Labour's 'tick box' approach. 'With their targets and bureaucratic control, Labour have actually created a system that forces NHS staff to follow rules that can actively cause harm to the health of patients,' the Conservative leader said in a 2009 speech. In place of the centralised box-ticking culture, the Tories will try and apply their localism agenda to the NHS.

The key reforms the Tories will seek to push through are likely to be procedural and structural rather than ideological – with the scrapping of the targets culture likely to be their top priority. 'There is a wealth of evidence that targets distort clinical priorities, lead to worse outcomes for patients and have produced a demoralised workforce whose expertise in delivering healthcare is constantly second-guessed,' a party policy paper states. The Tories have pledged to replace targets with 'practice-based commissioning'.

The party which created the internal market (a system where the money followed the patient) under Ken Clarke after the 1987 general election is once again set to seek to construct a patient-focused service, with a pledge of 'outcomes not targets' driving clinical decisions. To achieve this the patient is likely to be empowered to operate 'side by side' with the medical profession through a series of measures to be introduced by an incoming Conservative administration – although Cameron and his team will be mindful that the last thing a frequently revamped NHS requires is another wholesale restructuring. Instead the party is likely to embark on a series of policy shifts which in their totality will refocus the NHS around the needs of patients – dubbed as the 'the patient will see you now, Doctor' approach.

The Conservatives are committed to introducing 45,000 additional single rooms – meaning, the party says, that any inpatient will be able to select a single room 'if they want one'. The Conservatives have also pledged to finally remove mixed-sex wards from all hospitals – something which Tony Blair promised in 1997 but never achieved. The party is committed to reversing Labour's reduction in A&E services and maternity units, and will halt the move away from localised services towards megalithic polyclinics. They have also pledged to preserve local and district hospitals.

Choice is also likely to feature in the Tories' policy plan, with a commitment to allow those suffering from chronic conditions to use new data sets 'about the results of people's treatment in the NHS, not the processes that produced those results' to determine in which hospital they are treated. In order to plug the gap between expectations and expenditure the party is likely to dismiss calls for a system of charging. Instead, as Andrew Lansley has stated, the focus will be on pay restraint, efficiency savings and through the upside of 'payment by results'.

Another area where the Tories are offering radically different solutions to the current government is over access to patient records. The national programme for IT is currently projected to cost over £12 billion and is running four years behind schedule. The system is designed to keep all patient records on one giant central database, and they would be accessible to any authorised person working within the NHS. The Conservatives also plan to store such records centrally, but to host them on a secure platform supplied either by Google or by one of their commercial competitors. They would make health records accessible only to patients, and their hospital doctors and GPs. However, GPs – and even patients – would be able to amend and update the records online.

The Tories also appear set to alter the structure of the NHS by phasing out the strategic health authorities introduced by the Labour government. They have promised to introduce an NHS constitution and to encourage all NHS hospitals to become NHS trusts. But those expecting a right-wing rethink of the fundamentals of the health service are likely to be disappointed with the final Tory health blueprint. The desire to wrest the middle ground off Labour, and to out-poll the government on the crucial 'who do you trust to run the NHS' index, means the party is unlikely to propose overly bold or controversial reforms.

Whilst the Conservatives have pledged to increase spending on the NHS in real terms, the new Chancellor's first Budget is likely to show very small increases rather than any dramatic year-on-year growth. Instead the party will seek to spend smarter by, for example, pressing primary care trusts to adopt more efficient practices and developing a system which awards successful clinical outcomes rather than target hitting. In essence the Conservatives are seeking to drive the NHS to do a lot more, with just a small fraction more in real expenditure. A system of payment by results should, the party believes, see centres of excellence expand and poorly performing units either reform or fail to attract patients.

The Conservatives' health policy paper *Outcomes not Targets* states:

> With process targets abolished and patients exercising greater choice based on information about results, a whole new culture will emerge within the NHS. Instead of worrying about what politicians and bureaucrats think, NHS professionals will have powerful incentives to focus wholly on achieving better patient care. Any reason to structure activity around the interests of politicians simply falls away. Instead, NHS activity will be based around the needs and wishes of patients.

Despite a radical edge to some aspects of their health policies, the Tories' plans are unlikely to meet with universal approval. The right wing of their own party is likely to press for bolder reforms which recognise the fact that Labour's huge investment in the NHS has not delivered the results expected. The Conservative commentator Tim Montgomerie has criticised the party for falling into the trap of pledging year-on-year increases when, as Andrew Lansley himself has predicted, overall government spending is going to have to be reduced significantly. Given the fact that NHS resources have more than doubled since Labour came to office, yet outcomes have fallen in many areas, this pressure for more than simply efficiency savings from an incoming Tory administration is likely to persist – although in the early years Cameron's position is likely to hold.

Reform at the outcome end of the spectrum is central to the Tories' approach, with the party appearing set to rework the GP contract and framework and the dental contract. In order to free up money to focus on the patient, the party is also expected to overhaul the NHS's drug policy and tackle the system of pricing employed by NICE. The future of NICE, a body which has its detractors, appears secure. However, the pharmaceutical lobby and the huge NHS IT lobby expect to see systems of value-based pricing and a culture of risk-sharing agreements being introduced.

The party has issued a clear commitment to ensure that 'all new treatments that are clinically effective are made available'. This is a pledge which will result in some potentially testing conversations between ministers and pharmaceutical giants if, for example, the NHS is to be able to afford to provide treatments for cancer which are often routinely available in other European healthcare systems.

As it strives to improve an organisation which has proved its capacity to absorb vast increases in spending without equivalent outcomes, the Conservative Party is likely to fight the forthcoming election with an assault on 'ministerial meddling' and the targets culture. What that precisely translates into beyond polling day is at this stage less clear – and, as some will point out, if ministers are not engaged then what else should they be doing? However the party's 2007 NHS Autonomy and Accountability Bill pledged the creation of an independent NHS board to allocate regional health budgets free from political control. In this vein the party also pledges to 'release NHS staff from top-down interference and allow them to concentrate on doing what they do best: providing top-quality care to patients'.

The Conservative Party appears to have the political will to introduce some reforms to the NHS and to drive resources towards the front line of patient care. However, as they are likely to find out, treating a patient as large and as chronically ill as the NHS may require a prolonged dose of the strongest medicine.

Home affairs and justice

The Conservative Party has always traditionally been the party of law and order. Michael Howard established himself in the hearts of Conservative Party members with his 'prison works' slogan, and Edwina Currie brought the party faithful to their feet by waving handcuffs over her head during a speech to the party conference.

The Tories are determined to seize back the law and order territory, which always used to be – pre-Blair – theirs as of right. One of the most radical proposals they are putting forward is for US-style elected police commissioners, who would work with chief constables to bear down on crime in their areas. The need for these commissioners to be re-elected would add more urgency to their efforts and enable them to pressurise local borough commanders and chief constables to produce results.

Tacking youth crime and the scourge of anti-social behaviour will be a key focus for the new ministerial teams spread across the Home Affairs and Justice departments. Much of the offensive is likely to fall to shadow Home Secretary Chris Grayling if, as seems likely, he takes control of a department traditionally seen as notorious for the damage it can do to the careers of those who occupy this office.

The incoming Conservative administration is also likely face the logistically difficult and potentially expensive task of dismantling the half-built, and some conclude half-baked, ID cards scheme – although the new Labour Home Secretary, Alan Johnson, has already announced a significant scaling down of the project. In an intervention on 17 June 2009 Grayling said:

> We intend to scrap the ID card project as one of our first acts if we are successful at the election. I am increasingly concerned that the government is putting in place contractual arrangements that are designed to tie the hands of a future government, and I want to make the contractors absolutely aware that we do not intend to complete this work.

But beyond headline issues such as scrapping ID cards and giving police more freedom to pound the beat, the new government will find that issues of law and order and immigration can prove intractable, even when there is a clear political desire to act in line with public opinion. The mantra which served the Conservatives well in opposition – that Labour is 'soft on crime and soft on the causes of crime' – may be a difficult message to translate into a positive plan for action in government. With many of the traditional law and order issues now a matter for the Ministry of Justice, the incoming Tory Home Secretary may find that immigration, traditionally a Conservative strong point at the ballot box, weighs heavily on his in-tray.

Meanwhile Dominic Grieve, or any alternative Justice Secretary, will be charged with implementing a series of measures in the courts and penal system which impact upon offending rates. The Conservatives have presented the line that crime, terrorism and lax immigration laws and policies are interlinked, and that the UK can only be made safer and more secure if it deals firmly but fairly with those seeking immigration or asylum in the UK.

The home affairs and justice agendas, upon which the respective secretaries of state will work closely (unless the party reorganises departmental responsibilities), will focus on toughening the sentencing system, whilst simultaneously reforming the prison experience to reduce the likelihood of reoffending. The emphasis will be on applying the social justice agenda in such a way as to discourage offending and reoffending. The New Conservative agenda in this area owes much to Iain Duncan Smith and his Centre for Social Justice, and to David Davis and his libertarian crusade.

Crime and punishment

The Conservative Party is committed to toughening its treatment of offenders in a number of ways – most notably by ending the early release scheme. In a statement Dominic Grieve, shadow Secretary of State for Justice, said: 'Labour is giving criminals a break. They are releasing thousands of prisoners early and planning to water down sentences. We need punishment that fits the crime, enough prison places to hold all those sentenced by the courts, and a new focus on reforming offenders.'

Whilst Labour has said it will review the scheme in the autumn of 2009, the Tories believe they will require emergency extra prison places soon after taking office in order to accommodate an increase in prisoner numbers. The Justice Department will also seek to develop an 'honest sentencing policy' which ensures that criminals serve a minimum sentence handed down to them by the judge – rather than receiving release mid-way through their sentence. The party will also seek to develop the prison system to put a greater emphasis on rehabilitation in order to break the cycle of repeat offending by a large number of serial convicts.

Whilst there will be 5,000 new prison places over and above any Labour commitment, the Tories also want to develop a system of payment by results for rehabilitation trusts. By allowing private companies and third-sector bodies to become involved in the education, employment and rehabilitation of offenders, the Tories hope to bring down the catastrophically high rate of reoffending. As with other areas of social policy, Tory thinking in this area has been much influenced by the CSJ.

Victims of crime are to benefit from a new Victims Fund, paid for by offenders, and community sentences are to become 'tougher and more effective' – including a policy of withholding benefits from those who flout community sentences. American-style court orders whereby offenders are forcibly confronted with the consequences of their crimes may also be introduced.

To give greater power to the front line, the Tories are also committed to doubling the sentencing powers of magistrates to twelve months, and they have also pledged to repeal any new restrictions on their ability to issue suspended sentences. Measures to strip young offenders of their driving licence are also likely to be considered by an incoming Tory government, as well as restrictions on their ability to travel abroad.

In the document *Repair: Plan for Social Reform* the Conservatives postulate that a lack of social cohesion has led to an increase in crime. The document proposes tackling drug abuse and enhancing life changes through education. However, the Tories also say that empowering police to do their job is also fundamental. 'The bond between the police and the public must be rebuilt, and the first step will be cutting the paperwork which ties officers to their desks,' the document states. The creation of a new breed of directly elected police commissioners will be seen as an attempt to create a direct line of democratic accountability amongst those with operational control for combating crime.

Similarly the Tories have repeatedly pledged to scrap unnecessary paperwork such as stop and search forms to ensure police spend more time on the streets. The party will also strengthen stop and search powers to give police more capacity to respond urgently to the threat of serious crimes and reform the Regulation of Investigatory Powers Act to give the police more surveillance powers in routine cases.

The Tory justice team will also seek to get tough on knife crime so that anyone caught in possession of a knife is prosecuted, and to overhaul sentencing guidelines to ensure the presumption of a custodial sentence for anyone found guilty of a knife-related crime. In a speech during the Glasgow East by-election David Cameron said the presumption of prosecution was no longer a deterrent and pledged a 'presumption to prison'. He told an audience in the city: 'We have to send a clear message that carrying a knife on our streets is completely inexcusable and unacceptable in a civilised society.'

The question of drugs is likely to be one which features in the general election. Previous Tory attempts at a hardline policy have been undermined by personal admissions of drug use by shadow Cabinet members. In his own leadership election Cameron had called for a more relaxed and evidence-based policy on drugs, going as far as to suggest a World Health Organization or UN-wide effort to legalise drugs, although any shift in drugs policy is likely to be minor in the early years of a Tory administration. However, as the general election looms larger, the party has been taking a much tougher stance on drugs policy – including on the issue of the reclassification of cannabis.

The Tories believe strongly that they can win the public's confidence on law and order issues – and will be determined to introduce honesty into the immigration debate. However, the party is also acutely aware that the causes of crime may prove a more stubborn stain to remove from the fabric of society. This, Cameron believes, creates the need for a holistic approach – encompassing welfare, education, child poverty and the respect agenda – which is likely to require significant leadership time in No. 10. As he told his Glasgow East audience: 'If anyone thinks that criminal justice measures alone will halt the violence on our streets, then they do not understand the scale and the nature of the social breakdown that is its cause.'

Immigration

This has always been a difficult area for the Tories. They are aware that immigration features highly on the list of people's concerns, and that fear of uncontrolled immigration has fuelled the electoral successes of the BNP and (to an extent) UKIP. The strong showing of the BNP and the election of Nick Griffin and Andrew Brons in the European elections of June 2009 served to underline the importance of the immigration issue to voters in the United Kingdom. However, any attempt to lead with the issue, or to take too strong a line, would undo all of the success which they have achieved in decontaminating the Tory brand and ditching the 'nasty party' image.

The New Conservative line is that enforced multiculturalism and uncontrolled immigration are bad for community relations. The distrust and hostility which they have fostered have led to polarisation of views within communities and segregation between different communities. This in turn has helped to radicalise small sections of the immigrant community, which has inevitably led to the phenomenon of home-grown terrorism.

Specific measures which the Conservatives are advocating to counter these problems include offering English language tuition to all those who wish to receive it, whilst at the same time tackling cultural practices which they regard as unacceptable – such as forced marriages and female genital mutilation. They also promise to empower local authorities to deal with the particular circumstances of their areas.

The Tories in government would put a numerical ceiling on the number of immigrants allowed into the UK. Those potential immigrants who would be considered would have to be able to offer skills which were not currently available in the UK. The Tories would also place restrictions on the numbers of dependants who migrants would be allowed to bring in, or who would be allowed to follow on.

Another key Conservative policy was to advocate the formation of a border police force – a policy which the Labour government has since adopted with the formation of the UK Border Agency. The Tories would strengthen the numbers and powers of the agency. It would have responsibility not just for ensuring that illegal immigration became harder, but also for tracking down and removing those illegal immigrants who had evaded border controls.

The Conservatives are also committed to applying some greater form of eligibility test to those seeking to live and work in the UK. They will seek to grant immigration to those who will positively benefit the British economy. They would also increase the age limit for spouses to enter the UK to twenty-one and set English proficiency tests as part of a series of smaller immigration-related measures.

In order to mitigate the effects of further EU expansion, which could include the accession of Turkey, the Tories will seek to put in place transitional arrangements which restrict the residency and employment rights of nationals from new member states. This policy is being perceived as a direct attempt to prevent a future influx of cheap labour of the magnitude seen after the accession of countries such as Poland and Hungary to the EU.

The Tories believe that they have now gained sufficient trust from the British people to talk tough on immigration. They also believe that their cadre of MPs, PPCs and staffers are now sufficiently diverse that they can withstand and rebuff any accusations of racism.

Security and terrorism

The Conservative Party is no stranger to the threat of terrorism. In government it took on the IRA and its leadership itself was subject to a series of terrorist attacks, including the Brighton bombing in 1984. However, the rise of international terrorism means that home affairs and foreign affairs conflate. To reflect this, the party has pledged to produce a national security green paper which will form the basis of manifesto commitments in this policy area.

The green paper will say that foreign and domestic policy relating to terrorism must be treated as one. In order to meet this threat the Tories have pledged to introduce a Cabinet-level national security minister who will oversee a National Security Council and have control over a single national security budget. This position is likely to be assumed by Baroness Neville-Jones, the former diplomat who has served as chairman of the Joint Intelligence Committee.

Several Tory front- and backbenchers have intelligence backgrounds, some with actual experience in the field. There will be no shortage of experienced ministers to drive forward the Tory agenda in this area, although for understandable reasons their policies on this particular topic have not been fully announced.

Housing and planning

The Conservative Party believe that the housing market crash which followed on from the credit crunch means that there is a real need for a coherent housing policy which focuses on supply-side measures. This is despite the fact that many homeowners are unable or unwilling to sell their homes, and that thousands of unsold properties remain on the books of beleaguered property and construction companies. The Tories believe there are not enough houses of the right size at an affordable price in areas where people want to live.

In a foreword to the Conservative housing policy document David Cameron summed up the situation confronting the UK housing sector thus:

> Britain's housing market has been stuck in a vicious spiral of boom and bust. Under Labour we have built too few homes, in the wrong places and of the wrong kind, whilst the explosion of unregulated household debt has encouraged speculation on the housing market. We have swung from a crisis of affordability to a housing crash in a matter of months, with devastating effects on families, communities and the wider economy.

The property show presenter Kirstie Allsopp, also a Conservative policy advisor, went one further than the party's front bench when she called for the abolition of stamp duty in 2008 – although the party is showing a determination to think radically on housing issues. The Conservatives have pledged to scrap the duty for first-time buyers (up to £250,000) and will examine whether further reductions are affordable. In line with their opposition to the measure in the first instance, the Conservatives have also firmly pledged to scrap the controversial and partially introduced system of home information packs. In essence, Tory housing policy will be one of decentralisation, with the goal being the creation of community-led housing projects.

The Conservatives claim that Labour's changes to the planning system have resulted in developments skewed away from local need – fewer houses with gardens, not enough parking spaces and a lack of affordable housing. They say that they want to ensure that development is sustainable and does not infringe on green belt land, but they also want to ensure that decisions on new building are taken at a local rather than a national level. Incentive schemes to encourage new build in areas where it is needed will be put in place by an incoming Conservative administration. They have also pledged to scrap the Independent Planning Commission, which they see as being wholly at odds with their new localism and decentralisation agendas.

The party's housing paper *Strong Foundations* was given a mixed review by pressure groups. Measures to make better use of redevelopment of public buildings and greater incentives for affordable housing were broadly welcomed. However, measures to remove regional control of development and instead rely on loose alliances of local authorities lacked clarity, according to some observers.

Plans to develop new bodies – to be called local housing trusts – for those villages and towns which wish to develop new housing to benefit their community have also been given a generally positive welcome, although the details on this policy could present some complexities. According to the Conservatives these new bodies will have 'unparalleled power to develop new homes and other space for community use, subject only to the agreement of local people'.

The Tories are seeking to develop a policy which ensures the right kind of housing is built in the right area based upon local need balanced with environmental considerations. Other supply-side measures outlined by the Conservatives include:

- abolishing the unsuccessful regional planning system and regional housing targets
- incentivising new house building by matching local authorities' council tax take for each new house built for six years – with special incentives for affordable housing
- relaxing the rules which prevent thousands of habitable empty properties being used to house those on local authority waiting lists
- broadening access to the government's databases of surplus public sector land and buildings, to enable members of the public to identify vacant government land that should be available for house building.

The commitment to scrap unrealistic top-down housing targets was welcomed by housing groups, and commitments to support the green belt were also given a positive response. However, a commitment to reform density guidelines was described by the CPRE as 'alarming'. In April 2009 the CPRE said: 'Relaxation of these guidelines would risk unleashing a wave of development in the very green belts and countryside the Conservatives are pledged to protect.'

The Conservatives are also committed to a significant rethink, and decentralisation, of the planning process. The party says the inherently adversarial nature of the planning system ensures that all parties spend large amounts of time and money fighting each other, rather than seeking an agreed solution. The result, they claim, is that local communities, in particular, feel that their opinions are being ignored and that they are having development imposed upon them. To counteract this, the party has offered a series of specific pledges. They will ensure that the views of local residents are genuinely taken into account at the start of the planning process, by making pre-application consultations between developers and local people mandatory for major applications.

The Tories also want to enable councils to revise their current local plans to protect green belt land and prevent the imposition of eco-towns against local wishes. The policy blueprint details measures to reverse the classification of gardens as brownfield land and to allow councils to prevent over-development of neighbourhoods and stop what it describes as 'garden grabbing'. The party has made a guarantee that councillors will have the freedom to campaign and represent their constituents on planning issues.

As with other policy areas, the Tory's localism agenda has been applied to policy formulation in the area of housing and planning.

Local government

Under Margaret Thatcher the Conservatives had become highly suspicious of local government. Some 'loony left' councils had grossly abused their positions and squandered public money. Labour local authority leaders such as Derek Hatton and 'Red Ted' Knight had deliberately run up huge deficits. Ken Livingstone, sitting across the river from the Palace of Westminster in County Hall, had taunted Thatcher and her government on a daily basis with banners and an electronic sign chronicling the rise in unemployment.

The Tories of that era did not trust local authorities to operate without close oversight from central government. Faced with incompetent and irresponsible local authority leaders, the Thatcher government responded by curtailing the power of local authorities and starving them of resources – and the ability to allocate them. In the case of Livingstone, she went so far as to abolish the entire GLC just to get rid of him.

The New Conservative agenda is completely different. Philosophically they now believe in localism and in devolving power down to the lowest possible level. They want to transform local authorities from being the agents delivering centrally decreed services to becoming empowered bodies setting their own priorities and determining which services to deliver – and in what way.

The buzz phrase in CCHQ is 'post-bureaucratic'. In the internet age, the New Conservatives do not believe that local services can be centrally prescribed or centrally delivered. In a speech to the Local Government Association (LGA) conference in June 2009 David Cameron said 'In the post-bureaucratic age we can get citizens involved in the whole debate about what is spent, excite our politics and improve our administration. We must do it.'

The Conservatives are a strong force in local government – something which has not always been the case, even at times when the party was riding high in the polls. But in the period before a likely change in national administration, the tectonic plates often shift first in town halls and council chambers – and the Tories' position appears to bear out this notion, with the party now having around 10,000 councillors.

At the heart of the Conservatives' policy agenda for local government will be more localisation (or decentralisation depending on your perspective) and greater transparency. They also want to see greater value for money and renewed accountability at the local level. They will press ahead with measures to reduce the number of bodies relating to local and regional government, pledging for example to scrap the system of unelected regional assemblies. Instead, democratic controls will be put in place, through, for example, a system of on-demand directly elected mayors.

In the localism policy paper, the Conservatives said they wanted a shift in power and responsibility at the local government level. Amongst the proposed measures are promises to:

- enable local authorities to benefit financially when they deliver the housing that local people need
- give local authorities the right to retain the financial benefits arising from new business activity in their areas
- give local authorities a new discretionary power to decide on the level of business rates
- make the local government funding settlement more transparent
- freeze council tax rises until the recession is over.

Cameron also used his speech to the LGA to pledge greater powers to local bodies. But in exchange, and mindful of the serious spending constraints, he asked for efficiency savings in a system often notorious for poor financial controls and ill defined return-on-investment assessments. Cameron stressed that 'thriving local government' was at the heart of his vision for the country and called for 'new ideas, new activism and a new dynamism' at local level. He pledged that a Conservative government would devolve power 'downwards and outwards' and spelled out the areas where local government would gain more control.

To this end the Conservatives have pledged to:

- end Whitehall's capping powers, but give local residents the power to veto high council tax rises via local referendums
- drastically reduce the centrally imposed bureaucratic burdens that drive up council tax
- increase the freedom of local councils to act in the best interests of residents, by giving them a 'general power of competence'
- give local councils greater freedom to determine how they carry out their statutory regulatory duties
- end all forced amalgamations of local authorities.

The Tories have also pledged to remove the layers of bureaucracy that it believes are 'a straitjacket' and represent 'intrusive and ineffective inspection regimes'. They are therefore committed to the removal of process targets, the Comprehensive Area Assessment and regional strategies. They will also seek to mobilise a grassroots talent pool as they seek to create a new breed of local authority representatives. Caroline Spelman, the shadow Local Government Secretary, has said that standing for local election gives you 'direct involvement in improving your local area'. By generating a new culture of local activism, the party believes it can create a more responsive and representative system of local government.

In order to give freedom to local authorities to make decisions based on local need, the Conservatives have also committed themselves to a phased removal of ring-fencing. They will also examine new ways of enabling councils to raise funds on the bond market for special local projects. Councils will have more freedom to support vital local institutions, such as village shops and post offices, and even village pubs.

The party has also committed to reduce the number of quangos which regulate and oversee local government. Following what Cameron has described as 'pointless and vexatious complaints', an incoming Tory administration will scrap the Standards Board.

Regional development agencies will be stripped of their powers over planning, with local governments being given the power to establish their own local enterprise partnerships to take over development functions from RDAs. Some – if not all – RDAs may be abolished entirely. Specifically in relation to the regions, the Tories have pledged:

- to abolish all regional planning and housing powers exercised by regional government
- to abolish the Government Office for London and devolve its functions to London boroughs or the GLA
- to give local governments the power to establish their own local enterprise partnerships to take over development functions from RDAs
- to abandon plans to regionalise fire control, whilst providing new measures to enhance resilience in the case of a national emergency
- to impose parliamentary oversight on the Infrastructure Planning Commission and ensure that the concerns of local people are heard.

The Conservatives appear to be adopting a carrot and stick approach to local government. The incentive is greater localisation – but there is a price for greater freedom to determine how, where and on what money is spent. Cameron has, in return, asked local government to play its part in reducing, or at least capping, spending by councils and related bodies. Pointing to the debt crisis, the party will press for savings, innovation and greater transparency.

The Conservatives have also confirmed they will give local people a greater say on local government spending. Voters will be given a new right to block large increases in council tax, as mentioned above. It is hoped that this move would result in councils being forced to think seriously about efficiency savings rather than passing inflation-busting increases year after year.

Now, with the Tories the dominant party in local government, they have changed their attitude. The New Conservative government will allow local authorities to operate with increased freedom – but they will also ensure that local people have the power to rein in their local councillors if necessary. Quizzed by the author as to whether the Tories were serious about the localism agenda, the party chairman (and former leader of Bradford City Council) Eric Pickles simply replied: 'Localism is for real.'

Quangos

Whilst some of the Conservative plans inevitably mean the creation of new monitoring or regulatory bodies, David Cameron has set out on a personal mission to tackle the number of unelected quangos and to curtail their powers. Whilst he has stopped short of repeating Michael Heseltine's vow to light a 'bonfire of the quangos', they have been put on notice that a future Conservative administration will tackle the underlying rise in largely unaccountable government. Cameron used a speech in July 2009 to warn that the 'growth of the quango state' was 'one of the main reasons so many people feel that nothing ever changes, nothing will ever get done and that government's automatic response to any problem is to pass the buck and send people from pillar to post until they just give up in exasperated fury'.

Estimates on the number of quangos vary hugely, with the government estimating there to be 790, whilst the Taxpayers' Alliance claims that there are 1,162. At the upper end of the projection, quangos are currently spending some £60 billion. The Treasury has admitted that the 160 largest quangos spent £34 billion in 2008. Through answers to parliamentary questions, the Tories have also discovered that Gordon Brown created forty new quangos in his first two years as Prime Minister.

The quango concept runs counter to David Cameron's belief in more decentralised decision making. 'Too many state actions, services and decisions are carried out by people who cannot be voted out by the public, by organisations that feel no pressure to answer for what happens – in a way that is completely unaccountable,' he said in a July 2009 speech at the Reform think tank.

The Conservatives' approach will be to review each and every quango with a view to its abolition, reducing its size, or creating better systems of accountability. The Conservatives have suggested that many quangos are now 'lobbying organisations' and they have pledged to ban them from hiring consultants to lobby government. They have also stated that quangos should merely implement government decisions and that they should have no powers over the formulation of policy.

The party also wants quangos to halt mission and budget creep – whereby they stealthily entrench and extend their positions. The party states that 'no quango will have the power to stray outside the scope of its responsibilities . . . [and] they must operate wholly within the financial resources allocated to them by ministers'.

Ahead of the review the Conservatives have said that the media regulator Ofcom will be stripped of its policy-making functions and the Qualifications and Curriculum Development Agency will be scrapped. To date they have refrained from naming other targets, perhaps out of a desire to avoid starting the kind of arguments which they got into with Ofcom when they challenged the extent of its powers.

Of course many observers feel that the Tories are merely taking aim at easy targets and following a populist line in attacking the quangos. Some feel that, in government, they will be unlikely to follow through their rhetoric. Writing on the LabourList website, commentator Will Straw said:

> Politicians are meant to campaign in poetry and govern in prose. Today's speech by David Cameron on reforming quangos was a discordant harmony. One note was aimed at a populist 'slash and burn' audience and outlined the £64 billion cost of Britain's 790 to 1,100 quangos. The other was aimed at a more elite 'Sir Humphrey' audience and outlined that there were principles behind his approach. The problem is that the principles are so woolly and vague that they are unlikely to result in any cost savings at all.

That comment followed on from research for the BBC *Politics Show* which suggested that the Conservative policy plans would result in the creation of some seventeen new quango-type bodies and a commitment to abolish just two.

As part of their crusade against the explosion in public sector pay the Tories have quoted quangos as a prime example. Cameron has described the pay of some quango bosses as 'astonishing'. Apart from the BBC – always a favourite target of the Conservatives – the party has also singled out the bosses of Network Rail and the Post Office – both of whom earn over £1 million a year.

Those who doubt the Conservatives' will to take on what they refer to as 'the quango state' should think again. Their policies in this area are not just aimed at saving costs – although that is certainly an added bonus. They are also not just aimed at gaining cheap popularity and soft votes – although that is certainly another part of the attraction. The whole concept of quangos runs fundamentally counter to the New Conservative themes of democratisation, localism and moving into the post-bureaucratic age. This explains the off-the-record conversation which the author had with a very senior Conservative, who said that the relationship between senior quangocrats and their organisations would ultimately resemble that between Ann Boleyn's body and her head.

Transport

Developing an integrated transport policy has been an unfulfilled ambition of all governments since the Second World War. The Conservatives appear to be willing to countenance some radical thinking in order to achieve the elusive Holy Grail of a truly integrated transport system.

Plans for a £20 billion rail link between London, Birmingham, Manchester and Leeds are setting a new course for transport policy – although not every transport policy expert is convinced that it offers the solution to the nation's transport needs. Other experts – and large proportions of the business community – are also unhappy with the Tories' refusal to back the expansion of Heathrow airport. London mayor Boris Johnson's scheme for a brand new airport with high-speed rail links in the Thames estuary has attracted a lot of attention – and some support – but the scheme is not part of official Tory transport policy. The London mayor, however, is hoping to convert the party to the scheme before the general election manifesto is set in stone.

The Tories are adamant that a future Conservative government will cancel all moves for a third runway at Heathrow. They have repeatedly stated that they are opposed to what they claim are 'Labour's reckless plans for a new runway which would inflict major damage on the environment and the quality of life of millions of people'. In doing they are also rejecting the argument that extra airport capacity is needed to preserve Heathrow as a major passenger and cargo hub.

Theresa Villiers's announcement at the Tory conference in 2008 that the Tories would block the Heathrow expansion did much to put her career back on track. In making it she was strongly backed by David Cameron and by the environmental campaigner and Tory candidate for Richmond Park, Zac Goldsmith.

The Conservatives are also committed to ending BAA's monopoly over airport capacity in the south-east. They want to allow passengers to vote with their feet if they receive poor service and choose an airport run by a different operator – something which the Labour government has also now pledged to do. They also believe that the improvements that they will bring to the rail network will relieve some of the short-haul domestic demand for UK airports.

The Tories claim that in government they will improve Britain's transport system to strengthen the UK's economic competitiveness, provide better services for travellers and help reduce carbon emissions and the damage caused by climate change. The Conservatives' strategy for rail involves a major infrastructure commitment with the new high-speed rail link and new improved powers for the rail regulator. The pledged link between London, Birmingham, Manchester and Leeds will be joined with mainland Europe through the Channel Tunnel. The party also hopes that this will create jobs across the country, with a particular major boost for the economies of the West Midlands and the north, and provide a greener alternative to thousands of car and lorry journeys clogging up some of the busiest UK motorways.

To tackle over-crowding, improve services and ensure that the rail industry 'puts passengers first', the Conservatives will reform Network Rail. They plan to make it accountable to passengers and to transform the Rail Regulator into a powerful passenger champion with authority to block the bonuses of Network

Rail senior executives. They also intend to push for the development and implementation of an integrated railway timetable.

The Tories are also studying plans to allocate rail franchises for longer periods – perhaps extending them to as much as twenty years. This would provide companies with more security and encourage them to invest in their franchises. They are also examining plans for the creation of a dedicated rail freight line, to run the length of the country, as part of their plans to oversee a dramatic shift of freight from road to rail.

The Conservatives' approach to relieving the congestion on Britain's roads involves focusing on the worst bottlenecks, which will be tackled by a combination of new road building and improving the public transport system. This is part of their holistic approach to transport, neither championing one particular mode nor another, nor demonising drivers – something which the Labour government has been accused of doing. However, they have certainly not ruled out the introduction of some form of road user charging at some stage in the future.

The Tories are also committed to putting in place measures to deliver a national recharging network to encourage greener driving choices and the switch to electric and plug-in hybrid vehicles. They also aim to ensure that overseas lorries which use British roads will be made to contribute towards the cost of their maintenance, tackling a long-standing competitive disadvantage for domestic haulage companies.

The Conservatives will completely reverse the Labour government's policy of encouraging local councils to introduce local road pricing in return for vital transport funding. They will switch this spending into a Transport Carbon Reduction Fund, allowing local councils and voluntary groups to apply for funding for the green travel initiatives that will work best for their area – including projects to encourage cycling and improve real-time information and priority measures for bus services.

However, once in office the party may find that it has to yield to its critics – particularly in relation to aviation policy. The transport blueprint has won approval from some environmental and rail groups, but British business is still concerned that the policy is too heavily geared to environmental considerations. Some say that the debate about rail versus air is ultimately a 'false choice', and that greater capacity across all forms of transport will ultimately be required to ensure the UK retains its competitiveness.

Commenting on the Tory plans, David Frost, director general of the British Chambers of Commerce, said:

> This debate shouldn't be about either high-speed rail or a third runway at Heathrow. A fully thought-through transport vision would recognise that

improvements to both the UK's rail and air infrastructure are essential. Business understands the need to protect the environment. But refusing to listen to the needs of the economy on the issue of Heathrow expansion will hold back British business in the future.

Ultimately, as with every other policy area, it will largely come down to cost – raising the revenue to pay for integrating the existing transport structure and extending it where necessary. One of the big problems for both the current and incoming governments is the fact that the credit crunch has exposed some of the shortcomings of the PFI. A central plank of this scheme was that private enterprise would absorb the risk, in return for a premium. However, when schemes have failed as a result of the credit crunch, government has been forced to step in. One solution might be the formation of a National Infrastructure Investment Bank, which would use the government's strong credit rating to borrow money on favourable terms and which could also underwrite bonds which would be issued to finance specific infrastructure projects.

Tory policy relating to transport is well developed, but does not yet seem to be fully integrated. A solution to the immediate and medium-term problem of airport capacity in the south-east still needs to be found.

Voluntary sector

This is one of the Tories' priority areas and fits in well with their whole decentralisation agenda – which is one of their 'big ideas' in strategic policy terms.

Most Tories distrust big government, and for fiscal and philosophical reasons they would like to see the size of the state heavily pruned. However, the New Conservatives realise that you cannot simply withdraw services which people have come to depend on. Their solution is to fill that void with the voluntary sector – a Third Sector approach as opposed to a Third Way approach.

Margaret Thatcher was widely misquoted as saying that 'there is no such thing as society'. In fact what she was saying is that society is not an entity in and of itself – it is made up of individuals, families and voluntary associations. David Cameron has made it very clear that he does believe in society, but like Thatcher he looks beneath the surface to the component parts which make it up. So the Conservative Party official website states that 'we want to see a transformation in the role of community groups, social enterprises and the voluntary sector to help build a stronger society for all of us'.

The Conservatives are pledging that when they come to power they will support charities, voluntary groups, social enterprises and philanthropists by reducing the bureaucracy which they have to deal with. They have also pledged to reform the Gift Aid system to make it even more attractive to donors. They have promised to give government employees annual volunteering leave and to reform the complex, expensive and bureaucratic system currently in place for running criminal record checks.

However, the most radical proposals are reserved for their policy of using the third sector to take over roles, duties and functions currently performed by the state. They promise to introduce a new Voluntary Action Charity Fund and to make it easier for smaller charities to obtain government funding. Even more radical, they promise to set up an Office of Civil Society and to create social enterprise zones which will make it easier for social entrepreneurs to set up and operate enterprises aimed at tackling issues – such as drug abuse – which blight society.

Much of what the Tories will do in power is about reforming – and downsizing – existing government departments and functions. In the case of the voluntary sector, however, their proposals are radical – and might involve (at least initially) extra expenditure. However, the hope is that by boosting the role of the third sector, and diverting some of the funds to it which are currently absorbed by central government and quangos, they will get better value for money. Just as importantly, they hope that those who access public services will receive better – and more personalised – services.

Welfare and pensions

The Conservatives are coming to office pledging a dramatic shake-up of the country's welfare and pensions systems. At the heart of the party's plan will be a push towards a system of welfare into work and measures to defuse the pensions time bomb.

Speaking in February 2009, David Cameron was clear about the scale of the challenge his party will face. 'One of the biggest challenges facing the next government will be that of mass unemployment and how we can get Britain back to work,' he said.

Margaret Thatcher, Tony Blair and Gordon Brown all failed to devise and implement meaningful reforms to the welfare system. The challenge for David Cameron is no less than it was for his three predecessors, but the imperative to arrive at a viable solution is much greater. The current benefits system is unaffordable to a country already saddled with unprecedented debt, and the reform of the pensions system is just as urgent if the deficit in public finances is not to increase.

The Tories will have the DWP budget firmly in their sights when they get into government. This is not just because of the colossal cost to the government and to the taxpayer, but because of the incalculable cost to society of having so many people inactive and disengaged. This is the department where the Tories know they have to be the most radical. The current private sector pension system is in disarray and needs to be re-established. The current public sector pensions system is unaffordable and needs to be reined in. And something radical – and painful – has to be done to curb the huge cost of the benefits system – budgeted at £186 billion for 2009/10.

This really is a challenge which the Tories cannot duck, even if they wanted to. All the signs are, however, that they have every intention of meeting the challenge head on. There are not only vast savings to be made; they genuinely believe that if they can move as many people as possible from welfare dependency to paid employment they will be on well on the way to mending the UK's 'broken society'.

Welfare reform

An incoming Conservative administration will call time on a system which they claim has allowed generations to slip into dependency on benefits. They maintain that welfare dependency reduces life chances and creates a ghetto mentality, which in turn ultimately results in higher crime, poor health, child poverty and the erosion of the respect culture.

Labour's ability to assume the mantle of the party of radical welfare reform was dealt a blow in early 2009 when David Freud, the investment banker who advised former Work and Pensions Secretary James Purnell on how to get private sector engagement in moving people off welfare into work, moved over to join the Conservatives. According to *The Guardian*, a green paper which Freud authored put in place plans to 'finance the upfront costs of intensive work placement schemes from the subsequent savings to the welfare bill'. His plans were almost fully adopted in a green paper in December 2008 which the newspaper claimed deprived 'the Tories of their harder-edged welfare policies'. However, his subsequent decision to swap sides was widely read as a signal that Freud believed it would be a future Tory administration rather than Labour who would push through the necessary reforms to their ultimate conclusion. Freud is now seen as a future minister and working peer in the first Conservative term.

The Tories will also seek to keep the political pressure on the Labour government over the issues of welfare and unemployment. Conservative shadow Cabinet member Theresa May has accused ministers of failing to put in place the necessary reforms to the welfare system which would help the country to deal with the short-term effects of the global economic slump. As British joblessness continued to rise, May intervened in June 2009 with a warning that the government was 'continuing to sleepwalk' through the unemployment crisis and called on ministers to put in place the welfare reforms the country 'desperately needs'.

The Conservative Party supports the continued roll-out of the New Deal and has criticised the Labour government for cutting employment programmes in some parts of the country. The Tories believe that putting work at the centre of welfare policy will reduce poverty and enhance the health and life chances of hundreds of thousands of people currently inactive in the employment market.

A raft of welfare and community initiatives will seek to end long-term unemployment and break the dependency culture which the Conservative Party believes has been allowed to fester by a succession of administrations. The Tories have studied similar programmes deployed in countries such as the USA, Australia and the Netherlands, and they will put rights and responsibilities at the forefront of their attempt to reduce poverty, to cut the costs of failure and to enhance social mobility.

The favoured model with the Tories seems to be the 'Wisconsin model', whereby those who are out of work are presented with a 'ladder' which spells out the steps they will need to take to move up from welfare dependency to full paid employment – with incentives and penalties factored in along the way. The motto of the scheme is 'a hand up, not a hand out'. Jobseekers are provided with personal advisors and they are also offered catch-up classes. If, after a specified period of time (probably six months), they have not found paid employment, they will be made to enrol in welfare-to-work programmes.

The measures were set out in the Conservative Party's welfare policy, which also pledges tough sanctions on those who seek to avoid returning to work and who insist on remaining part of the benefits culture. The blueprint – entitled *Work for Welfare Repair* – set out clear policies in the employment and benefits arena.

In the foreword to the document David Cameron said that 'Labour's bureaucratic approach has failed'. He went on:

> We need a thorough overhaul of the way that benefits are administered. Our plans for welfare reform will help those who want to work into sustained employment, and cut benefits for those who refuse to work. They will give some of our most deprived citizens the opportunity to live independent and fulfilling lives. Above all, they will help more people contribute to the responsible society I want to achieve.

Under the Tory plans benefits will essentially become something which is earned, rather than being an automatic entitlement. The party wants a system through which every claimant potentially able to work is engaged in welfare-to-work activities aimed at helping them back into work 'as quickly as possible'. Those long-term unemployed who still cannot find work will take part in long-term community projects to help them get back into a working environment – and the Tories have said that they will restrict the benefits of those who fail to take part in the programmes.

A system of payment by results will be implemented for those in the state, private and voluntary sectors with whom a New Conservative government would work to deliver the new system. 'We will fund this extended programme by bringing the principle of payment by results to the return-to-work arena in the UK. The job of delivering our programmes will be contracted to third party providers from the private and voluntary sectors, including local authorities with relevant expertise. They will be paid when they get people into work,' the policy paper maintains.

The Conservatives will also reform the welfare system to 'strengthen families'. There is a commitment to end the 'couple penalty' in the tax credits system, and there are also plans which the party claims will help lift almost half a million children out of poverty.

Gordon Brown in opposition used to habitually refer to the massive welfare bill which the Tory government (and the taxpayer) had to pay as 'the price of failure'. With the DWP budget now approaching £200 billion, and more than five million Britons of working age economically inactive, that price of failure is now unaffordable. No Labour government has ever left power with unemployment lower than when it entered. It now looks as though this record will remain intact. In the three months up until May 2009 unemployment rose by a record 281,000. This pushed the headline figure up to 2.38 million, and in June it rose again to 2.43 million. At that rate, it is likely to have exceeded three million by the time of the general election.

The Tories, like the Labour government, will also have to address the difficult issue of care provisions when they form their next government. They have pledged to examine ways to create a more personalised framework for the provision of health and personal care services. They have also promised to make greater use of direct payments and individual budgets, which they say will give the elderly greater control over their care arrangements.

Pensions

The Conservative Party is acutely aware that the pensions time bomb is still ticking, and that the inevitable explosion is going to be made more severe by the country's recent economic woes. The current financial crisis has resulted in more people delaying the start of pension provision, and in an even greater squeeze on public sector pension pots. In the private sector, figures published by the actuaries Lane Clark & Peacock in August 2009 showed a pensions deficit amongst FTSE 100 companies alone of £96 billion. All parties are agreed that the pensions system needs dramatic reform. Equally, they all concede that no single system appears to offer all the solutions required to create sustainable incomes for a rapidly ageing population which will live longer and expect more.

Developed countries the world over are having to face up to the challenge of an ageing population. It is estimated that by 2050 the UK will have 54.7 economically inactive people for every 100 economically active people. That is a sharp increase from 2000 figures of 30.8 inactive people for every 100 active people. Making sure that older people have a secure and comfortable retirement is going to be a challenge, and the Tories are aware that they need to persuade people to start planning for their old age earlier.

The Tories believe that the government needs to be doing more to encourage people to save for their retirement, not penalising those that do. People are currently putting less and less money aside for their retirement and are hoping that the state will provide for them instead. This situation is exacerbated by the fact that most people substantially under-estimate the amount of money they will need to save in their pension to secure a comfortable retirement.

One reason which has been identified as contributing to this reluctance to save is that many people, particularly those on lower incomes and with less financial security, feel anxious about putting money away in a pension pot that cannot be touched until they near retirement. For many people, and particularly for women, not being able to access their own money, even in an emergency, is a substantial deterrent to saving. They worry that should they or a member of their family need the money (for example for medical treatment or because they were made redundant) then they could not access their own savings. Instead, they would rather save in an ISA or other savings vehicle. The Tories are looking at other countries to see if the UK could adopt their more flexible saving arrangements.

The Tories have pledged to raise the basic state pension in line with earnings rather than in line with pensions. This, they say, is in order to help stop the spread of means testing. It is likely, however, that they will have to scrap some of the means-tested benefits in order to pay for this pledge.

The Conservative Party has frequently stated that it believes that public sector workers do extremely important work and are entitled to security in retirement. However, it also believes that it would be irresponsible to ignore the rising cost of public sector pensions, with some estimates putting the deficit at £1.3 trillion. This situation is exacerbated by the current state of the economy and the public finances, the closure of defined benefit (DB) schemes in the private sector, and growing disparity between pension expectations in the public and private sectors.

The Tories also recognise the concern about the level of MPs' pensions and have always said that moving new MPs on to a defined contribution (DC) scheme is a crucial first step in any wider reform of public sector pensions. They are also committed to creating an independent Office for Budget Responsibility, which will carry out a comprehensive audit of all off-balance sheet liabilities, including public sector pensions.

The Conservatives also argue that DB schemes have come under huge pressure from taxation changes, the recession and increased stock market volatility. Whilst recognising that their long-term future maybe in doubt, the alternative (the DC scheme) places all the risk onto the employee, and the Conservatives are committed to retaining some aspects of DB schemes if they can.

One solution under consideration will be hybrid schemes, which do offer a means of retaining some element of DB provision, combining elements of both DB and DC to share risk. The UK is unique in requiring the mandatory indexation of deferred pensions and pensions in payment, with the resulting open-ended commitment that companies are forced to subscribe to. The next Conservative government is pledged to re-examine the introduction of conditional indexation, which they unsuccessfully tried to incorporate into the 2004 Pensions Act.

The Conservatives are advocates of voluntary adoption by companies of auto-enrolment in pension schemes, and they believe that introducing personal accounts should be subject to review upon their election. The party is concerned that personal accounts designed to help the less well off may not be as effective as some current savings vehicles, due to the cost of management charges.

Personal accounts, auto-enrolment, early access to savings and the future of DB schemes are currently the four main pension priorities for an incoming Conservative government. However, these initiatives alone are unlikely to defuse the pensions time bomb, and this area of policy is still under review and will be subject to further re-examination before and after the general election.

Going into government

The Tories have faced a dilemma in the run-up to the general election. They have set up an Implementation Team, whose job it is to plan for the transition into government. However, if they make the unit too large, or publicise its activities too widely, then they are in danger of being accused of complacency and presumption. However, if they had not established this unit, and if they had not allowed word of its existence to get out, they would have risked accusations of being amateurish and ill prepared.

The Implementation Team is headed up by Francis Maude, and he is assisted by Nicholas Boles, who has had experience as the head of Boris Johnson's transition team. There are, at the time of writing, only about half a dozen people working in the unit – some of whom have been seconded from large accountancy or management consultancy firms. In the first quarter of 2009 PricewaterhouseCoopers donated more than £100,000 of consultancy advice to the Tories. Other consultancies which have offered advice or seconded personnel to advise on efficiency and the transition include Grant Thornton, the European School of Management and Smith & Williamson.

The staffers and the secondees have been working closely with the Cabinet Secretary and senior civil servants as part of the standard procedure whereby the civil service is instructed to have preliminary meetings and discussions with potential incoming governments. They have also been receiving advice from Lord Turnbull, formerly Cabinet Secretary and head of the Home Civil Service.

Boles will have learned a lot from his former role with Johnson. The mayoral transition was not as smooth as it might have been, and the prime lesson will have been: be careful who you take in with you. Whilst some members of Team Boris have quietly and efficiently got on with their jobs away from the public eye, three deputy mayors have been forced out in a highly visible and politically damaging manner.

The functions of the Implementation Team are straightforward but crucial. Its members are charged with assessing policy proposals and drawing up timetables for their implementation in government. They are also charged with arranging the training of future ministers and with briefing them on the strengths and weaknesses of their future departments. Additionally, they have the task of assessing plans for government restructuring and ensuring that any such reorganisations would not have a negative impact on policy priorities. Finally, they have a role in identifying and assessing candidates to become special advisors and working peers in the new government.

The Tories have also been revisiting some of the findings of the James Commission, which identified £34 billion of savings ahead of the 2005 general election. They have hired the Boston Consulting Group, which used to employ Greg Clark, to advise them on where to make savings without having a severe detrimental effect on frontline services. If they can find substantial savings without impacting on those frontline services then their chances of securing a second term will be greatly enhanced.

The Tories admit in private that they have not yet decided whether to reshuffle the pack of Whitehall departments yet again. Gordon Brown has been hyperactive in this area, devising a department (DCSF) for his protégé Ed Balls and then creating a new super-ministry (BIS) for Lord Mandelson, who has seen him though some difficult times. Every time a department is restructured or merged, tens of millions of pounds – and several precious months of activity – are wasted.

As far as possible the Tories will avoid reorganising Whitehall departments. They realise that it not only costs money (which the government does not have), but also causes confusion and damages morale. Given that they plan to have a 100-day *blitzkrieg* to push their policies through, they cannot afford to indulge in dismantling some of Brown's structures for the sake of it. The only new department which they might construct (in homage to the efforts of Iain Duncan Smith and the CSJ) is a Ministry of Social Justice, but that will not be an immediate priority.

There is, however, serious talk about having both David Cameron and George Osborne based in Downing Street. Normally the Chancellor would operate from the Treasury on Horse Guards Road, but the physical distance between the twin architects of New Conservatism could possibly have a negative impact on the creative and harmonious relationship which has developed between them.

However, in an article in *The Independent* in August 2008 entitled 'How would Mr Cameron run his government?' Francis Maude is quoted as saying: 'The Blair–Brown style is all about central control. There would be a return to something much more like more conventional Cabinet government, with a strong Prime Minister showing leadership and direction at the top.' He added: 'To have a strong centre, you don't need a Prime Minister's Department. What you need is a strong Prime Minister who sets direction clearly. David Cameron will be more trusting of his colleagues, with their departments being held accountable but not constantly being second-guessed and interfered with.'

As the general election gets closer the contacts with the civil service will intensify. The Tories will have no choice but to beef up the Implementation Team – but they will find no shortage of volunteers from the private sector happy to offer their services. The nearer the general election looms, the clearer it will become that Maude (the midwife of the modernisation agenda) and Boles (although he is not yet even an MP) are two of the key players in Team Cameron.

The Tories have also been receiving assistance from a surprising source. Former Labour minister (and also the Labour Party's largest ever donor) Lord Sainsbury of Turville has set up the Institute for Government. He set it up because he believes that in recent years government has become inefficient. He cites the fact that Brown has appointed three secretaries of state for

Defence during his brief premiership, and that Tony Blair and Brown between them appointed eleven Europe ministers since 1997, as evidence of how dysfunctional government has become. The Tories have been working closely with this new institute, which is headed by the former Whitehall permanent secretary Sir Michael Bichard. They agree with Lord Sainsbury's thesis that constant reshuffles lead to bad government, and they have attended or sent representatives to all of the seminars which the institute has held to date.

Apart from the physical challenge of moving into government, the Implementation Team is also looking at some key policy areas. These are:

- developing a low carbon economy
- reforming the prison system and reducing the rate of reoffending
- reforming the NHS and decentralising decision making down to the local level
- reforming the welfare system, including some radical reforms such as the so-called 'Wisconsin model'
- reforming the education system and allowing (within reason) anybody to set up schools – the so-called 'Swedish model'.

The Tories have few frontbenchers who have experience of government – but they do have more than the handful Labour had in 1997. They also have several senior figures on the back benches who they could call upon if necessary – as they did with Ken Clarke. Other senior figures who could be pressed back into service include Peter Lilley, John Gummer and Stephen Dorrell. The Tories will also have some very talented policy makers at their disposal – in Parliament, at CCHQ and in the form of PPCs waiting to be elected.

All in all this is a very well-prepared government in waiting. Which is just as well, because they have unprecedented challenges to face – and just 100 days to make their mark and set the tone for the whole parliament.

Conclusion

If the Tony Blair handover to Gordon Brown was the most horrendous hospital pass in UK political history to date, the economic legacy which David Cameron and the Tories are about to inherit will certainly eclipse it. Brown's premiership has been one long binge in the last chance saloon on somebody else's credit card, and the Tories are going to have to pick up the tab.

There are, as my colleague Andrew Hawkins of ComRes frequently points out, only really three election slogans:

- Let us finish the job
- Don't let the other lot muck it up
- Time for a change.

Gordon Brown, possibly with signs of an economic recovery in evidence, will obviously rely on the first two. The Tories, however, will deploy the third – which is usually in any case the most powerful and the hardest to argue against. Their latest campaign slogan, 'Now for Change', closely echoes the 'Time for a Change' slogan. If they win – which they should – and if they manage to get to grips with the economic problems and the gargantuan budget deficit, then they in turn can deploy the first slogan in 2014 or 2015.

The author has consistently stated that he thinks that the Tories will win – and win big. The Tory high command is adamant that it has no such expectations, and the pollsters and psephologists back them up – pointing to the fact that the Tories need to achieve a swing of nearly 9 per cent to achieve any kind of majority at all.

Many Labour MPs (and some Tories) still think that a hung Parliament is a possibility. That is why both of the main parties have been keeping a close eye on the policies of the Lib Dems, and why they have been maintaining reasonably cordial relations with them. If there were a hung Parliament, however, the Tories would not be overly keen to form a government. They would allow Labour and the Lib Dems to form some kind of a coalition (or a looser arrangement) and to take all of the necessary unpleasant decisions which will need to be taken. Cameron is young enough, secure enough and confident enough to wait a while longer.

If the Tories score a narrow win, they will set out very early on what needs to be done to restore the economy, balance the books and reduce the bloated size of the state. There would then probably be one Budget and one Queen's Speech – and then another general election within eighteen months in order to secure a stronger mandate. There would also be some advantage to the Tories of a narrow win, in so far as the whips would find it easier to maintain discipline within the parliamentary party.

If, as the author suspects, the Tories achieve a thumping win (if not an actual landslide) then they will be free not just to pursue the necessary economic and fiscal measures, but also to start to implement their radical new localism agenda. This will be applied to all areas of policy, and would bring about a fundamental rebalancing of society away from big government. They would also hope that the sheer size of the majority would carry them through to a second term – despite the inevitable unpopularity of some of their fiscal measures.

Senior Tories have pointed out to the author that it is not the size of the swing needed which will be the factor in dictating the size of any majority – it is the ruthless targeting the party now practises. In the 2009 county council elections the Tories gained 250 extra council seats with just 37 per cent of the vote. That level of gain should only have been possible with a vote share of 40–42 per cent. The secret was in the targeting of winnable seats, and this is the creed which Lord Ashcroft has been preaching ever since 2005.

The expenses factor has been the big unknown in these calculations. The Tories were well ahead in the opinion polls when the row erupted, and they certainly did not need this distraction. However, the most likely scenario is that the whole affair will turn the traditional incumbency advantage on its head. Given that there are more than twice as many sitting Labour MPs as Tories, it can only really play in the latter's favour.

It has been said that politicians campaign in poetry, but govern in prose. Every election campaign has to have a narrative and the next one will not be an exception. The Labour Party will campaign on the issue of 'Labour investment' versus 'Tory cuts'. The Tories will respond by saying that the state is far too big – and remote. Their solution will be the localism agenda, devolving power down to the point where it is as close to the people as possible. This policy is bad news for Whitehall and quangos, but good news for local authorities, and also for the third sector and the emerging band of social entrepreneurs. It will be a battle between the diametrically opposed philosophies of 'the man in Whitehall knows best' and 'trust the people'. There can only one winner in that particular argument.

If localism is the 'big idea' which underpins the whole narrative, the number one (and number two and number three) priority for the New Conservative government will be cutting back the colossal public debt. Every permanent secretary of every Whitehall department, and every chief executive of every quango, will be asked a series of questions:

- Is this particular function a necessary one?
- Is it a function that your department (or your quango) ought to be undertaking?
- If so, can it be undertaken more efficiently and more cheaply?
- If not, is there a third-sector body which can do it better?

So, as we discussed at the start of this book, it really will be about the economy, stupid. But the Tories are utterly determined not to allow the Labour Party to pin the charge on them that they will be seeking to govern for the few, not the many. Any tax cuts, when they eventually come, will be targeted at the lower paid first. In an interview with Andrew Marr in July 2009 David Cameron said: 'Even the rich must bear their fair share in the effort to bring the debt burden down.'

Conservative Party chairman Eric Pickles has said that the general election campaign will be launched at the party conference in October 2009. He, and David Cameron and his senior colleagues, will be focused on winning power so that they can begin to address the country's parlous economic state, and then on keeping power so that they can begin to devolve power down to local authorities and third-sector groups and rebuild faith in the family. This will be a conservative government with both a large and a small 'c'.

Contributions from senior lobbyists

Below are some contributions from senior figures in the public affairs industry. They include those with strong links to the Tory Party, and those who are either non-aligned, or aligned with Labour or the Lib Dems. All are seasoned professional observers of the political scene. They have been asked (in approximately 200 words) to give their view on what the priority will be in the first 100 days of the New Conservative government.

Contributions

Hit the ground running, *blitzkrieg*, or whatever your favourite description is for a blizzard of action and announcements designed to convey decisiveness and a new government in charge of its own destiny, not the prisoner of events or of the markets.

David Cameron and George Osborne are utterly determined not to repeat what they see as Tony Blair's big mistake in 1997 of focusing largely on getting elected and much less on what to do next.

Whitehall mandarins have been impressed with the thoroughness of the 'preparing for government' programme run by Francis Maude and heavily influenced by both Ken Clarke and William Hague.

So expect some early populist moves: a review of Westminster boundaries to cut the number of MPs, the end of identity cards and plans for another runway at Heathrow and a purge on quangos, with RDAs at the top of the list.

But also look out for a second Finance Bill and very early agreement and announcements on where the public spending axe will fall. There may be immediate and painful cuts in schools, welfare and defence to enable the NHS budget to be protected and to give the government enough time to recover and to win a second term.

MICHAEL BURRELL, Vice Chairman Europe, Edelman

When David Cameron eventually walks through the door of 10 Downing Street, he will find an in-tray overflowing with urgent issues which demand his immediate attention. Top of the pile, of course, will be the state of the public finances.

Very near the top will be the whole issue of defence policy. This will include both operational and procurement matters, with budgetary pressures playing a key role. These decisions will be set out in the findings of a strategic defence review, the first major one since the 1990s, which will look at the resources required to meet operational needs. The review will be synergic with wider foreign policy and homeland security commitments. A likely outcome will be a major rationalisation of the means by which the UK procures equipment for its armed forces.

In defence, possibly more than anywhere else, a New Conservative government will have an opportunity to be iconoclastic, with sacred cows potentially under threat including everything other than the nuclear deterrent replacement (though even here a delay might be considered) and the CVF aircraft carrier procurement (safe provided the UK continues its commitment to an expeditionary foreign policy).

SIMON ELLIOTT, Managing Director, FD

There will be two priorities: sorting out the broken economy and healing the broken society. There will be a move away from big statism. The individual will be given important new rights and responsibilities. Symbolically, voluntary groups will become the first rather than the third sector.

In terms of style, Cameron will want to hit the ground running and get all the unpopular and difficult decisions out of the way immediately.

A Prime Minister's Office will be created which will in effect bring together the power bases of Nos 10 and 11, ensuring no damaging arguments between Cameron and Osborne.

A Cameron government will be neither the continuation of New Labour or a modern version of Thatcherism. In dreadful economic conditions, it will attempt to balance the rights of the individual with the need to protect the most vulnerable from the full impact of the market.

In a post-bureaucratic age, David Cameron will need to prove that Conservatives can deliver the aspirations and dreams of all the many elements that now make up British society.

Winning the election is the easy bit!

PETER BINGLE, Chairman, Bell Pottinger Public Affairs

There's no doubt that a Cameron administration will be refreshing, exciting and energetic. It will be a stark contrast to the last days of the Brown administration.

Expect the changes to flow rapidly from day one. In reality, there will be one main imperative on coming to power – to control public spending, with some exceptions.

The public mood will immediately lift after Election Day. The question is: how long will the honeymoon period last? Many have said that those aspiring to the next government should be careful what they wish for. The honeymoon period will probably end faster than ever before.

In the first few days there will be many parents of victory. These will be met with the tired smiles of others who have really done the work. There will be

no triumphalism from the new government. There will be an immediate and energetic application to the job in hand.
CHRIS LEWIS, CEO, Lewis PR

In the first hundred days and beyond, the economic climate will dictate the priorities of the next Conservative government. The need for spending restraint is likely to translate into an effort to reduce the number of quangos. There will be serious efforts to tackle waste, duplication and inefficiencies wherever possible – both in government departments and at the level of local councils. This will translate on the ground into the abolition of the regional development agencies, and possibly the Office for Government Commerce.

Education policy is one area where the Conservatives are pledging to be most radical. The party will move towards liberating state schools from local bureaucratic control – the weakest performers falling under the wing of the strongest – and providing the funding for new providers to set up schools where there is local demand.

Pledges to freeze council tax, abolish polyclinics, scrap the planned third runway at Heathrow airport, overturn the Local Government Act 2000 and reduce the bureaucracy faced by police will all be priorities.
NICK WOOD-DOW, Executive Vice President, Chelgate

There is a policy dichotomy at the centre of Cameron's Conservative Party. On the one hand they will be keen to drive reforms from the centre to deliver change, whilst on the other they will be keen to be seen to devolve power to the now mainly Conservative-run local councils.

This will impact tangibly upon the planning issues that relate to housing and energy policies. That the role of onshore wind farms in producing green energy has been airbrushed almost totally from the pages of the latest Conservative energy paper reflects this tension. Although it makes absolute environmental sense for there to be more onshore wind farms, they are deeply unpopular with many older shire Tory councillors. So in the first 100 days expect to see national planning statements being approved by Parliament, not just by the relevant minister, and energy initiatives to focus on anything but onshore wind.

With housing, local Conservatives are often against new homes being imposed upon local authorities through regional targets. So expect the scrapping of these targets and the introduction of incentives to deliver regional housing, such as increased funding for local authorities through the Revenue Support Grant and more freedom as to how they can spend their income.
MARK GLOVER, Managing Director, Bellenden Public Affairs

He may be many things, but David Cameron certainly isn't stupid. From day one he's going to be working to be re-elected. So David knows that he will have to use his first 100 days for radical shock therapy, if he's going to have any chance of putting the country on an upward swing come 2014. But promising radical therapy is not what gets you elected. So expect David to make a dramatic announcement at the end of his first fortnight. In a special TV address he'll say that the scale of the mess inherited from Labour is worse than anyone thought. It has forced him to tear up his manifesto and immediately slash government spending. And so he will break the (Labour-supporting) unions in the public sector and cut public sector salaries and pensions. And in a final flourish he will throw a bit of (literal) red meat to his old guard and announce an immediate end to the ban on fox hunting.

In the response to this whirlwind, the media will divide between hailing the new PM as a hero and labelling him a villain. But come 2014 David Cameron will be ready to tell us that the painful medicine has worked, and that he deserves our votes once more. . .

SACHA DESHMUKH, Chief Executive, Mandate Communications

The Queen's Speech will contain several reform bills to democratise public services, including a health bill abolishing centralised targets and an education bill enabling new schools to be set up where existing schools are failing. New legislation will provide for no-strike agreements and binding arbitration in essential public services. Indirect taxes will rise while any direct tax cuts in the first Budget will probably take the form of symbolic, post-dated cuts to inheritance tax and corporation tax.

The biggest change under a New Conservative government will be the speed with which it moves to bring green policies to Britain. The National Grid will be forced to buy energy from homes at a set tariff, and we will all be incentivised to separate our rubbish, invest in domestic renewable energy generation and insulate our properties.

ADRIAN PEPPER, Managing Director, Pepper Media

Unlike in Tony Blair's first 100 days, when the sun just kept shining and only popular decisions needed to be made, the UK's mounting debt crisis will require immediate attention. Reducing central government spending and the impact of doing so will dominate much of the headlines during this period. The size of a Conservative majority will be critical as the spending cuts will fall on constituencies and backbenchers naturally fight for local interests.

Pointing the finger of blame at the previous administration and dismantling chunks of costly Labour policies and failed structures will help Cameron through this tough period and establish a new policy direction. Major changes will be enacted to Brown's financial regulation regime with a greater role for the Bank of England and mechanisms introduced for independent oversight of public finances. The need to devolve power down to the people whilst saving money will see steps taken to reduce the number of quangos and to boost the transparency of decision making in central government and Parliament. On Europe, publication of a bill for a referendum on the Lisbon Treaty is expected. Major Labour projects, such as ID cards, will be ended. And not forgetting the green agenda, ruling out a third runway at Heathrow and measures to boost green technology investment are expected.

DAVID BEAMER, Director, Politics Direct

Any feelgood factor will be hard to create following the next election – with the enormity of the current economic situation weighing down any new government. But getting a grip on the economics must be the first priority and Cameron and Osborne have the opportunity to do so with a Budget likely to take place within the first month.

The first Cabinet meeting will set in train a rapid spending review that will be forced to reduce public expenditure significantly – but will ensure a relative carve out for NHS spending – a totemic Cameron promise.

The first Conservative Budget for twelve years is likely to place a premium on support for small and medium businesses with promised moves on corporation tax and national insurance. Watch out for the heralded moves on stamp duty and inheritance tax too – the core pledges which catapulted the Conservatives ahead of Labour in 2007. Mervyn King is likely to get what he wants even before the first Budget and macro prudential supervision for the financial services sector will be handed back to the Bank of England.

Watch out for one thing that might not make its way into the Conservative manifesto – for fear of antagonising the public sector unions this side of a general election: radical reform of public sector pensions. The Conservatives may feel they have the political traction to end defined benefit public sector pensions for new joiners – a move that in the medium to long term would help to address public sector costs and would be a seismic political move in the early days of a new government.

IAIN ANDERSON, Director and Chief Corporate Counsel, Cicero Consulting

The first 100 days of a David Cameron government will not be Tony Blair, Summer of 1997. The course is already set – 'Austerity Britain' – and the public will not support any glitzy PR blitz.

Of course, the sight of a new leader, Cabinet and government taking power elicits media fascination; and we can expect announcements on social policy legislation in areas such as health, education, welfare and the environment, to provide momentum for the Conservatives' 'big idea', of localised responsibility. But Austerity Britain will be the overriding priority – how could it credibly be otherwise?

Visualise new Chancellor George Osborne burning the midnight oil, poring over Treasury books to produce a detailed economic plan to maintain election manifesto spending promises (on the NHS and international aid) whilst reducing public debt and plotting a course to pull Britain out of recession. Expect bad news early, to manage expectations. David Cameron's task will be binding Cabinet colleagues into the plans, which will involve real spending cuts.

The main short-term issue will be Europe. If the Lisbon Treaty's still up for grabs after the general election, new Foreign Secretary William Hague will immediately want to set the date of a ratification referendum (making it clear the Conservatives would campaign for a 'no' vote). If the treaty is already in force, then we'll all be finding out what 'We won't let matters rest there' actually means!

DARREN CAPLAN, Director of Public Affairs, Brands2Life

In the same way that New Labour had to show that it was different from previous Labour administrations when it came to office in 1997, so too David Cameron's Conservative government will have to distance itself from conceptions about being the 'nasty party'. Those early days set the tone for the rest of the administration and whilst introducing some populist measures, Cameron will want to avoid accusations of being just like the party of old. Given the state of the economy and public finances there will be decisions to be made with winners and losers. These choices will show people what a Cameron Conservative Party really looks and feels like and what compassionate Conservatism means to the day-to-day lives of people.

Cameron's talk of implementing a 'green revolution' has to be proved by his immediate actions and policies on entering government. Is there any substance to the rhetoric of his four years as leader or will it be business as usual for a Conservative administration, placing the emphasis on traditional economic growth, tax cuts and so on? If he wants to be any more than a 'one-term wonder' then Cameron has to set out his economic, social and environmental vision in the first 100 days.

DR STUART THOMSON, Bircham Dyson Bell, author of Public Affairs in Practice

David Cameron will seek to use his first 100 days to establish the politics, people and policy of his administration. The failure of Blair to use his first term to do anything other than secure a second has become a cautionary mantra amongst Cameroons, but in reality it will be a template they might find difficult to avoid.

On politics, expect to see vast coverage of 'opening the books of Labour failure' – public audits and the like will be used to feed the public psyche of a devastating Labour legacy. On people the first 100 days will be used to establish the wider government team – key individuals fresh to the public such as Michael Gove, Andrew Lansley and Jeremy Hunt will have their profiles broadened and Cameron will be looking for them to respond and demonstrate the depth of quality of his new Cabinet.

On policy, expect to see a quick three-month comprehensive spending review and significant bills on reform of welfare, education and local government – and new fiscal responsibility structures. Finally, watch out for the big surprise – are David and George planning their own 'Bank of England moment' to really hit the ground running?

CHARLES LEWINGTON, Managing Director, Hanover Communications

This will be the 'government of thrift'. Labour confirmed in the Budget in April 2009 that the UK will accumulate a £1.2 trillion debt over the next five years – the biggest in history.

Before the recession, the Conservatives' plan was all about redefining their social agenda. No more 'nasty party'. The economic crisis changed the focus and perhaps the direction. Winning the battle over the economy and fixing the blame on Gordon Brown will be central to the Tory election campaign. It will almost certainly secure them victory.

But empty public coffers will bring a tremendous challenge along with that victory. The Tories have committed to introducing an 'austerity Budget' within days of coming to power. Quangos, defence contracts, ID cards, IT projects and spending plans are already lined up for the chop. Scaling back free childcare could be on the cards.

The big social issues of education, welfare and health are still on the table, particularly Michael Gove's education reform agenda. But these issues take time, money, patience and legislation to address. A clear agenda on the economy will be critical to confront a grim economic reality. This will define the first 100 days and beyond.

SUZY AWFORD, Partner and MD, DLA Piper

The honeymoon had better be good. A Cameron government will need to be quick to communicate that it has a firm grip on the economy and can win the support and confidence of both the private sector and the nation. The pressure will be on to deliver a better economy and better government sooner rather than later.

I think the first 100 days will see a lot of cutting action one way or another. Note the Boris approach to cutting communications budgets and the implicit Cameron desire to reduce public spending and waste and increase competition. Maybe to kick off, a Cameron government will propose a streamlined Cabinet, cut inheritance tax and abolish a few quangos.

Public services will be on the front line of change; with greater involvement from the private and independent sectors and inevitable cuts in funding. The first 100 days will definitely see a far more competitive environment emerging and, of course, the Conservatives will be desperate for things like the new schools model, which would allow independent organisations to set up schools, to feature large.

Good or bad, it is after the honeymoon when the real pitfalls will open. Either way, it won't be 1997.

GILL MORRIS, Managing Director, Connect

The first 100 days will be like a remake of 'The Axeman Cometh'. Very tough decisions lie ahead, which means, in all but name, heavy cuts to public spending. Cameron and his coterie are instinctive tax cutters and the economic malaise, the inheritance of a weak economy, will give them short-term cover for a broader programme of public sector cuts. So where is the axe likely to fall? Health and international development are safe; everything else is in the firing line but big changes will be dependent upon the size of the majority.

Hung Parliament/under 25-seat majority: Gently as she goes . . . with the potential need for Unionists or Liberal Democrats, many of the ambitions of the manifesto will be watered down and only the most modest changes will be implemented. The leadership will have to watch out for the 'march of the soloist' – rogue MPs with single issues on their mind. Europe could cause ructions for Cameron's government before they've even moved into second gear. Cameron will go for easy hits like scrapping ID cards – a popular measure that will also save a few billion pounds.

50–100-seat majority: Expect a bonfire of the quangos as RDAs, SHAs and local government offices get abolished. Controversially, the military could be persuaded to accept savage cuts to the Army, Navy and RAF in exchange for greater funding of operations in Afghanistan.

Over 125-seat majority: Think the unthinkable . . . perhaps the TV licence fee will be consigned to UKTV Gold? Pay-per-view technology exists and the Conservatives argue for choice. The question is, where will Mark Thompson find another salary and expense account that earns him over £800,000?

JOHN LEHAL, Managing Director, Insight Public Affairs

The political history of Britain shows that with depressing regularity, Conservative governments come in having to sort out the economic woes left to them by the outgoing Labour administration. This new Tory government will have that same challenge.

With the exception of the most faithful around Gordon Brown, almost everyone accepts that spending will be cut and that the incoming administration will need a cohesive plan to tackle the enormous debt. My additional worry for the new administration is that the spectre of inflation could well come back to haunt us. Huge amounts of money have been pumped through the economy by the government and the Bank of England, and the new administration will need to keep a keen eye on this too.

ANDREW CUMPSTY, Chairman, Enterprise Forum

After years in opposition, the Conservatives must hit the ground running and deliver key election commitments. There is limited scope for radical economic reform but David Cameron must demonstrate a firm grip on the economy. Labour's economic legacy and the state of the books must be addressed. An immediate audit of all departments will be ordered – exposing the true state of public sector finances, branding Labour's rule a failure and justifying tough limits on public spending.

Education and welfare will dominate the Queen's Speech, as Cameron sees radical reform as the way to fix Britain's 'broken society' – allowing parents, charities and others to set up new state schools and overhauling the welfare system. There will be an NHS Bill to establish an independent board, reducing ministers' day-to-day control.

Cameron has refused to cut health spending, so efficiency savings will be found in other areas. The Tories need populist wins and easy ways to save money – they'll scrap Labour's pre-election Budget promises and drop the identity card programme, saving billions. Expansion of Heathrow will be stopped and mandatory home information packs abolished. Plans to increase the inheritance tax threshold from £300,000 to £1 million will be announced.

CHRIS WHITEHOUSE, Managing Director, The Whitehouse Consultancy

The first Conservative government since 1997 will want to make its mark and will know that momentum early on is key.

In the first few weeks, the following can be expected: immediate announcements on scrapping ID cards and stopping the third runway at Heathrow; a statement from George Osborne that the public finances are worse than expected; and Cabinet meetings to agree cuts in public spending across the board with the exception of health and international development.

Osborne will create the Office of Budget Responsibility to keep the public finances in order and will announce that the Bank of England will regain its powers over banking regulation and macro prudential regulation, leading to a slimmed-down FSA; there will be a number of eye-catching announcements on the low carbon economy; Gove will announce new freedoms for schools; Lansley will set up a new independent board to run the NHS on a day-to-day basis, with a new emphasis on public health; and Cameron will start his new career as an international statesman with visits to Washington, Berlin and Paris.

The Tories' first Budget will freeze council tax for one or two years and will abolish the proposed rise in national insurance contributions, but the rest will be public spending cuts and rises in 'acceptable' forms of tax such as alcohol and tobacco duty or stealth tax rises. The Tories will watch Labour's leadership election closely to see who will lead the new opposition.

GRAHAM MCMILLAN, Chief Executive, Open Road

Back in September 2008, College Public Policy sponsored an event which saw the launch of *The Plan: Twelve Months to Restore Britain*. The book showed how an incoming government could seek to put the country on the right track. It was clearly a pitch to the Conservative leadership. The authors of *The Plan*, Daniel Hannan MEP and Douglas Carswell MP, could back then only dare to dream that their policies might catch Cameron's eye. The expenses scandal, however, has been transformational for localists in the Conservative Party.

The Milton Keynes speech in the middle of the scandal allowed Cameron to lay out his plans for a 'massive redistribution of power from central government to local government'. Cameron went on to talk about 'local control over schools, housing, policing' and 'the right to initiate local and national referenda'. The localists within the party heralded the Milton Keynes speech. One suggested that 'the new centre right stands to diffuse control over our centralised system of politics and public services the way it dispersed control of the commanding heights of the economy a generation ago'.

Every new government needs some eye-catching policies in the first 100 days to signal change and freshness. The Tories have no Guantanamo to shut down. Instead a new constitutional arrangement with the British people forged in the first 100 days and based on the localist creed allows the party to create some sense of enthusiasm for the new administration. By bringing back economic rectitude to Britain, the party will be forced to chose austerity over euphoria. Early May 2010 (if that's when the election is held) is likely to be very different to the heady days of early May 1997 but at least the party has *The Plan*.

ROBBIE MACDUFF, Partner, College Public Policy

Assuming the Conservatives win the general election, a day of reckoning will have arrived. After twelve years of Labour's reckless spending, expect to see David Cameron and George Osborne make an immediate and decisive effort to stabilise the public finances. Even an emergency Budget has been rumoured.

A Conservative government will be focused on making sure taxpayers' money reaches frontline areas of delivery in fields like healthcare and education. That means that all programmes and initiatives will be put under the microscope. Labour's quangos, especially, will come under scrutiny. The Infrastructure Planning Commission will, for example, be abolished. Capital works programmes which are non-core or environmentally damaging also face the axe. There are likely to be early decisions on a third runway at Heathrow and a second one at Stansted. The National Grid may well be rapidly overhauled to prepare for decentralised energy sources.

The ID card scheme will be scrapped. The first Cameron Budget will surely contain the promised reduction in inheritance tax from the 2007 party conference. Some have even speculated that final salary pension provision for civil servants and MPs may be quickly reviewed.

With a bit of luck, the age of new realism and reconstruction will soon be dawning.

SIMON NAYYAR, Managing Director, Public Policy, Citigate Dewe Rogerson

Gordon Brown is ensuring the private sector economy is being effectively flattened under unbearable public debt. Paying this back has to be the Tories' immediate priority via declared cuts in public expenditure of up to 30 per cent in the first few months; and tax rises on all except small businesses, which should see their tax burden fall. In social policy areas, the new government will make legislation on school reform a priority, via parent-inspired 'community schools'. They will also move legislation to reduce the number of MPs by 200 and create an elected Upper House of 200 legislators.

CHRIS GUYVER, Managing Director, Quintus

Clearly the Conservatives will inherit a very tight public spending position and we should expect an immediate review of government spending with all areas, except health, fair game for cutbacks. Whilst the focus will be on curbing inefficiencies, there will inevitably be some frontline services that will fall. The Sure Start scheme, aimed at low-income households with young children, is one obvious area destined for cuts. There will be some difficult decisions that will need to be taken in traditional Tory areas like defence. Some of the large defence projects may face slimming down under a Conservative Defence Secretary.

Another key area for the first 100 days will be Britain's international relations.

We should expect a much cooler approach to Europe whilst relations with the US will be a priority.

Gordon Brown came to No. 10 talking big about constitutional change. David Cameron has made similar noises and it will be interesting to see what he can actually deliver. Early in a new parliament is always the best opportunity to be radical.

MARK ADAMS, Managing Director, Foresight Consulting

Prime Minister David Cameron's first action will be to finalise his Cabinet and other ministers. Most of his shadow Cabinet ministers are expected to move into their equivalent government posts, but many middle and junior ranks will be open to the new Tory MPs. A National Security Council is expected, answerable directly to the Prime Minister.

Clearly the economic inheritance will dominate Cameron's first days and probably the rest of the parliament. The government will move very quickly. The budget deficit may well prove greater than has been announced and the blame will be placed squarely on the outgoing Labour government. Cabinet ministers will be flexible and will agree a programme of public expenditure cuts, which Treasury officials will have prepared beforehand, with only the health and international development budgets due to be exempt. These will be announced in an emergency Budget in June (assuming an early May general election), with some overall increase expected in the tax burden.

However, ministers will show that they are moving to fulfil other electoral promises. The removal of unnecessary targets from education, health and policing will be a priority, coupled with devolving powers to professionals. The Queen's Speech in mid-May, for a parliamentary session to the autumn of 2011, will be another opportunity, particularly for education reforms, reducing carbon emissions and protecting the independence of the civil service.

The next parliament will be very different from its predecessor, given how many MPs will have left at the general election, voluntarily and involuntarily. An early test of Cameron's belief in Parliament is whether he will let Conservative MPs choose their own chairmen, and even members, of select committees.

KEVIN BELL, President Regional, UK/Africa, Fleishman Hillard

What surprised many people about the early days of New Labour in May 1997 was the decisive character with which it acted then. The party's policies had been well trailed in the preceding period, yet it still kept one or two things – such as independence for the Bank of England – firmly up its sleeve.

To show that 'things have changed', the Conservative Party will doubtless be aiming to do something similar, should they, as many anticipate, win in 2010. Boldness rather than diffidence will be the order of the day, and it seems likely that the Bank of England will again be the institution used to illustrate that, with responsibility for banking supervision to be tilted firmly back in its direction for the first time since the BCCI crisis. This will require primary legislation, and a long bill at that, so it will be words rather than deeds that characterise this act.

Meanwhile, Philip Hammond MP, or whoever assumes the mantle of Chief Secretary to the Treasury, will have to initiate the painful process of making cuts in public spending. A bold Tory government will require those to be made within the 2010/11 financial year, with an immediate freeze on hiring, salary hikes and perks for the public sector. Spending programmes from 2011/12 onwards will experience dramatic weight loss!

JON MCLEOD, Chairman, Corporate Communications & Public Affairs, Weber Shandwick

Abbreviations

A&E – Accident & Emergency
AM – Assembly Member
APPG – All Party Parliamentary Group
ASI – Adam Smith Institute
BA – Bachelor of Arts
BNP – British National Party
BT – British Telecom
CCHQ – Conservative Campaign Headquarters
CCO – Conservative Central Office
CEBR – Centre for Economics and Business Research
CIPR – Chartered Institute of Public Relations
CPRE – Campaign to Protect Rural England
CPS – Centre for Policy Studies
CRD – Conservative Research Department
CSJ – Centre for Social Justice
DB – defined benefit (pension)
DBIS – Department for Business, Innovation and Skills
DC – defined contribution (pension)
DEFRA – Department for Environment, Food & Rural Affairs
DIUS – Department for Innovation, Universities and Skills
DTI – Department for Trade & Industry
ERM – Exchange Rate Mechanism
EU – European Union
FCO – Foreign & Commonwealth Office
FE – further education
FSA – Financial Services Authority
GDP – gross domestic product
GLA – Greater London Authority
GLC – Greater London Council
GP – general practitioner
IEA – Institute for Economic Affairs
IMF – International Monetary Fund
IT – information technology
LSE – London School of Economics
MBA – Master's in Business Administration
MEP – Member of the European Parliament
MoD – Ministry of Defence

MP – Member of Parliament
MSP – Member of the Scottish Parliament
NAO – National Audit Office
NFU – National Farmers' Union
NHS – National Health Service
NICE – National Institute for Health and Clinical Excellence
OECD – Organisation for Economic Co-operation and Development
ONS – Office of National Statistics
PFI – Private Finance Initiative
PMQs – Prime Minister's Questions
PPC – prospective parliamentary candidate
PPE – politics, philosophy and economics
PPS – parliamentary private secretary
PR – public relations *or* proportional representation
QC – Queen's Counsel
RDA – regional development agency
RUFC – Rugby Union Football Club
SNP – Scottish National Party
TA – Territorial Army
UKIP – UK Independence Party
UN – United Nations

Bibliography

Douglas Carswell and Daniel Hannan, *The Plan: Twelve Months to Renew Britain*, Douglas Carswell & Daniel Hannan, 2008.

The Class of 2010, Madano Partnership, 2009.

Francis Elliott and James Hanning, *Cameron: The Rise of the New Conservatives*, HarperPerennial, 2007.

Simon Lee and Matt Beech, *The Conservatives under David Cameron: Built to Last?*, Palgrave Macmillan, 2009.

Tim Hames and Valerie Passmore, *The Times Guide to the House of Commons 2005*, Times Books, 2005.

Kieron O'Hara, *After Blair: David Cameron and the Conservative Tradition*, rev. ed., Icon, 2007.

Colin Rallings and Michael Thrasher, *Media Guide to the New Parliamentary Constituencies*, Local Government Chronicle Elections Centre, 2007.

John Turnbull, *Vacher's Parliamentary Profiles*, Dod's Parliamentary Communications, 2006.

Edward Vaizey, Michael Gove and Nicholas Boles, *A Blue Tomorrow: New Visions for Modern Conservatives*, Politico's, 2001.

Websites

http://ukpollingreport.co.uk
http://www.totalpolitics.com
http://www.electoralcommission.org.uk
http://www2.politicalbetting.com
http://www.iaindale.blogspot.com
http://order-order.com
http://conservativehome.blogs.com
http://www.conservatives.com
http://www.kingsfund.org.uk
http://www.ifs.org.uk

Index